OUTDOORS

D0018128

# NORTHERN CALIFORNIA
# CABINS & COTTAGES

**TOM STIENSTRA**

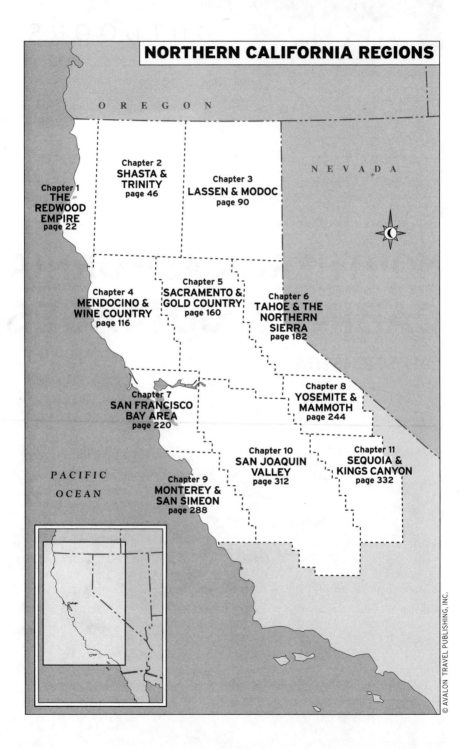

# NORTHERN CALIFORNIA REGIONS

OREGON

NEVADA

**Chapter 2**
**SHASTA & TRINITY**
page 46

**Chapter 3**
**LASSEN & MODOC**
page 90

**Chapter 1**
**THE REDWOOD EMPIRE**
page 22

**Chapter 5**
**SACRAMENTO & GOLD COUNTRY**
page 160

**Chapter 4**
**MENDOCINO & WINE COUNTRY**
page 116

**Chapter 6**
**TAHOE & THE NORTHERN SIERRA**
page 182

**Chapter 7**
**SAN FRANCISCO BAY AREA**
page 220

**Chapter 8**
**YOSEMITE & MAMMOTH**
page 244

**Chapter 10**
**SAN JOAQUIN VALLEY**
page 312

**Chapter 11**
**SEQUOIA & KINGS CANYON**
page 332

PACIFIC

OCEAN

**Chapter 9**
**MONTEREY & SAN SIMEON**
page 288

© AVALON TRAVEL PUBLISHING, INC.

# Contents

Best for Water Sports      Most Luxurious
Best for Fishing      Best for Families
Best for Horseback Riding      Most Romantic
Best for Winter Sports      Most Secluded
Best for Beach Access

**Including:**

Crescent City      Klamath River
Del Norte Coast      Leggett
Eel River      Lost Coast
Eureka      Pacific Coast
Fortuna      Petrolia
Garberville      Smith River Recreation Area
Humboldt Coast      Trinidad

**Including:**

Bella Vista      Lewiston
Big Flat      Lewiston Lake
Castella      Mount Shasta
Coffee Creek      Orleans
Dunsmuir      Red Bluff
Hyampom      Sacramento River
Klamath River      Shasta Lake
Lake Red Bluff      Shasta-Trinity National Forest
     Somes Bar

# Defining Cabins and Cottages

The purpose of this book is to provide a resource of cabins and cottages, from romantic to rustic, that are available for rent in Northern California. The territory covered spans from San Simeon to Mount Whitney in the south and all the way north to the Oregon border.

Recreational opportunities that are available near each cabin are also featured. With the array of outdoor activities in Northern California, you can enjoy many things, including beachcombing for sea shells, hiking to a gorgeous lookout, fishing for trout, or soaking in mineral hot springs. The result is a book that features opportunities for outdoor recreation by day, with a roof over your head—plus separate walls and privacy—by night. Our goal is to put the best of Northern California right in your hands, whether for a one-night getaway or a full vacation.

Each cabin or cottage listed in this guidebook provides self-contained, stand-alone lodging. They range from luxurious cottages and vacation home rentals to rustic tent cabins and yurts. Many are part of a resort, lodge, ranch, campground, or rental company. Each lodging is a separate building or unit, and would be suitable for couples, families, or singles who want more privacy than at a bed-and-breakfast and more personality than at a typical hotel or motel. The cabins and cottages in this guide are constructed from a variety of materials, including pine logs, redwood, canvas, and in rare cases, fiberglass, such as for luxury yachts that can be rented at their moorings in San Francisco and Oakland.

Each listing in *Moon Northern California Cabins & Cottages* is located in or near a major outdoor recreation area, including five national parks: Redwood, Lassen Volcanic, Yosemite, Sequoia, and Kings Canyon. In addition, the length of the Pacific coast from San Simeon to Oregon is also featured, along with the Sierra Nevada and its foothills, and the Sacramento and San Joaquin valleys.

*Moon Northern California Cabins & Cottages* provides everything you need for an enjoyable weekend getaway or a week-long vacation centered around outdoor recreation, with a cabin or cottage—or yurt, chalet, or yacht—that's right for you.

# How to Use This Book

## ABOUT THE MAPS

This book is divided into chapters based on regions; an overview map of these regions precedes the table of contents. Each chapter begins with a region map that shows the locations and numbers of the cabins or cottages listed in that chapter. For a directory of map symbols, please see page 355.

## ABOUT THE PROFILES

Each profile includes an introduction to the lodging facility, an overview of the grounds, facilities, and amenities as well as recreation opportunities available on-site or within a short drive.

Cabins and cottages marked by the **BEST** symbol are highlighted in the author's Best Cabins and Cottages list.

### Facilities

This section conveys the number of cabins or cottages available, whether kitchen facilities are available, whether linens and towels are provided, and if not, what you should bring to sleep comfortably, and whether private or communal bathrooms and showers are available. Amenities inside the cabins (such as fireplace, hot tub, and air-conditioning) as well as on the property (such as swimming pool, restaurant, and picnic area) are also mentioned here.

### Reservations and Rates

This section notes whether reservations are required or recommended. It also discusses the rates for each cabin, which often range due to cabin size, amenities, time of week, and time of year. If there are additional fees for extra persons or pets, this will be noted here. If there are package deals, that will also be noted. If a cabin is open during part of the year, those dates will be mentioned.

Contact information, including address, phone number, and website address, if available, for the featured cabin will be included.

### Directions

This section provides mile-by-mile driving directions from the nearest major town.

## ABOUT THE ICONS

The icons in this book are designed to provide at-a-glance information on activities that are available on-site or nearby.

- 🏃 Hiking trails
- 🚴 Biking trails
- 🏊 Swimming
- 🎣 Fishing
- 🚤 Boating (includes motorboats, canoes, kayaks, sailboats, and personal watercrafts)
- ❄️ Winter sports (includes downhill skiing, cross-country skiing, snowshoeing, snow mobiling, snowboarding, and ice skating)
- ♨️ Hot or cold springs
- 🐾 Pets are permitted
- 👨‍👩‍👧 Popular with families
- ♿ Wheelchair accessible

## ABOUT THE RATINGS

Every lodging option in this book is rated on two scales.

### Luxury

This scale of 1 to 5 rates the comfort level of the cabin or cottage. Generally, a place with more amenities will receive a higher ranking.

### Recreation

This scale of 1 to 5 rates the accessibility of on-site or nearby activities; it does not rate the number of activities available, nor the level of expertise needed to participate in them.

# INTRODUCTION

COURTESY OF CAMANCHE NORTH SHORE

# Finding Your Own Golden Pond

The idea for this book first came after watching one of my favorite movies, *On Golden Pond*.

It seemed to me that many people want to find their own Golden Pond; that is, a little cabin, cottage, or chalet in a beautiful spot—sometimes romantic, sometimes amid great recreation opportunities—and always a private hideaway. This search spanned the width of the state in hopes of finding every cabin and cottage rental from San Simeon to Mount Whitney, then stretched across Northern California up to Oregon. The result is a collection that ranges from some of the most luxurious and expensive accommodations available to some of the most primitive and cheap, as well as everything in between. Perhaps in these pages, you can find your own Golden Pond.

Northern California features some of the most beautiful landscape on earth. Each region offers something compelling and unique, providing everyone with the opportunity for a stellar getaway. The outdoors is good for the soul. Adventures can refresh the spirit. And the experience can be enhanced greatly by staying in a cabin or cottage. In fact, I can't think of enjoying a better time in California than spending the day hiking, boating, fishing, or sightseeing and spending the night in a little cottage or cabin.

Who knows, maybe you will find your own Golden Pond.

*—Tom Stienstra*

# Questions to Ask When Reserving a Cabin

Each write-up in this book contains detailed information about cabin facilities, surroundings, and rates. But cabin features and policies may change, so it's always best to verify what you expect to find there. If you confirm important details when you make your reservation, you can make the most of your time in the outdoors once you've arrived at the cabin.

Most cabin owners will be more than happy to answer your inquiries to ensure that they can meet your expectations. Here are some questions you may want to ask:

## CABIN FEATURES
• How many people can the cabin accommodate? What size are the beds?
• Does the cabin have its own bathroom with a tub or shower?
• Does the cabin have all linens provided, or should I bring sleeping bags, pillows, and towels?
• Does the cabin have electricity? If not, are flashlights or lanterns provided?
• Does the cabin have heat? If it has a woodstove or fireplace, is firewood available on-site?
• Does the cabin have kitchen facilities? What about pots and utensils? Trash bags and cleaning supplies?
• What kind of view does the cabin have?
• How close is the cabin to other structures on the property? Are road noises audible?

## PROPERTY AND SURROUNDING FEATURES
• Does the property have a barbecue or fire grill where I can cook outside?
• Are there any restaurants or grocery stores nearby?
• Is the cabin a single unit or duplex-style? Is it situated very close to other cabins, where I might hear my neighbors?
• Where is the nearest gas station?

## POLICIES
• What methods of payment are accepted?
• What is the cancellation policy?
• Are additional guests or visitors permitted? Are there extra fees?
• Are children permitted?
• What is the policy for pets? If pets are allowed, are there any extra fees?

# Best Cabins & Cottages

## ❰ Best for Water Sports

**Sugarloaf Cottages Resort,** Shasta and Trinity, page 73. Sugarloaf provides a great escape overlooking Shasta Lake. This is a great spot for trout fishing and bass fishing, as well as a preeminent destination for all water sports.

**Rollins Lakeside Inn,** Sacramento and Gold Country, page 168. Visitors here beat the summer heat by swimming or waterskiing on Rollins Lake and then retreating to their fully equipped, air-conditioned cabins.

**Zephyr Cove Resort,** Tahoe and the Northern Sierra, page 202. With an astounding mile of Tahoe beach frontage, this lakeside retreat is perfectly situated for water-sports enthusiasts—and an adjacent marina offers boat rentals and guided tours of the lake.

**Snug Harbor Resort,** San Francisco Bay Area, page 235. Waterfront cabins with docks and a full-service marina give boaters everything they need for a Delta adventure.

**Lakeshore Resort,** Sequoia and Kings Canyon, page 336. These cozy cabins are just off Huntington Lake, which is great for swimming, fishing, and waterskiing and is known for its classic summer sailing regattas.

## ❰ Best for Fishing

**Casa Rubio Bed and Breakfast,** The Redwood Empire, page 25. Anglers love this place's proximity to some of the state's best steelhead and salmon fishing, while others come for whale-watching, long beach walks, and comfortable accommodations.

**Burney Mountain Guest Ranch,** Lassen and Modoc, page 92. With an on-site casting pond and guided fishing trips, this resort caters to anglers—but it also offers trail rides and access to great hiking trails in Shasta National Forest.

**Lake Front Cabins,** Yosemite and Mammoth, page 263. Built in the 1950s as fishing retreats, these classic cabins still offer great access to June Lake and are just a short walk from the marina.

**Vermilion Valley Resort,** Sequoia and Kings Canyon, page 334. Anglers come here for a rustic tent cabin experience and to fish for trout in Edison Lake and Mono Creek.

## ❰ Best for Horseback Riding

**Burney Mountain Guest Ranch,** Lassen and Modoc, page 92. This fishing, horseback riding, and hiking resort offers trail rides that lead into Shasta National Forest.

**Childs Meadow Resort,** Lassen and Modoc, page 105. This high-mountain retreat has on-site corrals and easy access to riding trails.

**Highland Ranch,** Mendocino and Wine Country, page 130. Riders can explore over 100 miles of trails around this understated country spread.

**Greenhorn Creek Guest Ranch,** Tahoe and the Northern Sierra, page 184. Giddyup and go at this dude ranch spread on 600 acres—family friendly activities like cookouts and hayrides are the name of the game.

**Hunewill Guest Ranch,** Yosemite and Mammoth, page 250. This working ranch is the real deal, and it offers guests numerous opportunities to join in on riding, roping, and cattle drives.

**Owl's Nest,** San Joaquin Valley, page 322. Just outside of Yosemite's southern entrance, this peaceful place offers comfortable A-frames and loads of trail-riding opportunities.

## ◖ Best for Winter Sports

**Mount Shasta Resort,** Shasta and Trinity, page 52. This deluxe resort at the foot of glorious Mount Shasta offers winter ski packages, and some of its cabins have outdoor hot tubs.

**Cabins at Strawberry,** Sacramento and Gold Country, page 173. Just five miles from Dodge Ridge Ski Area, these kitchen-equipped cabins provide a cozy place to rest up after a day on the slopes.

**Bear River Lake Resort,** Tahoe and the Northern Sierra, page 212. Winter draws snowmobile enthusiasts to this comfortable mountain retreat with access to 75 miles of trails.

**Tamarack Lodge Resort,** Yosemite and Mammoth, page 273. This classic lodge is a winter-sports paradise; it offers 28 miles of groomed trails perfect for cross-country skiing or snowshoeing, and it's just three miles from Mammoth Mountain.

**Dinkey Creek Inn and Chalets,** Sequoia and Kings Canyon, page 342. These fully equipped A-frames can accommodate six people, making them a great crash pad for families who want to cross-country ski, showshoe, or snowmobile right from their doorstep.

## ◖ Best for Beach Access

**White Rock Resort,** The Redwood Empire, page 24. Set on sand dunes or low bluffs, these modern cabins provide ocean-facing decks and hot tubs.

**Howard Creek Ranch,** Mendocino and Wine Country, page 118. Walk the three-mile stretch of sandy coast just a stone's throw from these four cabins—or hit the beach on horseback.

**Agate Cove Inn,** Mendocino and Wine Country, page 120. Photo-ops abound at these picture-perfect oceanfront cottages set amid cypress trees.

**Dillon Beach Resort,** San Francisco Bay Area, page 222. These cottages near Tomales Bay attract beachcombers and kayakers, and offer access to some of the region's richest clamming beds.

**La Playa Hotel Cottages,** Monterey and San Simeon, page 292. Just a couple of blocks from Carmel Beach, these five serene cottages offer easy access to surf, sand, and sunsets.

## ◖ Most Luxurious

**Carter House Inns,** The Redwood Empire, page 34. This is the finest lodging in Humboldt County; the on-site restaurant—acclaimed for its wine selection—will serve you a multicourse meal right in your private cottage.

**Auberge du Soleil,** Mendocino and Wine Country, page 152. This highly praised resort sets the standard for opulence with its lavish Mediterranean-style cottages, fine dining, and full-service spa.

**Manka's Inverness Lodge,** San Francisco Bay Area, page 224. Uniquely appointed accommodations and a fantastic restaurant await at this upscale Point Reyes retreat, once a hunting and fishing lodge.

**Ahwahnee Cabins,** Yosemite and Mammoth, page 257. Visitors here find gorgeously appointed cottages and superb dining in a world-class Yosemite Valley setting.

**Post Ranch Inn,** Monterey and San Simeon, page 300. Guided hikes and individualized spa treatments are just some of the services available at this super-luxe property splendidly situated on the Monterey Coast.

## ◖ Best for Families

**Trinity Mountain Meadow Resort,** Shasta and Trinity, page 64. This rustic resort in the Trinity Alps offers hiking, swimming, arts and crafts, and an early dinner hour just for kids.

**Emandal Farm,** Mendocino and Wine Country, page 119. This working farm lets kids pitch in with chores or splash around in the Eel River—and everyone gathers for family-style meals featuring organic produce grown on-site.

**Costanoa,** San Francisco Bay Area, page 236. Kids will dig checking out the elephant seals at nearby Año Nuevo State Reserve, and parents will appreciate the range of lodging options and amenities at this spectacular ocean-view property.

**Yosemite Lakes,** San Joaquin Valley, page 318. With plenty of organized activities and easy access to Yosemite's west entrance, this is the kind of place the whole brood can appreciate.

**Montecito-Sequoia Lodge,** Sequoia and Kings Canyon, page 348. This popular family camp offers loads of outdoor activities, buffet meals, campfires, and sing-alongs.

## ◖ Most Romantic

**Pine-Gri-La,** Shasta and Trinity, page 61. Privacy is what you'll find at these custom-built cabins with stellar mountain views.

**Albion River Inn,** Mendocino and Wine Country, page 124. This lovely coastal property features 20 romantic cottages with amenities like fireplaces, whirlpool tubs, and private decks.

**Gables Cedar Creek Inn,** Sacramento and Gold Country, page 175. For a weekend away that doesn't cost a fortune, bunk down at the Hideaway, a cozy log cabin nestled in redwoods.

**The Cottage Inn at Lake Tahoe,** Tahoe and the Northern Sierra, page 196. These unique cottages-for-two feature stone fireplaces and lots of Old Tahoe charm.

**Dancing Coyote Beach,** San Francisco Bay Area, page 223. Scenic Point Reyes National Seashore has miles of beaches for hand-in-hand strolls, and the sleeping loft at Dancing Coyote Beach's Sky Cottage is a snug place to bunk at night.

**The Homestead,** San Joaquin Valley, page 323. Not far from Yosemite's southern entrance, these finely crafted cottages feature log beds, fireplaces, and private patios.

## ◖ Most Secluded

**Patrick Creek Lodge,** The Redwood Empire, page 26. Way up by the Oregon border, this forested property offers a private cabin and several other phone-free accommodations.

**Marble Mountain Ranch,** Shasta and Trinity, page 48. Once you've arrived at this ranch set deep in Klamath National Forest, there's no reason to leave; recreational opportunities abound and the all-inclusive packages see that all your needs are met.

**Mill Creek Resort,** Lassen and Modoc, page 103. You'll have to fill the tank to get here, but once you've arrived you'll have great access to Lassen Volcanic National Park from this rustic resort.

**Vermilion Valley Resort,** Sequoia and Kings Canyon, page 334. Enjoy lakeside accommodations, boat rentals and shuttle service, horseback riding, and all the fishing and hiking you want at an elevation of 7,650 feet.

**Mono Hot Springs Resort,** Sequoia and Kings Canyon, page 335. People set out for this remote retreat in the magnificent Sierra National Forest for its on-site hot springs and its superb hiking trails.

# THE REDWOOD EMPIRE

COURTESY OF CASA RUBIO

## BEST CABINS & COTTAGES

**❰ Best for Beach Access**
White Rock Resort, **page 24**

**❰ Best for Fishing**
Casa Rubio Bed and Breakfast, **page 25**

**❰ Most Secluded**
Patrick Creek Lodge, **page 26**

**❰ Most Luxurious**
Carter House Inns, **page 34**

# Visitors come from around the world to the Redwood

Empire for one reason: to see the groves of giant redwoods, the tallest trees in the world. On a perfect day in the redwoods here, refracted sunlight beams through the forest canopy, creating a solemn, cathedral-like effect. It feels as if you are standing in the center of the earth's pure magic.

But the redwood forests are only one of the attractions to this area. The Smith River canyon, Del Norte and Humboldt Coasts, and the remote edge of the Siskiyou Wilderness in Six Rivers National Forest all make this region like none other in the world.

On sunny days in late summer, some visitors are incredulous that so few people live in the Redwood Empire. The reason why is the same one that explains why the trees grow so tall: rain in the winter — often for weeks at a time — and fog in the summer. If the sun does manage to appear, it's an event almost worthy of calling the police to say you've spotted a large, yellow Unidentified Flying Object. So most folks are content to just visit.

Three stellar areas should be on your must-see list for outstanding days of adventure: the redwood parks from Trinidad to the Klamath River, the Smith River Recreation Area, and the Lost Coast.

I've hiked every trailhead from Trinidad to Crescent City. The hikes feature some of the best adventuring in Northern California. A good place to start is Prairie Creek Redwoods State Park, where you can see fantastic herds of Roosevelt elk. Then head over to the beach by hiking Fern Canyon, where you walk for 20 minutes at the bottom of a canyon adjacent to vertical walls covered with ferns, and then continue north on the Coastal Trail, where you'll pass through pristine woodlands and fantastic expanses of untouched beaches. All the trails through the redwoods north of the Klamath River are winners; it's just a matter of matching up your level of ambition to the right hike.

The Smith River Recreation Area is equally gorgeous. The Smith is one of the last major free-flowing rivers in America. Wild, pristine, and beautiful, it's set in a series of gorges and bordered by national forest. The centerpiece is Jedediah Smith State Park and its grove of monster-sized redwoods. South Fork Road provides an extended tour into Six Rivers National Forest along the South Fork Smith River, with the option of visiting many of the largest trees in Jedediah Smith State Park. The turnoff is on U.S. 199 just northeast of the town of Hiouchi. Turn right, cross two bridges, and you will arrive at a fork in the road. Turning left at the fork takes you along the South Fork Smith River and deep into Six Rivers National Forest. Turning right at the fork takes you to a series of trailheads for hikes into redwoods. Of these, the best is the Boy Scout Tree Trail.

The Lost Coast is often overlooked by visitors because of the difficulty in reaching it; your only access is via a slow, curvy road through the Mattole River Valley, past Petrolia, and out to a piece of coast. The experience is like being in suspended animation — your surroundings are peaceful and pristine, with a striking lack of people. One of the best ways to capture the sensation is to drive out near the mouth of the Mattole, then hike south on the Coast Trail long enough to get a feel for the area.

Compared to other regions in California, this corner of the state is somewhat one-dimensional. The emphasis here is on exploring the redwoods and the coast and, to some extent, fishing. Most of the cabins here are designed with that in mind; they're basic, rustic (with a few noteworthy exceptions), and among the most economical in the state.

Carter House Inns in Eureka ranks at the top of the luxury scale. It's a romantic getaway with an emphasis on fine cuisine and upscale lodging. Other high-quality spots include View Crest Lodge and Bishop Pine Lodge.

For beach and ocean lovers, White Rock Resort has park-model cabins with beach frontage, and Casa Rubio Bed and Breakfast has similar frontage and beach access, and hot tubs, too.

On the opposite end of the spectrum is Riverwalk RV Park with clean and simple cabins providing the basic elements you need.

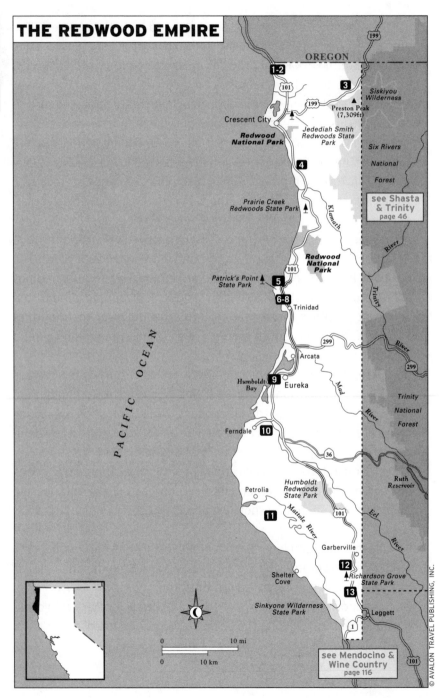

THE REDWOOD EMPIRE

# The Redwood Empire
# Cabins & Cottages

# 1 WHITE ROCK RESORT

**BEST**

Del Norte Coast, off U.S. 101 in Smith River

**Luxury rating:** 4　　　　　　　　　　　　　　**Recreation rating:** 3

Here's an example of a new breed of cabin rentals, and it's in a class of its own. These little cabins are packed full of amenities and seem much larger than their approximate 500- to 600-square-foot size. Inside each there's a bedroom, sleeping loft, kitchen, full bath, and small living area with a cathedral ceiling.

Situated on a low bluff or sand dune, the cabins are spaced fairly close together in two rows facing the ocean. The smaller cabins are closest to the ocean, while the larger units, with fireplaces, are in the second row. Each cabin has its own deck with spa and landscaping. A walking path to the beach is located between cabins three and four.

When you arrive, the smell of freshly baked bread usually fills the air. It's part of the resort's service, and the management says they really want you to feel at home. If the bread doesn't do the trick, maybe the complimentary bottle of wine, champagne, or sparkling cider will get you into vacation mode.

The decor is mostly contemporary. All cabins are individually owned, so, in turn, each is unique. All have heating systems.

The design of these cabins makes them ideal for groups. You want a good setup for the family? You got it. You want to go fishing with your buddies? It works. You want romance? There's potential.

For details about the area, refer to Casa Rubio Bed and Breakfast (see next listing).

## Facilities

White Rock Resort's 25 cabins sleep four adults or one family. Each cabin has a bathroom with shower/tub, fully equipped kitchen, and deck with spa. Some units have fireplaces. Cable television, a VCR, a stereo, and a complimentary bottle of wine, champagne, or sparkling cider are provided. Laundry facilities are available, and a restaurant is within walking distance. Barbecues are available on request. The resort is suitable for children. Smoking is prohibited. Pets are not allowed. Linens and towels are provided.

## Reservations and Rates

Reservations are recommended during the summer. Rates are $175 per night for an oceanfront cabin, $135–150 for an ocean-view cabin. There is a 10 percent discount for seven days or more. For more than four people, $15 per person per day is charged. Additional people are accepted with prior approval. There is a two-night minimum on weekends and three-night minimum on holidays. Major credit cards are accepted. Contact White Rock Resort, 16800 U.S. 101 North, Smith River, CA 95567, 707/487-1021 or 888/487-4659, fax 707/487-1063, website: www.whiterockresort.com.

### Directions

From Crescent City, drive north on U.S. 101 for approximately 20 miles to within 0.25 mile of the Oregon-California border. The resort is on the left.

# **2** CASA RUBIO BED AND BREAKFAST

BEST **(**

Pacific Coast, off U.S. 101 in Smith River

**Luxury rating:** 3                                                    **Recreation rating:** 3

Panoramic ocean views and easy beach access are the highlights here. With each lodging unit varying greatly in size and amenities, you can tailor your stay according to the number of people in your group and their needs. Each cabin or house is stocked with either croissants or muffins, juice, and coffee. Brookings, Oregon, 10 minutes north, has several good restaurants. My favorite is the Mexican place on the west side of the highway on the north end of town.

Most of the property has upgraded facilities. All lodging provides private entrances, a plus.

Casa Rubio is on Pelican Bay, which forms at the mouth of the Winchuk River, right on the California-Oregon border. You'll probably see plenty of seagulls, seals, and otters during your stay. Whale-watching traditionally starts in mid-December and continues through spring. The best times to see these magnificent mammals are the periods between storms, when the skies clear, the wind dies, and the ocean calms. These conditions seem to arrive each year around Christmas and New Year's, then again in mid-March and April.

Surfing is available north of the property. The beach is just a short walk from your cabin, through a well-kept garden. And, of course, there are plenty of fishing opportunities since you're in one of the best angling areas in California. There's superb steelhead fishing on the Smith River during the winter, and giant salmon to be had during the fall. Take your pick.

## Facilities

Casa Rubio has one cabin, along with a studio, a suite, and a "nest," set just to the south of the main house; all vary in size and amenities. All lodgings have a full bathroom, and two units have fully equipped kitchens. The cabin has a fireplace. Barbecues are available on request. Most units have a deck, and the largest house has a woodstove. Continental breakfast is provided. The facility is suitable for children. No smoking is allowed. Female dogs are allowed with prior permission. Linens and towels are provided.

## Reservations and Rates

Reservations are recommended during the summer. Rates are $78–158 per night, with a discount after five days. Additional guests are $15 per night per person. Children under eight are allowed only in the studio. Children under walking age are free. Contact Casa Rubio Bed and Breakfast, 17285 Crissey Road, Smith River, CA 95567, 707/487-4313 or 800/357-6199, website: www.casarubio.com (virtual tour available).

## Directions

From Crescent City, drive north on U.S. 101 for approximately 20 miles to Crissey Road, within 800 feet of the Oregon-California border. Turn left and drive a short distance to the resort on the right.

---

## 🖪 PATRICK CREEK LODGE                                    BEST �ā�

Smith River Recreation Area, off U.S. 199 near Gasquet

🎿 ⛵ 🛶 ❄️ 🐕 👪

**Luxury rating:** 3                                    **Recreation rating:** 4

---

This place captures the best of California's north woods and water. It is pretty, clean, and more of a little-known getaway spot than anything else.

After checking in, you drive to the back of the lodge on a curving, rising gravel road, ending at a cottage set above the lodge in the forest, quiet and private. The cottage has two bedrooms, a bathroom, plus a kitchen and a big main room. It is ideal for a large family, buddies on a fishing weekend, or a group of friends using the cabin as headquarters for a Smith River–based vacation.

In addition to this cabin, the lodge offers 16 rooms in various styles (10 of them upstairs) in two buildings. There are no telephones or televisions in the rooms, which for many is ideal for a wooded hideaway. The decor is country-style, homey and comfortable.

At the inn, a pretty trail provides access to the confluence of Patrick Creek and the Smith River.

Note that this place was becoming something of a legend regarding the grumpy owners who ran the place. They didn't discriminate against anybody; they treated everybody bad. In 2005, the operation was revamped by new owners, and of all the upgrades, the people-factor upgrade is the best news of all.

For a place you can reach by pavement, it is way out there, near the California-Oregon border on U.S. 199. It is near the point where Patrick Creek enters the Smith River, one of the last major undammed streams in America. It takes nearly two hours of driving from Eureka to get here, so if you add another 300 miles from San Francisco, you can figure on almost a day of saddle time before you can pull up to the hitching post. The prime adventures are exploring the Middle Fork Smith River, which is accessed on U.S. 199. There are many pullouts along the river with short trails down to beautiful spots. This is one of the most beautiful river gorges in California that you can reach by car.

## Facilities

Patrick Creek Lodge has a two-bedroom cabin and a lodge with four rooms, three two-bedroom suites, two continental rooms, and another building with six motel-style rooms. No telephones are available in the rooms or cabins; telephones are provided in the lodge lobby, and a public pay phone is just outside the entrance. There is a television with satellite hookup in the lodge lobby, as well as in the cabin. An on-site restaurant serves meals 7 A.M.–10 P.M. daily and a popular champagne brunch 10 A.M.–2 P.M. on Sunday. All pets are expressly prohibited, including in vehicles in the parking lot. Smoking is allowed in two rooms. Bedding and towels are provided.

## Reservations and Rates

Reservations are recommended. The fee for the cabin in the summer is $129.50 per night for two, $209 per night for six people. A surcharge is added if you're reserving for only one night. Lodge rooms start at $90 per night for two. Contact Patrick Creek Lodge, 13950 U.S. 199, Gasquet, CA 95543, 707/457-3323, website: www.patrickcreeklodge.com.

## Directions

From Crescent City, drive north on U.S. 101 for five miles to U.S. 199. Bear right (east) on U.S. 199 and drive past the towns of Hiouchi and Gasquet. From Gasquet, continue eight miles to well-signed Patrick Creek Lodge on the left (north side of the road).

# 4 CAMP MARIGOLD GARDEN COTTAGES

Klamath River, off U.S. 101 near Crescent City

🏃 🚴 🛶 ❄ 🐕 👫

**Luxury rating: 2**                                    **Recreation rating: 4**

Camp Marigold is set on 3.5 landscaped garden acres bordering redwood forests. The area offers boundless activities and world-famous scenery. It is surrounded by Redwood National Park, towering redwoods, Pacific Ocean beaches, driftwood, agates, fossilized rocks, blackberries, Fern Canyon, Lagoon Creek Park, and the Trees of Mystery. Plus, it's just two miles from the Klamath River.

Both rustic cottages and lodge rooms are available. The cottages are rustic but not primitive. The decor is mostly rustic-country. The lodge rooms are designed for sleeping and not much else; they're set up to accommodate up to 15 people, and separate restrooms for men and women provide adequate facilities.

Collectively, it seems best designed for groups or family meetings. Note that this park also operates an RV camp. This gives the place the feel of being primarily designed as a base of operations for outdoor adventure, not a luxurious, romantic getaway.

There are many trails on the property, as well as blackberry vines—picking is great in the fall. Horseshoe pits are available.

The nearby Klamath River offers opportunities for fishing for salmon in the fall and eel in the spring. Given your proximity to the Redwood Empire and the Pacific Ocean, you can wander and explore for days. A treat especially for families, the Trees of Mystery attraction lies just a mile south of the cottages. This popular vacationer's rest stop is best known for two things: trees that have been grown in many odd configurations and the dinosaur-sized Paul Bunyan and Babe (the blue ox) statues next to the parking lot. Trees of Mystery has a popular gift shop and a parklike setting.

Remember to bring warm clothing for early- and late-hour outdoor recreation; summers can be foggy here, so pack extra layers.

## Facilities

Camp Marigold has 15 cabins and a six-bedroom lodge. There are 10 studio-style cabins, 2 one-bedroom cabins, and 3 two-bedroom cabins. All cabins have modern bathrooms; some have kitchens or equipped kitchenettes. The group lodge has a fully equipped kitchen and sleeps up to 20 people. Small leashed pets are permitted. Smoking is allowed. Linens are provided.

## Reservations and Rates
Reservations are recommended. Cabins rent for $65 per night; the lodge rents for $300 per night for the first 10 people, $5 for each additional person (maximum 20). Major credit cards are accepted. It's open year-round. Contact Camp Marigold Garden Cottages, 16101 U.S. 101, Klamath, CA 95548, 707/482-3585.

## Directions
From Eureka, drive 60 miles north on U.S. 101 to the campground, which is 4 miles north of the Klamath River Bridge, on the right side of the road.

# 5 BISHOP PINE LODGE
Humboldt Coast, off U.S. 101 in Trinidad

**Luxury rating:** 4                    **Recreation rating:** 4

The Humboldt Coast near Trinidad is highlighted by Patrick's Point State Park and its outstanding views, short hikes, and beaches; forests with Sitka spruce, Bishop pine, and redwoods; ocean fishing; whale-watching; and the ease of just leaning against a rock and watching all that water out there.

Bishop Pine Lodge is near the best of the outdoors, just a few minutes' drive from both Patrick's Point State Park and the town of Trinidad. The lodge consists of neat, well-kept small cottages. Each cottage has a small kitchen, bathroom, and living area/bedroom. Although a television is provided, you can always drape a towel over it, or if it's in a cabinet, you can close the doors.

One element some visitors find off-putting is the cottages' luminous paint job, including front doors that are fire-engine red and bright green. Also note that although the lodge is *near* the ocean, it is in the woods. Some newcomers are disappointed to discover neither ocean views nor a feeling of being close to the ocean. The ocean is close by, but it is a two- to three-mile drive to reach a beach.

The nearby must-do spots feature the Seascape Restaurant at Trinidad Head, a great beach just north of the parking lot here, and, of course, Patrick's Point State Park. The Rim Trail at Patrick's Point follows a two-mile route on the edge of the bluff around three sides of the park; several short cutoff trails take visitors to coastal lookout spots. Among the featured lookout spots are Mussel Rocks, Agate Beach, Rocky Point, Patrick's Point, Abalone Point, and Palmer's Point. I recommend hiking the Rim Trail and exploring all of these side trails, as each provides a different glimpse of this special place.

Nearby, just south of Trinidad, is the Cherry Heights Casino, highlighted by an excellent dinner-only restaurant with a spectacular ocean view.

## Facilities
Bishop Pine Lodge has 13 cottages, each a different size with unique interior designs. Most have kitchens and all have bathrooms, telephones and televisions. Well-behaved pets are permitted for $10 per day. Bedding, linens, and towels are provided. For units with kitchens, or for each person more than two, add $10 per day. No smoking is allowed.

## Reservations and Rates
Reservations are recommended and are often required in peak months: June, July, and August. Fees range $90–110 per night per couple. The lodge is closed for a few weeks in early spring and late fall. Contact Bishop Pine Lodge, 1481 Patrick's Point Drive, Trinidad, CA 95570, 707/677-3314, fax 707/677-3444, website: www.bishoppinelodge.com.

## Directions
From Eureka, drive north on U.S. 101 for 20 miles to Trinidad and take the Trinidad exit. At the stop sign, turn left and drive west under the freeway a short distance to Patrick's Point Drive. Turn right on Patrick's Point Drive and drive 1.9 miles to Bishop Pine Lodge on the right side of the road.

## 6 EMERALD FOREST
Humboldt Coast, off U.S. 101 near Trinidad

Luxury rating: 2                                    Recreation rating: 4

This campground is on 12 acres of redwoods with the ocean at Trinidad Head only about a five-minute drive away. It's a nice spot, with friendly folks and an abundance of recreation available nearby.

The accommodations are a mix of fairly rustic, old-fashioned, and modernized. After all, this is a campground first and foremost, with the cabins provided as a bonus. A large recreation hall holds a kitchen—great for large families or groups.

The proximity of woods and water provides the reward here. The camp is set amid redwoods on Patrick's Point Drive, only a five-minute drive from Patrick's Point State Park. This drop-dead gorgeous park is famous for the Rim Trail, an easy hike that peeks in and out of the forest onto panoramas of the ocean.

On the best days, Trinidad is one of the prettiest places on earth. The harbor is gorgeous, with a protected, rock-strewn bay providing a launch point for fishing trips and crabbing. Just to the north of Trinidad Head is a pretty and expansive beach, ideal for walks, and best at low tide when it seems to stretch on forever. The hike to the top of Trinidad Head is also outstanding, with long-distance ocean views; you'll find the trailhead  next to Seascape Restaurant, known for its fantastic crab omelets and sandwiches.

## Facilities

Emerald Forest has 15 cabins with kitchens. A playground, minimart, and coin laundry are available. A recreational hall with fireplace, kitchen, and a seating capacity of 40 is on-site. Leashed pets are permitted by advance approval. An RV campground is on the property. Activities include a video arcade, a playground, horseshoes, volleyball, and badminton. Smoking is prohibited. Bedding, linens, and towels are provided, as well as a daily service with a change of towels and trash removal.

## Reservations and Rates

Reservations are recommended in the summer. Cabins cost $85–249 per night, depending on the size of your party. Two-night minimum stays are required on weekends and holidays; off-season discounts are available. Pets permitted with a $10 per night fee plus $50 deposit. Day-use is $5 per person. Tent and RV sites are available. Major credit cards are accepted. It's open year-round. Contact Emerald Forest, 753 Patrick's Point Drive, Trinidad, CA 95570, 707/677-3554 or 888/677-3800, fax 707/677-0963, website: www.cabinsintheredwoods.com.

## Directions

From Eureka, drive north on U.S. 101 for 28 miles to Trinidad. Take the Trinidad exit, turn left at the stop sign, and drive a short distance under the freeway to Patrick's Point Drive. Turn right on Patrick's Point Drive and drive about a mile north to the campground on the right side of the road.

# 7 SYLVAN HARBOR RV PARK AND CABINS

Humboldt Coast, off U.S. 101 near Trinidad

🏃 🛶 ➡️ ❄️ 👫

**Luxury rating:** 3                                     **Recreation rating:** 4

Sylvan Harbor is most often used as a base camp for anglers. It is designed as an RV park and fish camp. Cleaning tables and canning facilities are available both on-site and a short distance from the boat hoist at Trinidad Pier. If you plan on using the boat hoist at the pier, check in advance for the operation schedule.

Since this privately operated park is primarily set up for RVs, the cabins are more of an option than its centerpiece. All three cabins are in the campground. In the summer, when visitor numbers are highest, RVs may be parked in the area near the cabins. In fall and spring, when RV numbers are low, these spots are usually empty.

The decor varies. These are old-style cabins that have been revamped. They have relatively new decks. Each cabin comes with a fully equipped kitchen—everything you need to set up house while you're on vacation. But note that the cabins do not have microwaves or electric coffeemakers.

Sylvan Harbor is on Patrick's Point Drive, a road lined with towering redwoods, only about a mile outside the small port town of Trinidad. Beauty surrounds Sylvan Harbor on all sides for miles around. Visitors come to enjoy the various beaches, to go agate or driftwood hunting, or to hike the various trails at nearby Patrick's Point State Park.

## Facilities

The cabins have kitchens, telephones, cable television, decks, and gas barbecue grills. Coin laundry, LP gas, multiple fish-cleaning tables, three fish smokers, and canning facilities are available. No smoking is allowed. Pets are not permitted. Linens and towels are provided.

## Reservations and Rates

Reservations are recommended in summer months. Rates are $67 per night or $348 per week for a one-room cabin for two, $3 per additional guest. No credit cards are accepted; pay by cash or by check if pre-approved. Contact Sylvan Harbor RV Park and Cabins, 875 Patrick's Point Drive, Trinidad, CA 95570, 707/677-9988, website: www.sylvanharbor.com.

## Directions

From Eureka, drive north on U.S. 101 for 28 miles to Trinidad. Take the Trinidad exit, turn left at the stop sign, and drive a short distance under the freeway to Patrick's Point Drive. Turn right and drive a mile to the campground.

# 8 VIEW CREST LODGE
Humboldt Coast, off U.S. 101 in Trinidad

**Luxury rating:** 4  **Recreation rating:** 4

Most cabins, lodgings, and campgrounds on the Humboldt Coast have no ocean view, even though they are close to the water. View Crest, on the other hand, didn't get its name by accident. Although there is a road to look across, the seven cottages here provide a mix of glimpses and views of the ocean and the coast, each one different from the next. The best? Cottage 5, perhaps. Though everybody has their own opinion.

The first thing you notice upon arrival is not the view but the extraordinary landscaping at the entrance. It's so inviting that people let themselves right in. The cabins are clean, comfortable, and fully equipped, including the kitchen. The owners recently added a hot tub to one of the cottages, making it ideal for honeymooners and romantic getaways. Note that some of the cabins are positioned apart from the rest, and some are duplex style.

Besides the ocean views and the cute cottages, another feature keeps people coming back time after time: the birds. Hundreds of swallows often perform uncanny flying displays, doing dipsy-doos in a swirling maze just before sunset. Many have nests at the cottages. This aerial display can be your send-off for a great vacation at Trinidad, which may include trips to Patrick's Point State Park, one mile north, and (farther north) Big Lagoon, Prairie Creek Redwoods State Park, and Redwood National Park.

Finally, while it can be easy to arrange a stay at View Crest during the week, it can be extremely difficult during good-weather weekends. For weekends, book your trip as far in advance as possible.

## Facilities
View Crest Lodge has 11 cottages made up of separate units and duplexes. Cottages each have a bathroom and a kitchen with cookware and utensils. Duplexes also have a mini-refrigerator and coffeepot. Most have cable television and telephones. Some have hot tubs or Jacuzzis. No smoking is permitted. Restaurants, a grocery store, a boat hoist, and fishing trips are available four miles south in Trinidad. An adjacent campground and RV park are available on the property. No pets are permitted. Linens and towels are provided.

## Reservations and Rates

Reservations are recommended. Cabin rates range $80–160 per night, depending on the size of the cabin, with a two-day minimum stay on weekends. Contact View Crest Lodge, 3415 Patrick's Point Drive, Trinidad, CA 95570, 707/677-3393, website: www.viewcrestlodge.com.

## Directions

From Eureka, drive north on U.S. 101 for 22 miles to the second Trinidad exit, for Seawood Drive. Take that exit to the stop sign, turn left, and drive west under the freeway a short distance to Patrick's Point Drive. Turn right and drive two miles to View Crest Lodge on the right.

## 9 CARTER HOUSE INNS                                  BEST (

Eureka, off U.S. 101

**Luxury rating:** 5                                    **Recreation rating:** 4

Forget rustic. Forget primitive. Forget mosquito repellent. Just remember your wallet because you're going to need it. And, oh, is it worth the price for a special, memorable stay when you want to be pampered. If you're looking for a quiet getaway near exceptional outdoor activities, but you don't want to forgo first-class accommodations and the finest food and wine, then you've hit the jackpot here.

Located in Eureka's historic district, alongside Humboldt Bay, Carter House Inns consists of four Victorian structures, including Bell Cottage and Carter Cottage. The cottages have four-poster beds, antique furnishings, double-headed showers, in-room entertainment centers, and honor bars. All inn rooms and cottages include complimentary full breakfast and afternoon and evening refreshments. The inns' Restaurant 301 holds a *Wine Spectator* Grand Award and features a wide selection of vintage wine. The garden supplies the restaurant with fresh produce. Carter House Inns is considered the finest accommodation in Humboldt County, and the restaurant's food is superb.

Now let's talk about the cottages; that's why they're in this book. Carter Cottage is a completely self-contained unit, luxurious and private, and ideal for a honeymoon or romantic vacation. It is spacious and decorated with bright, sunny colors and a modern flair. Amenities include a deep marble spa tub, two marble fireplaces, a private deck with bay view, and a state-of-the-art kitchen. Now get this: One of the inns' chefs, at your request, will prepare and serve you a five- or nine-course dinner, with or without wine selections, right in your cottage. There's an extra fee, of course, but don't you feel pampered?

The other units at Carter House Inns are cottage-like, most accurately described as inn rooms with kitchen facilities. However, for groups, Bell Cottage can be rented in its entirety as a single unit. Bell Cottage is a refurbished 1800s structure with three separate suites, each with its own bathroom, marble fireplace, television, VCR, and stereo/CD player. A fully equipped kitchen and other common areas are available within the building.

Carter House rents traditional inn rooms; that is, without kitchen facilities. It's across the street from the hotel and has five suites, all with private baths. One suite has a whirlpool tub. There are no telephones or televisions.

## Facilities

Carter House Inns has one cottage, five cottage rooms, 23 inn rooms, and a restaurant. Accommodations include spacious rooms and full bathrooms; some rooms have in-room entertainment centers, marble fireplaces, and honor bars. Carter Cottage has a fully equipped kitchen. Although children can be accommodated, the inns are more suitable for adults. No smoking is allowed. Comfy beds, pillows, linens, and towels are provided.

## Reservations and Rates

Reservations are recommended during the summer. Rates range $155–595 per night, which includes a full gourmet breakfast, wine and hors d'oeuvres in the late afternoon, and evening tea and cookies. For more than two people, $25 per person per night is charged. No pets are allowed. Major credit cards are accepted. Contact Carter House Inns, 301 L Street (at 3rd Street in Old Town), Eureka, CA 95501, 707/444-8062 or 800/404-1390, fax 707/444-8067, website: www.carterhouse.com.

## Directions

From U.S. 101 southbound in Eureka, turn right (west) on L Street and drive two blocks to the inn's lobby on the right side.

## 10 RIVERWALK RV PARK
Humboldt Coast, off U.S. 101 in Fortuna

🏃 🏊 🛶 🏕 👫

**Luxury rating:** 2                    **Recreation rating:** 3

Location, location, location is what you have here. The park is in fairly close proximity to a number of exceptionally scenic spots and recreational opportunities. And as with horseshoes, close does count here. You're 20 miles from the ocean and Humboldt

Bay, and a few miles north of stands of old-growth redwoods in Grizzly Creek Redwood State Park and Humboldt Redwoods State Park. Other side-trip options include touring the giant sawmill in Scotia and accessing the nearby Eel River and one of its tributaries, the Van Duzen River. There's a great fishing spot for salmon in October, where the Van Duzen enters the Eel. Please note that the Van Duzen's waters can fluctuate greatly, making it dangerous to enter on occasions when the waters are high; at other times, during low water levels, it may be closed to fishing.

As for the accommodations, Riverwalk offers four one-room cabins and one two-room cabin. The one-room cabins can sleep four, and the two-room cabin sleeps six. They're clean and simple, providing the basic elements you need. The log-frame beds have foam mattresses. Each cabin has a porch with swing, barbecue, and picnic table. This is also an RV campground.

## Facilities

Riverwalk RV Park has four one-room cabins and one two-room cabin. A restroom with showers, group kitchen facilities, a coin laundry, a recreation room, a small store, and modem hookup in the office are available. A pool and a spa are open during the summer season. The park is suitable for children. Leashed pets are allowed. No smoking is permitted in the cabins. Linens are not provided, so bring towels and sleeping bags or bedding.

## Reservations and Rates

Reservations are recommended during the summer. Rates are $36–60 per night. For more than two people, $4–5 per person per night is charged. Children under age four are free. Pets cost $5 per night. Major credit cards are accepted. Contact Riverwalk RV Park, 2189 Riverwalk Drive, Fortuna, CA 95540, 707/725-3359 or 800/705-5359, fax 707/725-7809, website: www.riverwalkrvpark.com.

## Directions

From Eureka, drive 16 miles south on U.S. 101 to the Kenmar/Riverwalk Drive exit. Turn right (west) and drive to the end of the off-ramp. Turn right (west) and drive 0.25 mile to the park entrance on the right.

## 11 MATTOLE RIVER ORGANIC FARM'S COUNTRY CABINS
Lost Coast, off Mattole Road near Petrolia

🏃 🚴 🛶 ❄ 🐕

**Luxury rating:** 3                                    **Recreation rating:** 4

There is no place on earth like the Lost Coast, and on the Lost Coast, there is no place like Mattole River Country Cabins. The Lost Coast is in remote southern Humboldt County, completely isolated and shielded by natural boundaries: the Pacific Ocean to the west, Humboldt redwoods to the east, Bear River Ridge to the north, and the King Mountain Range to the south. The road here is long and twisty, combining dirt, asphalt, and gravel. It's a destination you have to earn.

The coast is an unusual blend of remote farm country and ranchlands in a river valley that extends to isolated beaches, rocky coastal outcrops, and tidelands where few ever venture. In the center of the Mattole River Valley is Mattole River Country Cabins, featuring inexpensive rental cabins, perfectly situated for adventuring on the Lost Coast. The cabins come with small kitchens, so once you've set up camp, you can turn this trip into a do-it-yourself special.

But get this: Even though there are five cabins, they are numbered 2, 5, 6, 7, and 9; there are no cabins numbered 1, 3, 4 or 8. It's just the way things are out here. The best cabin by far is number 9. It has a woodburning stove, skylights, and decks in the back and front; it's totally secluded and separate from the other units. It is private, quiet, and pretty. The decor is rustic and comfortable.

In addition to the scenic area drives to the coast, there is excellent hiking and biking in the summer. One good trip for hiking or biking is a drive out to the end of Lighthouse Road, where you'll find a trailhead for the Lost Coast Trail just beyond the Bureau of Land Management's Mattole Campground. From here, take the abandoned jeep trail for three miles out to the Punta Gorda Light Tower—a day trip with superb coastal views.

### Facilities
Mattole River offers seven cabins, each with a bathroom and kitchen. Cookware and utensils are provided. Small grocery stores are nearby in the towns of Petrolia and Honeydew. Pets are permitted with no extra fee. Bed linens and towels are provided.

## Reservations and Rates

Reservations are recommended. Cabin rates range $65–100, depending on the number of beds and amount of privacy. Contact Mattole River Organic Farm's Country Cabins, 42354 Mattole Road, Petrolia, CA 95558, 707/629-3445 or 800/845-4607.

## Directions

From San Francisco, take U.S. 101 north past Garberville and Redway to the South Fork Road/Honeydew exit. Take that exit, cross the Eel River, and turn left. Continue on Bull Creek Road through Rockefeller Grove for 24 miles to Honeydew. In Honeydew, drive over the Mattole River Bridge, turn right on Mattole Road, and drive three miles. Look for Mattole River Organic Farm's Country Cabins (white cabins, blue trim) on the left side of the road.

# 12 RICHARDSON GROVE RV PARK & FAMILY CAMP

Redwood Empire, off U.S. 101 near Garberville

**Luxury rating:** 2 _                                    **Recreation rating:** 3

This private camp provides a nearby alternative to Richardson Grove State Park. Here you can enjoy cabin rentals near the state park, known for its grove of giant redwoods and excellent hiking.

Richardson Grove RV Park & Family Camp is family-oriented, with volleyball and basketball courts and horseshoe pits. It is also set up for group outings and religious retreats. In fact, the place is owned and operated by the Northern California/Nevada District Assemblies of God. "We are dedicated to assisting you in impacting lives for Jesus Christ in this beautiful wooded mountain setting," I was told. Yet when contacted later to confirm prices, they were grouchy as hell.

The facilities are fairly rustic but inexpensive. Two log cabins that each sleep 4 are open to the public. A church dorm can accommodate up to 30. Though the cabins are small and primitive, they're clean. The park provides a base camp for a retreat in the dramatic Redwood Empire; note that a large campground with 100 sites for tents and RVs is the major part of the operation.

The adjacent South Fork Eel River may look like a trickle in the summer, but there are some good swimming holes available. It also provides good steelhead fishing in January and February. There is especially good shore-fishing access here, as well as to the south in Cooks Valley (check Department of Fish and Game regulations before fishing).

## Facilities
Richardson Grove Campground's log cabins sleep 4, but one can handle up to 8 people. Restrooms, showers, an RV dump station, a playground, a coin laundry, a grocery store, LP gas, and ice are available. A kitchen facility with refrigeration and food storage capabilities for large or small groups is also available. No linens or towels are provided. Visitors should bring sleeping bags, pillows, and towels.

## Reservations and Rates
Reservations are recommended. Log cabins rent for $28 per night in summer, $22 per night in winter. Group rates are available. Major credit cards are accepted. It's open year-round. Contact Richardson Grove Campground, 750 U.S. 101, Garberville, CA 95542, 707/247-3380, fax 707/247-9806, website: www.redwoodfamilycamp.com.

## Directions
From the San Francisco area, take U.S. 101 north to Piercy. Continue two miles north to the park entrance (nine miles south of Garberville).

# 13 REDWOODS RIVER RESORT
### Eel River, off U.S. 101 near Leggett

**Luxury rating:** 3                                           **Recreation rating:** 4

Woods and water. For many, that's all you need for a vacation setting, and that's what you get here at Redwoods River Resort. The woods are the big redwoods; this area is the southern gateway to the Redwood Empire, which features excellent hiking. The water is the South Fork Eel River, which provides a few hidden swimming holes in summer and fishing for steelhead in winter. In fact, the resort has 3,000 feet of river frontage. A hiking trail leads from the resort to the Eel River, a walk of about 350 yards.

To make it work, many pick Redwoods River Resort. It offers several choices for accommodations, but most choose the well-furnished cabins. The key questions with every cabin include: Is there a bed with fresh sheets? Is there a bathroom with a shower?

Is there a kitchen? The answers here are yes, yes, and yes for most of the cabins, and that makes it a winner.

The decor is simple, clean, and comfortable. Each cabin is unique. Primitive cabins are also available—what they call camping cabins. The camping cabins provide you the opportunity to save a few bucks by staying in a nonfurnished unit and using the resort's campground facilities.

Redwoods River Resort is in a 21-acre grove of redwoods on U.S. 101, at an elevation of 700 feet. Richardson Grove Redwoods near Garberville is a must-do side trip. The Lookout Point Loop Trail here provides a tour through giant redwoods, culminating at a canyon rim over the South Fork Eel River. Giant redwoods approaching 300 feet tall and an estimated 1,000 years old are the highlights of Richardson Grove, while younger redwoods, fir, and tan oak trees fill out the forest.

## Facilities

Redwoods River Resort has six standard cabins, one deluxe cabin, and two camping cabins. Eight lodge rooms have kitchenettes. Standard cabins provide bathrooms with showers, fully equipped kitchens, and woodburning stoves, and sleep up to six. The deluxe cabin has the same amenities plus a full bathroom. Camping cabins have two sets of bunk beds and a table, and can sleep up to four. A bathhouse is available. All cabins have barbecues and fire pits and full use of resort facilities. That includes a heated swimming pool (summer only), playground, recreation room, minimart, coin laundry, group kitchen, evening campfire (summer), and organized summer activities. Firewood is available. Leashed pets are allowed only in two cabins and two lodge rooms during the off-season. Linens and towels are provided in the standard cabins. In the camping cabins, you must bring your own sleeping bags, pillows, and towels.

## Reservations and Rates

Reservations are recommended. Double occupancy rates for standard and deluxe cabin rentals are $80–90 per night, camping cabins are $35 per night, and lodge rooms are $75–125 per night in summer. A two-night minimum stay is required on weekends and holidays. Pets, when allowed, are $10 per pet per night in rooms. Major credit cards are accepted. The resort is open year-round. Contact Redwoods River Resort, 75000 U.S. 101, Leggett, CA 95585, 707/925-6249, fax 707/925-6413, website: www.redwoodriverresort.com.

## Directions

From the junction of U.S. 101 and Highway 1 in Leggett, drive north on U.S. 101 for seven miles to the campground entrance.

# Other Cabins & Cottages in the Region

**Bear Basin Lookout & Pierson Cabin,** Smith River National Recreation Area, Six Rivers National Forest, 1330 Bayshore Way, Eureka, CA 95501, 707/457-3131, website: www.fs.fed.us/r5/sixrivers/recreation/smith-river/lookout.

**Kamping Kabins,** Crescent City Redwoods KOA, 4241 U.S. 101 North, Crescent City, CA 95531, 707/464-5744, website: www.koa.com.

**Kamping Kabins,** KOA Eureka, 4050 North U.S. 101, Eureka, CA 95503, 707/822-4243, website: www.koa.com.

**Patrick's Point State Park Yurt,** 707/677-3570 or 707/488-5555. Reservations at 800/444-PARK (800/444-7275) or online at www.ReserveAmerica.com.

# SHASTA
# AND TRINITY

COURTESY OF LAKEVIEW TERRACE RESORT

## BEST CABINS & COTTAGES

**❰ Most Secluded**
Marble Mountain Ranch, **page 48**

**❰ Best for Winter Sports**
Mount Shasta Resort, **page 52**

**❰ Most Romantic**
Pine-Gri-La, **page 61**

**❰ Best for Families**
Trinity Mountain Meadow Resort, **page 64**

**❰ Best for Water Sports**
Sugarloaf Cottages Resort, **page 73**

# At 14,162 feet, Mount Shasta rises like a diamond in

a field of coal. Its sphere of influence spans a radius of 125 miles, and its shadow is felt everywhere in the region. This area has much to offer with giant Shasta Lake, the Sacramento River above and below the lake, the McCloud River, and the wonderful Trinity Divide country with its dozens of pretty backcountry lakes and several wilderness areas. This is one of the best regions anywhere for an outdoor adventure – especially hiking, fishing, power boating, rafting, and exploring.

In this area, you can rent cabins that are truly set near remote, quiet wilderness, and that offer the potential for unlimited adventures. Of all the regions in this book, this is the easiest one in which to find a cabin in a secluded setting near great recreation opportunities. That is the main reason people visit.

The most upscale lodging is offered by the Mount Shasta Resort, where to play golf you have to wear a shirt with a collar. That rule is something of an anomaly for an area known for great outdoors recreation, one where even the nicest restaurants will allow you to dine in your hiking boots.

There are hundreds of destinations, but the best are Shasta Lake, the Trinity Alps and its surrounding lakes and streams, and the Klamath Mountains, known as "Bigfoot Country" by the locals.

Shasta Lake is one of America's top recreation lakes. It is the one destination that is big enough to handle all who love it. The massive reservoir boasts 370 miles of shoreline, cabin rentals, 11 marinas, and 400 houseboat rentals. A remarkable 22 species of fish live in the lake. Many of the cabin rentals feature decks with lake views. In addition, getting here is easy — a straight shot off I-5.

At the charmed center of this beautiful region are the Trinity Alps, where lakes are sprinkled everywhere. It's also home to the headwaters for feeder streams to the Trinity River, Klamath River, New River, Wooley Creek, and others. Trinity Lake provides outstanding boating and fishing, and just downstream, smaller Lewiston Lake offers a quiet alternative. One advantage to Lewiston Lake is that it is always full of water, even all summer long, making for a very pretty scene. Downstream of Lewiston, the Trinity River provides low-cost rafting and outstanding shoreline access along Highway 299 for fishing for salmon and steelhead.

The neighboring Klamath Mountains are well known as Bigfoot Country. If you drive up the Forest Service road at Bluff Creek, just off Highway 96 upstream of Weitchpec, you can even find the spot where the famous Bigfoot movie was shot in the 1960s. Well, I haven't seen Bigfoot, but I have discovered tons of outdoor recreation. This remote region features miles of the Klamath and Salmon Rivers, as well as the Marble Mountain Wilderness. Options include canoeing, rafting, and fishing for steelhead on the Klamath River, or hiking in to your choice of more than 100 wilderness lakes.

# SHASTA & TRINITY

OREGON

Klamath National Forest

Six Rivers National Forest

Klamath Mountains

Marble Mountain Wilderness

Scott River

Copco Lake

Iron Gate Reservoir

Meiss Lake

Yreka

Klamath National Forest

Lake Shastina

Shasta-Trinity National Forest

▲ Mt Shasta (14,162ft)

Russian Wilderness

Mt Eddy (9,025ft) ▲

Weed

Mt Shasta

Shasta-Trinity National Forest

Castle Crags State Park

Trinity Lake

Trinity Alps Wilderness

McCloud River

Shasta Lake

Whiskeytown Shasta-Trinity NRA

Lewiston Lake

Weaverville

Whiskeytown Lake

Whiskeytown Shasta-Trinity NRA

Redding

see Lassen & Modoc page 90

Six Rivers National Forest

see The Redwood Empire page 22

Mad River

Ruth Reservoir

Trinity National Forest

Sacramento

Tehama State Wildlife Area

Red Bluff

0    10 mi

0    10 km

see Mendocino & Wine Country page 116

see Sacramento & Gold Country page 160

Orleans

Weitchpec

Klamath

Trinity

Salmon River

© AVALON TRAVEL PUBLISHING, INC.

# Shasta and Trinity Cabins & Cottages

# 1 MARBLE MOUNTAIN RANCH

**BEST C**

Klamath River, off Highway 96 near Somes Bar

🏃 ⛰ 🚣 🏊 ❄ 👫

**Luxury rating:** 3                                                 **Recreation rating:** 5

This is as much a hideout as a hideaway. Marble Mountain Ranch is set deep in Klamath National Forest along Highway 96, the curving two-laner that runs along the Klamath River. So right off, this spot is extremely remote. Hey, some people think the town of Yreka along I-5 is remote, right? Well, from Yreka, it's another two hours of driving to get to Marble Mountain Ranch. Because of that remoteness, this ranch offers complete, self-contained vacation packages. You not only have the opportunity for cabin lodging, but three meals a day and a major activity each day. The most popular activities are rafting on the Klamath, horseback riding, wilderness pack trips, salmon and steelhead drift-boat fishing, and mountain biking. Put it all together and you may just want to make this your permanent hideout.

The decor is country-cottage style with quilts and pictures. All units are heated, but air-conditioning is available only in the deluxe homes. A beautifully landscaped pool and spa area adds a nice touch for such a remote setting.

At Marble Mountain Ranch, all guests share home-style meals with other guests and staff in the dining facility. Meals are bountiful and include home-baked breads and desserts, salads, vegetables fresh from the garden, and select meats smoked and roasted over native hardwoods. Adventure-seeking attracts most people to the ranch for the first time, but it is the meals that often bring them back.

For the price, the cabins are well-equipped. But if you can book the deluxe lodge homes, that's the way to go for a more woodsy comfort. The grounds of the ranch feature vegetable gardens and many fruit trees. Swimming is available down the trail at the river or at any of several "secret" swimming holes nearby. This is a great place to bring youngsters; the ranch features a play gym, swings, and a small petting zoo with bunnies and miniature goats.

Most summer visitors will arrange at least one day of rafting on the Klamath River. The company Access to Adventure (800/552-6284) offers trips that are "Mild to Wild." That means you can match the trip with the level of white-water excitement you can handle. This section of the Klamath is one of its prettiest, a mix of oak woodlands and conifers. With that mix comes a wide variety of wildlife, outstanding for bird-watching.

## Facilities

Marble Mountain Ranch has 11 cabins and two deluxe lodge homes. Cabins and lodges vary in size and can accommodate 2–7 people. Each cabin provides full bathrooms and fully stocked kitchens or kitchenettes. Many have decks and four have woodstoves. A game room and weight room are available. Therapeutic massage is available for a fee. No smoking is allowed. Pets are discouraged. Linens and towels are provided.

## Reservations and Rates

Reservations are accepted. Rates are $75 per night for a cabin for two, plus $15 per additional person; $100 per night for two for units with a kitchen; and $200 for a home for five with two bedrooms. Rates for lodging, three meals, and a major activity are $200 per day per adult and $175 per day per child. Major credit cards are accepted. The ranch is open year-round, weather permitting. Contact Marble Mountain Ranch, 92520 Highway 96, Somes Bar, CA 95568, 530/469-3322 or 800/552-6284, fax 530/469-3321, website: www.marblemountainranch.com.

For rafting trips, contact River Country Rafting, 530/493-2207, or Access to Adventure, 800/552-6284. For a fishing guide, contact Wally Johnson in Seiad Valley, 530/496-3291.

## Directions

From Redding, drive north on I-5 to Yreka and Highway 263. Turn north on Highway 263 and drive to Highway 96. Turn west on Highway 96 and drive 63 miles to Happy Camp, then continue another 30 miles to the ranch on the left.

From Eureka, drive north on U.S. 101 just past Arcata to Highway 299. Take Highway 299 east and drive for 50 miles to Willow Creek and Highway 96. Turn north on Highway 96 and drive 47 miles to Somes Bar and continue 7.5 miles to the ranch on the right.

# 2 SANDY BAR RANCH CABINS
### Klamath River, off Highway 96 near Orleans

Luxury rating: 3        Recreation rating: 5

Sandy Bar Ranch features a collection of little redwood cabins in a valley on national forest land, about a mile from the town of Orleans. They are inexpensive for what you get, with each cabin providing a separate bedroom, with side beds (platform couches) in the living room, plus a full kitchen. With a grocery store located about a mile away, cooking can help keep the price of your trip down. A café is nearby as well. A unique quality of Sandy Bar Ranch is an extensive organic garden with fruit and flowers. There is also a fruit tree nursery and homemade crafts. Special nursery programs are offered at various times during the year.

The decor, if you call it that, is rustic. Each unit is heated and all have air-conditioning. Outdoor decks face the river, a big plus.

Sandy Bar Ranch is nestled in a beautiful valley carved out by the Klamath River. It serves as a gateway to the trails and rivers of the Klamath-Siskiyou mountains. This is one place where nature has used a broad brush in its artwork, with beauty touching everything. The Klamath River tumbles around boulders, into gorges, and then flattens into slicks, all framed by a high canyon and bordered by forest. Abundant birdlife  and wildlife live in this area, and from late summer through fall, fish as well, as steelhead and salmon arrive in their annual migrations up the Klamath.

In the summer, April–August, water conditions are perfect for rafting, and in July, the temperatures warm up considerably for swimming. For expert rafters, the nearby Cal Salmon, a tributary to the Klamath River, is one of the best little-known whitewater rafting rivers in California. The best put-in spot is near the town Forks of the Salmon. From here, the first five miles are Class II+—and then it really sizzles, with Class IV and V rapids. Last Chance Rapid is a Class V that features a mind-bender of a drop that will have your heart leaving your body for what seems like an eternity.

## Facilities
Sandy Bar Ranch has four one-bedroom redwood cabins that sleep four, each with full kitchen (with utensils) and bathroom. Pets are permitted. A grocery store and café are within a mile. Linens and towels are provided.

## Reservations and Rates
Reservations are accepted. Cabin rates are $88 per night or $528 per week for two people, with a minimum stay of one week in summer and two nights on weekends and holidays. Each additional person is $10 per night. A flat fee of $10 is charged for dogs. There are discounts for children. Contact Sandy Bar Ranch, P.O. Box 347, Orleans, CA 95556, 530/627-3379, website: www.sandybar.com.

For rafting, contact Klamath River Outfitters, 530/469-3349.

## Directions
From Eureka, drive north on U.S. 101 just past Arcata to the junction with Highway 299. Turn east on Highway 299 and drive to Willow Creek. At Willow Creek, turn north on Highway 96 and drive 43 miles, passing the town of Weitchpec, to the town of Orleans. In Orleans, turn left at Ishi Pishi Road and drive 0.75 mile. Look for Sandy Bar Ranch Cabins on the right side of the road.

From I-5, drive to Redding and Highway 299 E. Take Highway 299 east 120 miles to Orleans. Continue over the bridge to Ishi Pishi Road. Turn right and drive 0.75 mile to the cabin rentals on the right.

# 3 STEWART MINERAL SPRINGS

Shasta-Trinity National Forest, off I-5 near Weed

**Luxury rating:** 3                          **Recreation rating:** 4

In an area where Shasta's fabled Lemurians (tiny, mysterious beings that live in underground caves lined with gold) are said to reign, you probably figured there was a place like Stewart Mineral Springs near Mount Shasta—a therapeutic retreat with mineral baths, saunas, massage service, and Native American-style purification sweats. Well, if you did, you figured right. But before you laugh it off as some New Age curiosity, consider first that the treatment here actually works. You will leave feeling like a whole new person.

Stewart Mineral Springs is on the northern slope of Mount Eddy, across the Shasta Valley from giant Mount Shasta. It's in the woods on property bordering the Shasta-Trinity National Forest. There are five cabins available, along with motel-style rooms, small apartments, and tepees. The cabins are rustic but comfortable and include bedding. The tepees have two cots and covering for the dirt floor, but no bedding. Some guests bring air beds. Kitchenettes are provided in the cabins and apartments. There is a small restaurant on the premises.

The decor is rustic/comfortable, with queen-size beds. The cabins are heated. There is no air-conditioning. Bathrooms are provided in all lodging choices; that is, except for tepees, of course.

Stewart Mineral Springs is an old resort—over 100 years old. The cold, streaming Parks Creek flows through the property a short distance from the mineral baths. The magic happens in the combination of hot mineral baths, saunas, or sweats followed by a jump into the cold creek. One of the perpetual challenges here is to go from one to the other. Providing you survive, that is.

A few other notes: No campfires are permitted; violators will be thrown out; some clothing-optional areas are tolerated; and a variety of mineral baths and massages are available.

## Facilities

Stewart Mineral Springs has five cabins, six apartments, six tepees, dorm rooms, an A-frame house, and spaces for tent camping and RVs. Four conference tents are available. Kitchenette facilities are provided in the cabins and apartments. A restaurant is available. Therapeutic mineral baths, massages, saunas, and purification sweats are available. Reservations are not required for mineral baths, but you must have an appointment for a massage. While nudity is not promoted, it is tolerated if discreet. No smoking is allowed. Pets are not permitted. Linens and towels are provided in the cabins. Linens are not provided in the tepees; be sure to bring a sleeping pad, sleeping bag, and pillow.

### Reservations and Rates
Reservations are recommended. The fee is $69 per night per cabin and $59–89 for an apartment room. Tepees are available at $24 per night double occupancy, with a $5 charge for each additional person to a maximum of five. An A-frame cabin that can sleep 10 is available for $325 per night, with a two-night minimum stay. The fee for a mineral bath is $15 for guests at Stewart Mineral Springs, $20 for day-use visitors. Contact Stewart Mineral Springs, 4617 Stewart Springs Road, Weed, CA 96094, 530/938-2222, fax 530/938-4283, website: www.stewartmineralsprings.com.

### Directions
From Redding, drive north on I-5 just past the town of Weed. Take the Edgewood exit, turn left at the stop sign, and drive a short distance (under the freeway) to Old Highway 99. Turn right on Old Highway 99 and drive a short distance to Stewart Springs Road. Turn left and drive four miles to Stewart Mineral Springs.

## 4 MOUNT SHASTA RESORT          BEST (

Mount Shasta, off I-5

🚶 🚴 🏊 🎣 🏊 ❄️

**Luxury rating:** 4                    **Recreation rating:** 5

This is the kind of place where you expect the finest. That is, the finest in lodging, dining, surrounding natural beauty, and recreation. At Mount Shasta Resort, your expectations are met.

From the moment you drive in, you are put on notice that this is the most deluxe golf club and resort setting open to the public in the region. The first rule is that men have to wear shirts that have collars. Let me tell you, there are guys in Siskiyou County who don't own a shirt with a collar. So right off, you've got a sense that it's something of an exclusive place, and so it is.

The resort is at the foot of Mount Shasta. The views from the fairway and from the restaurant are simply stunning, making it one of the prettiest golf courses in Northern California. The course is a professionally designed 18-hole course situated on 126 acres of forest and rolling terrain, a challenge to amateurs and professionals alike. The trees are very sturdy, ideal for wrapping your golf clubs around after you miss yet another shot. Heh. No, that kind of behavior is not tolerated.

The chalets are fairly new, quite beautiful, and well-furnished. The decor is woodsy and yet beautiful, definitely an upscale feel. They come in one- and two-bedroom units and include private bathrooms, full kitchens (with cherry-wood cabinetry), living rooms with gas fireplaces, televisions, telephones, and sleeper sofas. And did I mention the tiled entry provides ski racks, coat racks, and storage for golf clubs? Some of the units have their own decks with private hot tubs. The chalets are set amid ponderosa pines across the road from the resort headquarters, within range of the north shore of nearby Lake Siskiyou.

This is not Golden Pond, where cabins sit on the lake's shore. It is rather Siskiyou County's finest golf resort, a jewel that matches the grandeur of nearby Mount Shasta.

## Facilities

Mount Shasta Resort has 30 one-bedroom chalets, 20 two-bedroom chalets, and 15 motel-style Woodland rooms. All chalets have furnished bedrooms, bathrooms, and kitchens. Some have decks with private hot tubs. A restaurant, bar, golf course, golf lessons, pro shop, and tennis courts are available on the property. No smoking is allowed. Pets are not permitted. Linens and towels are provided.

## Reservations and Rates

Reservations for lodging and tee times are recommended. Rates for one-bedroom chalets for two people are $154–169, two-bedroom chalets are $190–239, and Woodland rooms for two people are $99–119. A two-night minimum stay is required in summer, a three-night minimum stay on holiday weekends. A deposit is required. Off-season discount rates are available, as are golf, ski, and midweek packages. Restaurant and spa facilities are on-site. Major credit cards are accepted. The resort is open year-round. Contact Mount Shasta Resort, 1000 Siskiyou Lake Boulevard, Mount Shasta, CA 96067, 530/926-3030 or 800/958-3363, golf course information (PGA pro Jeremy Dunkason) 530/926-3052, website: www.mtshastaresort.com.

## Directions

From the town of Mount Shasta on I-5, take the Central Mount Shasta exit (Exit 738) and drive to the stop sign. Turn west and drive a short distance to Old Stage Road. Turn left and drive 0.25 mile to a Y at W.A. Barr Road. Bear right on W.A. Barr Road and drive to the stop sign. Continue straight for one mile to the signed entrance for Mount Shasta Resort on the left.

# 5 LAKE SISKIYOU RESORT
### Mount Shasta, off I-5

🏃 🚴 🛶 🚐 🐕 👫 ♿

**Luxury rating:** 2                                          **Recreation rating:** 5

Native American legend has it that Mount Shasta was created when the Great Spirit poked a hole in the sky and made a tepee out of the fallen pieces. Sitting at the base of giant Mount Shasta is Lake Siskiyou—a true jewel. This artificially constructed lake is in one of the prettiest settings in the United States. It was created for the sole purpose of recreation—not to store water for farmers—so while reservoirs in the California foothills get drained, Siskiyou remains full.

Lake Siskiyou Resort provides a huge campground complex that is tucked into the forest so visitors don't get their style cramped. RV rentals, lodging units, and cabins are also available. They are clean and set up to provide an advanced form of camping. That is, you bring your sleeping bag and towels. The decor is rustic. All units are heated and have swamp coolers. All cabins have kitchens equipped with utensils.

Many anglers use this as a base camp for a vacation, camping in relative luxury, then fishing or swimming at Lake Siskiyou, or climbing or trekking at Mount Shasta.

Virtually in the shadow of Mount Shasta, Lake Siskiyou is almost always full and offers a variety of recreation options. From the resort, the lake is within walking distance and provides a swimming beach protected by a buoy line and cool, clean water. An excellent boat ramp is available and a 10-mph speed limit is strictly enforced and keeps the place quiet. In the summer months, the lake gets a lot of traffic from swimmers, sunbathers, and anglers.

## Facilities

Lake Siskiyou Resort has 11 RV rentals and 25 lodging units available, including cabins. A campground with both RV sites and tent sites is on the property nearby. Drinking water, flush toilets, showers, a playground, propane, a grocery store, coin laundry, and RV dump station are available. There are also marinas, boat rentals (canoes, kayaks, motorized boats), free boat launching, a fishing dock, a fish-cleaning station, and a swimming beach with buoy line. A free movie plays every night in the summer. No smoking is permitted. Pets are allowed during daylight hours or for day-use visitors, but are not allowed for overnight users. Linens and towels are not provided. Bring your own sleeping bag, pillow, and towel.

## Reservations and Rates

Reservations are recommended. RVs rent for $50–140 per night, $5 for each additional vehicle per night. A two-night minimum stay is required on weekends, three nights on holiday weekends. Major credit cards are accepted. It's open April–October, weather permitting. Contact Lake Siskiyou Campground and Marina, P.O. Box 276, Mount Shasta, CA 96067, 530/926-2618 or 888/926-2618, website: www.lakesis.com.

## Directions

From the town of Mount Shasta on I-5, take the Central Mount Shasta exit and drive to the stop sign. Turn west and drive a short distance to Old Stage Road. Turn left and drive 0.25 mile to a Y at W.A. Barr Road. Bear right on W.A. Barr Road and drive past Box Canyon Dam. Two miles farther, turn right at the entrance road for Lake Siskiyou Campground and Marina and drive a short distance to the entrance station.

## 6 ABODE AWAY
Mount Shasta off I-5

**Luxury rating:** 4            **Recreation rating:** 5

© SUSAN MORRIS

The Mount Shasta region is truly a four-season paradise, the last great unspoiled area in California that hasn't yet been discovered by hordes of people. There is plenty of clean air and clean water; in fact, I think it has the best-tasting water anywhere. Renting a private chalet or cabin close to the city of Mount Shasta provides a unique opportunity to experience the outdoor pleasures that the area provides without driving long distances each day. Another bonus is that the town of Mount Shasta has full services and caters to visitors; you'll be greeted by a small-town friendliness that is hard to find nowadays.

The various one-of-a-kind cabins and chalets at Abode Away provide the amenities of home. The Dacha is a two-story, two-bedroom, two-bath home with, yes, two woodstoves. The home has decks and breathtaking views of Mount Shasta and can accommodate up to eight people. This home is full of personality and has theme rooms, including Bear's Den, Jungle John, Captain's Quarters, and a bathroom named the Frog Pond.

The Lodge is situated in the pines just outside city limits and has three bedrooms and two bathrooms. It is set up for relaxation at the end of the day and includes extensive decks, a big-screen television, DVD player, table tennis, and foosball. Smaller cabins are also available.

So what are the activities? Spring and summer recreation includes white-water rafting and kayaking, stellar fishing, hiking, golfing, horseback riding, swimming, boating, and water sports. Many come to the area just to climb mighty Mount Shasta, which has an elevation of 14,162 feet; local guide services are available. In the late summer and early fall there is berry picking. Winter activities include ice skating, cross-country and downhill skiing, snowboarding, snowshoeing, snowmobiling, sled-dog excursions, and ice fishing. The Mount Shasta Board and Ski Park is just a few miles from the town of Mount Shasta.

The busiest time of year is the Fourth of July, when the town of Mount Shasta hosts the largest small-town foot race in the world. The little town of 3,600 swells to double its size and hosts walking and running races, a street fair and parade, live music, a barbecue, and a superb fireworks show at Lake Siskiyou.

## Facilities
Abode Away has a variety of private vacation rentals ranging from cozy cabins to three-bedroom lodges and chalets. Each home has bathrooms with showers, fully stocked kitchens with microwaves, television, heating, and laundry facilities. Paper products are provided. A complimentary amount of firewood is provided in homes with woodstoves. Some of the rentals have additional amenities such as big-screen televisions, DVD and VCR players, air conditioning, and wireless Internet service. No smoking is allowed. Pets may be allowed in some of the homes; call for details. Linens and towels are provided.

## Reservations and Rates
Reservations are recommended. The fee is $125–300 per night with an additional charge for extra people, depending on the home. A cleaning fee of $45–75 is also charged. There is a two-night minimum and a three-night minimum on holidays; it's open year-round. Contact Abode Away, 506 South Old Stage Road, Mount Shasta, CA 96067, 530/926-4836, website: www.abodeaway.com.

## Directions
From Redding, drive north on I-5 for approximately 60 miles to the town of Mount Shasta and the Central Mount Shasta exit. Once in town, call 530/926-4836 for specific directions to your particular lodging rental.

# 7 CAVE SPRINGS/DUNSMUIR CABINS

Upper Sacramento River, off I-5 in Dunsmuir

🚶 🚴 🚐 ❄️ 🐴 👫

**Luxury rating:** 3                    **Recreation rating:** 4

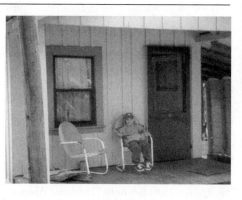

About an hour's drive north of Redding in the town of Dunsmuir you'll find Dunsmuir Cabins. The cabins are in different locations near the Upper Sacramento River. The units range from California box construction cabins to guest homes along the river. Some are small and rustic; others are upscale and gorgeous with decks overlooking the water. But all are on or close to the Upper Sacramento River. All have full kitchens and larger units have televisions. The best way to get started on this trip is to call the owner of Cave Springs, Louie Dewey, at 530/235-2721, and discuss what best fits your expectations.

The main attraction here is the Upper Sacramento River. In July 1991, the river was the site of the worst inland toxic spill in the history of California when a Southern Pacific freight train derailed at Cantara Loop, just north of Dunsmuir. But the river is back, all the way back.

In the time since that catastrophe, what is known as the "Genesis Effect" has taken place. The aquatic food web of the river was reestablished, from algae to caddis larvae, and this provided the foundation for the recovery of the trout fishery. It is once again considered one of the best trout streams in America, and is easily accessible from the adjacent interstate highway. The trout population has now stabilized, providing not only a stellar fishery, but an example of how nature reversed a human-caused cataclysm—and in that sense, it is considered a living laboratory.

The recovery effort has put Dunsmuir Cabins back in business as the best place to stay along the Sacramento River for visitors who want to fish, explore, hike, or even kayak this now-famous trout stream. This location is also about a half-hour's drive from the Mount Shasta Ski & Board Park, making Dunsmuir a year-round destination.

Hikes are available nearby at Castle Crags State Park and, of course, at Mount Shasta to the north and in the nearby Eddy Range to the west. There are several excellent driving tours as well. The best three are: 1) from south of Dunsmuir, take the Castle Crags State Park exit and drive past the state park and continue up the mountain for awesome views of the Crags; 2) from within the town of Mount Shasta, take the Central Mount Shasta exit and continue up the Everitt Memorial Highway all the way to Panther Flat at 7,400 feet; and 3) from Dunsmuir, drive to Lake Siskiyou and turn left for the drive up to Castle Lake, set at 5,450 feet, for incredible views of Mount Shasta to the east.

## Facilities

Dunsmuir Cabins accommodations come in a wide variety of lodging styles, from box construction cabins to guest homes along the river. Cabins include full kitchens. Pets are permitted. Linens and towels are provided.

## Reservations and Rates

Reservations are recommended. Rates range $40–375 per night. Major credit cards are accepted. Contact Dunsmuir Cabins, c/o Cave Springs Resort, 4727 Dunsmuir Avenue, Dunsmuir, CA 96025, 530/235-2721 or 888/235-2721, website: www.cave springs.com. For a fishing guide/tour service, contact Jack Trout Flyfishing International & Mount Shasta Scenic Tours, 530/926-4540, website: www.mtshasta.com. For fishing supplies and information, contact Ted Fay Fly Shop, 530/235-2969, website: www.tedfay.com; or Dunsmuir Flyfishing Company, 530/235-0705.

## Directions

From Redding, drive north on I-5 for 52 miles to Dunsmuir. Take the Central Dunsmuir exit. Turn left onto Dunsmuir Avenue, continue through the underpass, and drive one mile to Cave Springs Reosrt on the left at 4727 Dunsmuir Avenue.

# 8 RIPPLE CREEK CABINS

Shasta-Trinity National Forest, off Highway 3 near Trinity Lake

**Luxury rating:** 3                                   **Recreation rating:** 4

Sure, there are a ton of cabin rentals in the vicinity of Trinity Lake. But each one is unique, and so it is at Ripple Creek Cabins.

This resort is in the Trinity River Valley, about a 15-minute drive north of Trinity Lake. The cabins are nestled along a creek in a forest setting. On the inside, the cabins are well-furnished with a knotty-pine interior, often with a woodstove—a nice touch. Each cabin is different in its

design, but all provide the goodies a family needs: bedrooms, bathrooms, kitchens, and living rooms. Considering the relative remoteness of the place, most visitors find the accommodations far better than expected. For many, this is what a cabin-based vacation should be, both inside and out.

This area is very popular for hiking, with many outstanding trips in the vicinity. My personal favorite is the all-day hike to Mount Eddy (elevation 9,025 feet). It offers one of the most outstanding views anywhere in Northern California. On the climb up, you pass Deadfall Lakes, then rise up the west side of Mount Eddy. Only in your last steps to the top does Mount Shasta suddenly come into view to the east, a moment you will never forget. A detailed story about the hike my wife and I took to the Eddy summit is available for guests at Ripple Creek.

But there are many other options, including a series of wilderness trailheads along Highway 3, as well as along Coffee Creek Road nearby to the south. A map of Shasta-Trinity National Forest is a must.

## Facilities

Ripple Creek has six cabins and one large group cabin. Each cabin is unique. Bathrooms with showers, fully stocked kitchens, a woodstove, and electric heat are provided. Each cabin has a private yard, picnic table, and barbecue. Laundry facilities, a recreation room, and a play area with volleyball, badminton, and horseshoes are available nearby. A country store is four miles away. No smoking is allowed in rooms. Pets are permitted, but pet owners are requested to bring pet beds. Linens and towels are provided.

## Reservations and Rates

Reservations are recommended. The double-occupancy rate is $104 per night and $655 per week. For four people in the group cabin, the rate is $159 per night. A one-week minimum stay is required in summer. Off-season discounts are available. The pet charge is $10 per pet per stay. No credit cards are accepted. You can pay by cash or by check with prior approval. Contact Ripple Creek Cabins, Route 2, Box 4020, Trinity Center, CA 96091, 530/266-3505, website: ripplecreekcabins.com.

## Directions

From Redding, turn west on Highway 299 and drive 40 miles to Weaverville and Highway 3. Turn north on Highway 3 and drive 40 miles (just past Coffee Creek Road) to Eagle Creek Loop. Turn left and drive 1.5 miles to the Ripple Creek Cabins entrance on the right.

# 🟨 ENRIGHT GULCH CABINS
Trinity Lake, off Highway 3 near Trinity Center

🏃 🏊 🚣 🐕 👫

**Luxury rating:** 3                              **Recreation rating:** 4

Enright Gulch Cabins is a settlement of deluxe housekeeping cabins and motel units located a short distance to the north of giant Trinity Lake (think fishing, swimming, boating, and waterskiing), as well as wilderness trailheads for day hikes to Boulder Creek, Lake Eleanor, and up Swift Creek. These are the main recreation draws. The historical significance of the area adds a special perspective.

Enright Gulch received its name when it was patented as a placer gold mine in 1877. During the construction of Trinity Dam in the late 1950s, houses from the small community of Stringtown (which was later buried under the waters of Trinity Lake) were moved onto the property among the cedar, fir, and pines next to the small creek that flows through the area. That is how this resort was created. The place has a history like no other cabin rental resort in California.

These cabins now offer not only a bit of history, but also an oasis of comfort, peace, and privacy in a natural setting. The decor is country style, comfortable and updated, with many antiques.

The one potential drawback is that because of the sloping curves of the access road, medium to large boats cannot be trailered in. Boat owners looking for a headquarters for a Trinity Lake adventure should make sure they can trailer their boats in and out of the resort without a problem, or find other lodging closer to the lake.

There are two unique attractions nearby: Carrville Dredger Pond (for fishing) and Alpen Cellars (for wine-tasting). Carrville Dredger Pond is less than a half mile from Enright Gulch. It's fed by year-round springs, it's stocked regularly with rainbow trout, and it's open to fishing all year. Alpen Cellars, a top winery, is a short drive from the resort. Visitors are always welcome for wine-tasting.

## Facilities
Enright Gulch Cabins has four cabins, with one or two bedrooms, that sleep 2–8 people. There are also motel-style rooms. All are heated. A fully-stocked kitchen, heat, and deck with barbecue are provided. No smoking is allowed. Pets are permitted but must be attended at all times. Linens and towels are provided.

## Reservations and Rates

Reservations are recommended. The double-occupancy rate is $110 per day or $620 per week for a one-bedroom cabin, and $130 per day or $730 per week for a two-bedroom cabin; it's $5 per day or $30 per week for each additional person. Pets are $10 per day or $30 per week. There is a $100 deposit. A three-night minimum stay is required in summer. Major credit cards are accepted. Contact Enright Gulch Cabins, Highway 3 North, P.O. Box 244, Trinity Center, CA 96091, 530/266-3600 or 888/383-5583.

## Directions

From Redding, turn west on Highway 299 and drive 40 miles to Weaverville and Highway 3. Turn north on Highway 3 and drive 32 miles (2 miles north of Trinity Center) to Enright Gulch Road (private, gravel road). Turn left and drive 0.2 mile to the resort.

## 10 PINE-GRI-LA                                              BEST ◖

Upper Sacramento River, off I-5 near Castella

**Luxury rating:** 4                              **Recreation rating:** 5

COURTESY OF WWW.SHASTACABINS.NET

Folks around here try to keep Pine-Gri-La a secret. For instance, I was asked not to print the specific directions to their cottage rentals. In fact, the owners do not give out the directions to the public, but provide them only to those who have reserved a stay. That's because the cottages are extremely hidden and charming, ideal both for a family adventure getaway or a romantic hideaway. The owners want to keep it that way. So no one will be driving by, peeking in the windows, or trying to get a preview of the place.

The rentals are located roughly in the vicinity of Castle Crags State Park near Castella, 45 miles north of Redding. The cottages are set in the only privately occupied parcel in the Trinity Divide country of the Shasta-Trinity National Forest, roughly a 25-minute drive from I-5. So what you have here is a high-mountain wildland—yet with a gorgeous cottage to stay in as a launch point for your vacation. That's right, all the comforts of home in the wilderness.

The three cottages are named Bear, Country Chalet, and Deluxe, and all have full kitchens and decks with gorgeous views. These cottages are custom-built mountain cabins. They are not motel units, park model units, RV cabins, or residential houses.

They are built for privacy and sleeping comfort. Your only "neighbors" are deer and bears strolling about the tall firs, the pines, and the wildflowers—and the trout doing laps in the nearby lakes. The Trinity Divide is loaded with trout. Gray Rocks, Castle Crags, and Mount Shasta loom over the landscape. Three sleeping cabins can be rented to accommodate large groups.

There are several bedroom options. The decor is beautiful and comfortable with lots of natural wood. All units are fully heated.

One more note: The owners told me they often sleep in the cottages to judge and assure the quality of each. The real reason, I later figured, is so they too can feel like they're on a stellar vacation.

## Facilities
Pine-Gri-La has three customized cottages that can sleep 2–10 people, along with a small lodge. The cottages have full kitchens, heat, and decks. There are also three sleeping cabins available to accommodate additional persons in your party. No smoking is allowed. Pets are not permitted. Families are welcome. Linens, pillows, and towels are provided.

## Reservations and Rates
Reservations are recommended. The base rate is $150–200 per night for cabins sleeping 2–10; children are $1 for each year of age. Sleeping cabins, which accommodate 5–11 people, are $125 per person. A three-night minimum is required in summer, a two-night minimum the rest of the year. Major credit cards are accepted. It's open year-round. Contact Pine-Gri-La, P.O. Box 100, Castella, CA 96017, 530/235-4466, website: www.shastacabins.net.

## Directions
From Redding, drive north on I-5 for 45 miles to Castella and the Castle Crags State Park exit. Take that exit and drive a short distance to the stop sign. Turn left and drive under the highway underpass and continue 0.25 mile to the gas station/store on the left. Turn left and park; a pay phone is available. Phone 530/235-4466 for specific directions to your cottage.

# 11 BEST IN THE WEST RESORT
### Upper Sacramento River, off I-5 near Castella

🏃 🏕 🚣 🛶 🐎 👫

**Luxury rating:** 3                    **Recreation rating:** 4

This park is in the Upper Sacramento River Canyon, within close range of excellent fly-fishing for rainbow trout. The park is split by a small road, with the cabins on one side and an RV park on the other. The RV park is landscaped with shaded sites and lawns. The proximity to Castle Crags State Park, the Sacramento River, and Mount Shasta makes the location a winner.

The Best in the West Resort is a small resort situated among pines, cedars, and firs. The cabins are arranged around a courtyard alongside little Mears Creek. A short walk brings you to the forests, birds, animals, and wildflowers. Azaleas scent the air in spring and blackberries abound in late summer. As with all the camps, cabins, and cottages in

the Sacramento River Canyon, passing trains are common and can alarm those with heightened sensibilities. Others say they don't even hear the trains, and in fact, some say the sound of the trains is comforting.

The decor is country-style. All facilities are modern and fully equipped. All units are heated.

The Upper Sacramento River is again becoming one of the best trout streams in the west, with easy and direct access off an interstate highway. The trout population has recovered since the devastating spill from a train derailment that occurred in 1991. The Sims area provides access to some of the better spots for trout fishing, particularly from mid-May through July. The technique that works best here is nymphing with a Copper John and Prince Nymph and short-lining with a strike indicator.

In the spring, from April through mid-June, this is also a great section for rafting, with several Class III runs in the vicinity. The town of Mount Shasta, 20 miles to the north, has golf courses and restaurants. If you want to literally get away from it all, a trailhead about three miles east on Sims Flat Road climbs along South Fork, including a terrible, steep one-mile section near the top, eventually popping out at Tombstone Mountain.

## Facilities

Best in the West Resort has six cabins with 1–3 bedrooms with queen-size beds, along with a large A-frame lodge that sleeps 14-plus. The cabins sleep 6–8 people and have a full bath, deck, woodburning stove, television, and full kitchen with utensils. An RV campground is also on the property, but separated by a small road. Restrooms, hot showers, cable television, coin laundry, and a playground are available. Pets are allowed. No smoking is permitted in cabins. The cabins are not wheelchair accessible. Linens and towels are provided.

## Reservations and Rates

Reservations are accepted. Prices generally range $50–75 per night though there are exceptions, such as for groups. It's open year-round. Contact Best in the West Resort, 26987 Sims Road, Castella, CA 96017, 530/235-2603, website: www.eggerbestwest.com.

## Directions

From Redding, drive north on I-5 for about 40 miles to the Sims Road exit. Drive one block west on Sims Road to the campground on the left.

## 1 2 TRINITY MOUNTAIN MEADOW RESORT BEST C

Coffee Creek, off Highway 3 near Trinity Alps

**Luxury rating:** 2                                   **Recreation rating:** 4

If you want children to learn to love the wilderness and have a great outdoor experience, this is one of the best places imaginable to bring them. That is because Mountain Meadow Resort is like a wilderness retreat, set at the edge of the Trinity Alps Wilderness near Big Flat and the Coffee Creek Road wilderness trailheads. All meals are provided, you sleep in a snug cabin, a solar-heated swimming pool with a gorgeous view is available, and special programs and meals are set up for kids. So for many families, this is the ideal getaway.

The cabins are on the rustic side but make a good fit for the location. Hey, any cabin that has a bed, linens, shower, and towels gets a gold star when considering the comfort factor, even if it is set on the edge of never-never land. The units are heated.

The resort is set for children to enjoy a variety of crafts and activities that are scheduled throughout the week. An early dinner for children is supervised by staff and followed by organized games. That means the adult dinner hour is quiet and private. That's right, parents get some down time from being parents. This doesn't mean there aren't plenty of family activities available. The whole family can participate in volleyball, badminton, horseshoes, and sing-alongs by the campfire.

A real plus is the swimming pool. There are sun chairs set with dramatic panoramas of the surrounding canyon and mountain country. Even though this is the mountains, it can get hot here, and jumping in that swimming pool—especially with the surrounding scenery—is often euphoric.

For ambitious hikers, the nearby wilderness trailhead at the end of Coffee Creek Road provides the jump-off to beautiful Caribou Lakes. This is an all-day trip, nine miles one-way to the first lake. This trip is best done in three days, backpacking style, with a rest day in the middle at a base camp to explore and swim in the three lakes.

## Facilities

Trinity Mountain Meadow Resort has 10 cabins and a small lodge. The cabins have beds and bathrooms. A deck with a barbecue is available. There is no kitchen; three meals a day are provided, including a separate early dinner for children. A swimming pool, laundry facilities, recreation room, and small bar are available. Smoking is not permitted in cabins. No pets are allowed. The resort is especially designed for families. Linens and towels are provided.

## Reservations and Rates

Reservations are required. Rates for cabins for two people are $840 per week; child rates are $580 per week for a child over 10, $420 per week for a child under 10. There's no charge for children under 2. Rates include three meals per day. A one-week minimum stay is required in summer, while three nights are the minimum in June and September. No credit cards are accepted. The resort is open in summer, with opening and closing dates determined by the weather. Contact Trinity Mountain Meadow Resort, Star Route 2, Box 5700, Trinity Center, CA 96091, 530/462-4677, website: www.mountainmeadowsresort.com.

## Directions

From Redding, turn west on Highway 299 and drive 40 miles to Weaverville and Highway 3. Turn north on Highway 3 and drive 38 miles (past Trinity Lake) to Coffee Creek Road. Turn left and drive 20 miles to Trinity Mountain Meadow Resort near the end of the road.

# 13 BONANZA KING RESORT

### Coffee Creek, off Highway 3 near Trinity Lake

**Luxury rating: 3**                                    **Recreation rating: 4**

Bonanza King Resort encompasses eight acres in a mountain meadow setting of pines, fur, and cedar along Coffee Creek. Right there is one reason why some overlook it. The other reason is that once most visitors to the area reach Trinity Lake, they stay; few head onward just beyond the lake and turn left on Coffee Creek Road. Yet this is where Bonanza King Resort is hidden. So, you get a good deal of privacy if you go the extra mile.

The housekeeping cabins are fully equipped and well-maintained—and have heat. The cabins are spaced apart from each other, and each has its own front yard, backyard, and driveway. The decor is cozy and comfortable, and cabins are well furnished. The grounds are covered with plenty of green grass, edged by flower beds, and border Coffee Creek and a national forest filled with a sea of conifers. You'll be within close proximity of Trinity Lake, as well as several outstanding trailheads for day trips to wilderness lakes. The property also offers a playground for kids.

Nearby Coffee Creek is a mountain stream fed by snow from the Trinity Alps. This is stocked with trout by the Department of Fish and Game, and there are a few swimming holes as well. If you drive up Coffee Creek, there are sections where boulders are piled high along the river. These are mining tailings from the gold rush days, kind of like a living history lesson.

Many other adventures await nearby. Trinity Lake is only three miles to the south, the Coffee Creek trailhead for access to the Trinity Alps Wilderness is 20 minutes at the end of Coffee Creek Road, and there are several other trailheads along both Coffee Creek Road and nearby Highway 3.

In the winter, the surrounding mountains provide good cross-country skiing and snowshoeing. It's a good thing that Bonanza King Resort is open year-round.

## Facilities

Bonanza King Resort has seven cabins that sleep 3–7 people. All have bedrooms, bathrooms with showers, furnished kitchens, living rooms, and heat. A porch holds a barbecue and a picnic table. A washing machine and clothesline are available. A country store and café are nearby. Activities include swimming, volleyball, badminton, basketball, horseshoes, croquet, and Ping-Pong. No smoking is allowed. Leashed pets are permitted. Linens and towels are provided.

## Reservations and Rates

Reservations are recommended. Double-occupancy rates range $85–100 per day and $595–700 per week. There is a $10 per day per person charge for extra guests; children under three are free. Additional persons in tents or campers are not permitted. A one-week minimum is required in summer, with a two-night minimum the rest of the year, when open. A deposit is required for reservations. Special arrangements are required for check-in after 6 P.M. Major credit cards are accepted. It's open year-round, weather permitting. Contact Bonanza King Resort, HC 2, Box 4790, Trinity Center, CA 96091, 530/266-3305, website: www.bonanzakingresort.com.

## Directions

From Redding, turn west on Highway 299 and drive 40 miles to Weaverville and Highway 3. Turn north on Highway 3 and drive 38 miles (past Trinity Lake) to Coffee Creek Road. Turn left and drive 0.5 mile to the resort on the left.

# 14 WYNTOON RESORT

Trinity Lake, off Highway 3 near Trinity Center

🏃 🚲 🏊 🛶 🚐 🐕 🚻 ♿

**Luxury rating:** 3                                                    **Recreation rating:** 5

This huge resort is an ideal family vacation destination. Set in a wooded area covering 90 acres on the north shore of Trinity Lake, it provides opportunities for fishing, boating, swimming, and waterskiing, with lake access within walking distance. The lake sits at the base of the dramatic Trinity Alps, one of the most beautiful regions in Northern California.

The cottages are clean and well furnished, with air-conditioning and heaters. For some, the area can seem hot and a bit dusty, so air conditioners get a lot of use in summer—along with nearby Trinity Lake. The decor is cozy and comfortable, with minimum fluff.

Trinity Lake is California's third-largest reservoir, yet because of the long drive required for most to reach it, it receives far less use than the other big recreation lakes in California, such as Shasta, Oroville, Folsom, New Melones, Pine Flat, and Kaweah. The 145 miles of shoreline feature hundreds of secluded coves and beaches. During the summer, water surface temperatures rise to a comfortable 80°F and even higher, ideal for water sports.

The backdrop for all of this is the Trinity Alps Wilderness, a huge wildland covering more than 500,000 acres and best known for pristine lakes and high alpine ridges. Some excellent day hikes nearby are routed into the edge of the wilderness.

Though most visitors come between the Fourth of July and Labor Day weekends, the spring and fall are outstanding times. Wildflowers can be brilliant in the area from mid-April through May, and in the fall, the autumn foliage peppers the hills with color.

## Facilities

Wyntoon Resort has 19 one- and two-bedroom housekeeping cottages that include fully equipped kitchens and air-conditioning. A swimming pool, clubhouse with kitchen, recreation pavilion (with bingo on Wednesday and Saturday nights during the summer), shuffleboard, children's playground, and a store round out the amenities. An RV and tent campground is also located on the property. No smoking is allowed. Leashed pets are permitted. Linens and towels are provided.

## Reservations and Rates

Reservations are recommended. The double-occupancy rate is $100–155 per night, with discounts for weekly stays. The fee per pet is $10, or $8 per night for a week. A two-night minimum stay is required on weekends, and a three-night minimum is required on holiday weekends. Discount rates are available September 7–May 17. Major credit cards are accepted. It's open year-round. Contact Wyntoon Resort, P.O. Box

70, Trinity Center, CA 96091, 530/266-3337 or 800/715-3337, fax 530/266-3820, website: www.wyntoonresort.com.

## Directions
From Redding, turn west on Highway 299 and drive to Weaverville at Highway 3. Turn north on Highway 3 and drive to Trinity Lake. At Trinity Center, continue 0.5 mile north on Highway 3 to the resort on the right.

## 15 PINEWOOD COVE
### Trinity Lake, off Highway 3 near Trinity Center

**Luxury rating:** 2                                              **Recreation rating:** 4

© MIKE NICHOLS

This is a privately operated camp with full boating facilities at Trinity Lake. Its location is a highlight, with its own boat dock and small marina. That means this is the kind of place you tow a boat to, set up camp in one of the cabins, then enjoy yourself for a week on the lake—boating, skiing, swimming, fishing, or exploring the many hidden coves and shoreline points. The elevation is 2,500 feet.

The park has a full spectrum of offerings for lodging, with park-model cabins, trailers, and an A-frame cabin, along with campsites for tents and RVs on the property. The decor is country-lodge style, with a variety of wood finishes.

Trinity Lake is huge at 17,000 acres. It's big enough to provide plenty of room for all types of water sports. Yet it is sufficiently remote that large numbers of boaters almost never descend on the place. The lake's warm surface temperatures make it a haven for families with youngsters desiring water recreation. It warms up by late June and by midsummer can be like a giant bathtub, great for tubing.

One frustrating element is that after light winters, the lake can be subject to drawdowns, especially in August. Most of the water is sent via an underground pipe over to the Sacramento Valley, where it is exported to points south. That means less water for Trinity and a lot of bare, exposed shore in some years.

But it is a big lake, and once you're on the water, the levels matter little, as there is still plenty of lake to explore. The fishing is often good, including some of California's best fishing for smallmouth bass in late winter and spring, and good prospects for rainbow trout in late spring and summer. In winter, the place is virtually abandoned.

## Facilities

Pinewood Cove has 15 park-model cabins and 1 A-frame cabin. Kitchens are provided. An RV park, campground, and marina are on the property. Amenities include restrooms, showers, a coin laundry, an RV dump station, a recreation room, a grocery store, a boat dock with 32 slips, a beach, and boat rentals. No smoking is allowed. Pets are not permitted in cabins. Pillows are provided, but linens and towels are not. Bring your own bedding or a sleeping bag.

## Reservations and Rates

Reservations are recommended in the summer. For park-model cabins, the rate is $945 per week for four people (these can sleep six); for the A-frame, the rate is $95 per night or $665 per week for up to five people. A one-week minimum stay required in summer and most holidays. Major credit cards are accepted. It's open mid-April through October. Contact Pinewood Cove Campground, 45110 State Highway 3, Trinity Center, CA 96091, 530/286-2201 or 800/988-5253, website: www.pinewoodcove.com.

## Directions

From Redding, turn west on Highway 299 and drive to Weaverville. In Weaverville, turn right (north) on Highway 3 and drive 14 miles to the campground entrance on the right.

## 16 TRINITY ALPS RESORT

Near Trinity Lake, off Highway 3 at Stuart Fork

**Luxury rating:** 2                                          **Recreation rating:** 5

I've heard a few cases where romantic cottage getaways can require reservations a year or more in advance. That is almost never the case for cabin rentals set up for family summer vacations; that is, except for a few rare exceptions—and Trinity Alps Resort is one of those exceptions.

Reservations are often needed a year in advance to get a cabin here, and if you want a vacation during prime time—from Fourth of July through Labor Day weekend—well, you usually have to sign up on a waiting list and hope for a cancellation. There's a reason for this. Everything is designed at Trinity Alps Resort as the ultimate, fun, camp vacation. In other words, you show up and turn off the outside world for a week.

The resort is big—43 cabins on 90 acres. It is located on Stuart Fork, a pretty stream that pours out of the Trinity Alps, just 1.5 miles from Trinity Lake. There is a lot of action all the time. Every night, there could be a game of bingo, a talent show, or square dancing.

If the cabins appear rustic when you first arrive, it's because they were built in the 1920s. The interiors have been remodeled, of course. Although they provide the basic necessities for a week's stay—beds, kitchen, bathroom with shower, and some with a small living room—many visitors just bring their sleeping bags, pillows, and towels (or rent linens from the resort) and use the cabins as a base camp for exploring the area and hanging out at the lake. In fact, five of the cabins are set right above swimming holes on Stuart Fork. These cabins are named Kern, Lassen, Modoc, Tehama, Lake, and Solano.

The nearby outdoor recreation is outstanding, of course. The Stuart Fork arm of Trinity Lake often provides excellent trout fishing, and the lake is outstanding for all water sports, especially waterskiing. In addition, if you drive another mile to Bridge Camp at the end of Trinity Alps Road, a trailhead provides access to the Trinity Alps Wilderness, used mostly by overnight backpackers.

### Facilities

Trinity Alps Resort has 43 cabins and three apartment-style lodge rooms. Beds, kitchens with oven and refrigerator, and bathrooms with showers are provided. A restaurant, barbecue, and community center with nightly activities are available nearby. Activities include basketball, volleyball, and tennis courts. Smoking and pets are permitted. Linens and towels are not provided. Bring a sleeping bag or rent linens for $20 from the resort. Be sure to bring a towel.

### Reservations and Rates

Reservations are required. Rates range from $845 per week for 4 people to $1,275 for up to 10 people. Apartments for 4 cost $655. A one-week minimum stay is required from May through early September. Credit cards are not accepted. Discounts are available during the off-season. Pets are free. Contact Trinity Alps Resort, 1750 Trinity Alps Road, Trinity Center, CA 96091, 530/286-2205, website: http://trinityalpsresort.com.

### Directions

From Redding, turn west on Highway 299 and drive to Weaverville and Highway 3. Turn right (north) on Highway 3 and drive 13.5 miles to the Stuart Fork Bridge and Trinity Alps Road. Turn left and drive 1.5 miles to the resort.

## 17 TRINITY LAKE RESORT
Trinity Lake, off Highway 3 near Trinity Center

🏃 🚲 🏊 ⛴ 🚤 🐕 👫

**Luxury rating:** 3                                          **Recreation rating:** 4

Trinity Lake Resort is still better known as Cedar Stock Resort, its former name. By any title, it features excellent housekeeping cabins sized to sleep 4–12 people, ideal for a vacation at Trinity Lake.

The decor is comfortable and rustic, with a warm, woodsy theme.

Trinity Lake is a giant reservoir at the foot of the Trinity Alps that is sometimes overlooked from being in the shadow of its even bigger sibling, Shasta Lake, north of

Redding. It is a great lake for boating, waterskiing, swimming, and fishing by virtue of quiet water and few speedboats. With 145 miles of shoreline, it is big enough to provide plenty of room for every type of user. To stay out of the northwest winds, most water-skiers prefer the sheltered western shoreline. Yet bass fishers prefer the hidden fingers and coves along the eastern shoreline, so they almost never get in each other's way.

If hiking is a favorite activity, there is a trailhead to the Trinity Alps Wilderness near the resort, as well as many day hikes, along with non-wilderness mountain-bike rides.

The cabins here are available by the week from mid-June through early September, when families usually visit the lake. Special two-day deals are available April–June, when anglers are more apt to visit. Major discounts are available during the off-season.

With the new owners comes new service, and that now includes sheets, pillows, and towels with your rental. The cabins provide a stove with oven, sink, and small refrigerator; it's a good idea to bring a large ice chest so you have plenty of room for produce and beverages. All cabins are equipped with cookware, plus a nearby barbecue. A restaurant, grocery store, marina, and boat ramp are all close at hand.

## Facilities

Trinity Lake Resort has housekeeping cabins sized to sleep 4–12. A kitchen, bathroom, cookware, and dishes are provided, and a barbecue is available nearby. Amenities include a restaurant, grocery store, marina, boat rentals, and launch ramp. Pets are permitted with an additional nonrefundable $40 cleaning fee. Linens and towels are provided.

## Reservations and Rates

Reservations are often required during summer. From June 1 to September 3, a four-person cabin rents for $575 per week. From April 1 to June 15, a four-person cabin rents for $350 for two nights and includes a fishing boat and $25 credit toward dinner. The resort is open year-round. In the off-season, a four-person cabin rents for $65 per night or $400 per week. Contact Trinity Lake Resort, 45810 State Highway 3, Trinity Center, CA 96091, 530/286-2225 or 800/982-2279, fax 530/286-2665, website: www.trinitylakeresort.com.

## Directions

From I-5 at Redding, turn west on Highway 299, drive over Buckhorn Summit, and continue to Weaverville. In Weaverville, turn right on Highway 3 and drive about 15 miles to Cedar Stock Road. Turn right on Cedar Stock Road and drive a short distance to the resort office.

# 18 TSASDI RESORT CABINS
Shasta Lake, off I-5 near Lakehead

**Luxury rating:** 4            **Recreation rating:** 5

The first thing most people want to know about this place is how to say Tsasdi. It is pronounced SAUZ-dee, but no matter how you say it, this is a great resort near the head of Shasta Lake.

It includes a gorgeous deck overlooking the lake, a swimming pool, beautiful rooms, and cabins with private decks and picnic tables—all within close range of Shasta Lake. Don't get the idea that these are lakeside cabins. These cabins are on a hillside about 100 feet above the water, but there is direct lake access via a stairway. The 20 cabins offer views of the Sacramento River arm of Shasta Lake. The cabins are in good shape, with knotty-pine walls and air-conditioning. The cabins are always clean and well maintained by owners who live here year-round. A bonus is that if you have your own boat, you can dock it here for free as long as you stay.

Shasta Lake is the number-one boating recreation lake in California. It is a huge lake, with 370 miles of shoreline and five major lake arms. Shasta can have a surface temperature of 80°F, which has given the lake a reputation as best for hot weather, warm water, gobs of suntan lotion, and lots of fun.

An overlooked bonus is that fall is one of the more beautiful times to visit, when the hillsides are brought to life by the autumn colors and there is relief from the summer heat.

## Facilities
Tsasdi Resort has 20 air-conditioned cabins sized at one, two, and three bedrooms; all feature bathrooms, fully equipped kitchens, cable television, decks with a picnic table, and barbecues. A swimming pool is available. Free boat slips are nearby. The town of Lakehead has a grocery store. There are no boat rentals at Tsasdi's, although they can be found nearby at Antlers, Lakeshore, or Sugarloaf Marinas. Pets are permitted. Linens and towels are provided.

## Reservations and Rates
Reservations are recommended. Cabin rates are by the week in summer, ranging from $900 for a cabin that sleeps 4, to $1,725 for one that sleeps 9, to $1,925 for a

modular home that sleeps 12. In the off-season, Labor Day to the Thursday before Memorial Day Weekend, it is possible to rent a cabin by the night for as low as $85. Boat docking is free. Contact Tsasdi Resort, 19990 Lakeshore Drive, Lakehead, CA 96051, 530/238-2575 or 800/995-0291, website: http://tsasdiresort.com. For a trout fishing guide on Shasta Lake, call Gary Miralles at 530/275-2278, website: www.shastatackle.com.

## Directions

From Redding, drive 24 miles north on I-5 to the town of Lakehead. At Lakehead, take the Lakeshore/Antlers exit (Exit 702). At the stop sign, turn left, drive under the freeway, and arrive at Lakeshore Drive. Turn left on Lakeshore Drive and drive two miles, then look for the sign for Tsasdi Resort on the right side of the road.

# **19** SUGARLOAF COTTAGES RESORT

**BEST C**

Shasta Lake, off I-5 near Lakehead

**Luxury rating: 4**　　　　　　　　　　　　　　**Recreation rating: 5**

Sugarloaf Cottages Resort has some of the most loyal patrons in Northern California. To these people, Sugarloaf is like a second home for a vacation every year. Same time, same place, right down to the same cottage. If you want to join in the fun, it is critical to make your reservation very early, as soon as possible. Often there is space available for summer beginning in January, and that is when you must strike.

The reason for the consistent bookings is that Sugarloaf provides a great escape overlooking Shasta Lake. All of the cottages are near the lakeshore. The two-bedroom townhouse cottages face the lake, and the three-bedroom, two-bath cottages have panoramic views of the lake. They are very cozy and beautiful inside, with A-frame-style bedrooms paneled with knotty pine. They come loaded. You pretty much need to bring nothing except your toothbrush.

Sugarloaf is on the upper end of Shasta Lake, on the Sacramento River arm, a short drive from I-5 at Lakehead. Boat docking, free with a cottage rental, is within short walking range of the cottages. This is a great spot for trout fishing and bass fishing, as well as a preeminent destination for all water sports.

## Facilities

Sugarloaf Cottages Resort has 15 cottages in one-, two-, and three-bedroom layouts. Air-conditioning, full all-electric kitchens, bathrooms with showers, and cable for television hookups (you bring your own television) are provided. A marina offers boat launch, boat moorings, boat rentals, gas, houseboats, and a store with tackle shop and bait. Moorage is free with cottage rental. Nearby recreation includes volleyball, basketball, and horseshoes. Pets and smoking are permitted. Linens and towels are provided.

## Reservations and Rates

Reservations are recommended. The weekly rates range from $970 for a cabin for 2 people to $1,980 for up to 12. Pets are allowed with a $10 fee. Major credit cards are accepted. The resort is open year-round, weather permitting. Contact Sugarloaf Cottages Resort, 19667 Lakeshore Drive, P.O. Box 768, Lakehead, CA 96051, 530/238-2448 or 800/953-4432, website: www.shastacabins.com.

## Directions

From Redding, drive north on I-5 to Lakehead and the Lakeshore/Antlers Road exit (Exit 702). Take that exit to Lakeshore Drive. Turn left and drive three miles to the resort entrance on the left. Turn left and drive to the cottages on the left.

# 20 LAKESHORE INN & RV
### Shasta Lake, off I-5 near Lakehead

**Luxury rating:** 3                                    **Recreation rating:** 4

Some of the best views of Shasta Lake are from the Lakehouse Cottage here at Lakeshore Inn & RV. The cottage features a deck that provides a beautiful lookout of the Sacramento River arm of Shasta Lake. The rest of the property is a mini-village, with rustic cabins and an RV park. The cabins are extremely popular. If you want to stay, make your reservation as early as possible, because many cabins are often booked a year in advance.

The decor is old-style rustic, clean and comfortable, with some of the best cabin views anywhere on the lake.

The grounds are sprinkled with ponderosa pines and oaks, but the big draw here is Shasta Lake, California's number-one recreation lake. A nearby boat ramp and private marina are available. Shasta Lake is a massive reservoir with 370 miles of shoreline, with all water sports available. In addition, getting here is easy, a straight shot off I-5. The fishing is great for bass, with high catch rates, and good for trout and salmon, and some surprise catfish caught as well.

This is the one place where there is plenty of room for everybody. Even on the most crowded weekends, with thousands of boats on the water, it seems like a giant party with everybody happy, lathering up with sunscreen, and drinking lots of liquids. If you want to escape the festivities, just head into one of the quiet coves; there are thousands of them.

## Facilities

Lakeshore Inn & RV has seven one-bedroom cabins and three two-room cabins with fully equipped kitchenettes, private bathrooms with showers, and cable available for television (but you must bring your own television). The Lakehouse Cottage sleeps six and has a full kitchen, lawn with a picnic table and fire pit, barbecue, and an RV site attached. Leashed pets are permitted. An RV park, large swimming pool, bar, restaurant, store, playground, picnic area, game room, hot showers, laundry facilities, dump station, and wheelchair-accessible restrooms (at the main lodge) are available nearby. Family barbecues are held on Sunday during the summer 5–9 P.M. Live music is scheduled most weekends. A marina and boat rentals are available nearby. Linens and towels are provided.

## Reservations and Rates

Reservations are required (summers often fill in advance). Rates are $85–120 per night ($195 for lakeside). A four-night minimum stay is required in summer with advance reservations. Off-season discounts are available. The pet fee is $5 per night. Major credit cards are accepted. It's open year-round. Contact Lakeshore Inn & RV, 20483 Lakeshore Drive, Lakehead, CA 96051, 530/238-2003, fax 530/238-2832, website: www.shastacamping.com.

## Directions

From Redding, drive north on I-5 for 24 miles to the Lakeshore/Antlers Road exit (Exit 702) in Lakehead. Take that exit, turn left at the stop sign, and drive under the freeway to Lakeshore Drive. Turn left on Lakeshore Drive and drive one mile to the park.

# **21** ANTLERS RESORT
### Shasta Lake, off I-5 near Lakehead

**Luxury rating:** 3                                 **Recreation rating:** 5

Antlers Resort is a great place on Shasta Lake. The cabins are in a rustic setting amid oaks and pines. They are beautifully furnished and include decks that overlook the lake. The decor is country-style. For many visitors, that's all they need for a vacation getaway.

But that's just the start. The resort is on the Sacramento River arm of the lake near the town of Lakehead, a short drive from I-5. This is a great spot for waterskiing and all other water sports, as well as fishing. Getting on the water in a boat is the appeal that usually brings vacationers here.

Out-of-towners arriving for a summer vacation will likely first notice the heat.

Afternoon temperatures in the 90s and low 100s are common. You might wonder if you can take a full week of it. Stop your wondering. For starters, all the cabins are air-conditioned, and you've got the lake right next to you. Shasta Lake is like a giant swimming pool in the summer, with surface temperatures ranging 75–82°F, perfect for water play, swimming, and all boating.

The cabins are designed with pine interiors and come clean and fully furnished. You can even see the lake and marina from the picture windows—as well as from the decks with barbecues. The lodge is equally nice, with a dining room, pool table, and small bar.

Antlers has successfully dealt with the one big problem here—lake drawdowns in late summer—by installing a floating marina system where the marina and docks move up and down the shore according to water levels. Boat launching and parking are easy and ample, respectively.

## Facilities

Antlers Resort has 11 cabins in one-, two-, and three-bedroom layouts. Air-conditioning, full all-electric kitchens, showers, private decks with barbecue, and televisions are provided. Laundry service is available. A swimming pool is available on-site. A marina offers boat launch, boat moorings, boat rentals, gas, houseboats, and a store with tackle shop and bait. A boat mechanic is available. Pets are permitted but must be attended at all times. Smoking is permitted. Linens and towels are provided.

## Reservations and Rates

Reservations are recommended. Cabin rates are $1,119 per week for a one-bedroom cabin that sleeps 6, $1,539 for a two-bedroom cabin that sleeps 10, and $1,805 for a three-bedroom cabin that sleeps 12. A one-week minimum is required in summer. Occasional discounts available year-round. Small-boat moorage costs $7. The pet fee is $10. Major credit cards are accepted. The resort is open year-round, weather permitting. Contact Antler's Resort, 20679 Antlers Road, P.O. Box 140, Lakehead, CA 96051, 530/238-2553 or 800/238-3924, fax 530/238-2340, website: www.shastalakevacations.com.

## Directions

From Redding, drive north on I-5 for 25 miles to Lakehead and Antlers Road. Take that exit and continue a short distance to Antlers Road. Turn right at Antlers Road and drive (it curves to the left) until the road dead-ends at Antlers Resort.

# **22** STEELHEAD COTTAGES
Trinity River, off Highway 299 near Big Flat

🏊 🛶 🚐 ❄️ ⛺ 🚹

**Luxury rating: 3**  **Recreation rating: 4**

Money can make a difference, especially if you don't plan on spending much, yet want a first-class vacation. There's a place on the Trinity River that solves this dilemma, where you can stay in a cabin at night and play in the river by day for as little as $63 per night. And an extra $29 to $39 (for a double) will get you an inflatable kayak for a day on the Trinity River, including all gear, with a nominal fee for a shuttle ride, from Bigfoot Rafting.

The cabins are on the northeast side of the highway, across the road from the river, on a half moon–shaped driveway. They are well furnished, clean, and comfortable, with the grounds sprinkled with pines. The decor is country-style with knotty pine interiors. There are four one-bedroom cabins and one two-bedroom cabin. All are fully heated. It is walking distance to a small beach along the river.

In the summer, many visitors take advantage of the excellent rafting. You get a chance at pure exhilaration doing a sport that is far easier to learn and safer than most people believe. In a survey I conducted of rafting companies in the west, this trip at Big Flat on the Trinity River turned out to be the least expensive among hundreds of white-water adventures.

Near Big Flat, the Trinity is a "pool-and-drop" river. That is, it consists of long, deep pools sprinkled with sudden riffles and drops, making it perfect for rafting. Class II and III rapids such as Hell Hole, The Slot, Zig-Zag, Fishtail, Pinball, and others occur every five minutes or so, providing short bursts of thrill, then short rests to regain your composure. Most of the rapids are Class II, nothing serious, just fun and ideal for youngsters. For a river trip with a cottage, this is the cheapest deal around.

Fishing on the Trinity River is free, with a current state license, of course. A bonus is that this area has many of the best spots on the entire river for fishing from shore. This is the appeal of Big Flat, a little one-store settlement along Highway 299, about a 90-minute drive either way from Eureka or Redding.

## Facilities

Steelhead Cottages has five cabins, each with a full bathroom, kitchen with utensils, and propane heat. Picnic tables and barbecues are available, and a fish-cleaning station, horseshoe pits, a small grocery store, and a restaurant are nearby. A fish smoker is also available. Smoking and pets are not allowed. Linens and towels are provided.

## Reservations and Rates

Reservations are recommended June–November. Cottages rent from $63 per night for two to $89 per night for four. It's open year-round. Contact Steelhead Cottages, 31221 State Highway 299W, Junction City, CA 96048, 530/623-6325 or 800/742-3785, website: www.steelheadcottages.com. For rafting information, contact Bigfoot Rafting, 530/623-3012, website:bigfootrafting.com.

## Directions

From I-5 at Redding, turn west on Highway 299 and drive through Weaverville, continuing for 23 miles to Big Flat. Look for Steelhead Cottages on the right side of the road. If you are coming from U.S. 101 at Eureka, drive north to Arcata. Just past Arcata, turn east on Highway 299 and drive through Willow Creek, continuing for 40 miles to Big Flat. Look for Steelhead Cottages on the left side of the road.

# 23 LAKEVIEW TERRACE RESORT
### Lewiston Lake, off Highway 299 near Weaverville

**Luxury rating: 3**                                          **Recreation rating: 5**

Lewiston Lake has just about everything. It's a treasure of a lake—surrounded by alpine beauty, always full, good for trout fishing, set near Trinity Alps, and with cabins for lodging. But it is what Lewiston does not have—loud, high-powered jet boats—that makes it most special. A 10-mph speed limit guarantees quiet water, making your experience at Lewiston intimate and tranquil, yet retaining prospects for great adventure. This makes Lewiston Lake an ideal place for a small boat, especially a canoe. When you paddle across the lake, the conifer-lined mountain slopes can reflect on the lake surface, with the only sound being the dipping of paddles, leaving little whirlpools with every stroke. From the far shore of the lake, you can see the snow-covered Trinity Alps.

It has become a popular destination for fly fishers casting near the tules near Lakeview Terrace. There can be an impressive surface rise near sunset here, so good that fly fishers will drive long distances for the chance to cast to it.

And if you are out on the lake, whether in a canoe, one of the rental boats, or even a float tube, not once will you cringe at the far-off roar of a high-powered V-8 engine echoing across the lake, followed a moment later by the arrival of a speedboat barreling in your direction at 50 mph. It won't happen because there are none. There never will be. Lewiston Lake will always be quiet and peaceful.

The cabins are distant enough from the resort's RV park to provide privacy. Each cabin has a picnic table and a barbecue, making them fine for evening celebrations after a day of fishing. They are little, red with green roofs, and have clean interiors.

The decor is clean and comfortable, with each cabin having its own personality. There are no phones and no televisions, so in other words, this is an escape hatch from city life.

## Facilities
Lakeview Terrace has 12 cabins sized at one, three, or five bedrooms, along with an adjacent resort and RV park. Each cabin has one or more bedrooms, a living room, dining area, fully equipped kitchen, and bathroom with shower. Picnic tables with barbecues are provided nearby. Beach mooring is available with boat and motor rentals. A swimming pool and a coin laundry are available. Leashed pets are permitted only by prior arrangement. Linens are provided. Towels are available for rent.

## Reservations and Rates
Reservations are required. Fees range $86–173 per day or $542–1,090 per week, depending on the size of the cabin and number of people in your party. A one-week minimum stay is required in summer. Pet fee is $10. Major credit cards are accepted. Contact Lakeview Terrace Resort, HC 01, Box 250, Lewiston, CA 96052, 530/778-3803, fax 530/778-3960, website: www.lakeviewterraceresort.com.

## Directions
From I-5 at Redding, turn west on Highway 299, drive over Buckhorn Summit, and continue for 5 miles to the Lewiston-Trinity Center turnoff. Turn right on Trinity Dam Boulevard, drive about 10 miles (5 miles past Lewiston), and look for Lakeview Terrace Resort on the left side of the road.

# 24 TRINITY RIVER LODGE RV RESORT
Trinity River, off Highway 3 near Lewiston

**Luxury rating: 2**                    **Recreation rating: 4**

In some rural areas, the nearby locations become a more important consideration than the luxury level of accommodations. Trinity River Lodge RV Resort is one of those places.

Its location is everything—along the Trinity River near the town of Lewiston, yet just a short drive north to Lewiston Lake or a bit farther to giant Trinity Lake. River or lake, take your pick. Several outstanding hiking trails start within a half-hour's drive.

The cabins are rustic and the trailer decor is typical.

This is not a luxury-style romantic hideaway but primarily a family and outdoor enthusiast's campground that provides the bonus opportunity of renting a furnished trailer for the night. The park has shaded green lawns sprinkled with maples and the adjacent natural beauty of the Trinity River—all amid forested mountains. Wildlife is often abundant, with deer roaming the grounds daily. Eagles, ospreys, herons, and ducks frequently fly past. For anglers, the adjacent Trinity River provides excellent fishing opportunities for brown trout and, in the fall, for migrating salmon and steelhead.

Other nearby recreation includes excellent low-cost rafting (ideal for families, with the rapids rated Class I and Class II) and golf.

## Facilities

Trinity River Lodge RV Resort has five furnished trailers and one cabin. Cable television is available. The resort is designed primarily as a campground with restrooms, hot showers, coin laundry, a store, a recreation room, a library, a clubhouse, a recreation field, volleyball, and horseshoes available. A swimming lagoon is nearby. Some facilities are wheelchair accessible. There is lake fishing less than 10 minutes away. Smoking is permitted, as are leashed pets. Linens and towels are provided.

## Reservations and Rates

Reservations are recommended. The fee is $80 per night per cabin, $40 per night for trailers. Major credit cards are accepted. It's open year-round. Contact Trinity River Lodge RV Resort, P.O. Box 137, Rush Creek Road, Lewiston, CA 96052, 530/778-3791 or 800/761-2769.

## Directions

From Redding, go west on Highway 299, drive over Buckhorn Summit, and continue for five miles to County Road 105. Turn right on County Road 105 and drive four miles to Lewiston. Turn right at Trinity Dam Boulevard and drive six miles, crossing the Trinity River. Just after the bridge, turn left on Rush Creek Road and drive three miles to the second campground on the left.

# 25 SILVERTHORN RESORT

Shasta Lake, off Highway 299 near Bella Vista

🏊 🛶 🚐 🐴 👫 ♿

Luxury rating: 3                                    Recreation rating: 5

Shasta Lake is so giant, with 370 miles of shoreline, that each lake arm can feel like a different lake. Silverthorn Resort offers a remote launch point for your Shasta vacation because it's on the relatively distant Pit River arm of the lake.

Silverthorn Resort is well known among those who love Shasta for its array of deluxe houseboats, various lake cabins, and location near excellent fishing and boating. Each cabin offers a cozy yet rustic atmosphere. They come complete with kitchen conveniences, covered patios, gas barbecues, and more. Though set in the pines, the cabins are within walking distance of the marina and a restaurant. Cabin 7 has a fantastic view of Shasta Lake, and Cabin 8 has a breathtaking view from the large second story deck. In addition, Cabin 3 is wheelchair accessible. The decor is rustic and clean.

But sooner or later, you will see the houseboats here that have everybody on the lake gawking and talking. These are among the most luxurious houseboats ever built and available to the public, including several that have 1,500 square feet of cabin and deck space and will sleep 16. One even has a hot tub.

Silverthorn is also the place of legends. Merle Haggard, the great country singer, once owned the resort and had a giant houseboat built that included a hole in the floor next to the dining table—so he could fish while eating dinner!

The Pit River arm of Shasta Lake hides many secrets. The calm, clear water in front of the resort, though, is well known as a great site for waterskiing. Upstream a five-mph speed limit protects quiet water for excellent fishing for bluegill, crappie, and catfish; it's probably the best area of the lake for panfish. The immediate vicinity of Silverthorn is good in the spring for bass and trout as well.

## Facilities

Silverthorn Resort has eight cabins with layouts for 2–8 people. One is wheelchair accessible. Swamp coolers, all-electric kitchens, bathrooms with showers, and televisions are provided. Houseboat rentals range from $2,390 per week for 10 people to a deluxe model for $6,990 per week for 16 people, depending on the size and furnishings. Off-season discounts are available. A marina provides boat launch, boat moorings, boat rentals, houseboats, and a store with tackle shop and bait. A recreation room includes a pizza pub and a pool table, video games, Ping-Pong, and music. Pets and smoking are permitted. Linens and towels are provided.

## Reservations and Rates

Reservations are recommended. Rates for cabins range $115–265 per night and $720–1,600 per week, depending on size and number of people. A three-night minimum stay is required. Major credit cards are accepted. Cabins are available May–September; houseboats are available year-round. Contact Silverthorn Resort, P.O. Box 1090, Bella Vista, CA 96008, 530/275-1571 or 800/332-3044, website: www.silverthornresort.com.

## Directions

From Redding, turn east on Highway 299 and drive 7.5 miles to Bella Vista and Dry

Creek Road. Turn left on Dry Creek Road and drive nine miles to a Y in the road. Bear left at the Y and continue to Silverthorn Resort.

# 26 RIVERSONG VILLAGE
Shasta-Trinity National Forest, off Highway 3 in Hyampom

🏃 🚴 🏊 🎣 🦌 📷

**Luxury rating:** 2                                               **Recreation rating:** 4

Where the heck is Hyampom?

Isn't that the point?

This hideout is literally in the middle of nowhere, but you already knew that. The nearest place of note is Hayfork. No, that is not one of those pointy-tooled objects with a long handle known as a pitchfork. Hayfork is actually a town. Like I said, isn't that the point?

By now you have probably figured out that this isolated retreat is set up primarily for disappearing from the world. Some people also go fishing, hunting, or exploring around in the nearby river.

A few may remember RiverSong Village as "Ziegler's Trails End" under the previous owner. It is on the South Fork Trinity River on the edge of remote Shasta-Trinity National Forest, about 50 miles west of Redding. Each cabin has an individual character and is decorated accordingly. All have a casual and comfortable feel.

The cabins are painted green and set amid a massive lawn. Picnic tables are set outside each cabin. The resort grounds are landscaped with shade and fruit trees, flowers and shrubs, and a picnic area. The entire property has a laid-back, country feel. A swimming hole and beach on the river lie within walking distance.

This is a good area for viewing wildlife, especially ospreys, bald eagles, and blue herons cruising the stream. The area is something of a fishing and hunting retreat, with guide services available in season.

I'll tell you something else. If you are looking to avoid a sheriff trying to serve you with a subpoena, he or she will never find you out here.

## Facilities
RiverSong Village has seven cabins in one- or two-room layouts. Air-conditioning, full kitchens with utensils and microwaves, bathrooms with showers, and televisions with VCRs are provided. A barbecue, horseshoe pits, breakfast service, pool table, and VHS movies are available. A general store is nearby. Pickup from Hyampom Airport

is available with advance arrangement. No smoking is allowed in the cabins. Pets are permitted. Linens and towels are provided.

## Reservations and Rates
Reservations are recommended. The rates start at $55 per night for two with a two-night minimum stay and $330 per week; it's $10 for each additional person, $10 for pets. Major credit cards are accepted. It's open year-round, weather permitting. Contact RiverSong Village, 108 Main Street, P.O. Box 150, Hyampom, CA 96046, 530/628-4929 or 800/566-5266, website: www.riversongvillage.com.

## Directions
From Redding, drive west on Highway 299 for 27 miles to Douglas City and Highway 3. Turn left (south) on Highway 3 and drive 24 miles to Hayfork and Hyampom Road. Turn right and drive 24 miles to the resort.

# 27 CAMP DISCOVERY
### Lake Red Bluff/Sacramento River, off I-5 near Red Bluff

**Luxury rating:** 1                                                    **Recreation rating:** 3

When the gates at the Red Bluff Diversion Dam on the Sacramento River are closed, it creates Lake Red Bluff, where waterskiing, birdwatching, hiking, and fishing are popular activities. This occurs from April through early September every year.

Camp Discovery contains a series of campsites, group camps, and picnic areas, plus six screened cabins operated by the Forest Service. It's

COURTESY OF THE RED BLUFF RECREATION AREA

popular for groups to reserve the cabins, which together provide space for up to 48 people. Staying at the cabins, however, isn't much different than camping: You are responsible for bringing everything you need. The sleeping arrangements are four double-platform beds in a common room. This is primitive but clean. There is no heat or air-conditioning.

The cabins are rented as one big unit to groups only, or to singles who are willing to rent the entire facility.

Created by the Red Bluff Diversion Dam, Lake Red Bluff has become a backyard swimming hole for local residents during the summer, when the temperatures reach the high 90s and low 100s almost every day. Two boat ramps are nearby.

Adjacent to Lake Red Bluff are the headquarters for Camp Discovery, a visitor information center, where visitors check in when they arrive. This also includes a fish-viewing station, where you can occasionally see migrating salmon passing up the fish ladders to get past the Red Bluff Diversion Dam.

There are no beaches at Lake Red Bluff, but there is a large grassy area on the west bank where people sunbathe and swim. This is the only practical area for wading and swimming because the water temperatures are far lower out on the main lake body. Only the hardy few who can tolerate cold water try swimming here, though many will attempt a quick dip in summer to cool off from the 100°F temperatures. Waterskiing is popular at Lake Red Bluff, as this area is often less windswept than the wide-open lakes in the foothills, making its flat surface ideal. However, many avoid risking a fall because of the stunning shock of the cold water.

In mid-September, the gates at the dam are opened, draining the lake. Overnight, it is transformed again to the Sacramento River. This allows salmon and steelhead to migrate unimpeded through the area.

## Facilities
Camp Discovery has 11 screened cabins that can each accommodate a maximum of eight people. Drinking water, showers, vault and flush toilets, a fish-viewing plaza, and two covered eating areas that accommodate up to 100 people are available. In the group camp area, there are two large barbecues, electrical outlets, lockable storage, five large picnic tables, a comfort station with showers and sinks, and an amphitheater. Two boat ramps are nearby. No linens (nor beds) are provided. Bring a sleeping pad or air mattress plus a sleeping bag.

## Reservations and Rates
Reservations are required. The fee per night is $150 for up to 100 people. It's open April–October. Contact Camp Discovery, Lake Red Bluff Recreation Area, 1000 Sale Lane, Red Bluff, CA 96080, 530/527-1196 or 530/527-2813, website: www.srdc.tehama.k12.ca.us.

## Directions
From I-5 at Red Bluff, turn east on Highway 36 and drive 100 yards to the first turnoff at Sale Lane. Turn right (south) on Sale Lane and drive 0.5 mile to the campground at the end of the road.

# Other Cabins & Cottages in the Region

**Bigfoot Campground and RV Park,** P.O. Box 280, Junction City, CA 96048, 530/623-6088 or 800/422-5219, website: www.bigfootrvcabins.com.

**Dunsmuir Springs Cottages,** 4146 Prospect Avenue, Dunsmuir, CA 96025, 530/235-4863, website: www.dunsmuirsprings.com.

**Fawndale Lodge & RV Resort,** 15215 Fawndale Road, Redding, CA 96003, 530/275-8000, 530/275-1863, or 800/338-0941, website: www.fawndale.com.

**Girard Ridge Lookout,** Shasta-Trinity National Forest, McCloud District, 530/964-2184.

**Mount Shasta KOA,** 900 North Mount Shasta Boulevard, Mount Shasta, CA 96067, 530/926-4029, website: www.koa.com.

**Premier RV Resort,** 280 North Boulder Drive, Redding, CA 96003, 530/246-0101 or 888/710-8450, website: www.premierrvresort.com.

**Trinity Canyon Lodge and Resort,** 27025 Highway 299 West, Junction City, CA 96048, 530/623-6318, website: www.trinitycanyonlodge.com.

# LASSEN
# AND MODOC

COURTESY OF BURNEY MOUNTAIN GUEST RANCH

## BEST CABINS & COTTAGES

## Mount Lassen and its awesome volcanic past seem

to cast a shadow everywhere you go in this region. At 10,457 feet, the mountain's domed summit is visible for more than 100 miles in all directions. It blew its top in 1914, with continuing eruptions through 1918. Although it's now dormant, the volcanic-based landscape dominates Lassen's vast sphere of influence.

In terms of lodging, many resorts are remodeling and upgrading their cabins and cottages, and new operations are opening with quality accommodations in appealing settings. There are lodges here that are set up for the high-end fly-fishing crowd and others that are just one step above camping.

The top cabins include those at Drakesbad Guest Ranch – the epitome of what many desire in this area – as well as Burney Mountain Guest Ranch. Drakesbad, for example, is the only place in the region where visitors get stellar accommodations and meals in a setting on the edge of wilderness in a national park. (The place is often completely booked far in advance.) A number of cabin rentals designed as fish-camp lodges surround Lake Almanor, the highlight of which is Lassen View Resort. One of the most economical deals is at Eagle Lake Cabins, especially for anglers with their own boats who are determined to catch large trout.

Of all the areas covered in this book, this region has the least number of romantic getaway spots. It caters instead primarily to outdoors enthusiasts. And Lassen is one of the best places to lace up the hiking boots or spool new line on a reel. It's often off the radar scope of vacationers, making it one of the few national parks where you can enjoy the wilderness in relative solitude.

Lassen Volcanic National Park is easily explored along the main route, the Lassen Park Highway. Along the way, you can pick a few trails for adventure. The best hikes are the Summit Climb (moderate to challenging), best done first thing in the morning, and Bumpass Hell (easy and great for kids) to see the sulfur vents and boiling mud pots. Another favorite for classic alpine beauty is Shadow Lake Trail.

Unique features of the area include its pumice boulders, volcanic rock, and spring-fed streams from the underground lava tubes. Highlights include the best still-water canoeing and fly-fishing at Fall River, Big Lake, and Ahjumawi State Park.

Nearby is Burney Falls State Park, along with the Pit River and Lake Britton, which together make up one of Northern California's best recreation destinations for families. This is also one of the best areas for fly-fishing, especially at Hat Creek, Pit River, Burney Creek, and Manzanita Lake. For more beautiful settings, visit Lake Almanor and Eagle Lake, both of which provide cabin rentals and excellent fishing and boating.

And there's more. In remote Modoc County, you'll find Lava Beds National Monument and the South Warner Wilderness. Lava Beds is a stark, pretty, and often lonely place. It's sprinkled with small lakes full of trout, is home to large-antlered deer that migrate in after the first snow (and after the hunting season has closed), and features a unique volcanic habitat with huge flows of obsidian (dark, smooth, natural glass formed by the cooling of molten lava) and dacite (gray, craggy volcanic flow). Lava Beds National Monument boasts 445 caves and lava tubes, including the 6,000-foot Catacomb tunnel. Nearby is pretty Medicine Lake, formed in a caldera, which provides good trout fishing, hiking, and exploring.

# LASSEN & MODOC

Upper Klamath Lake

Klamath Falls

Klamath River

Lower Klamath NWR

OREGON

0    10 mi

0    10 km

Meiss Lake

Lower Klamath Lake

Tule Lake

Tule Lake NWR

Lava Beds National Monument

Clear Lake Reservoir

Goose Lake

Modoc National Forest

Modoc

National

Forest

Medicine Lake

**139**

Big Sage Reservoir

Alturas

**395**

see Shasta & Trinity page 46

Shasta

National Forest

**49**

South Warner Wilderness

**89**

Ahjumawi Lava Springs State Park

Big Lake

River

Pit River

**299**

Moon Lake

MacArthur-Burney Falls State Park

Fall River Mills

Burney

**299**    **89**

**1**

**89**

**2**

Thousand Lakes Wilderness

**3**

Old Station

**4**

Lassen

National

Forest

**5-6**

Eagle Lake

**395**

NEVADA

**44**    **7**

Lassen Peak (10,457ft)

**89**

Lassen Volcanic National Park

Caribou Wilderness

**44**

**8**

Susanville

**36**

**11**

**36**

**A3**

Honey Lake

**9**  **10**

Chester

**13-14**

Mountain Meadows Reservoir

Tehama State Wildlife Area

**12**

**15**

Lake Almanor

**89**

Antelope Lake

Plumas

National

Forest

**395**

**99**

see Sacramento & Gold Country page 160

N Fork

Feather River

Quincy

see Tahoe & the Northern Sierra page 182

**70**

**70**

Chico

Middle Fork Feather River

© AVALON TRAVEL PUBLISHING, INC.

# Lassen and Modoc Cabins & Cottages

# ◼ BURNEY MOUNTAIN
# GUEST RANCH                              BEST ◖

Hat Creek, off Highway 89 in Burney

🚶 🛶

**Luxury rating:** 3                                      **Recreation rating:** 4

Those who love to fly-fish should apply here. Horseback riders and hikers can check in as well. This modern guest ranch on 120 acres caters to people from around the world who come mainly for some of the best fly-fishing in California. It's not a western dude ranch at all; it's a fishing, horseback riding, and hiking resort. A fishing pool opened in 2005.

Burney Mountain Guest Ranch opened in 1998 with two newly built duplex units (each housing two "cabins"). The cabins have a wide variety of sleeping options. The decor is country/comfortable. All units are heated and have air-conditioning.

Rates include all meals and fishing. What you get here is friendly, personalized service and a low-key atmosphere. The property is surrounded by Shasta National Forest, with Lassen and Modoc National Forests nearby. A golf course is nearby.

The cedar-sided cabins are situated alongside a casting pond, about 20 feet apart. The 400-square-foot cabins have white-painted walls and are tastefully decorated. Each has a private bathroom with shower and tub. There are no kitchen facilities, since meals are provided in the lodge.

A day's activities might include fishing in nearby Hat Creek, Pit River, or Fall River. Professional fishing guides are available, costing about $200 for a half day. If you don't want to fish, you can hike or ride horseback on trails that lead into Shasta National Forest. The Pacific Crest Trail is a popular choice; it actually crosses the driveway. Regular rides are available to beautiful 129-foot Burney Falls and Baum Lake; an extra fee is charged for riding.

The ranch owners say no one should get bored here because they ensure that every guest has an opportunity to participate in the activities that they enjoy. For instance, couples often split up for the day, with one going fishing and the other going riding, bird-watching, or merely relaxing and reading; then they meet up again at dinner.

## Facilities

Burney Mountain Guest Ranch has four cabins, each with bathroom and porch, that sleep up to five people. There are no kitchen facilities, but complimentary meals are provided in the lodge. There is a deluxe suite in the lodge. Fishing guides and horseback riding guides are available for a fee. Pets are allowed only when approved in advance. No smoking is permitted. Linens and towels are provided, and there is daily maid service.

## Reservations and Rates

Reservations are recommended. Cabins are $175–195 per night for double occupancy, with package deals for fishing or horseback riding. Children under three are free. This price includes three meals per day. The ranch is open April–October. Major credit cards are accepted. Contact Burney Mountain Guest Ranch, P.O. Box 1426, Burney, CA 96013, 530/335-4087, website: www.burneymtn.com.

## Directions

From Redding, drive east on Highway 299 to Burney and continue for five miles to the junction with Highway 89. Continue straight on Highway 299 for 2.7 miles to Hat Creek Powerhouse #2 Road. Turn right and continue up the red dirt road to the guest ranch.

# **2** RIPPLING WATERS RESORT
Hat Creek, off Highway 89

**Luxury rating:** 3                                      **Recreation rating:** 4

You wouldn't think a little resort on the side of the highway in a remote part of California would have a full house all summer, would you? Wrong. You'd better have reservations or you can forget about staying here. The attraction? It's shaded, it's pretty, there's good fishing right next to the resort on Hat Creek, and it's fairly close to a lot of great getaways.

Each cabin is different, set among tall pines and cedars, along Hat Creek. Cabin 1 is probably the most popular because it's creekside and has the best bathroom, with a tub and shower. Cabin 2 is a close second, with a private deck overlooking the creek. Cabin 5 has a bedroom door that opens to the creek, a feature many people like. Cabin 6 has a carport and trellised deck with barbecue, and although it is farthest from the creek, it's the most secluded cabin. The decor is theme-related and varies from cabin to cabin.

The elevation here is 3,700 feet, and while most summer days are warm and sunny, here's a hint about winter: They provide flannel sheets. What does that tell you? It can get butt-cold in winter, that's what.

Rippling Waters Resort is in Lassen National Forest and is within easy walking distance of a secluded section of Hat Creek. Three smaller creeks run through the property and guests have use of a private pond. If this isn't enough for you, within 20 miles are Pit River, Fall River, Lake Britton, Baum Lake, McArthur-Burney Falls

State Park, the lava tubes at Subway Caves, and Thousand Lakes Wilderness. You have almost an endless supply of fishing and hiking options.

## Facilities

Rippling Waters Resort has one studio and five one-bedroom cabins with fully equipped kitchens, including microwave and coffeemaker, and full bathrooms with shower. Most cabins have a deck, woodstove, and living room. Barbecues are provided, but bring your own charcoal. Facilities include a trout pond, campfire area, a small gift shop, fishing supplies, a play area for children, horseshoes, basketball, and a banquet room. The resort is suitable for children. Call for details regarding pet policies. No smoking is permitted. Linens are provided. Bring your own towels.

## Reservations and Rates

Reservations are required starting July 1. The fee is $110–175 per night for two persons; the seventh night is free. For additional people, $15 per person per night is charged. Children ages five and under are free. With a reservation, a two-night minimum stay (three nights on holiday weekends) is required. Major credit cards are accepted. Contact Rippling Waters Resort, 16241 Highway 89, Hat Creek, CA 96040, 530/335-7400.

## Directions

From Redding, drive east on Highway 299 to Burney and continue for 5 miles to the junction with Highway 89. Turn right (south) on Highway 89 and drive 14 miles to the resort on the left.

## ❸ RIM ROCK RANCH
Off Highway 44 near Old Station and Lassen Volcanic National Park

🏃 ⛵ 🐕 👪

**Luxury rating: 3**                                    **Recreation rating: 4**

Rim Rock Ranch is named after the Hat Creek Rim of the northern Lassen volcanic plateau country but is better known for its proximity to Hat Creek and Lassen Volcanic National Park. Hat Creek is a fine trout stream, well-stocked along Highway 89 to the north, with access points from several Forest Service camps along the road. But some people staying in cabins at Rim Rock Ranch just walk right across the street and start fishing. Note that the special wild trout section of Hat Creek, entirely catch-and-release using artificial lures with single barbless hooks, is off Highway 299.

The place was formerly named Padilla's Rim Rock Resort. But since those days, the resort has been renovated throughout, and the new owners promise to make this a great destination and launch point for adventure.

If hiking is your thing, Lassen Park, of course, is famous for its great trails, ported thermal activity, wilderness lakes, and the two-hour (one-way) Lassen summit climb, which offers an outstanding view to the north of Mount Shasta. The resort is 14 miles from the northern park entrance at Manzanita Lake.

The cabins at Rim Rock Ranch run the gamut when it comes to quality. Two new log cabins are really quite nice and come completely furnished with everything but towels.

A little country store fronts the property, a cute place that the owners call "the biggest little store in Shasta County." A lot of trips have been salvaged thanks to that store, because no matter what you forget, it is likely to have it.

## Facilities

Rim Rock Ranch has 10 cabins of varying sizes and ages, plus two motel units. Bathrooms and kitchens (or kitchenettes) with cookware and utensils are provided. A small grocery store is on the property. Call for details regarding pet policies. Linens are provided. Bring your own towels (towels are provided in motel units).

## Reservations and Rates

Reservations are accepted. Cabin rates range $60–115 per night, depending on the size and age of cabin. A two-night minimum stay is required. Discounted weekly rates are available. Motel units cost $45 per night. Major credit cards are accepted. Contact Rim Rock Ranch, 13275 Highway 89, Old Station, CA 96071, 530/335-7114, website: www.rimrockcabins.com. For fishing information, phone Vaughn's Sporting Goods in Burney at 530/335-2381.

## Directions

From Redding, take Highway 44 east for 48 miles to the junction with Highway 44/89. Continue north on Highway 44/89 and drive 14 miles to Old Station. Continue for two miles and look for Rim Rock Ranch on the right side of the road.

## 4 HAT CREEK RESORT
Hat Creek, off Highway 44/89 in Old Station

| Luxury rating: 3 | Recreation rating: 4 |
| --- | --- |

The major pastime here is fishing for trout—rainbows, brookies, and browns—in Hat Creek. You see, the Department of Fish and Game makes regular plants on Hat

Creek along Highway 89 throughout the summer, and that keeps the fishing enthusiasts coming.

The 10 cabins at Hat Creek Resort are situated among tall pines and next to a grassy area, with Hat Creek flowing by. Cabins 3A and 4A sit right along the creek and are the most popular because of the creek views. Cabin 7 is the most private and is aptly nicknamed the Honeymoon Cottage; it's behind the lodge and features a forest setting. The resort is on 20 acres adjacent to Lassen National Forest.

The decor is country-rustic, 1930s' style. All units are heated.

A bonus for those with horses is that a six-stall "horse motel" and corral, troughs, and feeders are on-site. An RV park is also on the premises.

The Pacific Crest Trail runs right next to Hat Creek Resort and provides hiking options; you can go this way or you can go that way. Ten miles from the property is the northern entrance to Lassen Volcanic National Park, a must-see with plenty of hiking (including the Mount Lassen summit climb) and exploring to do, as well as catch-and-release fishing at Manzanita Lake.

## Facilities

Hat Creek Resort has 10 cabins and seven lodge rooms. Cabins range from studios to three-bedrooms and can accommodate up to eight. Each has a fully equipped kitchen and bathroom with shower. There are no telephones or televisions. Amenities include a barbecue, laundry facilities, badminton, a tennis court, basketball, horseshoes, complimentary wagon rides on weekends, and a restaurant and store. The resort is suitable for children. Pets are allowed in the cabins only, and smoking is permitted with restrictions. Linens and towels are provided.

## Reservations and Rates

Reservations are recommended. The double-occupancy rate is $66–112 per night per cabin; the seventh night is free. Lodge rooms are $49–62 per night. Additional people are charged $7 per person per night. There is a two-night minimum. Major credit cards are accepted. Contact Hat Creek Resort, P.O. Box 73, 12533 Highway 44/89, Old Station, CA 96071, 530/335-7121, website: www.hatcreekresort.com.

## Directions

From Redding, drive east on Highway 44 to the junction with Highway 89 (near the entrance to Lassen Volcanic National Park). Turn north on Highway 89 and drive about 12 miles to the resort entrance on the right side of the road (if you reach the junction of Highway 89/44, you have gone three miles too far).

# 5 EAGLE LAKE CABINS
Eagle Lake, off Highway A1 in Spaulding

🚴 🛶 🚤 🦌 👫

**Luxury rating:** 3                                       **Recreation rating:** 4

With every blessing, there seems to come a curse. So it is at Eagle Lake. This lake has big trout, real big: 18- to 20-inchers on average, with 5-pounders pretty common. The documented lake record was a smidgen over 11 pounds, and there are reports of even bigger fish. That is the blessing. The curse? It's the wind. It can really howl out here on the edge of the high desert in Lassen County, whipping huge yet shallow Eagle Lake to a froth, a common enough event to earn the respect of nearly every visitor.

What to do? No problem. You go and hide out in your cabin until the wind dies down—which will likely be the next morning—and then head out again. You'll book your cabin through Heritage Land Company, which operates a rental business from the little town of Spaulding Tract, set on the western shore of the lake. The 45 cabins available for rent include bathrooms, kitchens, and propane heat. Some of the cabins have views of the lake. No linens or towels are provided, so you should bring a sleeping bag, pillow, and plenty of towels, or you'll be in a heck of a fix. Think of your stay here as being more like a fish camp than anything else.

The decor varies greatly, anything from basic-rustic to lakefront elegance. There are many bedroom options available, from a simple studio to four-bedroom with lake views and decks.

The boat ramp is only a half mile from the cabins, making it a snap to get from bed to the lake. It's a good thing, too, because with that wind, you need to be out very early. Get out at dawn, get your fishing done, and get the heck off the water. Though there are days when it never blows (most commonly in the fall), in summer your fishing day is often over by 10 A.M. By 10:30 A.M., you're fishing on borrowed time. By 11 A.M., you're a fool. And by noon, if you're still out there and the wind is roaring, I'll start praying I don't have to fish you out of Davy Jones's locker.

Note that the fishing season at Eagle Lake is different from other areas of California. It runs from Memorial Day weekend through December 31.

## Facilities
There are 45 cabins in various sizes, each with a bathroom and kitchen. Cooking utensils, dishes, and silverware are provided. A boat ramp is a half mile away. A nearby RV

park has a small store and grocery stores are available in Spaulding Tract and Stones Landing. Dogs and smoking are permitted in some facilities, prohibited in others. No bedding or towels are provided. Bring your own sleeping bag and towels.

## Reservations and Rates

Reservations are required. Cabin fees range $60–295 per night, depending on the size of the cabin. Weekly rates are also available. There's a two-night minimum stay on weekends. Major credit cards are accepted. Contact Eagle Lake Cabins (Heritage Land Company), 686-920 Spaulding Road, Eagle Lake, CA 96130, 530/825-2131, fax 530/825-2139, website: www.eaglelakeheritage.com.

## Directions

From Redding, drive east on Highway 44 to Highway 44/89. Turn right on Highway 44/89 and drive 45 miles to Highway 36. Continue east on Highway 36 for about four miles to County Road A1. Turn left on County Road A1 and drive to Spaulding on the shore of Eagle Lake. In Spaulding, turn right on Spaulding Road and drive 1.5 miles. Look for the sign for Heritage Land Company on the right side of the road.

# 6 EAGLE LAKE RV PARK & CABINS
Eagle Lake, off Highway A1 near Spaulding

**Luxury rating: 2**                                    **Recreation rating: 4**

Eagle Lake RV Park & Cabins has become something of a headquarters for anglers in pursuit of Eagle Lake trout, which typically range 18–22 inches, the largest average trout of any lake in California. A nearby boat ramp provides access to Pelican Point and Eagle Point, where the fishing is often best in the summer. A full-service store on the premises is a great plus—and the owners have a way of stocking just what you need for your trip but forgot to bring. That also means no special trips into town for supplies are necessary. No worrying, just vacation time: lounging beside Eagle Lake, maybe catching a big trout now and then. Resident deer can be like pets here on late summer evenings, including bucks with spectacular racks. One night here, my boys, Jeremy and Kris, were stunned to see a pair of bucks with spectacular antlers walk right past as if these wild animals were tame.

The cabin rentals span such a wide spectrum in accommodations—from a primitive camping cabin to an all-furnished cabin—that the luxury rating should actually be 2, 3, and 4 because no one single number does the place justice. In short, there are two camping cabins (no heating or plumbing) that can sleep two or three, one fully furnished house that can sleep up to eight (heating, plumbing, and electricity included), one studio (with shower but without bedding) that sleeps up to four, and two trailers (with shower but without bedding) that sleeps four.

The rental house is the only option with separate bedrooms. The decor is basic and varies from place to place. A large RV park is on the premises.

Eagle Lake is the second-largest natural lake in California; it borders the high desert on the edge of the Great Basin. It offers long-distance views, crystal-clear water, and native trout that are beyond compare. One downer: The wind typically howls here most summer afternoons. So get out on the water at first light, catch your fish early, and then enjoy the rest of the day exploring the area.

## Facilities

Eagle Lake RV Park & Cabins has two camping cabins, one house, one studio, one trailer, and one mobile home. The house and mobile home are fully furnished, including bedding, kitchen facilities, and satellite television. There is a separate area on the property for RVs and another for tents only. Restrooms, showers, coin laundry, a sanitary disposal station, a grocery store, a recreation room, and a boat ramp are available. Smoking is prohibited. Leashed pets are permitted. Linens are provided in the house and mobile home. They are not provided in the studio, camping cabins, or the trailer; bring your own.

## Reservations and Rates

Reservations are recommended. Camping cabins are $37 per night for up to four people, the studio is $75 per night or $450 per week for up to six people, the trailer starts at $75 per night and $450 per week for up to four people, and the house is $145 per night and $750 per week for up to six. An additional $10 per night is charged for each additional person. A two-night minimum stay is required. Major credit cards are accepted. Eagle Lake is open late May to late November, weather permitting. Contact Eagle Lake RV Park & Cabins, 687-125 Palmetto Way, Eagle Lake, CA 96130, 530/825-3133 (May–December) or 530/243-3069 (January–April), website: www.eaglelakeandrv.com.

## Directions

From Red Bluff, drive east on Highway 36 toward Susanville. Just before reaching Susanville, turn left on County Road A1 and drive to County Road 518 near Spalding Tract. Turn right on County Road 518 and drive through a small neighborhood to the lake frontage road (look for The Strand). Turn right on Palmetto Way and drive eight blocks to the store at the RV park entrance.

# 7 MILL CREEK RV PARK
Lassen Volcanic National Park, off Highway 44 in Shingletown

**Luxury rating: 2**                  **Recreation rating: 4**

Mill Creek Park is set up primarily for RVs but has an area with small cabins and another with tent sites. It's small and intimate, the owners are friendly and helpful, and they'll tell you that is exactly how they plan on keeping it. The elevation is 4,000 feet, and the place is set amid towering pines and large oaks on the western slopes of Mount Lassen. The proximity to Lassen Volcanic National Park represents a key attraction.

Mill Creek Park covers 15 acres and includes a great 2-acre pond for fishing for bass or trout, as well as a pretty stream and a small waterfall. There are some easy walking trails on the property as well. With luck, you might catch a glimpse of some of the local wildlife that abounds in the area, including deer, sometimes black bears, and the rare antelope.

There are resident ospreys living above the pond in summer. Otters also live in the creek. The landscape here is quiet and gorgeous.

The cabins are rustic but inexpensive, and since the draw here is good hiking and fishing, most visitors don't mind. The four cabins are in the middle of a small campground that has seven tent sites and 16 RV sites. One cabin has been converted to handle up to nine people. All cabins have heating (two with propane, two with electric) and two have bathrooms. For the two cabins that do not have bathrooms, it is only a 15-foot walk to bathrooms. Each cabin also has a barbecue. For groups and families, a group picnic area with a massive barbecue is available across a meadow, about a quarter mile away. The road up to it is easy and wheelchair-accessible.

The park is 14 miles from the entrance to Lassen Volcanic National Park and Manzanita Lake. Another popular getaway is the drive on Highway 89 past the foot of Mount Lassen to the steaming mud pots, called Bumpass Hell. In addition, nearby Grace and Nora Lakes are rich in local history, including the ruins of a castle built by a local land baron many years ago, and Lake McCumber and Lake Almanor provide good fishing for bass and trout.

## Facilities

Mill Creek RV Park has four cabins, two with bathrooms. A laundry room, a group picnic area, a fishing pond, horseshoes, and a creek with a swimming area are available nearby. Leashed pets are permitted. Linens and towels are provided.

## Reservations and Rates

Reservations are recommended and a deposit is required. The rate is $40 per night for cabins without bathrooms and $60 per night for cabins with bathrooms; the seventh night is free. A two-night minimum stay is required for cabins. Major credit cards are accepted. It's open year-round. Contact Mill Creek RV Park, Shingletown, P.O. Box 267, Shingletown, CA 96088, 530/474-5384, fax 530/474-1236.

## Directions

From Redding, drive east on Highway 44 to Shingletown. In Shingletown, continue east on Highway 44 for two miles to the campground.

# 8 DRAKESBAD GUEST RANCH

Lassen Volcanic National Park, off Highway 89 near Chester

**Luxury rating:** 2           **Recreation rating:** 5

This is it. The kind of place you've fantasized about: a quintessential, picture-perfect rustic lodge with cabins located in one of the most beautiful meadows in California, secluded and low-key. This place really exists. At 5,700 feet in elevation, it's Drakesbad Guest Ranch.

There's just one problem: getting a reservation! It can take months in advance—or even years—to get a spot in July or August. The best hope is to get lucky and happen to squeeze in at the last minute because someone else canceled their trip, which occurs occasionally each summer. So the advice is to get on the cancellation list.

This place is unique in every way. Once you book a stay, expect rustic, modest accommodations on a guest ranch built in the late 1800s. It has been updated, of course, and is well furnished, cozy, and peaceful. The decor is beautiful, simple and rustic, with handcrafted furniture made from pine logs.

The meals are also excellent. Finding these qualities in such a remote setting always comes as a pleasant surprise to newcomers. All meals are provided in the lodge's dining room; vegetarian meals are available. Barbecues take place every Wednesday.

The road in is long, twisty, and dusty, and the place is on the edge of wilderness in a remote sector of a national park. That is why many celebrities have stayed here; the lodge provides a genuine hideaway where you aren't bugged by anything. In addition, the management is first-class, with a focus on quality of service.

Since there's no electricity in the cabins, kerosene lamps and propane heat are used. Leave your electrical appliances at home. But do bring your swimsuits—Drakesbad Guest Ranch was named for the warm-water hot springs that fill the pool. The springs keep the pool temperature toasty all summer.

The ranch has horse stables, and daily guided rides are provided for an extra fee. Fly-fishing and lessons in nearby Hot Springs Creek are also available; you can buy a fishing license at the ranch.

The hiking is unusual and fairly easy, with the highlight a 4.4-mile round-trip walk to Devils Kitchen. The trail leads directly from the lodge. You'll encounter steaming vents and boiling mud pots and fumaroles. For safety reasons, it is illegal to walk off the trail in this area.

So, don't you feel lucky?

## Facilities

Drakesbad Guest Ranch has four cabins, eight bungalows, one duplex, and six lodge rooms. There are no kitchen facilities, but the lodge provides three meals a day that are included in your rental rate. All units include a toilet and sink. Some have a shower, and a bathhouse is available. Amenities include a pool, a restaurant, laundry facilities, horseback riding and lessons, volleyball, table tennis, horseshoes, badminton, and croquet. A canoe is available at Dream Lake, a five-minute walk from the lodge. A Swedish massage therapist is on duty. No pets are allowed. Smoking is prohibited. Linens and towels are provided and there is daily maid service.

## Reservations and Rates

Reservations are required. The rate is per person but based on double occupancy of adults, with additional charges for extra people, but that charge varies according to whether the extra guest is a child or an adult. The rate is $155 per person per night or $802–1,137 per week. For ages 2–11, the fee is $77 per night or $458 per week. Additional guests are $114–128 per night. All prices include three meals a day. Major credit cards are accepted. A $10 national park entrance fee is added to each reservation. Holders of a Golden Eagle Pass or Lassen Volcanic National Park annual pass will be waived the $10 entrance fee. The ranch is open early June to mid-October, weather permitting. Contact Drakesbad Guest Ranch, 2150 North Main Street, Suite 5, Red Bluff, CA 96080, 530/529-1512, ext. 120, fax 530/529-4511, website: www.drakesbad.com.

## Directions

From Red Bluff, take Highway 36 east for 44 miles to the junction with Highway 89 (do not turn left on Highway 89 to the Lassen Volcanic National Park entrance). Continue east on Highway 36/89 to Chester and Feather River Drive/Warner Valley Road. Turn left (north) on Feather River Drive/Warner Valley Road and drive 0.75 mile to Warner Valley Road/Lassen Volcanic National Park. Bear left and drive 17.5 miles through national forest to the well-signed resort.

# 9 McGOVERN'S CHALETS

Lassen Volcanic National Park, off Highway 36 in Mineral

🚶 🚴 ⛷ 🚙 ⛵ ❄ 🐎 👫

**Luxury rating:** 3                                    **Recreation rating:** 3

I include McGovern's Chalets in this book simply because there are so few large cabins and cottages to rent in this area, the southern gateway to Lassen Volcanic National Park.

The chalets are modern buildings done in a woodsy style with an eclectic ensemble of furnishings from all over the world. All have the basic amenities you need, except for laundry facilities. And the kitchens are a bonus, since dining options are limited around here.

If you're looking for a large cabin or several cabins to house a family or group, with kitchen facilities and bathrooms included, then consider these two-story chalets.

You're within easy driving distance to Lassen Volcanic National Park, Lake Almanor, and Mill Creek. Day trips to these areas promise hiking, fishing, and exploring galore. In the winter, you can cross-country ski, snowshoe, or snowmobile close by.

This is a popular park for church groups and family reunions.

## Facilities

McGovern's Chalets has three cabins with fully equipped kitchens, three or four bedrooms, living room, dining room, and bathroom. The cabins have decks or patios, and barbecues are provided during the summer, but bring your own charcoal. Woodstoves and firewood are provided. There are no telephones or televisions. The cabins are suitable for children. Leashed pets are allowed. Smoking is permitted. Pillows, blankets, and quilts are provided, but linens and towels are not; bring your own or rent linens and towels for an extra fee.

## Reservations and Rates

Reservations are recommended. The rate is $80–150 per night per cabin, or up to $700 per week per cabin for up to 10 people. Pet fee is $5 per day, with a $50 deposit. Major credit cards are accepted. Contact McGovern's Chalets, 563 McClay Road, Novato, CA 94947, 530/595-3241, website: www.ovrentals.com.

## Directions

From Red Bluff, drive 43 miles east on Highway 36 to the town of Mineral and Highway 172. Turn right on Highway 172 and drive one-half block to Mount Lassen Avenue. Turn right and drive one-half block to Scenic Avenue. Turn right and drive 0.25 mile to the cabins on the right at 38228, 38234, and 38240 Scenic Avenue.

# 🔟 MILL CREEK RESORT                                            BEST 🅒
### Off Highway 172 near Lassen Volcanic National Park and Mineral
🏃 🚴 🛶 🐴 👫

**Luxury rating:** 3                                            **Recreation rating:** 3

Here's a place on the threshold of Lassen Volcanic National Park and near Lassen National Forest. It sits in the middle of a great outdoor recreation area, with good fishing and hiking nearby. I looked long and hard to find such a place.

The resort features nine rustic cabins, all sized at one or two bedrooms complete with a small kitchen and bathroom, at inexpensive rates. The cabins have been around for decades and have been refurbished. The decor is simple in design, with patchwork quilts and mountain scenes.

It turned out to be Mill Creek Resort, and it is just unknown enough that cabins are usually available. It sits east of Red Bluff at 4,800 feet in elevation, just off remote Highway 172, a little loop road off the main highway that bypasses Morgan Summit. The reason the resort gets missed by so many is that nobody takes the Highway 172 bypass by accident. In addition, there are no other businesses of any kind on Highway 172. So right off, you have a relatively secret spot.

A highlight here is nearby Mill Creek, and I mean the stream, not the town. The lodge owners can provide specific directions to the parking area and trailhead on your visit. It's great to take an evening walk along the stream, which babbles and wends its way around rocks and into pools.

Sooner or later, however, you will find yourself making the 15-minute drive north to the entrance of Lassen Volcanic National Park, then exploring for at least a day or two.

## Facilities

Mill Creek Resort has nine one- and two-bedroom cabins with bathrooms, kitchens, and propane heat. One cabin has a fireplace. Pets are permitted. No smoking. A small grocery store and restaurant are available at the lodge. Linens are provided.

## Reservations and Rates

Reservations are accepted. Cabin rates are $60–65 per night for a one-room cabin, $70–85 per night for a two-room cabin, with no minimum stay required (except for three-day holiday weekends). Contact Mill Creek Resort, 1 Highway 172, Mill Creek, CA 96061, 530/595-4449 or 888/595-4449, website: www.millcreekresort.net. For a recreation packet on the area, contact the Shasta Cascade Wonderland Association, 800/474-2782, website: www.shastacascade.com.

## Directions

From I-5 at Red Bluff, take the Highway 36 exit and drive east on Highway 36 to the town of Mineral. In Mineral, turn right on Highway 172 and drive six miles to the town of Mill Creek. Look for Mill Creek Resort on the right side of the road.

# 11 CHILDS MEADOW RESORT BEST [

Lassen Volcanic National Park, off Highway 36 in Mill Creek

[icons]

**Luxury rating:** 3 **Recreation rating:** 4

Do you dream about sitting on a cabin deck overlooking a picturesque meadow with mountains in the background? Well, you can do just that at Childs Meadow Resort (and your view is of Mount Brokeoff).

This 18-acre resort at 5,000 feet in elevation has a lot to offer. The two-bedroom chalets are spaced closely together and have full kitchens and bathrooms, with outside decks and porches. They are centrally located and are open year-round.

The decor is mostly natural woods, very cozy. One of the cabins has a hot tub.

In the summer, there are plenty of recreation opportunities. You can fish (catch-and-release only) or hike along Mill Creek, one mile away. The trailhead for Spencer Meadow Trail is just east of the resort alongside Highway 36, and it's a 10-mile round-trip to Spencer Meadow and an effervescent spring that is the source of Mill Creek. Horse corrals and troughs are available at the resort and there are riding trails in the area.

In the winter, you can cross-country ski or snowshoe right from the resort. Rentals are available, and winter backcountry touring by snowmobile is offered for an additional fee.

## Facilities

Childs Meadow Resort has five modular cabins, seven two-bedroom chalets, 16 motel rooms, and a campground. Cabins have fully equipped kitchens and bathrooms with shower/tubs. One has a hot tub, two have lofts. A restaurant, summer laundry facilities, a convenience store, horse corrals, cross-country ski rentals, a bathhouse, a group picnic area, horseshoe pits, a meeting room, and a wedding or reunion area are available. The resort is suitable for children. Pets are allowed only by prior approval. Smoking is permitted with restrictions. Linens and towels are provided, but if you bring your own you receive a 10 percent discount.

## Reservations and Rates

Reservations are required in the summer. Modular cabins are $75–175 per night; chalets are $300 for two days, $420 for three days, and $900 per week for up to four people. Additional guests are $5 per person per night. Motel rooms are $60–80 per night. Children under the age of one are free. There is a two-night minimum for chalets. Major credit cards are accepted. Contact Childs Meadow, 41500 Highway 36E, Mill Creek, CA 96061-3000, 530/595-3383 or 888/595-3383, website: www.childsmeadowresort.com.

## Directions
From Red Bluff, drive east on Highway 36 to the resort on the left (one mile east of the Mill Creek Bridge).

# 12 PLUMAS PINES RESORT
### Off Highway 89 on the west shore of Lake Almanor

🏃 🚴 ⛱ 🎣 🛥 👫

**Luxury rating: 3**                                    **Recreation rating: 4**

Many of the cabin and cottage rentals at Lake Almanor are on the east side of the lake, but Plumas Pines Resort is on the west side. Its one- and two-bedroom cottages with kitchens are popular and often book up a year in advance during the summer season. Set about 40 feet apart, the cabins are almost 800 square feet in size. They have been around for decades, and quite a bit of remodeling has taken place. A view of the lake can be seen

© SUZI BRAKKEN

from most of the cabins, and the lake access is just a short walk across the road.

The country-style decor is finished in natural woods. The cabins have two separate sleeping areas, one in a common room and one with a sliding door.

Plumas Pines is a full-service resort with lodge rooms, an RV park, and live music on weekends, so don't expect a serene setting with lots of privacy. What you do get, however, is service and convenience. You can come here for a week and probably never have to leave the resort for supplies.

A swimming beach is available but is only usable when the lake level is not down. All types of boating are permitted, including personal watercraft riding. Besides the myriad boating and fishing available on the lake, you can hike or bike on Lake Almanor Recreation Trail, a 9.5-mile paved trail that more or less parallels the shoreline of the lake.

## Facilities
Plumas Pines Resort has eight cottages, nine lodging rooms, and an RV park. The cottages have fully equipped kitchens and bathrooms. A barbecue, picnic table,

and gas fireplace are provided. Laundry facilities, a waterfront restaurant, a convenience store, a full-service marina, and boat rentals are available. The resort is suitable for children. Pets are allowed only when approved in advance. Smoking is permitted in some rooms. Linens and towels are provided, but there is no daily maid service.

## Reservations and Rates

Reservations are recommended for up to a year in advance during the summer. Cottages are $100 per night or $760–839 per week. An additional fee of $5 per person per night is charged for more than four people. There is a two-night minimum on weekends and a three-night minimum on holidays. Major credit cards are accepted. The resort is open year-round with limited winter facilities. Contact Plumas Pines Resort, 3000 Almanor Drive West, Canyon Dam, CA 95923, 530/259-4343, fax 530/259-3216, website: www.plumaspinesresort.

## Directions

From Red Bluff, take Highway 36 east for 44 miles to the junction with Highway 89. Continue east on Highway 36/89 to Lake Almanor and the junction with Highway 89 (2 miles before reaching Chester). Turn right on Highway 89 and drive 7 miles to Almanor Drive West. Turn left and drive 1 mile to the resort on the left. Check in at the store.

# 13 KNOTTY PINE RESORT
Lake Almanor, off Highway 36 near Chester

**Luxury rating: 3**　　　　　　　　　　　　　　　　　　　**Recreation rating: 4**

The cabins at Knotty Pines Resort are often booked a year in advance.

That known, most people who stay at Knotty Pine Resort either bring a boat, rent a boat, or do both. The activities are oriented toward boating, sailing, and fishing, and most visitors spend a lot of time on the water. The average water temperature during the summer is 60–70°F. As with most lake resorts, they book up early during the summer months.

The resort is on a peninsula on the east side of the lake. The lakefront log cabins are painted dark brown with red doors; inside, of course, is knotty pine paneling. The decor is rustic, often splashed with flowers, and clean and comfortable. They come with two bedrooms and are about 500 square feet. They have a queen bed and two twin beds.

These are traditional cabins, but they've been refurbished, so you'll have simple, updated appliances and fixtures. An available house has about 700 square feet with two bedrooms, a dining area, living room, and fireplace insert. The house sleeps six people and has a patio. The resort also has an RV park.

## Facilities

Knotty Pine Resort has five cabins and one guest house with fully equipped kitchen, including microwave. The bathrooms have been refurbished and have a tub/shower. Barbecues, a deck or porch, a picnic table, a television, and one complimentary boat slip per cabin are provided. Recreation includes a heated swimming pool, a recreation room with pool table, a full-service marina, bait and tackle, boat rentals, television, table tennis, and board games. The resort is suitable for children. Leashed pets are allowed by prior arrangement. No smoking is permitted. Linens and towels are provided.

## Reservations and Rates

Reservations are recommended. The fee is $140–175 per night per cabin or $840–1,050 per week. Call the resort for pet fees. There is a one-week minimum stay June–August. Major credit cards are accepted. The resort is open year-round, with limited winter facilities and off-season discounts. Contact Knotty Pine Resort, 430 Peninsula Drive, Lake Almanor, CA 96137, 530/596-3348, fax 530/596-4404, website: www.knottypine.net.

## Directions

From Red Bluff, take Highway 36 east to Chester and continue for five miles to Highway A-13. Turn right and drive about one mile to Clifford Drive. Turn right on Clifford and drive a short distance to Big Cove Road. Turn left on Big Cove and drive a short distance to Peninsula Drive. Turn right and drive to the resort on the left.

## 14 LITTLE NORWAY RESORT

Lake Almanor, off Highway 36 near Chester

**Luxury rating:** 3                                   **Recreation rating:** 4

This resort has been around for decades, and it's established itself as a full-service, friendly establishment. People return to Little Norway Resort year after year, and for that reason you need to make reservations early.

Little Norway Resort offers nine one- to four-bedroom cabins surrounded by tall pine trees on the peninsula of Lake Almanor. They can accommodate up to 10 people per rental and they're set up for groups due to their close proximity to one another; in some cases, cabins are spaced only several feet apart.

The cabins are small with knotty-pine paneling and are modestly decorated. They are old-style rustic, modest and clean. The mobile homes are more contemporary than the cabins, with more updated kitchens. The houses are the most spacious and inviting of the rentals. One two-story house has wood paneling, a vaulted ceiling, and an open stairway; it has the classic mountain cabin look and feel. All of the rentals have decks.

The cabins are within a couple hundred feet of the lake and marina, making it easy to access the lake and its activities. You can dock your boat here, and there's easy access for getting on and off the lake, which is at 4,500 feet in elevation. The resort is situated in a protected cove and it boasts the lake's largest boat fleet; you can rent everything from fishing boats to pontoon boats and from water-ski boats to personal watercraft. You'll have 52 miles of shoreline to explore at Lake Almanor. This is one of the truly outstanding fishing lakes in Northern California, and first-class guides are available for outings.

## Facilities

Little Norway Resort has nine cabins and two houses with fully equipped kitchens and full bathrooms with showers. Barbecues, decks, and a boat slip are provided, and some units have woodstoves. A full service marina, bait and tackle, and boat rentals are available. The resort is suitable for children. Leashed pets are allowed. Smoking is permitted. Linens and towels are not provided, but blankets and pillows are. There is no daily maid service.

## Reservations and Rates

Reservations are recommended. The fee is $90–160 per night per cabin or $540–990 per week. There is a one-week minimum for the cabins during the summer. Additional guests are charged $5 per night per person or $30 per week; the additional fee kicks in for the third person for one-bedroom rentals, for the fifth person for a two-bedroom rental, and for the seventh person for a four-bedroom rental. The pet fee is $10 per night or $60 per week. Major credit cards are accepted. Contact Little Norway Resort, 432 Peninsula Drive, Lake Almanor, CA 96137, 530/596-3225, website: www.littlenorway.net.

## Directions

From Red Bluff, take Highway 36 east to Chester and continue for five miles to Highway A-13. Turn right and drive two miles to Peninsula Drive. Turn right and drive two miles to the resort on the left.

# 15 LASSEN VIEW RESORT
Lake Almanor, off Highway 36 near Chester

🏃 🏊 🚣 ⛵ 🐴 👫

**Luxury rating:** 3                    **Recreation rating:** 4

Lassen View, an institution as a fish camp for 30 years at Lake Almanor, was sold in 2005 and will reopen in 2006 with many anticipated changes. Significant upgrades are expected in lodging; that's what new owners usually do first. Prices typically are raised shortly thereafter. A name change is also likely.

© SUZI BRAKKEN

Lassen View Resort is a place where you just tend not to worry about anything except the weather and having a good time, and how to catch the trout, salmon and smallmouth bass. And whereas a fair number of families stay here in the summer, it is better known as the number-one fishing and hunting retreat around in the spring and fall, respectively.

The cabins are rustic, done in western style, but upgrades are likely. They are in a campground on the eastern shore of Lake Almanor, a five-minute boat drive from one of the best fishing spots on the lake at Big Springs. This is a classic fish camp; that is, it has everything for the angler, including cabins, a tackle shop, a store, and a small marina with boat ramp and boat rentals. And there are guides and all the advice you can listen to.

Almanor is a very pretty lake, big (13 miles long) and often full, ringed by pines and firs, at 4,500 feet near Lassen National Forest. Chester, the small town at the north end of the lake, has supplies and a few restaurants, as well as a small airport. Nearby, there are many other recreation options, including a remote and beautiful section of Lassen Volcanic National Park, Butt Lake, Feather River, and thousands of acres of national forest.

## Facilities

Lassen View Resort has 12 cabins ranging 2–5 rooms. Each includes a full kitchen (stove, refrigerator, utensils), bathroom, small deck, and fire ring with grill. A small grocery store, tackle shop, seasonal snack bar, and coin laundry are available. A boat launch, dock, swimming area, small marina with boat and motor rentals, gas, and fish-cleaning facility are nearby. Activities include an arcade, horseshoes, and volleyball. Pets are permitted in the cabins as long as they are attended. There is also a campground. Restaurants are located in Chester, about 10 miles away. Linens, pillows, and towels are provided.

## Reservations and Rates

Reservations are recommended. Cabins range from $90 per night or $620 per week for a one-bedroom to $143 per night or $858 per week for a three-bedroom. Contact Lassen View Resort, 7457 Highway 147, Lake Almanor, CA 96137, 530/596-3437. For fishing guides, contact Roger Keeling, 530/258-2283, or Mark Jiminez, 530/596-3072.

## Directions

From I-5 at Red Bluff, turn east on Highway 36 and drive about 75 miles to the junction with Highway 89. Bear north on Highway 89/36 and, as you approach the lake, continue straight on Highway 36. Drive through Chester and across the spillway at the north end of the lake. One mile past a lakeside rest stop, turn right (south) on County Road A13 and drive about four miles. The road will cross over the Hamilton Branch, then junction with Highway 147. Turn right and drive about 200 yards to the well-signed resort entrance on the right.

# Other Cabins & Cottages in the Region

**Almanor Lakefront Village and Almanor Lakeside Resort,** 318 Peninsula Drive, Lake Almanor, CA 96137, 530/596-3959, website: www.lakealmanor resorts.com.

**KOA Lassen/Shingletown,** 7749 KOA Road, Shingletown, CA 96088, 530/474-3133, website: www.koa.com.

**Lake Almanor Resort,** 2706 Big Springs Road, Lake Almanor, CA 96137, 530/596-3337, website: www.lakealmanorresort.homestead.com.

**Little Mount Hoffman Lookout,** Shasta-Trinity National Forest, McCloud District, McCloud, CA, 96057, 530/964-2184.

**Vagabond Resort,** 7371 Highway 147, Lake Almanor, CA 96137, 530/596-3240.

**Wilson's Camp Prattville Resort,** 2932 Lake Almanor Drive West, Canyon Dam, CA 95923, 530/259-2267.

# MENDOCINO AND WINE COUNTRY

COURTESY OF HERITAGE HOUSE

## BEST CABINS & COTTAGES

**❰ Best for Families**
Emandal Farm, **page 119**

**❰ Best for Beach Access**
Howard Creek Ranch, **page 118**
Agate Cove Inn, **page 120**

**❰ Most Romantic**
Albion River Inn, **page 124**

**❰ Best for Horseback Riding**
Highland Ranch, **page 130**

**❰ Most Luxurious**
Auberge du Soleil, **page 152**

For many people, this region offers the best possible combination of geography, weather, and outdoor activities around. The Mendocino Coast is dramatic and remote, with several stellar state parks for hiking, while Sonoma Valley, in the heart of wine country, produces some of the most popular wines in the world. Add in the self-indulgent options of mud baths and hot springs at Calistoga and a dash of mainstream recreation at Clear Lake, Lake Berryessa, or any other lake, and you have a capsule summary of why the Mendocino Coast and the wine country have turned into getaway favorites.

For the most part, this is where people go for romance, fine cuisine, great wine, mineral springs, and anything else that comes to mind. To accommodate this type of high-end vacation, the lodging tends be pricey, especially in the Sonoma and Napa Valleys. You pay for your pleasures here. Auberge du Soleil has freestanding cottages that cost up to $3,000 per night, the most expensive rental in Northern California that I could find. The Heritage House is another romantic getaway where you can reward yourself without being too price conscious.

This region wouldn't be the best of both worlds if there weren't options on the other end of spectrum. Inexpensive cabins, primarily set up for family recreation, are available. Destinations include Clear Lake, Lake Berryessa, and Blue Lakes. If the shoe fits — and for many, it does — you can have a great time fishing, boating, and waterskiing.

The coast features romantic hideaways plus excellent adventuring and hiking. The Fort Bragg area alone has three state parks, all with outstanding recreation, including several easy hikes, many amid redwoods and along pretty streams. Fort Bragg also offers excellent fishing out of Noyo Harbor.

The driving tour of Highway 1 along the coast here is the fantasy of many, and it can live up to that fantasy if you don't mind the twists and turns of the road. Along the way, there are dozens of hidden beaches and untouched coastline where you can stop and explore and maybe play tag with the waves. The prize spots are MacKerricher State Park, Salt Point State Park, and Anchor Bay.

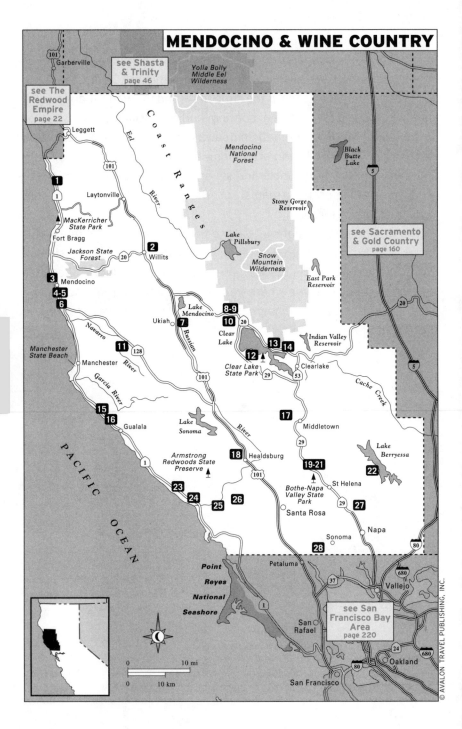

# MENDOCINO & WINE COUNTRY

see Shasta
& Trinity
page 46

Yolla Bolly
Middle Eel
Wilderness

see The
Redwood
Empire
page 22

Garberville

101

Leggett

101

Laytonville

1

**1**

MacKerricher
State Park

Fort Bragg

Jackson State
Forest

20

Willits

**2**

Mendocino
National
Forest

Black
Butte
Lake

5

Stony Gorge
Reservoir

Lake
Pillsbury

Snow
Mountain
Wilderness

East Park
Reservoir

see Sacramento
& Gold Country
page 160

**3** Mendocino

**4-5**
**6**

Navarro

Ukiah

Lake
Mendocino

**8-9**

**10**

20

**7**

Clear
Lake

Indian Valley
Reservoir

20

5

Manchester
State Beach

**11** 128

Manchester

Garcia River

Russian River

101

**13** **14**

**12**

Clear Lake
State Park

29

53

Clearlake

Cache Creek

**15**
**16**

Gualala

1

Lake
Sonoma

Armstrong
Redwoods State
Preserve

River

**17**

Middletown

29

Lake
Berryessa

**18** Healdsburg

101

**19-21**

**22**

PACIFIC OCEAN

**23**
**24**

**25**

**26**

Bothe-Napa
Valley State
Park

St Helena

29

**27**

Santa Rosa

Napa

Sonoma

**28**

80

Petaluma

37

Vallejo

680

Point
Reyes
National
Seashore

1

see San
Francisco Bay
Area
page 220

San
Rafael

24

680

0        10 mi

0        10 km

80

Oakland

San Francisco

© AVALON TRAVEL PUBLISHING, INC.

# Mendocino and Wine Country Cabins & Cottages

# ❶ HOWARD CREEK RANCH                    BEST ◖

Mendocino Coast, off Highway 1 near Westport

🏃 🐎 👫

**Luxury rating:** 3                                    **Recreation rating:** 4

Imagine this: a beautiful ocean-view cottage with a woodstove fired up when you want it, a hot tub and sauna, a 30-second walk to a long, pristine beach—all on the remote northern Mendocino Coast, one of the most divine stretches of ocean frontage anywhere.

Although life can't be like this all the time, it can last for as long as you decide to stay at Howard Creek Ranch. There are four cabins among its accommodations, including two with small, private hot tubs on the decks. There are also seven rooms in the renovated carriage barn and two in the historic farmhouse. A central hot tub and sauna are available; guests usually take turns on an individual couple basis, so privacy is always retained.

Everything near the cabins is cozy, pretty (flowers everywhere), and quiet. The grounds cover 40 acres and include a year-round creek. The ranch is a county-designated registered historical site, with a farmhouse built in 1871.

Yet all is not surreal. Those horses, llamas, sheep, cows, cats, and dogs roaming and grazing at the ranch are the real thing. One of the bonuses is that you can go for a private horseback ride, right down to the beach. What? You say riding a horse makes your butt sore? No problem: You can schedule a professional massage instead.

The property adjoins Westport Union Landing State Beach, about a 30-second walk from the cabins across the road and down to the beach. It's a long, sandy beach, and at low tide you can walk it for three miles. No, yer not dreamin'. From the cabins, the ocean is close enough not only to see, but to hear.

## Facilities

Howard Creek Ranch has four cabins, seven rooms in the renovated carriage barn, two in the farmhouse. Each cabin has a woodstove and bathroom (one has a nice outhouse). All have refrigerators and microwaves. Two cabins have hot tubs on their decks. A full ranch-style breakfast is provided, and barbecues are available. A fine restaurant is nearby, and a grocery store is three miles to the south in Westport. Linens and towels are provided.

## Reservations and Rates

Reservations are recommended. Rates range $75–185 per night depending on the level of accommodations. Contact Howard Creek Ranch, P.O. Box 121, Westport, CA 95488, 707/964-6725, fax 707/964-1603, website: www.howardcreekranch.com.

## Directions
From Fort Bragg and Highway 1, drive north 15 miles to Westport; continue north for 3 miles. At milepost 80.49, look for the turnoff to Howard Creek Ranch on the right. Turn right and drive a short distance in the valley to the ranch.

# **2** EMANDAL FARM                                      BEST **C**
Off U.S. 101 near Willits

🏃 🏊 🛶 👪 ♿

**Luxury rating: 2**                                **Recreation rating: 4**

It's not Old MacDonald's Farm, it's Emandal Farm—and it's gone organic. You'll still hear a moo-moo here and an oink-oink there, because cows, pigs, sheep, chickens, ducks, and turkeys live here on 1,000 acres of farmland and wooded open space bordering Mendocino National Forest.

What you get is pretty incredible: a primitive, redwood cabin; family-style meals served in a dining room; access to three miles of Eel River frontage; a five-acre bass lake; and the run of a working farm and its miles of wide-open space. And if you want to stay here, your only choices are August and September, since the farm is used for various group camps the remainder of the summer. Demand exceeds supply, so if you want a cabin, cross your fingers and call in early January; otherwise you'll probably end up on the waiting list.

This is a lot like camping because the cabins were built in the early 1900s, and not much has changed over the years. Each cabin has cold spring water, electricity, and queen beds and bunk beds. The facilities comprise a central bathhouse and restroom. Complimentary home-style meals are served three times a day, except for Sunday, when only one meal is prepared. Most of the food, including the meat, is grown organically on the farm. Fresh bread is made almost daily.

So what do you do? You swim in one of several swimming holes, you canoe on the small lake, you hike, you read, you lounge in a hammock, you spend time with your family. That's what it's all about. And if you feel like helping out with farm chores, you can pick berries, gather eggs, or dig potatoes. There's always a list of chores; of course, you can do absolutely nothing if you want.

## Facilities
Emandal Farm has 19 cabins and a campground. There are no kitchen facilities, but three meals per day Monday–Saturday and a meal on Sunday are provided. A central bathhouse offers hot showers and restrooms. The cabins have cold spring water and electricity. The farm is suitable for children. Pets are not allowed. No smoking is permitted. Some facilities are wheelchair accessible. Linens and blankets are provided but towels are not.

## Reservations and Rates

Reservations are recommended. The fee is $805 per week, double occupancy, and $196–560 per week for children, depending on age; call for nightly rates. Prices include most meals. Children under the age of two are free. A 10 percent service charge is added to the final bill. There is a two-night minimum on weekends. Major credit cards are accepted. The farm is open May–October only. Contact Emandal Farm, 16500 Hearst Post Office Road, Willits, CA 95490, 707/459-5439 or 800/262-9597, website: www.emandal.com.

## Directions

From U.S. 101 in Willits, turn east on East Commercial Street and drive 1.5 miles to a Y intersection. Bear left onto Hearst Willits Road/County Road 306 and drive 1.6 miles to Canyon Road/County Road 308. Drive straight ahead onto Canyon Road, cross a narrow bridge, then continue 4.3 miles to a Y intersection. Turn left on Tomki Road, cross a cement bridge, and continue for 1.6 miles to a T intersection. Turn right on Hearst Willits Road and drive 5.2 miles (crossing the Eel River) to a Y intersection. Bear right at the Emandal sign and drive a short distance (bearing right) to the farm at the end of the road.

# 3 AGATE COVE INN                                    BEST (
Mendocino Coast, off Highway 1 near Mendocino

**Luxury rating: 4**                                    **Recreation rating: 4**

High on a bluff in beautiful Mendocino sit eight quaint, charming cottages so appealing that they keep appearing on the covers of magazines and directories—posing as the poster cottages of the year. The reason for this is that these cottages at Agate Cove Inn have the right look, with an exquisite oceanfront location, as well as a comfortable, romantic ambience inside. In other words, they have it all.

All of the cottages are not created equal, nor are they all freestanding; some are in duplex units and two rooms are in a farmhouse. Most have decks, fireplaces, and large soaking tubs for two, but the big differences are the views; not all have ocean views. For the best views, and I mean dramatic coastline views, rent Obsidian Cottage or Emerald Cottage, located in a duplex unit. You'll pay a little more, but you get more.

Obsidian has an oversized room with double picture windows. The decor is an unusual country mix of floral wallpaper and bedspread with a black-and-white plaid couch and chairs. A white four-poster feather bed dominates the high-ceilinged room, and a sitting area with fireplace completes the picture. Emerald has an equally stunning view from the deck and the bed. It also has a multi-angled high ceiling, four-poster king bed, a soaking tub, and a fireplace. It is decorated with a bright, cheerful floral scheme of red, green, and yellow.

The inn is situated on two acres, amid 100-year-old cypress trees, near the edge of the quaint little village of Mendocino. The main farmhouse was built in 1860, and although it has been remodeled, the exterior looks much like it did originally, including the candlestick-style, white picket fence. Complimentary breakfast is served in the farmhouse kitchen, which offers more breathtaking views of the headlands and sea stacks. For details on the local area, refer to The Inn at Schoolhouse Creek (see next listing).

## Facilities

Agate Cove Inn has eight cottages and two inn rooms. All have private bathrooms. There are no kitchen facilities but a full breakfast is served. Most cottages have a deck and fireplace. Gift baskets, in-room massages, and wedding and reunion facilities are available. The inn is not suitable for children under 12. Pets are not allowed. No smoking is permitted. Linens and towels are provided.

## Reservations and Rates

Reservations are recommended. The fee is $199–309 per night per cottage, and inn rooms are $139–269 per night. A fee of $30 per night per person is charged for more than two people. Special packages are available. There is a two-night minimum on weekends and July–September, and a three-night minimum on holidays. Major credit cards are accepted. It's open year-round. Contact Agate Cove Inn, 11201 Lansing Street, Mendocino, CA 95460, 707/937-0551 or 800/527-3111, website: www.agatecove.com.

## Directions

From Mendocino and Highway 1, turn west on Little Lake Road and drive a short distance (0.1 mile) to Lansing Street. Turn right and drive 0.1 mile to the inn on the right (east side) side of the road.

# 4 THE INN AT SCHOOLHOUSE CREEK
Mendocino Coast, off Highway 1 in Little River

**Luxury rating:** 4                                                        **Recreation rating:** 4

This is a gorgeous spot where the pace slows and you can spend your mornings and evenings doing nothing but soaking in the surrounding beauty. The grounds are landscaped and pretty, with white picket fence, flowers, and 11 pristine cottages (as well as seven rooms in a separate lodge unit), often with ocean views. The cottages are cozy, clean, and intimate. They include woodstoves, small kitchens, and full baths. Rose, Heather, and Fuchsia Cottages all have decks with ocean views; Cypress and Willow have ocean views (but no decks); and Hawthorn has a forest-view deck and ocean glimpses.

The Inn at Schoolhouse Creek is in the town of Little River, 3 miles south of Mendocino and about 10 miles south of Fort Bragg. The inn is centered around the Ledford House, built in 1862 and nestled on eight acres of spectacular gardens, just east of Highway 1—and across from the ocean. There's a hot tub for four at the top of the meadow with fabulous ocean views; the best time for whale-watching is in the off-season, from Christmas through Memorial Day.

Many excellent hiking opportunities await nearby. Within a 15-minute drive are Van Damme State Park, the Mendocino Headlands, Russian Gulch State Park, Caspar State Beach, and Jug Handle State Reserve. A bit farther south is Navarro River Redwoods, and just north are Fort Bragg, Noyo Harbor, and Jackson Demonstration State Forest.

Excellent driving tours explore Highway 1. Adventurers can try spectacular scuba diving in shallows, sea kayaking in coves, and coastal fishing for salmon or rockfish. The fastest and easiest way to get a slice of this life is to drive to the town of Mendocino and take the short drive out to the Mendocino Headlands. The views, sunsets, and whale-spout viewing are all spectacular; a short, flat walk along the bluff provides a continuous lookout at the best of it.

A more secluded hike with an additional payoff is the five-mile round-trip in Russian Gulch State Park to see 36-foot Russian Gulch Falls. This is a divine waterfall, starting in a chute then staircasing in three steps, finally cascading off a huge boulder into a pool. The entire setting can be stunning, with ferns, giant downed logs, and a forest canopy.

## Facilities

The Inn at Schoolhouse Creek has 11 cottages extremely well furnished with woodstoves, small kitchens, telephones, televisions, and bathrooms; most have decks and ocean views. There are also seven inn-style rooms, most with ocean views. Pets are permitted by prior approval. Linens and towels are provided.

## Reservations and Rates

Reservations are strongly recommended. The fee ranges $140–235 per night for cottages, double-occupancy, with discounts for weekdays and the off-season. Lodge rooms are $130 per night. For each additional person add $15 per night; children under 12 are free. Rollaways or cribs cost $10. Contact The Inn at Schoolhouse Creek, North Highway 1, P.O. Box 1637, Mendocino, CA 95460, 707/937-5525, fax 707/937-2012, website: www.schoolhousecreek.com.

## Directions
From U.S. 101 at Cloverdale, take the Highway 128 exit, turn left at the stop sign, and drive west on Highway 128 to Highway 1. Turn north (right) on Highway 1 and drive 6.5 miles. Look for The Inn at Schoolhouse Creek on the right (east) side of the road.

# 5 HERITAGE HOUSE
Mendocino Coast, off Highway 1 in Little River

**Luxury rating:** 4           **Recreation rating:** 4

Heritage House is everything it claims to be: a romantic retreat on the rugged coastline with drop-dead gorgeous vistas, good food in an old lodge, and luxurious—often unusual—lodging. The inn has received a ton of publicity over the years, but it is well deserved. It's difficult to find fault with the place, but if I had to say that there are any negatives, it's that so much lodging has been crammed onto the 37 acres.

Lodging ranges from a basic motel-style room to secluded, luxurious accommodations situated on cliffs overlooking a dramatic section of the California coastline. You can also rent a water tower, Ivy 1 Cottage with a piano, or one of the bungalows where the movie *Same Time Next Year,* with Alan Alda and Ellen Burstyn, was filmed years ago. Take your pick, but remember: This is a place where upgrading your accommodations can make a huge difference, resulting in a memorable getaway. I suggest spending the extra money for a luxury cottage.

With a deluxe cottage, you most likely will get a private deck with panoramic ocean view, wet bar, dining table, large bedroom with king-sized bed, sitting area in front of a marble-faced fireplace, large bathroom with whirlpool tub for two, and tasteful, traditional decor.

The restaurant is housed in the 1800s-era, ivy-covered farmhouse. Breakfast and dinner are served here, and on weekends, brunch is available.

For details about the Little River area, refer to the description for The Inn at Schoolhouse Creek (see previous listing).

## Facilities

Heritage House has 65 cottages and three inn rooms. There are no kitchen facilities, but a restaurant is available. Amenities vary greatly, and some cottages have a fireplace or woodstove, deck, wet bar, and refrigerator. There are no televisions or telephones. Wedding and retreat facilities are available. Pets are not allowed. No smoking is permitted inside. Some facilities are wheelchair accessible. Linens and towels are provided.

## Reservations and Rates

Reservations are recommended. The fee is $125–425 per night per cottage. Additional guests are $20 per night per person. There is a two-night minimum stay on weekends. Off-season discounts are available. Major credit cards are accepted. Contact Heritage House, 5200 Highway 1, Little River, CA 95456-9503, 707/937-5885 or 800/235-5885, fax 707/937-0318, website: www.heritagehouseinn.com.

## Directions

From Mendocino, drive south on Highway 1 for approximately four miles to the town of Little River and Heritage House on the right (ocean) side.

## 6 ALBION RIVER INN    BEST (

Mendocino Coast, off Highway 1 near Albion

🥾 ♿

**Luxury rating:** 4                                    **Recreation rating:** 4

If you like your scenery rugged and breathtaking, your lodging luxurious, and your food divine, then consider Albion River Inn, a 10-acre spread several miles south of Mendocino. The 20 New England–style cottages perched high on a bluff overlooking dramatic coastline will make you feel like you're in Maine—although some might say you'll feel like you're in heaven.

Your cottage will likely have an ocean view, a deck, a sitting area with fireplace, plush furnishings, high ceilings, and a big whirlpool tub where you can lounge and enjoy your private view of the ocean. These cottages were designed to please, and they do. They are painted white and ooze romance. In the morning, you'll be treated to a made-to-order breakfast in the inn's restaurant, which has been praised by the food magazine *Bon Appétit*.

The acreage consists of gardens, lawns, and lookout points. The property is so beautiful that it is a popular place for weddings and special events. For details about the local area and recreation opportunities, refer to the description for The Inn at Schoolhouse Creek (see listing in this chapter).

## Facilities
Albion River Inn has 22 cottages with private bathrooms. There are no kitchen facilities but complimentary breakfast, coffee, tea, and wine are provided. Some cottages have decks, fireplaces, and whirlpool tubs. A restaurant is available. Pets are not allowed. No smoking is permitted. Some facilities are wheelchair accessible. Linens and towels are provided.

## Reservations and Rates
Reservations are recommended. The double-occupancy rate is $195–325 per night per cottage. Additional guests are $25 per night per person. There is a two-night minimum stay on weekends and a three-night minimum on holidays. Credit cards are accepted. The inn is open year-round. Contact Albion River Inn, 3790 Highway 1, P.O. Box 100, Albion, CA 95410, 707/937-1919 or 800/479-7944, fax 707/937-2604, website: www.albionriverinn.com.

## Directions
From Highway 1 in Mendocino, drive south six miles to the inn on the right (ocean) side.

# **7** VICHY SPRINGS RESORT
Ukiah, off U.S. 101

**Luxury rating:** 3                               **Recreation rating:** 4

At Vichy Springs Resort, your body likely will be fizzing, and it won't be from drinking sodas, but from the naturally carbonated mineral baths—the only warm, naturally occurring ones in North America. The "champagne" baths, the hot soaking pools, the Olympic-size swimming pool, and 700 acres with hiking trails make up the featured attractions here. As with other hot springs I found, the lodging is considered secondary to the hot springs and usually is viewed as a convenient place to hang out and sleep while enjoying the resort. You have a choice between cottages and inn rooms, and I strongly recommend a freestanding cottage, which is much more private and quiet.

This is a historic resort, built in 1854, and such notables as Jack London, Mark Twain, Robert Louis Stevenson, and U.S. presidents Theodore Roosevelt, Harrison, and Grant soaked their cares away here. The sulfurous, slightly rotten-egg smelling water is thought by some to have curative powers for the relief of stomach ailments and circulatory problems, the treatment of topical wounds and poison oak, and the relief of arthritis, gout, and rheumatism. The facilities are open for day use.

The one- and two-bedroom cottages have private bathrooms and are a step up from staying in the inn rooms. They have hardwood floors and redwood, oak, and pine furniture; the bathrooms are tiled with handmade Mexican paver tiles. The cottages feature fully equipped kitchens, and a complimentary buffet breakfast is served. Two of the cottages were built in 1854 and are recognized as the oldest buildings in Mendocino County. As you might guess, these historic cottages are the most requested, largely because London and Twain stayed in them.

In addition to the resort's 700 acres, attractions within a 30-minute drive include scads of wineries and microbreweries, three museums, the Russian River, Lake Mendocino, golf courses, Montgomery Woods State Park, and the Skunk Train.

## Facilities

Vichy Springs Resort has eight cottages and 12 inn rooms. The cottages have one or two bedrooms and include a fully equipped kitchen. A pool, hiking trails, massages, and facials are available. The resort is not suitable for children. Pets are not allowed. No smoking is permitted inside buildings. Some facilities are wheelchair accessible. Linens and towels are provided.

## Reservations and Rates

Reservations are recommended. The rates are $285–305 per night per cottage and $155–235 per night for inn rooms. Additional people are $40 per person per night. Breakfast and use of the mineral baths, swimming pool, and hot pools are included. A two-night minimum stay is required for certain periods. Major credit cards are accepted. It's open year-round. Contact Vichy Springs Resort, 2605 Vichy Springs Road, Ukiah, CA 95482-3507, 707/462-9515, fax 707/462-9516, website: www.vichysprings.com.

## Directions

From U.S. 101 in Ukiah, take the Vichy Springs Road/Central Ukiah exit and turn east on Vichy Springs Road. Drive for 1.3 miles and bear right to stay on Vichy Springs Road. Continue 1.7 miles to the resort on the right.

# 8 PINE ACRES BLUE LAKES RESORT
Upper Blue Lake, off Highway 20 north of Clear Lake

**Luxury rating:** 3                                   **Recreation rating:** 4

There are a half dozen Blue Lakes in California, but the twin set along Highway 20 north of Clear Lake are often the most overlooked. Vacationers miss them because they are in the shadow of nearby giant Clear Lake. Yet these lovely lakes offer good fishing for trout, especially in spring and early summer on Upper Blue Lake, and a decent chance the rest of the year. The long, narrow lakes are created from the flows of Cold Creek, which eventually runs into the East Fork Russian River and Lake Mendocino. With a five-mph speed limit in place, quiet boating is the rule. Swimming is good here. No waterskiing is permitted.

Pine Acres Resort is on Upper Blue Lake, known for its high water quality. The cabins here are a clear step above rustic and a clear step below luxury. They were remodeled in 2005. For many, it's a good, comfortable fit. They are well equipped, maintained daily, and best of all, within short range of the dock. People come here to either fish or swim in the lake.

Upper Blue Lake is stocked in the spring and fall with trout on a bimonthly basis, and at times has the most consistent catch rates in the region. The best trout fishing always happens in the cooler months, however, not in the hot summer, leaving frustrated visitors who show up in July wondering, "Where are all the trout I've heard about?" The answer is that they've either been caught already or they're hiding deep in the thermocline, where the water is cool and oxygenated. When that happens, it is better to switch than to fight. That means fishing instead for bluegill (during the day), largemouth bass (in the mornings and evenings), or catfish (at night). The size of the bass (occasionally over 10 pounds) can be a real stunner here, especially for anglers who think only Clear Lake has fish that big.

## Facilities
Pine Acres Blue Lakes Resort has five cottages, five motel rooms, one deluxe unit, and a campground. Some have kitchens. Microwaves, dishes, utensils, and televisions are provided. A clubhouse with kitchen facilities and woodstove is available for groups of up to 100. A sandy beach is on-site. No pets are permitted in cottages. Linens and towels are provided.

## Reservations and Rates

Reservations are recommended. Cottages without kitchens are $80 per night, cottages with kitchens are $95 per night, and the deluxe unit is $1,250 per night. Two-night minimum stays on weekends and three-night minimum stays on holidays are required. Additional guests are $5 per night; children under age two (with own bedding) are free. Major credit cards are accepted. It's open year-round. Contact Pine Acres Blue Lakes Resort, 5328 Blue Lakes Road, Upper Lake, CA 95485, 707/275-2811, fax 707/275-9549, website: www.bluelakepineacres.com.

## Directions

From Ukiah, drive north on U.S. 101 for 5 miles to the junction with Highway 20. Turn east on Highway 20 and drive about 13 miles to Irvine Street. Turn right on Irvine Street and drive one block to Blue Lakes Road. Turn right and drive two blocks to the resort.

# 9 THE NARROWS LODGE RESORT
### Upper Blue Lake, off Highway 20 north of Clear Lake

**Luxury rating:** 3                                         **Recreation rating:** 4

Not all cabins are created equal. At The Narrows Lodge Resort, the cabins are always in clean and tidy condition. Cabins 7, 8, 9, and 10 all have lake views. The grounds feature a lawn and shade trees, with the pretty waters of Blue Lake nearby. And since a campground is on the property, full facilities are available, including a boat dock. Its location aside, Upper Blue Lake is ideal, and when you put it all together, it can make for a great getaway in foothills of Lake County.

Upper Blue Lake is very pretty in the spring, when its azure blue waters are contrasted with the surrounding neon green hills. As summer turns the hills gold, the contrast with the water is even more striking. With a five-mph speed limit in place on the lake, tranquility reigns. For some, this lake thus becomes their favorite place.

The lake has trout, bass, crappie, bluegill, and catfish. Trout fishing is good in the spring and fall; go for bass in the spring and early summer. The weather gets very hot from mid-June through August and the cool, clear waters of the lake provide great relief. It's one of the best swimming holes you could ever want.

## Facilities

The Narrows Lodge Resort has five cabins of various sizes and 11 motel units. They are well furnished and include private bathrooms. Some have kitchens with utensils. A campground on the property offers modem hookups, a recreation room, boat rentals, a pier, a boat ramp, and a country store with fishing supplies, propane, and ice. Motel-style rooms are also available. Pets with no fleas are permitted by prior arrangement and must be attended at all times; some breeds are not permitted. Smoking is not permitted in some cabins. Linens and towels are provided.

## Reservations and Rates

Reservations are recommended. The rates range $65–88 double occupancy, to $125 for up to six per night, and $394–812 per week. Major credit cards are accepted. It's open year-round. Contact The Narrows Lodge Resort, 5690 Blue Lakes Road, Upper Lake, CA 95485, 707/275-2718 or 800/476-2776, fax 707/275-0739, website: www.thenarrowsresort.com.

## Directions

From Ukiah, drive north on U.S. 101 for 5 miles to the junction with Highway 20. Turn east on Highway 20 and drive about 11.5 miles to Blue Lakes Road. Turn right and drive to 5690 Blue Lakes Road.

# 10 LE TRIANON RESORT

Lower Blue Lake, off Highway 20 north of Clear Lake

**Luxury rating:** 3                                        **Recreation rating:** 4

Le Trianon Resort, set on Lower Blue Lake, is a big RV park that as a bonus provides 10 cabin rentals. This spot is considered a fishing enthusiast's special, with no waterskiing permitted, good trout fishing in spring and early summer—and a chance for giant bass.

Many anglers do not want anything fancy, but that doesn't always mean their nonfishing companions agree. The family cabins are furnished with bathroom, kitchen, and two bedrooms, each with a double and queen beds. Because the cabins are part of a large RV camping complex, the available facilities are extensive and not far away. A small store is usually well stocked, and in addition, a small marina offers a boat ramp and rentals.

And that gets us to the fishing, which is why Lower Blue Lake has become popular. Blue Lakes has quietly become a secret spot for local anglers searching for big bass. When the bite is turned off at Clear Lake, or when Clear Lake gets too crowded with skiers or tournament anglers, these locals head for Blue Lakes. That's because they know a secret.

It is surprising the size of the bass that can be caught in Lower Blue Lake, in some cases over 10 pounds. Crankbaits, such as the Speed Trap, can be very effective when cast parallel to the shoreline. Another trick here is to work a Brush Hog off of any kind of structure. This will give you a fair chance of catching a large bass. There is a five-mph speed limit on the lake; waterskiing and personal watercraft riding are prohibited. Swimming, sailing, sailboarding, kayaking, and canoeing are allowed.

## Facilities

Le Trianon Resort has 10 family cabins, each with a bathroom with shower, a family room, a fully equipped kitchen, and a porch. A large RV park is on the property with a playground, a boat ramp, boat rentals, fishing supplies, coin laundry, a snack bar, and a grocery store. No dogs are permitted in cabins. Smoking is permitted in cabins. No motorcycles are allowed. Those under 21 without parents are not permitted. Night security is provided, with a quiet time enforced 10 P.M.–9 A.M. Linens and towels are provided.

## Reservations and Rates

Reservations are recommended starting March 1 of each year. Rates are $80–100 per night and $465–595 per week for up to four people. Children under age three are free. Major credit cards are accepted. There is a three-day minimum on holidays. The resort is open May 23–October 4. Contact Le Trianon Resort, 5845 West Highway 20, Ukiah, CA 95482, 707/275-2262, fax 707/275-9416, website: www.letrianon.com.

## Directions

From Ukiah, drive north on U.S. 101 for five miles to the junction with Highway 20. Turn east on Highway 20 and drive 12 miles to 5845 West Highway 20.

# 11 HIGHLAND RANCH                    BEST (
Philo, off Highway 128

**Luxury rating:** 4                                      **Recreation rating:** 5

I really searched to find a large ranch that wasn't near the Sierra, and I found one—overlooking Anderson Valley, an area known more for wine than horses and fishing. The other surprise at Highland Ranch is that the management speaks English, Italian, French, and Spanish. The owner lived in Europe for 24 years and brought back a European clientele with him. This is not a dude ranch, but rather a relaxed, upscale country retreat for people who like horseback riding, hiking, and enjoying good food and drinks with people from all over the world. Put together a group of at least 14 people, and you can have the entire ranch to yourselves. The place was remodeled in 2005.

You'll have 247 acres of extraordinary redwood groves and open, grassy meadows next to pines and oaks to horseback ride and hike on, as well as the use of a trap-shooting range for ages 14 and older. Hendy Woods State Park and several private ranches adjoin Highland Ranch, so the horseback riding and hiking opportunities are enormous, with over 100 miles of trails in the immediate area. If you don't feel like leaving the vicinity of your cabin, you can play tennis, swim in the pool, read a book in a hammock under towering trees, fish in the four-acre bass pond, or make arrangements for a massage.

The staff wants you to enjoy the outdoors, but they also ensure that you aren't roughing it. Although there are many activities to choose from, horseback riding is the emphasis here, and there are daily rides for all levels of riders; English and western saddles are available. Twenty horses live at the ranch, and the owner jokingly refers to them as family. Horseback riding is included in your room fee, but riding lessons, massages, clay pigeon shooting, and baby-sitting are extra.

And when it's chow time, you head over to the dining room for a home-cooked, family-style meal, complete with cocktails and wine and beer from the local wineries and microbreweries. The dining room has the feel of an old-fashioned lodge, with a vaulted ceiling, long wooden tables with blue-checkered tablecloths, and deer head mounts hanging from wood-paneled walls. The lodge was built in the 1880s and has received additions and been remodeled over the years.

The one- to three-bedroom cabins have private bathrooms, fireplaces, and decks, and are situated under large redwoods. Most of the cabins are in duplex units, but two of the rentals are freestanding. A typical cabin has wood paneling; vaulted, beamed ceilings; a woodburning fireplace with large brick hearth; and a decidedly ranch-style look and feel. There are no kitchens, since meals are provided.

## Facilities

Highland Ranch has eight cabins with private bathrooms. There are no kitchen facilities, but all meals and drinks are provided. Amenities include tennis courts, horseback riding, clay pigeon shooting, mountain bikes, a bass lake, massage, yoga classes, baby-sitting, and conference facilities. The ranch is suitable for children. Well-behaved dogs are allowed. Smoking is permitted. Linens and towels are provided.

## Reservations and Rates

Reservations are recommended. The fee is $285 per night per person and $190 per night for children under age 12, and includes all meals and drinks. Infants are free. A 10 percent service charge is added to the final bill. There is a two-night minimum stay and a three-night minimum stay on holidays. Major credit cards are accepted. It's open year-round. Contact Highland Ranch, P.O. Box 150, Philo, CA 95466, 707/895-3600, fax 707/895-3702, website: www.highlandranch.com.

## Directions

From Cloverdale on U.S. 101, turn northwest on Highway 128 and drive about 35 miles to Philo. Continue 2.5 miles to Hendy Woods Elk Road. Turn left and drive 1.1 miles Highland Ranch entrance on left. If the entrance is gated, the tumbler-lock combination is 3600. Drive 4 miles to the ranch.

# 12 EDGEWATER RESORT

Clear Lake, off Highway 29 near Kelseyville

🏊 ⛵ 🛶 🐕 🚻

**Luxury rating:** 3                                      **Recreation rating:** 4

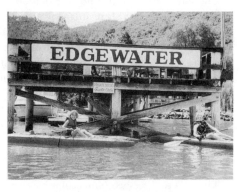

Soda Bay is one of Clear Lake's prettiest and most intimate spots, and this camp provides excellent access. Edgewater Resort is a large operation featuring eight furnished cabins, two houses, and an adjacent RV park and campground.

All cabins on the property have two bedrooms, bathrooms, and furnished kitchens and can sleep up to 4; the houses can sleep 8 and 12, respectively. The cabins have air-conditioning and cable television. Because a campground is on the property, many bonus amenities are provided. These include a 230-foot fishing pier, rentals of fishing boats or kayaks, and a swimming pool in the summer season. A recreation area is also available. This resort is very popular for groups, such as for reunions, because a clubhouse (accommodating up to 200 people and including a full kitchen) with lake views is available.

The recreational highlights of the place are boating, waterskiing, and fishing. Both waterskiing and fishing for bass and bluegill are excellent in Soda Bay, as it is sheltered from north winds; that means quiet water. The shore is tule-lined from Henderson Point all the way around to Dorn Bay—nearly three miles of prime fishing territory.

Maybe Clear Lake should be renamed Fish Lake or Green Lake, because its emerald green waters are full of fish. With high levels of nutrients and algae clouding the water, it is anything but clear—and you can thank nature for creating such a wonderful problem. You see, the lake's substantial nutrients—phytoplankton and algae—and a huge minnow population support a high carrying capacity. In simpler terms, a lot of aquatic food equals a lot of fish. Clear Lake produces more big crappie and greater numbers of catfish than any other lake in California, including yellow, blue, and channel catfish. In the 1970s, people said the lake had wall-to-wall crappie. In the 1980s, they talked about the wall-to-wall catfish, and in the 1990s, wall-to-wall bass. Now, in the 21st century, those same folks are saying that Clear Lake could be the first lake in Northern California to produce a 20-pound bass, and maybe even a world record.

Set amid the foothills of Lake County, Clear Lake is quite pretty, covering more than 40,000 surface acres. It is the largest natural freshwater lake within California's borders, and with Highway 20 running aside the eastern shore, it often seems full to the brim. The dozens of resorts and private campgrounds sprinkled along the 100 miles of shoreline accommodate huge numbers of visitors without making the area feel crowded. Reservations are strongly recommended in the summer.

## Facilities
Edgewater Resort has eight cabins that can sleep 4–12 people and include kitchens with microwaves and utensils, bathrooms with showers, air-conditioning, heat, and televisions. A campground is on the property; facilities include modem hookups, a game room, a general store, laundry, a swimming pool, horseshoes, volleyball, and Ping-Pong. A swimming beach, boat ramp, fishing pier, boat dock, and watercraft rentals are nearby. "Good dogs" are permitted in cabins, and a dog run is available at the beach. No smoking is permitted in the cabins. Linens and pillows are provided.

## Reservations and Rates
Reservations are recommended. The nightly rates are $140–190 for up to 4 people for the cabins and $350–450 for up to 12 people for the houses. Pets are $5 per night. Discounted winter rates are available. Major credit cards are accepted. It's open year-round. Contact Edgewater Resort, 6420 Soda Bay Road, Kelseyville, CA 95451, 707/279-0208 or 800/396-6224, website: www.edgewaterresort.net.

## Directions
In Kelseyville on Highway 29, take the Merritt Road exit and drive on Merritt for two miles (it becomes Gaddy Lane) to Soda Bay Road. Turn right on Soda Bay Road and drive three miles to the campground entrance on the left.

## 13 INDIAN BEACH RESORT
Clear Lake, off Highway 20 near Glenhaven

🏊 🚣 🚤 🐕 👫 ♿

**Luxury rating:** 3                                    **Recreation rating:** 4

You'll be sitting on 300 feet of lake frontage when you rent a cabin at Indian Beach Resort, but if you're like most visitors, you'll be out fishing instead of sitting along the lake's edge. When a resort offers a floating fishing dock with night lighting, you know that fishing is a priority. But if you do decide to sit for a spell, you'll have a view of the 10 lakeside cabins set amid oak trees.

The studio to two-bedroom cabins have fully equipped kitchens, bathrooms, and televisions, and some have a deck or porch. Four of the cabins are duplex units, and five are freestanding, plus a studio cabin. Up to 10 people can be accommodated in the cabins, depending on the rental. Here's the inside scoop on the cabins: The most popular cabins are Cabins 6, 8, and 9 because they're closest to the lake. Cabin 10 is the largest rental, with two bedrooms, two bathrooms, one queen bed, three double beds, and a sofa bed.

Indian Beach Resort is a good setup for a family or group because it also has a swimming beach with its own floating dock, a boat launch, a picnic area with barbecue facilities, a small store, bait and tackle, and even a Ping-Pong table. The facilities are in a protected cove, which means that when it gets windy on the lake, the water is calmer here. The resort is on the eastern edge of the lake in a centralized area that is full of activity, which means more urban conveniences are within a short distance.

## Facilities

Indian Beach Resort has 10 cabins with fully equipped kitchens and private bathrooms. Televisions are provided, but there are no telephones. Amenities include a picnic area with barbecues, Ping-Pong, a swimming area, a boat dock and launch ramp, and a small store with bait and tackle. The resort is suitable for children. Leashed pets are allowed. Smoking is permitted. One cabin is wheelchair accessible. Linens and towels are provided.

## Reservations and Rates

Reservations are recommended. The fee is $48–125 per night per cabin. Children under the age of two are free. The pet fee is $7 per night per pet. Major credit cards are accepted. The resort is open year-round. Contact Indian Beach Resort by mail at P.O. Box 648, Glenhaven, CA 95443, or at 9945 East Highway 20, Clearlake Oaks, CA 94423, 707/998-3760.

## Directions

From U.S. 101 in Ukiah, turn east on Highway 20 and drive about 45 miles to the resort on the right side of the road, at Clear Lake.

## 14 BLUE FISH COVE RESORT
Clear Lake, off Highway 20 near Clearlake Oaks

**Luxury rating:** 3                    **Recreation rating:** 4

You can have all that Clear Lake has to offer from Blue Fish Cove Resort: a cabin with fully equipped kitchen and deck close to the shoreline, a swimming beach, a lighted fishing pier, boat launch and dock, a hot tub, a small store with bait and tackle, boat rentals, and a game room with pool table and arcade. And what are your outdoor recreation options? You can swim, boat, and fish until you're tired out, then return to your cabin with your day's catch for a barbecue on your deck, maybe followed by a game of pool.

The cabins come in one- and two-bedroom sizes and can sleep up to five, depending on the rental. Three of the cabins are freestanding, and four are duplex style. Not all cabins have a lake view, so if you want one, ask for Cabin 5 or 7. They're clean and cozy and have a breakfast nook. The kitchens have everything you need, including a microwave, toaster, coffeepot with filter, cream and sugar, dishwashing soap, salt and pepper, and towels. All you have to remember to bring is the food.

For more information about Clear Lake, refer to the description for Edgewater Resort (see listing in this chapter).

### Facilities
Blue Fish Cove Resort has seven cabins with private bathrooms. Most cabins have a fully equipped kitchen, barbecue, cable television, balcony or patio, heater, and evaporative cooler. A lighted fishing pier, a fish-cleaning station, bass boat outlets, boat and personal watercraft rentals, bait and tackle, a pool table, a game room with arcade, a basketball court, horseshoes, and croquet round out the facilities. The resort is suitable for children. Leashed pets are allowed. Smoking is permitted. Some facilities are wheelchair accessible. Linens and towels are provided.

### Reservations and Rates
Reservations are recommended. The double-occupancy rate (except for Cabin 3, which is based on four people) is $60–120 per night per cabin, and $370–680 per week; discounts are available. Additional guests are $10 per night. The pet fee is $20 for the first night, then $10 per night thereafter, and a $100 damage deposit is required. Children under age five are free. Major credit cards are accepted. It's open year-round. Contact Blue Fish Cove Resort, 10573 East Highway 20, Clearlake Oaks, CA 95423, 707/998-1769, website: www.bluefishcove.com.

### Directions
From north of Ukiah on U.S. 101, or at Williams on I-5, turn on Highway 20 and drive to Clearlake Oaks and the resort on the left.

## 15 SERENISEA COTTAGES
Mendocino Coast, off Highway 1 near Gualala

🏃 🌊 🛶 🐴 👪

**Luxury rating:** 3                                  **Recreation rating:** 3

Serenisea Cottages is a fantasy-driven spot on the Mendocino Coast, featuring both company-owned and privately owned ocean-bluff cottages and homes for rent. For the highest quality, my advice is to reserve one of the privately owned cottages or homes, rather than going for one of the cabins on the property. Many cottages have decks with ocean views and hot tubs, and some have access to nearby sand beaches. There are 25 available, most well-furnished and all designed to provided a memorable vacation. They offer a wide variety of settings and conditions. For instance, 5 cottages allow pets and 10 allow youngsters under 16. Some are secluded in the forest.

This is a quiet and beautiful stretch of California coast. Touring Highway 1, exploring nearly deserted beaches, and enjoying ocean views make a perfect vacation for many. It's calm and still compared to the intense pace that many experience on a daily basis.

Nearby Gualala Regional Park provides an excellent easy hike, with the headlands-to-beach loop offering coastal views, a lookout of the Gualala River, and many giant cypress trees. Another good side trip is to Salt Point State Park, south of Serenisea, where there is a beautiful cove, a kelp forest, and native abalone grounds.

The nearby Gualala River is remote and pretty, and is the best of the smaller coastal rivers in Sonoma and Mendocino Counties. Families and novice rafters find that the Gualala River makes a great place to enjoy an easy float in a canoe or kayak. The river is very scenic, and rafters should be able to see lots of wildlife and birds. Swimming is good all along the lower river, which has a few deep swimming holes and even rope swings in a couple of places.

## Facilities

Serenisea has three cabins on its property and manages an additional 25 privately owned vacation homes and cottages in the Gualala-Anchor Bay area. Most of these cottages have decks, fireplaces or woodstoves, full kitchens, and televisions. They can sleep 2–8 people per night. Call for details regarding pet policies. Linens and towels are provided.

## Reservations and Rates

Reservations are required, and there is a two-night minimum stay on weekends. Fees for cottages range $95–160 per night. Vacation homes range $110–250 per night. Contact Serenisea Cottages, 36100 Highway 1 South, Gualala, CA 95445, 707/884-3836 or 800/331-3836, website: www.serenisea.com.

## Directions

On U.S. 101 north of Santa Rosa, turn west on River Road and drive 13 miles to Guerneville and Highway 116. Turn west on Highway 116 and drive about 20 miles to Highway 1 at Jenner. Turn north (right) on Highway 1 and drive 38 miles to Gualala. Continue on Highway 1 past Gualala for 3 miles and look for Serenisea on the west (ocean) side of the road.

# 16 ST. ORRES

Mendocino Coast, off Highway 1 near Gualala

**Luxury rating:** 3          **Recreation rating:** 3

The first time you drive past St. Orres, it's nearly impossible not to give the place a head-craning, full-out gawk. The reason is the unique architecture; it appears as if elaborate, rustic domed structures were lifted from Russia and deposited north of the town of Gualala, then sided with redwood. Maybe it's the dramatic ocean scenery on one side of Highway 1, along with the equally dramatic setting at St. Orres on the opposite side of the highway, that makes your brain go into overload. Whatever the reason, this is the kind of place that you don't forget.

There are 13 cottages and cabins dotted around the 12 acres, mostly hidden by the main lodge and the forest. From behind the hotel, a footbridge leads to 4 cottages and a cabin on the edge of a redwood forest. The most popular rental of this grouping is Treehouse, with a Franklin stove, French doors in the sitting area, a deck, a wet bar, a king-sized bed on an elevated level from the sitting area, and a bathroom with a big soaking tub and shower. This cottage rents for $220 per night. The Black Chanterelle has high ceilings, a sauna, and a large whirlpool tub. Wildflower is a small, rustic cabin that was originally built for logging crews. It has an outside shower with a forest view. Inside, there's a woodburning stove in the sitting area and a sleeping loft with a double bed and skylight. This is the most economical cabin at $120 per night.

In a more secluded area of the property sit eight other cottages, some with ocean views, that share a hot tub, sauna, and sundeck. The largest cottage is Osprey Cove, a two-story home suitable for families. It boasts a spacious deck, wood-burning stove, master bedroom with king-sized bed, bathroom with sauna, and private hot tub. Ocean views can be seen from this cottage, and a telescope is provided for whale- and bird-watching.

St. Orres also boasts a well-known gourmet restaurant and eight hotel rooms that are reached by climbing a heavy-timbered spiral staircase that circles—get this—a tree trunk. The rooms share three bathrooms. You want friendly, good-natured staff? You get that here.

Ocean and beach access are available across the highway. Two miles south is Gualala Point Park, adjacent to the mouth of the Gualala River. Headlands Beach Loop is an easy, 1.5-mile hike.

## Facilities

St. Orres has 13 cottages and cabins and eight hotel rooms. Only 1 cottage has a kitchen (the others have a refrigerator and coffeemaker), but a complimentary breakfast is provided. Fireplace or woodstove, deck, and whirlpool tubs are available in some of the rentals. Most of the facilities are not suitable for children. Pets are not allowed. No smoking is allowed. Linens and towels are provided.

## Reservations and Rates

Reservations are recommended. The double-occupancy rate is $120–420 per night per cottage or cabin and $90–105 per night for hotel rooms, with a charge of $30 per night per additional person. Full breakfast is included. There is a two-night minimum stay on weekends and a three-night minimum stay on holidays. Major credit cards are accepted. It's open year-round. Contact St. Orres, 36601 Coast Highway 1, Gualala, CA 95445, 707/884-3303, fax 707/884-1840, website: www.saintorres.com.

## Directions

On U.S. 101 north of Santa Rosa, turn west on River Road and drive 13 miles to Guerneville and Highway 116. Turn west on Highway 116 and drive about 20 miles to Highway 1 at Jenner. Turn north on Highway 1 and drive 38 miles to Gualala. Continue on Highway 1 past Gualala for 2 miles to St. Orres on the right.

# **17** PINE GROVE RESORT
Cobb Mountain, off Highway 29 near Middletown

**Luxury rating:** 2                    **Recreation rating:** 3

"One step up from camping" is the best description for the 16 cabins at Pine Grove Resort. This is a family-oriented resort, with activities designed for children. Coming here is much like taking your family to a large campground or rustic summer camp. Clear Lake is about 20 miles north, but once here, most people are content to hang out on the 33 tree-covered acres, spending their days swimming, playing basketball or volleyball, and using the recreation room. Evenings are usually spent sitting around the campfire, watching the weekly children's talent show, square dancing, or participating in a game.

The one- to three-bedroom cabins were built more than 50 years ago and not much has changed in them over the years. There is a dark-brown paint job on the outside and plywood walls on the inside. They have kitchens and bathrooms, but you must bring your own linens and towels. There are no telephones, televisions, or air-conditioning. Nine of the cabins are set along Kelsey Creek, and the favorite is Grapevine Cabin because it sits up on a hill and is the most private.

The highlights for most families are the two swimming pools and two wading pools; one pool actually is a spring-fed cold pool. The café is open daily for dinner and on weekends for breakfast. The snack bar at the pool area is open daily.

The resort also has a beer garden. The official motto here is "Relax and have fun."

## Facilities

Pine Grove Resort has 16 housekeeping cabins and a campground for tents, trailers, and RVs. The cabins have fully equipped kitchens, barbecues, and a deck or porch. Amenities include a café, a small store, two swimming pools, two wading pools, volleyball and horseshoe pits, a children's play area, a recreation room with Ping-Pong, pool table, and video games, and organized activities. The resort is suitable for children. Leashed pets are allowed. Smoking is permitted. Some facilities are wheelchair accessible. Linens and towels are provided.

## Reservations and Rates

Reservations are recommended. The fee is $99–145 per night per cabin, with discounts available for longer stays. Major credit cards are accepted. Contact Pine Grove Resort, 15969 Bottle Park Road, P.O. Box 44, Cobb, CA 95426, 707/928-5222, website: www.pinegroveusa.com.

## Directions

From Vallejo, drive north on Highway 29 past Calistoga to Middletown and the junction with Highway 175. Turn north on Highway 175 and drive 8.5 miles to Bottle Rock Road. Turn left and drive 0.5 mile to the resort on the right.

## 18 BELLE DE JOUR INN
Sonoma foothills, off U.S. 101 in Healdsburg

**Luxury rating:** 4                                  **Recreation rating:** 3

You'll have a romantic white cottage on a hill overlooking rolling hills and vineyards and situated next to an 1870s Italianate farmhouse when you stay at one of the cottages at Belle de Jour Inn. Or, you can stay in the most popular rental, the 800-square-foot Carriage House. Either way, you get a relaxing setting on six acres, in close proximity to wine touring and exploring rural Sonoma County and the Russian River.

Small details that make a difference are what you'll notice here, from the sheets dried in the sun to the fresh flowers and the landscaping. The grounds are beautifully manicured and include footpaths, benches, and even hammocks. It is a peaceful, serene setting made for relaxing. The cottages are adjoined, and each one is decorated with contemporary furniture and accents.

The Caretaker's Suite, once the caretaker's home, has a trellised entry deck, sitting area with fireplace, a king canopy bed, and a private bath with whirlpool tub for two. It rents for $275 per night. The Carriage House is on the second floor and features a vaulted ceiling, a king bed, sitting areas, a gas fireplace, a stained glass window, and a bathroom with whirlpool tub for two. The color scheme is in warm tones. This suite rents for $335 per night.

Complimentary full breakfast is served in the farmhouse each morning. The Windsor Golf Club is within a 15-minute drive of the inn.

## Facilities

Belle de Jour Inn has four cottages and the Carriage House, all with private bathrooms. There are no kitchen facilities, but a full breakfast is served. Features include a small refrigerator, telephone, fireplace, ceiling fan, air-conditioning, and television, and some cottages have whirlpool tubs. The inn is not suitable for children. Pets are not allowed. No smoking is permitted. Linens and towels are provided.

## Reservations and Rates

Reservations are recommended. The fee is $195–335 per night per cottage. There is a two-night minimum stay on weekends, a three-night minimum stay on holidays. Major credit cards are accepted. It's open year-round. Contact Belle de Jour Inn, 16276 Healdsburg Avenue, Healdsburg, CA 95448, 707/431-9777, fax 707/431-7412, website: www.belledejourinn.com.

## Directions

From U.S. 101 in Healdsburg, drive north to the Dry Creek Road exit. Take that exit and turn right on Dry Creek Road. Drive 0.5 mile to Healdsburg Avenue. Turn left and drive one mile to the inn entrance road on the right, across the street from Simi Winery. Turn right and drive up the tree-lined driveway to the inn.

# **19 WASHINGTON STREET LODGING**

Napa Valley, off Highway 29 in Calistoga

🏃 ≈ 🎿 🐾

**Luxury rating:** 3                                                 **Recreation rating:** 4

This is the place where souls get recharged, bodies get rejuvenated, and your brain takes a vacation. How? By taking advantage of the town's hot springs, mud baths, towel wraps, massages, and quality dining. In 24 hours, Calistoga finds a way to get inside you and realign your senses.

The cottages at Washington Street Lodging are clean, cozy, and pretty inside and out. Believe it or not, you can bring your pet. The first thing you notice is that the entire property is loaded with blooming flowers, and the place is well kept. The headwaters of the Napa River run right by the cottages. Although the Napa River here is more like a creek, the riparian woodlands provide a nice feel and setting, especially in the early evening. One special feature of Cottages 3 and 4 is the small deck overlooking the creek.

The only downer is for late risers during the spring, fall, and winter. Directly across the stream, behind the cottages, is an elementary schoolyard, and they have recess every morning for 20 minutes starting at 8:15 A.M. The shrieks can be irritating if you are trying to sleep. In summer, it's not a factor, since school is not in session.

Peace is what you come here for, and for the most part, it is peace that you will get. Calistoga has nine hot spring spas, all with mud baths and treatments that will make your skin glow. The full treatment, which includes a mud bath, hot mineral soak, towel wrap, and massage, will have you surrendering to the final euphoria. Problems? What problems? Taking a mud bath is like sinking into a cauldron of ooze; the hot soak will permeate and loosen every tight muscle in your body, and then the warm towel wrap will have you practically levitating with tingles. Finish it off with a session with a massage therapist, and your mission will be near complete; you will gleam for days. Even the most tightly wound souls will yield, and suddenly, in just a few hours, problems seem unimportant.

After reaching this state of harmony, the best way to integrate it into the real world is to visit one of the area's parks for a hike in a natural setting. There are three state parks nearby, two to the south of Calistoga, Bothe-Napa and Bale Grist Mill, and one to the north, Robert Louis Stevenson.

For information about other activities in the area, refer to the description for Cottage Grove Inn (see listing in this chapter).

## Facilities

Washington Street Lodging has five cottages, each with a small kitchen with microwave and/or stove, and a bathroom with shower. Pets are permitted. Linens and towels are included.

## Reservations and Rates

Reservations are strongly recommended, both for cottage rentals and for treatments at any of the spas. Cottages are $95–140 per night. There is a $15 per pet fee. Full spa treatments are about $100, with some less expensive options. Contact Washington Street Lodging, 1605 Washington Street, Calistoga, CA 94515, 707/942-6968 or 877/214-3869, website: www.washingtonstreetlodging.com.

## Directions

From Napa, drive north on Highway 29 for about 30 miles to Calistoga. At the flashing light, turn right on Lincoln Avenue and drive into downtown Calistoga. Turn left (north) on Washington Street and drive two blocks to 1605 Washington, on the left (west) side of the road. Limited parking is available near the cottages. Parking is available on the east side of Washington Street.

# 20 INDIAN SPRINGS
### Calistoga, off Highway 29

🏃 🏊 🎿 👪 ♿

**Luxury rating:** 4                                             **Recreation rating:** 4

At Indian Springs, you can almost roll out of bed and into a volcanic ash mud bath or Olympic-size mineral pool; that's the big advantage of renting a bungalow here. Almost everyone who stays here visits the full-service, historic spa on the premises or the local wineries—or both.

The resort is situated on 16 acres of volcanic ash and three thermal geysers. Thousand of years before the invention of resorts and spas, the local Native Americans built sweat lodges over the escaping steam, bathed in the warm water, and called this area Oven Place. When the Spaniards arrived in the 17th century, they named the area Agua Caliente. During the 1800s, Sam Brannan, the first California gold rush tycoon, bought the property and built an upscale resort, naming it Calistoga, a combination of California and Saratoga, a lavish East Coast resort. Later, Leland Stanford bought the property and at one time planned to build Stanford University here.

The current bathhouse and pool were built in 1913, and the cottages were added in the 1940s, although they have been refurbished recently. Today, Indian Springs is recognized as the oldest continuously operating thermal pool and spa in the state. The temperature of the naturally heated mineral pool fluctuates between 90°F and 102°F, depending on the season. The spa has a full range of services, including 15 different types of massage.

The 17 bungalows are actually duplex units, except for one freestanding cottage with a fully equipped kitchen. There is another cottage that is connected to the management unit, plus 24 rooms in the lodge. The duplex rentals have kitchenettes. The remodeling includes whitewashed walls, plank floors, fireplaces, down comforters, and front porches. Each bungalow has a hammock outside. With such nice facilities, it's too bad that the management is not consistently friendly and helpful to their guests and the public.

For details about other activities in the area, refer to the description for Cottage Grove Inn (see next listing).

## Facilities

Indian Springs has one freestanding cottage and one attached, 17 duplex-style bungalows, plus 24 rooms in the lodge. All have private bathrooms, front porches, barbecues, televisions, and air-conditioning. The freestanding bungalows have fully equipped kitchenettes. Amenities include a large mineral pool, a full-service spa with mud baths, a tennis court, croquet, bicycle racks, and hammocks. The lodging is suitable for children. Pets are not allowed. No smoking is permitted. One cottage is wheelchair accessible. Linens and towels are provided.

## Reservations and Rates

Reservations are recommended. The fee is $185–600 per night per cottage, with a charge of $15 per night per additional person. Major credit cards are accepted. It's open year-round. Contact Indian Springs, 1712 Lincoln Avenue, Calistoga, CA 94515, 707/942-4913, fax 707/942-4919, website: www.indianspringscalistoga.com.

## Directions

From Napa, drive north on Highway 29 for about 30 miles to Calistoga. At the flashing light, turn right on Lincoln Avenue and drive approximately 1 mile to Indian Springs on the right.

# 21 COTTAGE GROVE INN
Calistoga, off Highway 29

**Luxury rating:** 4                    **Recreation rating:** 4

Cottage Grove Inn is one of the few high-end lodges in Calistoga with deluxe cottages available. Sixteen of them—with vaulted ceilings, skylights, and hardwood floors—opened in 1996, and they were an instant hit. The location is great for travelers because the cottages are just off the main street, within easy walking distance of restaurants, shopping, the airport, and the spas.

No details were forgotten in the design of these cottages, which include front porches with rocking chairs, large bathrooms with deep whirlpool tubs for two, wet bars, down comforters on king-size beds, and custom-made furniture. Each cottage is decorated individually, and this is one of the few inns that doesn't have a cottage that stands out as being the most desirable or popular. Rose Floral Cottage has the appearance of a European country sitting room, with its two overstuffed lounge chairs with ottomans, coral hues, and an oil painting that hangs above the fireplace. The Pine Cottage has a huge, fluffy bed that requires a step stool to climb onto. Provence Cottage features a wrought-iron bed.

The cottages are spaced close together, but there are no adjoining walls with neighboring cottages. A private driveway leads to most of the cottages. Although there are no kitchen facilities, an expanded continental breakfast is served in the morning, and in the afternoon a buffet table with Napa Valley wines and a variety of cheeses is available to guests.

Hot-air balloon and glider rides are popular just a few miles north of here. For those of you who have never experienced either of these activities, be aware that they create completely different sensations. Ballooning creates little sensation other than a feeling of floating. It is usually quiet and serene in a balloon, except for the occasional hissing of the gas burner. A glider ride is also quiet and can sometimes feel like floating, but that is where the similarities end. The adrenaline rush you feel the first time the chain is unhooked, disconnecting your glider from the airplane that is towing you, is like nothing else. You suddenly realize that you are airborne in a capsule with wings but no engine, and it darned well better glide. Fortunately, it does glide, as you quickly discover, but you need to remember two things: 1) Bring a plastic bag, and 2) Don't allow the pilot to attempt to break his record for the number of circles completed when catching an uprising thermal draft … 19, 20, 21. … Where is that plastic bag?

## Facilities

Cottage Grove Inn has 16 cottages with private bathrooms. There are no kitchen facilities but a deluxe continental breakfast and afternoon wine and cheese are provided. Each cottage has a front porch, whirlpool tub for two, fireplace, small refrigerator, television with VCR, and wet bar. Children over 12 are welcome. Pets are not allowed. No smoking is permitted. One cottage is wheelchair accessible. Linens and towels are provided.

## Reservations and Rates

Reservations are recommended. The double-occupancy rate is $225–330 per night per cottage, plus $50 per night for each additional person. There is a two-night minimum stay on weekends. Major credit cards are accepted, and it's open year-round. Contact Cottage Grove Inn, 1711 Lincoln Avenue, Calistoga, CA 94515, 707/942-8400 or 800/799-2284, fax 707/942-2653, website: www.cottagegrove.com.

## Directions

From Napa, drive north on Highway 29 for about 30 miles to Calistoga. At the flashing light, turn right on Lincoln Avenue and drive approximately one mile into downtown Calistoga to the inn on the left.

# 22 LAKE BERRYESSA MARINA RESORT

Lake Berryessa, off Highway 121

🏊 🛶 🚤 👫

**Luxury rating:** 3                                    **Recreation rating:** 4

Lake Berryessa is the Bay Area's backyard water recreation headquarters, the number-one lake in the greater Bay Area for water sports, loafing, and fishing. This resort is on the west shore of the main lake, one of several resorts at the lake.

One thing that sets Lake Berryessa Marina Resort apart from the others is that it offers a series of park-model cabins, also called RV cabins, for rent. These are the extremely cute, clean cabins that are built off-site, then trailered in on wheels to their location. Lattice is added around the base of the unit, so it appears permanent, and a deck with a barbecue is added as well. For guests, it means having a cabin by the lakeside without having to spend a fortune. They work great, and though a bit small, the cabins feel more cozy than cramped, especially with the outside deck to provide extra room.

This resort makes a fine headquarters for a vacation at Lake Berryessa. When full, it is a big lake, covering some 21,000 acres with 165 miles of shoreline, complete with secret coves, islands, and an expanse of untouched shore (on the eastern side) that is off-limits to people. It is one of California's most popular lakes, and on weekends it is full of happy boaters zooming around, especially pulling kids in tubes or on wakeboards. It's also good for waterskiing.

During the week, the lake quiets down significantly, and that is when fishing is best. Trout fishing in the summer is often excellent for people who understand how to troll deep in the thermocline. A lot of the trout range 14–17 inches, and most anglers get up before dawn in summer and then troll at either Portuguese Cove or Skiers Cove, which are entrances to the narrows (especially the Rock Slide on the east side of the lakeshore) and the mouth of Markley Cove. The key in the summer is depth, trolling typically 25–35 feet deep using lures such as the Rainbow Runners, Triple Teaser (white with a red head), and Humdinger.

Lake Berryessa is loaded with bass in the spring, most ranging 11–14 inches. It is common to catch 20 or 30 bass in a day, casting a variety of lures—plastics are best—along protected shoreline coves. The east shoreline, from the vineyards on into the adjacent cove, is an excellent spot where bass hold from late March through early June. In addition, this lake has dozens and dozens of flooded islands where bass congregate during these times.

## Facilities

Lake Berryessa Marina Resort has 15 RV park cabins that sleep up to four, with beds, kitchenettes (no stove), small bathrooms with showers, living rooms, and outdoor decks with barbecues. Bring cooking and eating utensils, charcoal, and a lighter. The resort has coin laundry, complete marina facilities, boat rentals, houseboat rentals, supplies, and groceries. Pets and smoking are prohibited in the cabins. Linens and towels are not provided. Bring your sleeping bag, pillow, and towels.

## Reservations and Rates

Reservations are required and are available by phone and on the resort's website. Rates range $100–150 per night. A two-night minimum stay is required on summer weekends. There is a $15 fee for additional vehicles and a $10 fee for boat parking and launching. Major credit cards are accepted. It's open year-round. Contact Lake Berryessa Marine Resort, 5800 Knoxville Road, Napa, CA 94558, 707/966-2161, website: www.lakeberryessa.com. For boat-rental reservations, call 707/966-4204; for houseboat rentals, call 707/966-2827.

## Directions

From Vallejo, drive north on I-80 to the Suisun Valley Road exit. Take Suisun Valley Road and drive north to Highway 121. Turn north on Highway 121 and drive five miles to Highway 128. Turn left on Highway 128, drive five miles to Berryessa-Knoxville Road, turn right, and continue nine miles to 5800 Knoxville Road.

# 23 STILLWATER COVE RANCH
Sonoma Coast, off Highway 1 near Jenner

**Luxury rating:** 2                                    **Recreation rating:** 4

Inexpensive lodging with a dramatic oceanside setting on 50 acres is what you get at Stillwater Cove Ranch. You also get direct access to the ocean and Stillwater Cove Regional Park. The ranch is wedged between Salt Point State Park and Fort Ross State Historic Park. For ocean lovers and hikers who like their coastline on the rugged side, this is a perfect location.

Stillwater is a working farm, so you'll share the land with the resident chickens, white pigeons, geese, peacocks, and sheep—even a semi-tame wild pig. The lodging consists of two freestanding cottages, four large inn rooms with kitchenettes, and a bunkhouse with kitchen facilities. These buildings were constructed in the 1930s, and they haven't been updated much.

Teacher's Cottage and Cook's Cottage are the most private lodgings, and are also considered the most romantic. Cook's Cottage is nicknamed the Honeymoon Cottage; you'll have an ocean view from your deck. The cottages do not include kitchens, but hibachis are allowed on the deck and restaurants are nearby. Each cottage has a fireplace and two double beds. The other units have fully equipped kitchens. The Dairy Barn, or bunkhouse, is set up with eight bunk beds, two bathrooms with showers, and a wood-burning stove (free wood is provided for the Dairy Barn). You have to bring your own linens and towels. A maximum of 16 can be housed in the bunkhouse.

The views are great. You can spend hours scanning the coast.

## Facilities

Stillwater Cove Ranch has two cottages, four inn rooms, and a bunkhouse. One cottage has a fireplace. Conference facilities are available. The ranch is suitable for children. Leashed pets are allowed in some cabins. No smoking is permitted inside. Linens and towels are provided in all facilities except for the bunkhouse.

## Reservations and Rates

Reservations are recommended. The fee is $75–100 per night per rental (midweek discounts available) and $175 per night for the bunkhouse, with a $10 charge per night for each additional person. Special rates are available December–March and in July. There is a two-night minimum stay on weekends and a three-night minimum on holidays. Children under age three are free. Credit cards are not accepted. It's open year-round. Contact Stillwater Cove Ranch, 22555 Highway 1, Jenner, CA, 707/847-3227, website: www.media.malamud.com (then click Stillwater Cove Ranch).

## Directions

On U.S. 101 north of Santa Rosa, turn west on River Road and drive 13 miles to Guerneville and Highway 116. Turn west on Highway 116 and drive about 20 miles to Highway 1 at Jenner. Turn north on Highway 1 and drive 16 miles to the ranch on the right.

# 24 MURPHY'S JENNER INN AND COTTAGES

Sonoma Coast, off Highway 1 in Jenner

**Luxury rating:** 4                    **Recreation rating:** 3

Jenner Inn is at the mouth of the Russian River on the Sonoma Coast, 1.5 hours from San Francisco, 2.5 hours from Sacramento, and only 45 minutes from Santa Rosa. You just get in your car, point it to Sonoma County, and before you know it, you're there—"where the Russian River meets the sea."

When you arrive, you'll find little cottages and homes set on a coastal foothill at the mouth of the Russian River. This is Jenner-by-the-Sea. The main inn is below a prominent rock outcropping, and adjacent cottages and homes are nuzzled into the hillside. Rosebud and Rosewater are waterfront cottages with ocean and estuary views. They also have an adjacent grassy yard that slopes down to the water. This makes for an excellent put-in spot for kayaks or canoes. Riversea Cottage has an exceptional view of the bird refuge on Penny Island and the place where the Russian River meets the sea. Whale Watch Cottage features a great view of the ocean, Tree House is set for a river lookout, and Mill Cottage provides views of a meadow and stream. There are absolutely zero televisions, so you can quickly embrace the natural harmony of the coast.

No matter which way you turn, there are many side trips and adventures available. To the south are Sonoma Coast State Beach (5 minutes on Highway 1), Bodega Bay (20 minutes), and Point Reyes National Seashore (one hour). To the north on Highway 1 are Fort Ross (20 minutes) and Salt Point State Park (30 minutes). To the east on Highway 116 are the Russian River, the Russian River wine country (30 minutes), and Armstrong Redwoods State Park (30 minutes).

The closest quality adventure requires just a short drive south on Highway 1 to Shell Beach/Sonoma Coast State Beach. Shell Beach is a beautiful place, and with the trail to Arch Rock and good beachcombing at low tides, you can spend hours here. A hike starts just across from the entrance to Shell Beach, on the east side of Highway 1; follow the coastal trailhead for the Pomo-Ohlone Trail. The trail climbs up the foothills, providing beautiful views of the ocean to the west, and eventually gains the ridge for more great views, including those of Goat Rock at the mouth of the Russian River and a sweeping lookout of the coast.

## Facilities

Murphy's Jenner Inn and Cottages has four cottages, two homes, and 16 rooms divided into four buildings. Each cottage is unique, but most feature a kitchenette and full bath, with deck, hot tub, and fireplace available. Some cottages and rooms have telephones but none have televisions. A full breakfast is provided. Leashed pets are allowed in some units. Linens and towels are provided.

## Reservations and Rates

Reservations are recommended. Rates for cottages range $158–278 per night. Rooms range $98–268. The Osprey Home is $378 per night. A two-night minimum stay is required on weekends. Contact Murphy's Jenner Inn and Cottages, 10400 Coast Highway 1, P.O. Box 69, Jenner, CA 95450, 707/865-2377 or 800/732-2377, website: www.jennerinn.com.

## Directions

On U.S. 101 north of Santa Rosa, turn west on River Road and drive 13 miles to Guerneville and Highway 116. Turn west on Highway 116 and drive about 20 miles to Highway 1 at Jenner. Turn north on Highway 1 and look for Jenner Inn and Cottages on the right side of the road.

# 25 HUCKLEBERRY SPRINGS COUNTRY INN AND SPA

Russian River, off Highway 116 near Monte Rio

🚶 🏊 🚣 ❄ 〰

**Luxury rating:** 3                                              **Recreation rating:** 4

After passing through Monte Rio, a little town along the Russian River, I made the assigned right turn at Tyrone Road, though it's so small that I just about missed it. It turned out to be a narrow patch of asphalt that passes a few houses, climbs and turns to gravel, then dirt, and finally narrows even more, passing through a forest of some oaks and redwoods. There was no sign of any resort. "This can't be the right way," I said.

But it was, it turns out. A moment later, posted on a tree on the right side of the road, I spotted a small sign reading Huckleberry Springs, and in a few minutes, despite all my misgivings, I was pulling into a small parking place next to the lodge headquarters.

It also turns out that this is the most secluded setting for cabin rentals in this region, with four unusual little cabins nestled in the woods in the foothills south of the Russian River. The place is quiet and remote, yet at the same time close enough for canoeing, hiking, fishing, or just playing in the river. The only downer is that you must drive to take part in the area's outdoor recreation.

The cottages at Huckleberry Springs are like nothing I've seen anywhere. The Cherry Barrel, believe it or not, is literally that—a giant barrel that has been converted into a room, with a pine ceiling and a skylight, along with a bathroom; it's the most unusual cabin imaginable.

Another, Spring Hill, is reached via a five-minute walk up a steep hill. You are rewarded with a small custom-made cottage with a deck and a view of the valley, a bed set high in a loft accessible by a built-in ladder, and a skylight. It is absolutely quiet, and if you're lucky, you might even see shooting stars at night through the skylight.

## Facilities

Huckleberry Springs has four cottages, each with a bathroom, television, and VCR. No telephones are provided in the cabins. At the lodge, a telephone, video library, and restaurant-style dining are available. Facilities include a small swimming pool and spa with a gazebo. A private massage cottage offers spa treatments, including massage, facials, and reflexology for an extra charge. Children must be over 15. Linens and towels are provided.

### Reservations and Rates

Reservations are required. The rate for cabins ranges $130–150 per night, double occupancy, $225 for triple occupancy for Orchard Cottage, including a full hot breakfast. Contact Huckleberry Springs Country Inn, P.O. Box 400, Monte Rio, CA 95462, 707/865-2683 or 800/822-2683, fax 707/865-1688, website: www.huckleberrysprings.com.

### Directions

From Rohnert Park, take Highway 116 northwest. Continue on Highway 116 past Sebastopol and Guerneville. Four miles past Guerneville, at an intersection with a stop sign, go straight (Highway 116 veers to the right) and enter Monte Rio. Turn left on the Bohemian Highway, drive a short distance over the Russian River, then turn right on Main Street. Continue on Main Street through Monte Rio. One mile past the firehouse, turn right on Tyrone Road. Drive 0.5 mile, then bear right on Old Beedle Road and continue for one mile to Huckleberry Springs.

## 26 THE FARMHOUSE INN

Russian River, off Highway 116 near Forestville

**Luxury rating:** 4                                              **Recreation rating:** 3

New owners, eight newly renovated cottages, a restaurant in a Victorian farmhouse, and a new, upscale attitude and ambience are what you'll find at The Farmhouse Inn. The innkeepers have completed a $500,000 renovation of the existing facilities and six acres, and now they're turning their attention to adding eight additional cottages. If you liked the place before, you'll most likely love it now.

The Farmhouse Inn specialty is luxury, with all attention directed toward privacy, quiet, excellent food, and romance. What do you do here? Well, when they sell gift baskets with names like "Sensuous" and "Romance," what do you think you do here? And this certainly is the right place for romance: saunas and double-jetted whirlpool tubs for two, wood-burning fireplaces with Italian tile, breakfast delivered to your cottage if you like, feather beds and pillows with handcrafted bedding, oversized furniture, and a four-star restaurant. The setup is so lovely and upscale that it's popular for weddings, and special packages are available.

Cottages 6 and 7 are the largest, with a separate living room, and Cottages 3 and 5 are the smallest, with canopy beds. The favored unit is Cottage 7, which has a raised king bed and customized bedding made from fine European textiles. The suite is decorated in taupe, silver, and black. Good things can come in small packages, and that is the scenario with Cottage 5. It is a dramatic room, decorated in tangerine and ruby, with a wrought-iron canopy bed and white lace duvet cover. Each room is decorated individually and the effect is sophisticated luxury, with a touch of traditional and country decor.

A full gourmet breakfast is served in the conservatory-style dining room or on the outdoor terrace. Or, a deluxe continental breakfast can be delivered to your cottage. The restaurant overlooks a small vineyard and courtyard fountain. Dinner is served Thursday through Sunday, and live, classical guitar music is sometimes played.

Three-night, midweek packages are offered that include lodging and activities such as tours of small wineries in Sonoma County and the Russian River Valley, excursions to local culinary businesses, and bicycling, canoeing, and hot-air ballooning. The emphasis is on cuisine and adventuring, and up to 16 persons can be accommodated each week.

## Facilities

The Farmhouse Inn has eight adjoining cottages/rooms. There are no kitchen facilities, but a full gourmet breakfast is provided, and a restaurant is on-site. Each cottage has a private bathroom, fireplace, sauna, double-jetted whirlpool tub for two, shower, small refrigerator stocked with water, and television and VCR. Amenities include a pool, spa, sundeck, movie library, gift baskets, and massage and aromatherapy. Wedding and meeting facilities are available. The inn is not suitable for children. Pets are not allowed. Smoking is not permitted. One cottage is wheelchair accessible. Linens and towels are provided.

## Reservations and Rates

Reservations are recommended. The double-occupancy rate is $175–299 per night per cottage, plus $25 per night for each additional person. Major credit cards are accepted. The inn is open year-round. Contact The Farmhouse Inn, 7871 River Road, Forestville, CA 95436, 707/887-3300 or 800/464-6642, fax 707/887-3311, website: www.farmhouseinn.com.

## Directions

From U.S. 101 in Santa Rosa, drive on U.S. 101 to the north end of Santa Rosa and the River Road exit. Take that exit and drive west on River Road for 7.1 miles to the inn on the left.

## 27 AUBERGE DU SOLEIL

**BEST** ☾

Napa Valley, off Highway 29 in Rutherford

🚶 🏊 ♿

**Luxury rating:** 5      **Recreation rating:** 4

© LOU HAMMOND & ASSOCIATES

When a resort's motto is "a place without reality checks," you know it's out of the ordinary.

Understated luxury is dominant among the 11 spacious, airy, Mediterranean-style cottages. Private terraces and expansive views overlook the Napa Valley. The facilities are tucked away on a gently sloping hill situated in an olive grove and on 33 acres. Auberge du Soleil translates to Inn of the Sun, and it emanates a quietly cheerful and serene setting.

People who lodge here usually fit into one of two categories: very rich or lucky souls who work for companies that are in the black and reward their executives with a business retreat. How do I know that? Well, a freestanding cottage rental goes for $2,500–3,500 per night, the highest priced listing in this book, so it's pretty easy to figure out that the average person can't fork over money like that.

The cottages have an abundance of terra cotta tile, adobe-style walls, vaulted ceilings, fireplaces, and oversized, white-painted French doors with shutters. The furnishings are simple yet elegant, with king-size beds and Frette linens, overstuffed chairs, wet bars and small refrigerators stocked with wines and cheeses, and a basket of snacks. The bathrooms are indulgent, with a skylight, a large tub, double sinks, oversized towels, two different types of bathrobes, candles, and fragrant bath salts.

The Napa Valley has a reputation for some of the best food in California, and Auberge du Soleil's restaurant rates near the top. The executive chef, Robert Curry, has established a reputation as one of the finest in the wine country. In 1981, when the restaurant opened, its chef at the time, Masataka Kobayashi, was considered by many to be one of the top 10 chefs in the world. The restaurant's wine list holds a *Wine Spectator* award.

The extras you get here include 24-hour room service, a top-quality restaurant with bar and private dining rooms, a large swimming pool, tennis courts, a fitness center, a $2 million full-service spa—even a sculpture garden with a collection of large-scale sculptures. If this sounds like your kind of place, here's my suggestion for staying here without completely draining your savings: rent one of the 39 suites or rooms, since they start at $450 per night and you get almost the same amenities as staying in a private cottage. It's still a lot of money, I know, but heck, doesn't that sound better than $3,500 per night? Then again, if you have to ask the price, maybe you're having a reality check in a place that doesn't have reality checks.

## Facilities

Auberge du Soleil has 11 cottages and 39 inn rooms and suites. There are no kitchen facilities. Fireplaces, telephones, wet bars, televisions, and air-conditioning are provided in each unit. Amenities include a restaurant and lounge, 24-hour room service, a full-service spa, a boutique, a pool with sundeck, tennis courts and instruction, a gym with hot tub and steam rooms, meeting rooms, picnic areas, art gallery, and concierge services. The facilities are not suitable for children under 16. Pets are not allowed. Smoking is not permitted in designated areas. Some lodging is wheelchair accessible. Linens and towels are provided.

## Reservations and Rates

Reservations are recommended. The fee is $2,500–3,500 per night per private cottage, and $450–1,650 for inn rooms and suites. There is a two-night minimum stay on weekends and a three-night minimum stay on holidays. Major credit cards are accepted. It's open year-round. Contact Auberge du Soleil, 180 Rutherford Hill Road, Rutherford, CA 94573, 707/963-1211 or 800/348-5406, fax 707/963-8764, website: www.aubergedusoleil.com.

## Directions

From Napa, drive north on Highway 29 to Highway 128 east. Turn east on Highway 128 and drive one mile to a fork in the road. Bear left at the fork and continue on Highway 128 to the Silverado Trail. Turn left on the Silverado Trail and drive a short distance to Rutherford Hill Road. Turn right and drive 0.25 mile to the resort on the right.

# 28 SONOMA CHALET
Sonoma, off Highway 12

**Luxury rating:** 4                                          **Recreation rating:** 3

You'll think you've stepped into an alpine lodge when you enter Sonoma Chalet, only it's in the Valley of the Moon, the heart of the Sonoma wine country, and is a five-minute drive from downtown Sonoma. Three storybook cottages sit on the 3.5-acre hillside property, along with a Swiss-style farmhouse with four inn rooms. Amid towering eucalyptus trees and surrounded by pastures, the cottages are perfect for a quiet getaway; they're close to wine tasting, great cycling routes, shopping, and touring Jack London State Historic Park.

The freestanding cottages and inn rooms are filled with antiques, collectibles, and unique bric-a-brac, and have fireplaces or woodstoves, clawfoot bathtubs, and decks or porches. The inn has a reputation for quirky touches. The most popular rental is Sara's Cottage, which is the most private and is reached by crossing a wooden bridge. Amenities include a good-sized bathroom with clawfoot tub, woodstove, loft, hardwood floors with Oriental rugs, and antiques and collectibles from the 1800s to the 1950s. The size of the cottages ranges 400–600 square feet.

A complimentary breakfast of fresh juice, coffee, fresh fruit, cereal, breads, and pastries is served in the dining room, on a deck overlooking a 200-acre ranch, or it can be delivered to your cottage on request. A garden hot tub and bicycles are available for guests.

Of course, the main attraction of the Sonoma Valley for vacationers is wine tasting. Within three miles, on the east side of Sonoma, are Sebastiani, Ravenswood, Buena Vista, and Gundlach Bundschu wineries. Sonoma Mission Golf Course, an 18-hole course, is six miles away.

A few miles up Highway 12 is Jack London State Historic Park, where London created his dreams and became one of America's truly great writers and philosophers. It was also here that those dreams were shattered, first by a fire that devoured his ranch home, then by an illness at age 40 from which he never recovered. You can visit London's cottage, winery ruins, barns, and distillery. A one-mile walk on the Lake Trail leads to a small pond that was a favorite recreation area for London and his guests.

## Facilities
Sonoma Chalet has three cottages and four inn rooms and suites. The cottages have no kitchens, but a complimentary continental breakfast is served. Private bathrooms and air-conditioning are provided in the cottages. There are no televisions or telephones in the units. A garden hot tub is available. Pets are not allowed. No smoking is permitted. Linens and towels are provided.

## Reservations and Rates
Reservations are recommended. The fee is $185–225 for cottages and $110–170 for inn rooms. There is a two-night minimum stay on weekends. Major credit cards are accepted. It's open year-round. Contact Sonoma Chalet, 18935 5th Street West, Sonoma, CA 95476, 707/938-3129 or 800/938-3129, website: www.sonomachalet.com.

## Directions
From Sonoma and Highway 12, turn west on West Napa Street and drive five blocks to West 5th Street. Turn right and drive approximately 0.75 mile to the end of the road. Continue straight ahead onto a gravel road and drive a short distance to Sonoma Chalet.

# Other Cabins & Cottages in the Region

**Bell Haven Resort,** 3415 White Oak Way, Kelseyville, CA 95451, 707/279-4329 or 877/279-4329, website: www.bellhaven.com.

**Cloverdale KOA,** P.O. Box 600, 26460 River Road, Cloverdale, CA 95425, 707/894-3337, website: www.koa.com.

**DeHaven Valley Farm and Country Inn,** 39247 North Highway 1, Westport, CA 95488, 707/961-1660 or 877/334-2836, website: www.dehaven-valley-farm.com.

**Dr. Wilkinson's Hot Springs Resort,** Calistoga, CA, 94515, 707/942-4102.

**Harbor House Inn,** 5600 South Highway 1, Elk, CA 95432, 707/877-3203 or 800/720-7474, website: www.theharborhouseinn.com.

**Manchester Beach KOA,** P.O. Box 266, Manchester, CA 95459, 707/882-2375, fax 707/882-3104, website: www.koa.com.

**Mount View Hotel,** 1457 Lincoln Avenue, Calistoga, CA 94515, 707/942-6877 or 800/816-6877, website: www.mountviewhotel.com.

**The Old Milano Hotel,** 38300 Shoreline Highway 1, Gualala, CA 95445, 707/884-3256, website: www.oldmilanoho.com.

**Willits KOA,** P.O. Box 946, Willits, CA 95490, 707/459-6179, fax 707/459-1489, website: www.koa.com.

**Wishing Well Cottages,** P.O. Box 487, Fort Bragg, CA 95437-0487, 707/961-5450 or 800/362-9305.

# SACRAMENTO AND GOLD COUNTRY

COURTESY OF DORRINGTON INN

## BEST CABINS & COTTAGES

**◖ Best for Water Sports**
Rollins Lakeside Inn, page 168

**◖ Best for Winter Sports**
Cabins at Strawberry, page 173

**◖ Most Romantic**
Gables Cedar Creek Inn, page 175

# From a distance, this section of the Sacramento

Valley looks like flat farmland extending into infinity, with a sprinkling of cities and towns interrupting the view. But a closer look reveals a landscape filled with Northern California's most significant rivers—the Sacramento, Feather, Yuba, American, and Mokelumne. All of these provide water recreation, in both lakes and rivers, as well as serve as the lifeblood for a series of wildlife refuges.

This is an area for California history buffs, with Malakoff Diggins State Historic Park and Piety Hill Cottages located in the center of some of the state's most extraordinary history: the gold rush era. In addition, Malakoff Diggins has one of the least expensive cabin rentals that I could find – $35 a night.

There are relatively few cabin rentals in the Sacramento Valley and nearby foothills. The ones that are here are either on lakes, such as Camanche, Rollins, Oroville, and Red Bluff, or are getaways in historic towns. These rentals, more than those in any other area of Northern California, represent the middle range of both pricing and accommodations—but also some of the best deals.

Timing is everything in love and the great outdoors, and so it is in the Central Valley and the nearby foothills. Spring and fall are gorgeous here, along with many summer evenings. But periods of 100-plus temperatures always occur in the summer.

That's what gives the lakes and rivers such appeal, though, and in turn, why they are treasured. Take your pick: San Joaquin Delta near Stockton, Lake Oroville in the northern Sierra, Folsom Lake outside Sacramento . . . the list goes on. On a hot day, jumping into a cool lake makes water more valuable than gold, a cold drink on ice worth more than silver. These have become top sites for boating-based recreation and fantastic areas for water sports and fishing.

In the Mother Lode country, three other lakes − Camanche, Amador, and Pardee − are outstanding for fishing. The guidebook *Foghorn Outdoors California Fishing* ranks three of this chapter's lakes among the top 10 lakes for fishing in the state − Lake Oroville and Lake Camanche make the list for bass and Lake Amador makes it for bluegill and catfish − no small feat considering the 381 other lakes they were up against.

For touring, the state capital and nearby Old Sacramento are favorites. Others prefer reliving the gold mining history of California's past or exploring the foothill country, including Malakoff Diggins State Historic Park.

# SACRAMENTO & GOLD COUNTRY

see Shasta & Trinity page 46

see Lassen & Modoc page 90

see Tahoe & the Northern Sierra page 182

see Mendocino & Wine Country page 116

see San Francisco Bay Area page 220

see San Joaquin Valley page 312

© AVALON TRAVEL PUBLISHING, INC.

# Sacramento and Gold Country Cabins & Cottages

# 1 BUCKS LAKE LODGE
Plumas National Forest, off Highway 89 near Quincy

🏃 🛷 🚣 🐕 👫

**Luxury rating: 3**                                     **Recreation rating: 5**

Bucks Lake is one of Northern California's greatest destinations for reclaiming the simple life—taking a cabin by the lake and heading out in a boat each day to try to catch "Walter."

The lake is at 5,237 feet in Plumas National Forest, about a 25-minute drive from the town of Quincy, so it feels remote. It is also very pretty, and the cabins, nearby marina, boating, and fishing answer dreams for water enthusiasts.

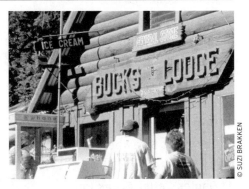

© SUZI BRAKKEN

When you open the door of your Bucks Lake Lodge cabin in the morning, you will notice immediately the smell of pine duff, the clear air, the blue-green water, and the purity of all the nearby streams. The cabins at Bucks Lake Lodge are not luxurious, but they're nice enough, woodsy-looking, and well-suited for families. They can handle couples or groups up to 8. The Timberline Inn also has 12 lodge rooms.

The decor varies, but the cabins are always clean and comfortable. The cabins are located across the street from the restaurant, bar, and store. Timberlineline Inn is located a few hundred yards away, and is set up like a motel with oak furnishings and air-conditioning.

What makes Bucks Lake a winner for so many is the fishing for rainbow trout in the 11- to 15-inch class by trolling or fishing from shore with bait. There's also the chance for mackinaw trout in the 20-pound range by using deepwater trolling or jigging techniques. Bucks Lake is one of the most consistent producers of trout in California, with the best spot by Rocky Point near where Bucks Creek enters the lake. Another good spot is the old river channel near where Mill Creek enters the lake.

Each spring, usually in early May when the lake first becomes accessible, the mackinaw fishery is the source of tremendous anticipation. You never know what you might get—a nice 5-pounder, a trophy 20-pounder, or perhaps the next state record in the 40-pound class. The fishing is best for these giant mackinaw trout just after the lake clears of ice, typically in early May, and stays good until hot weather arrives for summer in July.

Enough 15- to 20-pounders have already been caught to make some believe that a state-record fish may be caught here one day. I call that fish "Walter," just like in the movie *On Golden Pond*.

## Facilities

Bucks Lake Lodge has 11 cabins, with kitchens, sized for groups of 2–8. Lodge rooms are also available. A small marina, boat ramp, boat and motor rentals, general store, and restaurant are available nearby. Pets are permitted. Both smoking and nonsmoking cabins and rooms are available. Linens are provided. There is no room service.

## Reservations and Rates

Reservations are recommended. Cabin rates range from $77 (for 2) to $125 (for up to 8) per night. Timberline Lodge rooms are $85–110 per night. Major credit cards are accepted. Dogs are $10 per night. Contact Bucks Lake Lodge, P.O. Box 236, Quincy, CA 95971, 530/283-2262, website: www.buckslakelodge.com.

## Directions

From Oroville, drive north on Highway 70 to the junction with Highway 89. Turn south on Highway 89/70 and drive 11 miles to Quincy. In Quincy, turn right at Bucks Lake Road and drive 17 miles to Bucks Lake.

# 2 BUCKS LAKE MARINA

Plumas National Forest, off Highway 89 near Quincy

**Luxury rating: 2**                    **Recreation rating: 5**

© TOM RATH

Vacationers flock here year after year because they know exactly what they'll get: great fishing, beautiful mountain scenery, fresh air, and the same cabin they've stayed in for years. Maybe their grandparents even rented one of these cabins decades ago, since they were built in the 1930s.

What visitors find is almost identical to what Grandma and Grandpa experienced; that is, except for the personal watercraft. There are one- and two- bedroom cabins with lake views, and they accommodate 2–5 people, depending on the cabin. They each have a kitchen, a bathroom, and the basics—no frills added. The decor is rustic. There are no televisions or telephones, but a pay telephone is available at the marina. Situated about 50 yards above the lake under pine and fir tree cover, the cabins are spaced about 20 feet apart.

Although you'd think that everyone who stays here wants to fish and boat, this is not always true. Horseback riding is popular in this area. In the fall, you'll see hunters.

Bucks Lake Lodge—with a restaurant, store, lounge, and game room—is within walking distance of the cabins here at Bucks Lake Marina.

For more information about Bucks Lake, refer to the description for Bucks Lake Lodge (see previous listing).

## Facilities

Bucks Lake Marina features eight cabins and an RV campground. Each cabin has a fully equipped kitchen and a bathroom with shower. A fire pit and porch are provided. A small store, boat dock, and full-service marina, bait and tackle, and boat and personal watercraft rentals are available. One set of linens and towels is provided. There is no daily maid service; bring extra towels.

## Reservations and Rates

Reservations are required in the summer. The fee is $85–99 per night per cabin, or $575–685 per week. A pet fee of $10 per night per pet is charged. There is a one-week minimum during the summer. The cabins are suitable for children. Up to two leashed pets are allowed per cabin, not to be left unattended. No smoking is allowed. Major credit cards are accepted. It's open early May through early November, weather permitting. Contact Bucks Lake Marina, P.O. Box 559, Quincy, CA 95971, 530/283-4243, website: www.buckslakemarina.com.

## Directions

From Oroville, drive north on Highway 70 to the junction with Highway 89. Turn south on Highway 89/70 and drive 11 miles to Quincy. In Quincy, turn right at Bucks Lake Road and drive 16.5 miles to the lake and the second resort on the right.

## 3 SIERRA SHANGRI-LA
Yuba River, off Highway 49 near Downieville

**Luxury rating:** 3                                        **Recreation rating:** 4

The Yuba River is one of the prettiest rivers to flow westward out of the Sierra Nevada. The stretch of river near Downieville is especially gorgeous, flowing from the drops of melting snow from the Sierra crest, with deep pools and miniature waterfalls, often edged by slabs of granite and punctuated with boulders. In the spring, it can be a wild and cold force of water, running blue-white during peak snowmelt. In the summer and fall, it greens up, warms considerably, and takes on a more benign demeanor in its routed canyon course.

From the cabins at Sierra Shangri-La, you can watch the changing faces of this dynamic river. The North Fork Yuba River passes within ear range of the cabins here. Several cabins have views of the river canyon, but from all of them you will feel the magnetism of moving water.

The decor is country-style with knotty-pine wood paneling, hardwood floors, and comforters on the beds. It is peaceful and quiet.

The reason more people don't know about the Yuba or the secluded cabins near its banks is their remoteness. There is no direct way to get here. Even with the best route on Highway 49, you will discover that calling it a "highway" is a mighty stretch. This two-laner is constructed like a narrow pretzel, probably built on an old stagecoach route where grades had to be lengthened by curving the roads in order to give the horse teams a breather.

The secluded Sierra Shangri-La is on the canyon bottom at 3,300 feet in elevation. The cottages with the best river views are Blue Jay, LaVista, Flycaster, and Jim Crow, while three rooms in the upper level of the lodge also provide great views. By the way, the resort gets its name from the nearby magnificent Shangri-La wall of river stone.

This stretch of river is good for fly-fishing for both rainbow trout and brown trout, and is decent for swimming and rafting out of Goodyear's Bar. The resort has a good swimming hole on the North Fork Yuba within walking distance of the cabins. Another good one is upstream at Union Flat Campground near Quartz Point, six miles east of Downieville on Highway 49.

## Facilities

Sierra Shangri-La has eight one- and two-bedroom cabins, each with a bathroom, kitchen, and fireplace. A lodge offers three bed-and-breakfast rooms with river views. No pets are permitted. Smoking is prohibited. Linens and towels are provided.

## Reservations and Rates

Reservations are advised. Cabin rates are $85–195 per night for two, depending on the size of cabin, season, and length of stay; it's $20 for each additional person. A minimum stay of a week is required in July and August; weekly rates are $800–1,200 for two people. The three bed-and-breakfast rooms at the lodge are rented by the night, $70–115 per night, depending on the season. It's open April–December. Contact Sierra Shangri-La, P.O. Box 285, Downieville, CA 95936, 530/289-3455, website: www.sierrashangrila.com.

## Directions

From Auburn, take Highway 49 north to Nevada City and continue (the road jogs left at Nevada City, then narrows) to Downieville. Continue three miles east on Highway 49 and look for the sign for Sierra Shangri-La on the right side of the road.

# 4 MALAKOFF DIGGINS STATE HISTORIC PARK

Off Highway 20 near Nevada City

**Luxury rating:** 1                                    **Recreation rating:** 3

A trip here is like a walk through history. Malakoff Diggins State Historic Park is the site of California's largest "hydraulic" mine. Huge cliffs have been carved by mighty streams of water, a gold mining technique involving the washing away of entire mountains to find the precious metal. This practice began in the 1850s and continued for many years. Several major gold-mining operations combined hydraulic mining with giant sluice boxes. Hydraulic mining was a scourge to the land, of course, and legal battles between mine owners and downstream farmers eventually ended this method of mining.

The park also contains a 7,847-foot bedrock tunnel that served as a drain. The visitor center has exhibits on life in the old mining town of North Bloomfield. Tours of the numerous historic sites are available during the summer.

The cabins are near a small lake in the park and are one of the cheapest deals in California at $35 a night. Consequently, as you might expect, the accommodations are primitive. There really isn't much to them except for a couple of bunk beds and a picnic table. Sleeping arrangements are in a common room. There is a woodstove for heat, with wood for sale nearby.

There isn't even electricity, so bring everything, just like on a camping trip. By now you have probably figured out that this isn't where you come if you don't want to rough it.

The drive in from Nevada City is slow and circuitous, with the last mile quite steep, so take your time and enjoy the sights along the way. The park is at 3,400 feet in elevation.

## Facilities

Malakoff Diggins State Historic Park has three primitive cabins along with a state park campground for tents and RVs. A group area is also available. No electricity is provided. A picnic table, woodstove, and two double bunk beds that can accommodate up to eight people are provided inside each cabin. A fire pit and picnic table are also provided outside each cabin. Drinking water and flush toilets are available (except mid-November through February) nearby. Pets and smoking are not permitted. Linens and towels are not provided; bring your own sleeping bag and pillow.

## Reservations and Rates

Reservations are recommended. Call 800/444-PARK (800/444-7275) and ask for "Malakoff Diggins Speciality Camps," or visit the website www.ReserveAmerica.com

for Memorial Day through Labor Day. For the off-season, call the visitor center at 530/265-2740. Cabins cost $35 per night. The park is open year-round. Contact Malakoff Diggins State Historic Park, California State Parks, Goldrush District, 23579 North Bloomfield Road, Nevada City, CA 95959, tel./fax 530/265-2740.

### Directions
From Auburn, drive north on Highway 49 to Nevada City and continue 11 miles to the junction of Tyler Foote Crossing Road. Turn right and drive 16 miles (in the process the road changes names: Cruzon Grade, Back Bone Road, Der Bec Road, North Bloomfield Road) to the entrance on the right. The route is well-signed; the last 2 miles are quite steep and the last mile is dirt.

## 5 PIETY HILL COTTAGES
Nevada City, off Highway 49

**Luxury rating:** 3                    **Recreation rating:** 3

Situated smack dab in the charming little Victorian town of Nevada City, these cottages combine the best of a bed-and-breakfast inn with a traditional cottage rental. The cottages are nestled in the Sierra foothills, at 2,500 feet in elevation, and set in an updated 1930s auto court.

All of the nine one- to three-room cottages have been nicely refurbished with cheerful, eclectic touches, giving them a homey, comfortable feel. Some have separate bedroom options, along with a sleeping area in the common area. The cabins are spaced closely together around a garden and a tree-shaded grassy courtyard. Flower gardens permeate the one-acre property.

The vintage-style decor is fresh with wallpaper, quilts, and antiques.

White Birch Cottage has a full kitchen and private garden and is the largest rental. Apple Blossom Cottage also has a private garden. Maple Cottage has a woodburning stove (firewood provided). Walnut Cottage is considered the most romantic and features a claw-foot tub. All of the bathrooms are small but nicely remodeled. What's more, you can have a full, hot breakfast delivered right to your cottage or garden. A continental breakfast can be substituted for a lower rate.

Nevada City, a Victorian-theme town of about 3,000, has a historic playhouse (Mark Twain spoke here), antique stores, and small museums. Victorian Christmas festivities are held between Thanksgiving and Christmas, and you must make reservations early for lodging, since this is the most popular event of the year in Nevada City.

The Empire Mine State Park in nearby Grass Valley offers hiking, biking, and equestrian trails. If you're a history buff, check out the the park's museum and grounds, which comprise the site of the world's largest-producing gold mine during its heyday.

Within a 40-minute drive of Nevada City, you'll find an abundance of recreational opportunities, including hiking, biking, and fishing in the Tahoe National Forest and Grouse Ridge areas east of Highway 20. Just north of town on Highway 49 is the Yuba River, with good stretches for fishing, kayaking, and rafting, as well as hiking trails. Boating and water sports are available at Scotts Flat Reservoir east of Highway 120 and at Bullards Bar Reservoir and Englebright Lake, west of Highway 20 or north of Highway 49.

## Facilities

Piety Hill has nine cottages with kitchenettes; one cottage has a full kitchen. The cottages have full baths, air-conditioning and heat, telephones, televisions, and modem hookups. A gazebo-covered spa is available in season. A complimentary hot breakfast is provided. The cottages are suitable for children. No pets are allowed. No smoking is permitted in cabins. Linens, towels, and daily maid service are provided.

## Reservations and Rates

Reservations are recommended. The fee is $100–170 per night per cabin and includes a full breakfast and hot and cold beverages. An additional charge of $20 per night per adult and $10 for children ages 3–12 is charged for more than two people. Children under three are free. Rates are slightly higher during November and December. Weekly and corporate rates are available. There is a two-night minimum stay on weekends and a three- to four-night minimum stay on holidays. Major credit cards are accepted. Contact Piety Hill Cottages, 523 Sacramento Street, Nevada City, CA 95959, 530/265-2245 or 800/443-2245, fax 530/265-6528, website: www.pietyhillcottages.com.

## Directions

From Auburn, drive north on Highway 49 to Nevada City. Take the Sacramento Street exit to Sacramento Street. Turn left and drive three blocks to the cottages on the left.

# 6 ROLLINS LAKESIDE INN                    BEST
Sierra foothills, off I-80 near Colfax

Luxury rating: 3                                    Recreation rating: 4

Rollins Lake is in the canyonlands of the Sierra foothills at 2,100 feet in elevation, north of Colfax off I-80. Here at Rollins Lake, right where the foothills meet the forest, a resort with cabins offers a surprising variety of water sports and recreation.

With its nine well-furnished cabins, Rollins Lakeside Inn is the focal point of the lake. Each of the cabins comes complete with everything you need, including cookware and bed linens, as well as things you don't need, such as cable television. No problem with the latter; just throw a towel over it. The cabins also have air-conditioning.

There is a choice between studio-style and two-bedroom cabins. The decor is country Victorian and rates high on the cute scale.

This area is not only where the valley grasslands rise and give way to conifers, but also where the snow line starts in winter. The result is a reservoir that spans the spectrum from very hot in summer to very cold in winter, with great transition periods in the spring and fall. The summer heat makes excellent conditions for waterskiing, boating, and swimming, and the spring and fall transitions are great for trout and bass fishing. In spring and early summer, when afternoon winds are common out of the west, the lake is also popular for small sailboats and sailboarding.

Rollins Lake's two extensive arms cover 26 miles of shoreline, in addition to long stretches of open water near the lower end of the lake. Excellent for waterskiing, these long stretches have water surface temperatures ranging 75–80°F in the summer. Most anglers choose to fish well up the lake arms, either for bass in the coves during the morning and evening in the summer, or for trout near where the feeder streams enter the lake. The latter is where the lake's water is coldest; trout are naturally attracted to the cool water temperatures, oxygenated flows, and the abundant food supply during the hot months.

There are several other lakes in the immediate region, including Englebright, Collins, and Scotts Flat, but only Rollins has cabin rentals.

## Facilities

Rollins Lakeside Inn has nine cabins, each with full kitchen, television, heat, and air-conditioning. A solar heated pool, a laundry room, horseshoes, volleyball, and table tennis are available. A boat ramp and marina with boat rentals (aluminum boats with motors, canoes, and paddleboats) are about a half mile away. Call for details regarding pet policies. No smoking is permitted. Linens and towels are provided.

## Reservations and Rates

Reservations are accepted. Cabins that sleep up to four start at $130–140 per night for up to four people, $800 per week; cabins that sleep up to eight start at $175–200 per night and $1,100 per week. A furnished home on the lake rents for $600 for three nights or $2,000 per week. A two-night minimum stay is required, with a three-night minimum stay on holidays. Contact Rollins Lakeside Inn, P.O. Box 152, Chicago Park, CA 95712, 530/273-0729, website: www.rollinslake.net.

## Directions

From Auburn, drive northeast on I-80 for about 20 miles to Colfax and Highway 174. Turn north on Highway 174 (a winding, two-lane road) and drive 3.7 miles (bear left at Giovanni's Restaurant) to Orchard Springs Road. Turn right on Orchard Springs Road and drive about a mile to Rollins Lakeside Inn.

# ⑦ CAMANCHE NORTH SHORE

Central Valley foothills, northeast of Stockton

🚴 🏊 ⛵ 🚤 👫

**Luxury rating:** 3                                **Recreation rating:** 4

Lots of cool water, hot sun, eager fish, and well-kept housekeeping cabins....

Isn't it about time you had some fun?

That's what inspires trips to Camanche Lake, the closest lake to the Bay Area of those in the Central Valley foothills northeast of Stockton. Camanche is a big lake, covering 7,500 acres and 53 miles of shoreline, with enough lake arms, coves, islands, and a canyoned inlet on the Mokelumne River to hide many secrets.

What makes Camanche Lake work for a weekend visit is a gated development called Camanche North Shore, a series of rentals in prefab homes that are designed like cottages in large grassy areas. Because the operation is gated with an entry kiosk, visitors are guaranteed a quiet time 11 P.M.–8 A.M.

The rentals range from a one-bedroom to four-bedroom units. There are combinations of kings, queens, twins, and sofas. The decor is condo/country-style, clean and comfortable. All have both heat and air-conditioning.

On a recent trip, I headed out on the lake, cruising across the peaceful emerald waters shortly after dawn. The trout were jumping, leaving beautiful, washtub-sized swirls. Two golden eagles cruised overhead in tandem, and the fresh, white wake behind my boat made working at an office job seem like a sentence at a state prison.

Like most California lakes, Camanche is filled in May, and as the Central Valley turns gold, the high, emerald water is a beautiful contrast to the surrounding bronzed foothills. As summer takes over and the water heats up, there is ample room for waterskiing and personal watercraft, which are restricted to various areas by speed limits. User conflicts between personal watercraft riders and anglers are kept to a minimum due to the size of the lake and its enforced rules.

The fishing is excellent for bass and often good for trout and bluegill. Camanche is known as a structure lake; that is, there is a lot of underwater structure where the bass hang out. They can be teased into biting with plastic worms such as Senkos or Brush Hogs. The trout fishing is also very good, with trolling the best along Hat Island and along the old river channel.

## Facilities

Camanche North Shore has eight housekeeping cottages for up to 4 people, four residential housekeeping cottages for up to 10 people, four motel rooms, and a marina with boat rentals, a coffee shop, grassy campsites, and RV sites. No pets are permitted in cabins. Linens and towels are provided.

## Reservations and Rates

Reservations are recommended and are often required during summer months. Housekeeping cottages that sleep 4 cost $126 per night. Residential housekeeping cottages that sleep 10 run $263 per night. A $120 security deposit is required. Discounts are available by the week, month, and season. Contact Camanche North Shore, 2000 Camanche Road, Ione, CA 95640, 209/763-5121, website: www.camancherecreation.com. For fishing information, contact The Fisherman's Friend, Lodi, 209/369-0204.

## Directions

From Stockton, drive east on Highway 88 to the town of Clements. Just east of Clements, bear left on Highway 88 and drive six miles to Camanche Parkway. Turn right and drive seven miles to the Camanche North Shore entrance gate.

# 8 DORRINGTON INN
### Off Highway 4 near Arnold and the Calaveras Big Trees

**Luxury rating:** 4                          **Recreation rating:** 4

Folks call this area "The Big Trees," as in, "I'm heading up to The Big Trees." That's because the Calaveras Big Trees make this region special, along with the Stanislaus River (where rafting, swimming, and fishing abound). Also popular are trips "up the hill" to Lake Alpine, Bear Valley Ski Area, and all the way to Ebbetts Pass and a great trailhead for the Carson-Iceberg Wilderness.

Dorrington Inn makes a great

headquarters, not only because of its location, but because of its truly intimate cottages. The interiors are knotty pine and decorated in alpine style. Five of the chalets have a queen-sized bed upstairs and a queen downstairs. One chalet has two twins upstairs and a queen downstairs. There are also three lodge rooms. All units have heating and air conditioners.

With fluffy down comforters and a fireplace, you get the perfect mix of rustic with modern style. A light breakfast is also provided—delicious croissants and muffins, along with fresh fruit, juice, cheese, and freshly roasted coffee. Complimentary port or wine is available each evening in the Common Room.

This great little spot is on Highway 4 in the Sierra Nevada, east of Arnold, at an elevation of 5,000 feet. The legendary Pony Express once rode through, and the entire area is filled with history. The primary destination for most visitors is easily accessible Calaveras Big Trees and its two trails, North Grove Loop and South Grove Loop. These trees, of course, are known for their tremendous diameters, not height; it can take a few dozen people linking hands to encircle even one.

The only complaint about this area is made by anglers. The Stanislaus River, along Highway 4, supports a puny fishery of a few very small trout. To get anything decent, you need to make the long drive up the hill to Spicer Meadows Reservoir. But the pluses far outshadow that solitary minus. Rafting is excellent on the lower Stanislaus. Hiking is also stellar, with a great, easy hike around Lake Alpine, a superb wilderness trailhead for day hikes up at Ebbetts Pass and, for the ambitious, up at Highland Lakes.

## Facilities

Dorrington Inn has cabins available in different configurations, offering a choice of two queen beds (one in a loft), one queen, or one king. A fireplace, small refrigerator, television, and kitchen are provided. A common room with a book and film library is also open to guests. Pets are allowed in the chalets only, by prior arrangement. No smoking is allowed indoors. Linens and towels are provided.

## Reservations and Rates

Reservations are recommended. Chalet rentals are $99–169 per night, with a two-night minimum stay on weekends and a three-night minimum stay on holiday weekends. Rates are charged on a per-room per-night basis, single or double occupancy, plus $10 for each extra person. Lodge rooms are $89–129. Contact Dorrington Inn Cottages, 3450 Highway 4, P.O. Box 4446, Dorrington, CA 95223, 209/795-2164 or 888/874-2164, website: www.dorringtoninn.com.

## Directions

From Stockton, turn east on Highway 4 and drive into the Sierra Nevada. Continue past Arnold for six miles to Dorrington. Look for the Dorrington Inn on the right (south) side of the road.

# 9 CABINS AT STRAWBERRY                    BEST (

Dodge Ridge, off Highway 108 east of Sonora

**Luxury rating:** 4                          **Recreation rating:** 4

The cabins here are gorgeous, with stream settings and plenty of privacy. Some have decks that overlook the Stanislaus River. All of the cabins are three-bedroom, two-bath units that can accommodate up to eight. Each of the bedrooms has a queen bed, plus there is a queen sofa bed in the living room. The cabins feature modern rustic decor with a fireplace, vaulted ceilings, a breakfast bar, and an updated kitchen.

The decor is completed in a fishing scheme with knotty-pine wood paneling and ceiling fans. All units are heated.

The location is excellent, beside the South Fork of the Stanislaus River at 5,230 feet, just five miles from Dodge Ridge Ski Area and 1.5 miles from the Pinecrest Lake turnoff. For more details about the area, see the listings for Pinecrest Lake Resort and The Rivers Resort in the Yosemite and Mammoth chapter.

Note that Strawberry Inn and Cabins at Strawberry were once owned by the same family. The cabins were sold to a new interest, and they now are competitors.

## Facilities

Cabins at Strawberry has eight cabins with fully equipped kitchens. Each cabin has a private bathroom, fireplace, barbecue, and deck. No more than two vehicles are allowed at each cabin. The cabins are suitable for children. One small pet is allowed in some of the cabins. No smoking is permitted. Some facilities are wheelchair accessible. Linens and towels are provided.

## Reservations and Rates

Reservations are recommended. The fee is $189 per night. For pets, a refundable $100 cleaning deposit is required. There is a three-night minimum stay. Major credit cards are accepted. It's open year-round. Contact Cabins at Strawberry, P.O. Box 109, Strawberry, CA 95375, 209/965-0885 or 888/965-0885, website: www.strawberrycabins.com.

## Directions

From Sonora, drive east on Highway 108 to the village of Strawberry (just past the turn for Dodge Ridge). Look for Strawberry Inn on the left (a store is on the right). Continue past the front of Strawberry Inn to the signed entrance for the cabins.

# 10 LAZY Z RESORT CABINS
Stanislaus National Forest, off Highway 108 near Twain Harte

**Luxury rating:** 4                **Recreation rating:** 3

The "swimming pool" at Lazy Z Resort is one of the most dramatic homemade pools at any resort in California. It looks more like a lake, as if the surrounding stone were carved out of mountain granite, complete with waterfalls that pour forth fresh water. Like a lake, it is not heated, but since air temperatures in the 90s are common during the summer, the water temperature is perfect. It's even warmer than a real lake would be because this "lake" is eight feet deep. The two adjacent hot tubs are a bonus. You can hop in and out from pool to hot tub to pool, and in short order start feeling refreshed.

The resort is designed for absolute minimal stress, and you notice it right away in the resort office, which has light classical music playing in the background. The 12 cabins follow that lead, all first-class accommodations, supplied with everything that you might need except for food and drinks.

The decor is country-modern, very tidy. All units are heated, and six cottages have air conditioning.

Lazy Z is just outside of Twain Harte, elevation 3,500 feet, right on the dividing line between oaks and pines in the summer, rain and snow in the winter. In the summer, this means you are out of the hot foothill country, just high enough to be in the shade of giant sugar pines. In the winter, it can be snowing like crazy uphill at the Dodge Ridge Ski Area near Pinecrest, but here at Twain Harte it will only be raining. Often you don't have to chain up your tires during winter storms.

The best-known recreation areas nearby are Stanislaus National Forest and the Stanislaus and Tuolumne Rivers; both bodies of water offer good fishing, swimming, and panning for gold. The best way to explore is with a map of Stanislaus National Forest that shows all backcountry roads and access points to the rivers. Within an hour's drive in the mountains, you'll find Beardsley Reservoir, Pinecrest Lake, Lyons Lake, and Dodge Ridge Ski Area.

But after taking a dunk in the resort's pool, maybe followed by a plunge into the hot tub, few visitors will feel like going anywhere else anytime soon.

## Facilities
Lazy Z Resort has 12 cabins and cottages of various sizes with bathrooms and fully equipped kitchens or kitchenettes. Some cabins have a fireplace, deck, or barbecue. A

swimming pool, hot tub, and clubhouse with a game room are on the property. The resort also has a horseshoe pit, table tennis, and walking trails. No pets are permitted, and smoking is prohibited. Linens and towels are provided.

## Reservations and Rates

Reservations are required. Cabin rates on weekends range $85–195 per night, with a two-night minimum stay required. Weekly discounts are available. Major credit cards are accepted. The resort is open year-round. Contact Lazy Z Resort, 22732 Middle Camp Road, P.O. Box 1055, Twain Harte, CA 95383, 209/586-1214 or 800/585-1238, website: www.lazyz.com.

## Directions

From Manteca on Highway 99, turn east on Highway 120 and drive 17 miles to Oakdale and Highway 108/120. Turn left on Highway 108/120 and drive to Sonora. Continue on Highway 108 for about 5 miles to Twain Harte. At Twain Harte, turn left at Mono Vista and drive a short distance to Longeway Road (a stop sign). Turn right at Longeway and drive about 3 miles to where it dead-ends at Middle Camp Road. Turn right on Middle Camp Road and look for the resort on the left side of the road.

# 11 GABLES CEDAR CREEK INN          BEST (

Stanislaus National Forest, off Highway 108 near Twain Harte

**Luxury rating:** 3                                    **Recreation rating:** 3

This is a romantic getaway spot, and for those of you used to the high cost of many of California's resort areas, you'll be surprised at how low the prices are at Gables Cedar Creek Inn.

For under $100 per night, you can get your own cozy cabin with fireplace, outside deck, antique furnishings, and romantic country decor. And guess what? It's clean, it's surrounded by towering pines and cedars, and it's close to snow skiing, fishing, hiking, golfing, and historic gold-rush towns.

Four of the cabins are duplex units, but the other three are freestanding. An expansive lawn area with outdoor furniture is available for all inn guests. Most of the cabins have fully equipped kitchens, except for The Love Nest and The Blue Room, which have kitchenettes. If you're part of a large group, try the two-story Creekside Home, which sleeps seven and includes a master suite with fireplace and sitting area, vaulted ceilings, gas fireplaces, a television, a deck, and plenty of windows allowing the sunlight inside.

By far, the most popular cabin is Hideaway, a secluded log cabin across the creek and accessible by crossing a stone bridge. It sits among redwood trees and has a partial view of the golf course. The Loft Room is next to the creek and has a kitchen and living room with woodburning stove downstairs, and a loft with a double mattress.

Golf lovers will be happy to know that the fourth fairway of the nine-hole Twain Harte Golf Club adjoins the property, and guests have been known to start golfing from this point, with permission of course. The town of Twain Harte has a number of restaurants and shops; the innkeepers can direct you. Heading east, Dodge Ridge Ski Area, with downhill and cross-country skiing and snowboarding, is just a 35-minute drive away. Pinecrest Lake has a variety of water sports and outdoor movies under the stars during the summer. Closer to home, free summer music concerts are held in the Twain Harte city park on Saturday evenings. A few blocks from the inn is Twain Harte Lake, a private recreational lake that's available to inn guests.

## Facilities

Gables Cedar Creek Inn has seven cabins and one house. Most of the cabins have fully equipped kitchens. Woodstoves or fireplaces plus telephones and televisions are included. The inn is not suitable for children. Leashed pets are allowed. No smoking is permitted. One rental is wheelchair accessible. Linens and towels are provided, and maid service is available by request.

## Reservations and Rates

Reservations are recommended. The fee is $83–108 per night per cabin, and $229 per night or $1,100 per week for the house. For more than two people, an extra fee of $10 per night per person is charged. The pet fee is $10 per night per pet; no dogs over 40 pounds are permitted. There is a two-night minimum stay on weekends and a three-night minimum on holidays. Major credit cards are accepted. The inn is open year-round. Contact Gables Cedar Creek Inn, P.O. Box 1818, 22560 Twain Harte Drive, Twain Harte, CA 95383, 209/586-3008 or 888/900-4224, website: www.gocedarcreek.com.

## Directions

From Sonora, drive east on Highway 108 to Twain Harte and Twain Harte Drive. Turn left on Twain Harte Drive and drive for 1.2 miles to the inn on the left.

# Other Cabins & Cottages in the Region

**Auburn KOA,** 3550 KOA Way, Auburn, CA 95602, 530/885-0990, website: www.koa.com.

**Bucks Lakeshore Resort,** P.O. Box 338, Meadow Valley, CA 95956, 530/283-6900, fax 530/283-6909, website: www.buckslake.com.

**Camanche Lake South Shore,** P.O. Box 206, Burson, CA 95225, 209/763-5178, website: www.norcalfishing.com (then click on Camanche).

**Lake Oroville Floating Camps,** Lake Oroville State Recreation Area, 530/538-2200, or Lake Oroville Visitor Center, 530/538-2219, reservations at 800/444-7275, website: www.ReserveAmerica.com.

**Loomis KOA,** 3945 Taylor Road, Loomis, CA 95650, 916/652-6737, website: www.koa.com.

**Placerville KOA,** 4655 Rock Barn Road, Shingle Springs, CA 95682, 530/676-2267, reservations at 800/562-4197, website: www.koa.com.

**Sacramento-West Old Town KOA,** 3951 Lake Road, West Sacramento, CA 95691, 916/371-6771 or 800/562-2747, reservations at 800/562-3403, website: www.koa.com.

# TAHOE AND THE NORTHERN SIERRA

COURTESY OF SHORE HOUSE AT LAKE TAHOE

## BEST CABINS & COTTAGES

❰ **Best for Horseback Riding**
Greenhorn Creek Guest Ranch, **page 184**

❰ **Most Romantic**
The Cottage Inn at Lake Tahoe, **page 196**

❰ **Best for Water Sports**
Zephyr Cove Resort, **page 202**

❰ **Best for Winter Sports**
Bear River Lake Resort, **page 212**

## Mount Tallac affords a view across Lake Tahoe like

no other: a cobalt blue expanse of water bordered by mountains that span miles of Sierra wildlands. The beauty is stunning. Lake Tahoe is one of the few places on earth where people feel an emotional response just by looking at it. Yosemite Valley, the giant sequoias, the Grand Canyon, a perfect sunset on the Pacific Ocean – a few other sights occasionally can evoke the same response. But Tahoe often seems to strike the deepest chord. It can resonate inside you for weeks, even after a short visit.

"What about all the people?" you ask. It's true that people come here in droves. But I found many spots that I shared only with the chipmunks. You can enjoy these spots, too, if you're willing to read my books, hunt a bit, and most importantly, time your trip to span Monday through Thursday.

This area has the widest range of accommodations: family resorts, romantic lakeside chalets, riverside cottages, dude ranches, fishing cabins, a remote forest hut, and even a lodge (Shore House at Lake Tahoe) where you can book a room, get married, have a wedding reception, and have your honeymoon, all presided over by the lodge owner, who is an ordained minister.

This region also has some of the most popular cabin rentals in California, including Sardine Lake Resort and Angora Lakes Resort, where you begin the reservation process by signing up on a cancellation list and then waiting for 10 years or so for someone to cancel. The reason? These two resorts offer the closest thing to an *On Golden Pond* setting in California.

Tahoe and the northern Sierra feature hundreds of lakes, including dozens you can drive to. The best for scenic beauty are Echo Lakes, Donner, Fallen Leaf, Sardine, Caples, Loon, Union Valley . . . well, I could go on and on. It is one of the most beautiful regions anywhere on earth.

The north end of the Sierra starts near Bucks Lake, a great lake for trout fishing, and extends to Bear River Canyon (and Caples Lake, Silver Lake, and Bear River Reservoir). In between are Lakes Basin Recreation Area (containing Gold, Sardine, Packer, and other lakes) in southern Plumas County, the Crystal Basin (featuring Union Valley Reservoir and Loon Lake, among others) in the Sierra foothills west of Tahoe, Lake Davis (with the highest catch rates for trout) near Portola, and the Carson River Canyon and Hope Valley south of Tahoe.

You could spend weeks exploring any of these places, having the time of your life, and still not get to Tahoe's magic. But it is Tahoe where the adventure starts for many, especially in the surrounding Tahoe National Forest and Desolation Wilderness.

One of California's greatest day trips from Tahoe is to Echo Lakes, where you can take a hiker's shuttle boat across the two lakes to the Pacific Crest Trail, then hike a few miles into Desolation Wilderness and Aloha Lakes. Yet with so many wonderful ways to spend a day in this area, this day trip is hardly a blip on the radar scope.

With so many places and so little time, this region offers what can be the ultimate adventureland.

# TAHOE & THE NORTHERN SIERRA

# Tahoe and the Northern Sierra Cabins & Cottages

# 1 GREENHORN CREEK GUEST RANCH

BEST (

North Plumas, off Highway 89 near Quincy

**Luxury rating:** 3

**Recreation rating:** 5

---

The folks here don't say "Hi" or "Hello" when you arrive. Instead, it's "Howdy, and welcome to Greenhorn Creek Guest Ranch." This is a genuine western dude ranch. Stay here for a few days and you might start feeling like a cowgirl or cowboy. Stay here for a week and you might not want to return home—not with the scrumptious chuckhouse chow, campfire cookouts, hayrides, trail and pony rides, fishing, western dancing, frog races, and guest rodeo.

With more than 600 acres of ranchland at 4,000 feet in elevation, plus the adjoining Plumas National Forest at your disposal, you'll have more choices than time to do all the things that make a greenhorn smile. Mom and Dad can leave the younger buckaroos at the kiddie corral, with child-care attendants and a full day of activities, while the older cowpokes explore the ranch by foot or horse, get riding instruction, fish for trout in the pond or one of the surrounding lakes or streams, or swim and sunbathe.

And when it's time to get some shuteye, hang your hat in a cozy wood-paneled cabin with private bathroom. The decor is comfortable western. There are porch swings at every cabin. These one- and two-bedroom units are grouped in rows of four adjoining cabins, with bunk beds for the kids.

The gang at Greenhorn Creek Guest Ranch knows all about making happy trails for their guests.

## Facilities

Greenhorn Creek Guest Ranch's 16 cabins and 11 lodge rooms can accommodate 2–7 people per rental. There are no kitchen facilities, but all meals are provided. The cabins have a bathroom with shower and a deck or porch. Amenities include an outdoor spa, heated pool, lounge, fishing pond, laundry room, recreation room with billiards, exercise room, petting zoo, horseback riding, dancing, volleyball, badminton, Ping-Pong, softball, horseshoes, a supervised children's program, and organized activities. Pets are not allowed. Smoking is permitted in some areas. Linens and towels are provided, and there is daily maid service.

## Reservations and Rates

Reservations are required. For stays less than one week, the fee is $253 per night per person for ages 16 and over, $162 per night for ages 6–15, $89 for ages 3–6, and free for under age 3. Weekly rates are $1,252–1,377 for ages 16 and over, $812–843 for ages 6–15, $353–392 for ages 3–6, and free for under age 3. Group rates are available for 10 or more people. A one-week minimum stay is required in June, July and August. Major credit cards are accepted. The ranch is open April–November, weather permitting. Contact Greenhorn Creek Guest Ranch, 2116 Greenhorn Ranch Road, Quincy, CA 95971, 530/283-0930 or 800/33-HOWDY (800/334-6939), fax 530/283-4401, website: www.greenhornranch.com.

### Directions
From Oroville, drive north on Highway 70 to the junction with Highway 89. Turn south on Highway 89/70 and drive 11 miles to Quincy. Continue 11 miles to Greenhorn Ranch Road. Turn left and drive two miles to the ranch on the right.

## 2 LONG VALLEY RESORT
Plumas National Forest, off Highway 89 near Quincy

**Luxury rating:** 3                                    **Recreation rating:** 4

This Plumas County setting at an elevation of 4,300 feet provides the ideal location for adventuring, hiking, fishing, and golf. One of the cottages at Long Valley Resort is a convenient launch point, along Highway 70/89 in Plumas National Forest country, at the threshold of adventure. There is nearby access to six golf courses in Graeagle, as well as a half dozen drive-to lakes in the Lakes Basin and some 50 lakes in the whole region. The star of the show is nearby Plumas-Eureka State Park, a very pretty park ideal for hiking.

The nine cottages at Long Valley Resort are about 30 feet apart, yet once you're inside, they are very private. Cottages 6, 7, and 8 have decks with views of a pretty meadow, which often holds deer or horses. A creek lined with cottonwoods runs along the edge of the meadow—a stunning setting when the trees turn color in the fall.

The decor is theme-related and varies from cabin to cabin. Themes include fishing, golf, winter, and railroad. All units are fully heated and have air-conditioning.

Fishing can be excellent at the nearby Middle Fork Feather River. The easiest access to the Middle Fork Feather from Long Valley Resort is to drive a half mile north on Highway 70/89 and turn left on Sloat Road. From there, drive about a mile, turn right, drive over the railroad tracks, continue a short distance to the river, and drive over the river. Here the road turns to dirt and traces along upriver for a spell; this is the fishing access.

## Facilities

Long Valley Resort has nine cottages (seven two-bedrooms with three beds, one one-bedroom with two beds, and one three-bedroom with three beds), and Cottage 11 has two bedrooms, three beds, and two bathrooms. Each has a bathroom and a kitchen with cookware and utensils. A motel with four rooms is also available, often used for overflow lodging. A grocery store/café is nearby. Pets are permitted in selected cottages by prior arrangement, $8 per night. No smoking is permitted indoors. Linens and towels are provided. Daily maid service is included.

## Reservations and Rates

Reservations are accepted. Rates are $75 per night or $380 per week, with a charge of $6 per day per additional person (more than two). A three-bedroom unit is $85 per night. A two-night minimum stay is required in season. Discounts are available for off-season and stays of three nights or more. Contact Long Valley Resort, 59532 Highway 70, P.O. Box 30121, Cromberg, CA 96103, 530/836-0754 or 800/887-6653, website: www.longvalleyresort.com.

## Directions

From Oroville, drive north on Highway 70 to the junction with Highway 89. Turn south on Highway 89/70 and drive 11 miles to Quincy. Continue through Quincy, drive 15 miles, and look for Long Valley Resort on the right side of the road.

# 3 LITTLE BEAR RV PARK
Long Valley, off Highway 70/89 in Blairsden

🚶 🚴 ⛵ 👫

**Luxury rating:** 1                     **Recreation rating:** 4

The cabins here are intended to accomplish two things: 1) get the tenters off the ground; 2) force the bears to have to knock. The cabins at Little Bear RV Park are primitive; that is, a few beds for sleeping, a table, and that's about it. Your reward: no bugs, no meandering bears, privacy, and hey, you're not on the ground. The cabins are in a ring around a community fire pit, which adds a camping feel to the place.

The decor is rustic-country, with plaid curtains. There is no heat or air-conditioning.

This privately operated park at 4,300 feet is set up primarily for RV campers, and they are what really make the place tick. Among the many nearby recreation attractions are outstanding and beautiful golf courses. Most venture out to Plumas-Eureka State Park, only seven miles away. A must-do side trip is the hike up Eureka Peak, elevation 7,447 feet. The panoramic view of the southern Sierra Nevada includes all the peaks of the Gold Lakes Basin, with Mount Elwell (7,818 feet) most prominent to the south, and Plumas National Forest to the north and west, crowned by Blue Nose Mountain (7,290 feet), Stafford Mountain (7,019 feet), and Beartrap Mountain (7,232 feet). It requires a three-mile round-trip with a climb of 1,150 feet.

## Facilities

Little Bear RV Park has four primitive cabins with no electricity, six cabins that have electricity along with a television and VCR, and 85 RV campsites. Each cabin has a double bed, a bunk bed, a table, and a deck with a chair, hammock, and picnic table, plus a community fire ring. Drinking water, showers, flush toilets, coin laundry, a grocery store, and ice are available. No smoking is allowed. Pets are not permitted in cabins. Linens and towels are not provided; bring your own sleeping bag, pillow, and towels.

## Reservations and Rates

Reservations are accepted. The rate is $30 per night for two for cabins without electricity, $40 per night for cabins with electricity, $8 for each additional person, and $4 for children ages 5–17. It's open mid-April through October 28. Contact Little Bear RV Park, P.O. Box 103, Blairsden, CA 96103, tel./fax 530/836-2774, website: www.littlebearrvpark.com.

## Directions

In Truckee, drive north on Highway 89 to Blairsden and the junction with Highway 70. Turn north and drive one mile to Little Bear Road. Turn left on Little Bear Road and drive a short distance to the campground.

# 4 GRAY EAGLE LODGE
Graeagle, off Highway 70/89

🏃 ≋ 🛶 🐕 👪 ♿

**Luxury rating:** 3                              **Recreation rating:** 4

For a midrange cabin rental in the Gold Lakes Basin, this is one of the best bets. There are some good cabins with great locations in this area, but none of them provide all of the amenities that you'll find at Gray Eagle Lodge, set in Plumas National Forest at almost 6,000 feet in elevation.

You'll get a private bathroom with shower in your rustic, wood-paneled cabin, and two complimentary meals a day, a big plus for families and vacationers who don't want to fuss with cooking. Gray Eagle Creek flows through the property, and some of the cabins are set along the creek. Alder Cabin is the largest, with two bedrooms and a creekside location. Poplar Cabin and Cedar Cabin also feature creekside settings.

The knotty-pine decor is comfortable. All units are fully heated.

The activity list is long and includes horseback riding and golfing nearby. Swimmers can enjoy one of the local lakes, or the ol' swimming hole at the base of little Gray Eagle Falls, which is within 200 feet of the lodge. Hikers' and anglers' options are plentiful. From the lodge, take the Smith Lake trailhead for one mile to reach the lake and its trout inhabitants, where a canoe is available for the first lodge guest to claim it. Continue on this trail for two miles to reach the top of Mount Elwell at 7,818 feet, with an elevation gain of 2,018 feet over the course of three miles. Other trails leading to pristine mountain lakes can be accessed.

The Gold Lakes Basin is a beautiful area with friendly people.

## Facilities
Gray Eagle Lodge has 19 one- and two-bedroom cabins, and two lodge rooms. There are no kitchen facilities, but complimentary breakfast and dinner are provided, and box lunches are available for an additional fee. Cabins include a bathroom with shower and a deck. There are no televisions or telephones in the cabins. A restaurant, lounge, recreation room, and evening campfire are available. The lodge is suitable for children. Leashed pets are allowed, with a two-pet limit per cabin. No smoking is permitted. One cabin is wheelchair accessible. Linens and towels are provided, and there is daily maid service.

## Reservations and Rates
Reservations are recommended. The fee is $195–235 per night for a one-bedroom cabin, $235–255 per night for a two-bedroom cabin. For more than two people, there is a fee of $70 per night per adult, $50 per night for ages 10–16, $35 per night for ages 2–9, and $20 for ages 3 and under. The pet fee is $20 per night per pet. There is a three-night minimum stay year-round and a five-night minimum stay when booking a year in advance. Major credit cards are accepted. It's open mid-May through mid-October, weather permitting. Contact Gray Eagle Lodge, 5000 Gold Lake Road, P.O. Box 38, Graeagle, CA 96103, 530/836-2511 or 800/635-8778, website: www.grayeaglelodge.com.

## Directions
From Truckee, drive northwest on Highway 89 toward Graeagle to the Gold Lake Highway (one mile before reaching Graeagle). Turn left on Gold Lake Highway (Forest Road 24) and drive five miles to the sign for Gray Eagle Lodge. Turn right and drive 0.3 mile to the lodge.

# 5 ELWELL LAKES LODGE

Lakes Basin, Plumas National Forest, off Highway 89 near Graeagle

🏃 🚵 🏊 🎣 ⛺ 👪

**Luxury rating:** 2                                    **Recreation rating:** 5

First, let's end the confusion. There is no Elwell Lake. Rather there is nearby Mount Elwell, 7,812 feet in elevation, and the lodge is named for the dozens of lakes in its shadow, including 23 within a three-mile radius of the lodge.

The cabins, both housekeeping cabins and tent cabins, provide a perfect base camp for exploring this area, whether you're hiking, fishing, boating, or sailboarding. Highlights include beautiful Long Lake, three-quarters of a mile away, where the lodge provides unlimited use of boats and motors for guests, and of course, the Mount Elwell Trail.

This lodge was first built in 1920 and is still owned and operated by the original family. When the lodge opened, almost all of the cabins were tent cabins. Only three tent cabins remain, and these are rented as extra rooms for those renting cabins, such as couples who wish to put the youngsters in a separate room for the night. Another highlight for families is the recreation building. It features a huge fireplace, a pretty view, and many books and games for those who want to stay at the camp.

Although the place retains its rustic qualities, all modern amenities are now provided. The cabins rest amid a pine forest, providing a classic alpine setting. They are wood-sided, often with metal roofs, and most have decks. Each cabin has all of the pots, pans, dishes, and linens you'll need, plus kitchen and bathroom facilities. All you need to bring is your food. The most popular cabin is the Cromwell, a two-person cabin in the woods on a seasonal creek.

The decor is simply country. All units are fully heated.

This is one of the best cabin locations in California for hiking to nearby mountain lakes. For newcomers to the lodge, climbing Mount Elwell is like being baptized. It is a three-mile hike one-way to the top, requiring a climb of 1,100 feet. Your reward is a spectacular view of the Lakes Basin, a landscape of granite, pine forest, and scattered lakes, looking like gem after gem.

Note that nearby Gold Lake Lodge (see next listing), less than a half mile to the north, and other lake and cabin settings in the area provide additional lodging opportunities.

## Facilities

Elwell Lakes Lodge has 10 cabins and 3 tent cabins, each fully equipped with bathroom, kitchenette, and barbecue. Guests have use of a boat on nearby Long Lake and full use of lodge facilities. No pets are permitted. Linens and towels are provided. For tent cabins, you must bring your own sleeping bag.

## Reservations and Rates

Reservations are required. Fees vary according to the size of the cabin. A small cabin for two people is $78 per night or $468 per week. A large cabin for up to six people is $147 per night or $878 per week. For additional space, tent cabins are available for $17 per night for two, with each additional person costing $8 per day. Weekly rates are available, with a one-week minimum required from mid-June through mid-September. No credit cards are accepted. It's open when the snow clears, usually from mid-June to October, weather permitting. Contact Elwell Lakes Lodge, P.O. Box 68, Blairsden, CA 96103, 530/836-2347, website: www.members.aol.com/elwellodge.

## Directions

From Truckee, turn north on Highway 89 and drive past the town of Clio to the Gold Lake Highway near the southern end of Graeagle. Turn left on Gold Lake Highway (Forest Road 24) and drive up the mountain. Turn right at the signed turnoff for Elwell Lakes Lodge (if you reach Gold Lake, you have gone too far) and drive a short distance to the lodge.

# 6 GOLD LAKE LODGE

Lakes Basin, Plumas National Forest, off Highway 89 near Graeagle

🚶 🚴 🛶 � 👪

**Luxury rating:** 3                                               **Recreation rating:** 5

The centerpiece of the Lakes Basin Recreation Area is Gold Lake, a beautiful sky-blue lake in a rock basin in the northern Sierra at 6,400 feet. It is the largest of the many lakes in the region, and the trout here can get huge. Several trailheads around the lake allow for outstanding hikes to smaller nearby lakes, and a pack station and stable are available near Gold Lake.

Perfect, right? There's more. Gold Lake Lodge, about a half mile north of Gold Lake near the Sierra crest at an even higher 6,620-foot elevation, provides both rustic and standard cabins, and a restaurant serves dinner and breakfast.

The one bugaboo that surprises newcomers all summer long is the wind at Gold Lake. The lake's location near the Sierra crest often causes what is called the venturi effect, especially in the afternoon, when wind is funneled through the mountain gap over the lake, picking up speed as a large mass of air is forced through a relatively small gap in the mountain ridge. Of course, the wind makes for great sailboarding and sailing, at least until it really howls. One protected cove is calm even when the rest of the lake is raging.

The cabins at Gold Lake Lodge are situated largely out of the wind and close to excellent short hiking trails. The standard cabins have full baths, but the rustic cabins do not, though detached facilities are offered. Breakfast, dinner, and supplies for a trail lunch are included in the price. There is also family-style dining.

The decor is basic country-style. All units are heated.

Although there is no docking or boat launch at nearby Big Bear Lake, in summer the lodge keeps one boat there, which is available only for guests. This pretty lake is a half-mile walk from the lodge and provides good trout fishing, often with higher catch rates than at Gold Lake, though the trout are far smaller. In addition, there is a recreation hall, a bonfire area, and outside games.

The trail from Gold Lake Lodge to the north shore of Big Bear Lake (6,485 feet) is one of several excellent short hikes. It is slightly downhill, losing about 200 feet, and from Big Bear Lake it is a short distance to Little Bear Lake and about a quarter mile to Little Cub Lake. You can then take a half-mile loop that skirts the southern shore of Long Lake (which is quite beautiful) then turns left and passes Silver Lake and Round Lake (6,714 feet in elevation) before heading back to the lodge. This great loop hike passes six lakes in all and covers about three miles.

## Facilities

Gold Lake Lodge has three rustic and six standard cabins, and an open tent cabin is available for extra space. Standard cabins provide a full bath; rustic cabins do not but have facilities nearby. No pets are permitted. Smoking is allowed. Linens and housekeeping are provided.

## Reservations and Rates

Reservations are required. Rates are $95–105 per night single occupancy for a rustic cabin or $155–171 per night double occupancy, $130–144 per night single occupancy for a standard cabin or $190–210 per night double occupancy. Additional people are $60–66 for adults, with discounts for children. There is a two-night minimum stay, with weekly rate discounts. Contact Gold Lake Lodge, P.O. Box 308, Graeagle, CA 96103, 530/836-2350, website: www.lakesbasin.com/gold/.

## Directions

From Truckee, turn north on Highway 89 and drive past the town of Clio to the Gold Lake Highway near the southern end of Graeagle. Turn left on Gold Lake Highway (Forest Road 24) and drive up the mountain. About 0.5 mile past the Lakes Basin Campground, turn right at the signed turnoff for Gold Lake Lodge and drive a short distance to the lodge.

# **7 PACKER LAKE LODGE**

Lakes Basin, Tahoe National Forest, off Highway 49 near Bassetts

**Luxury rating: 3**                                    **Recreation rating: 5**

What a place: old lakefront log cabins, good trout fishing, low-speed boating, one of the best trails in California for hiking—all set in Tahoe National Forest, where serenity reigns. No, you have not gone to heaven. You have gone to Packer Lake.

Packer Lake, at a 6,218-foot elevation, is at the foot of the dramatic Sierra Buttes. The trout fishing is decent here, but there are an additional 15 lakes with fishing within a five-mile radius in the Lakes Basin Recreation Area. Take your pick.

The most dramatic adventure of all, however, is hiking to the awesome and thrilling lookout at the Sierra Buttes. The trailhead is only about a mile away, at the foot of the buttes. From here, you climb 2,369 feet over the course of about five miles. The trail traces the mountain rim to the lookout, topped off by a stairway with 176 steps that juts out into open space—an eerie yet unforgettable experience. The view is astounding: hundreds of miles in all directions. It's one of my favorite hikes.

Packer Lake Lodge features 14 cabins, including low-cost log cabins (a bit on the raw side) all the way up to newer cabins with all-electric kitchens, bathrooms, and everything you need except food. A bonus is the small fishing boat that is supplied as part of the package for all cabin guests.

## Facilities
Packer Lake has 14 cabins varying in size and amenities, with eight providing bathrooms and kitchens. A small fishing boat is included in cabin rentals. A small dock, primitive boat ramp, and additional rental boats and canoes are available. A small restaurant is on the property. Linens and towels are provided.

## Reservations and Rates
Reservations are required. Cabin rates are $81 per day or $526 per week for a one-room sleeping cabin with no kitchen or bath, up to $135 per day or $1,165 per week for cabins with a kitchen and bathroom, depending on cabin size. It's open May to mid-October. Contact Packer Lake Lodge, P.O. Box 237, Sierra City, CA 96125, 530/862-1221. In the off-season (November–April), contact 2245 Beach Street, Apartment 2, San Francisco, CA 94123, 415/921-5943.

## Directions
From Truckee, turn north on Highway 89 and drive 25 miles to Sierraville. Turn left on Highway 49 and drive about 10 miles to Bassetts Store. Turn right (north) on Gold Lake Road and drive 1 mile. Look for the signed turnoff for Packer Lake/Sardine Lake. Turn left here, drive a short distance, and at the fork bear right (left goes to Sardine Lake) and drive 3.5 miles to Packer Lake.

# 8 SARDINE LAKE RESORT
Lakes Basin, off Highway 49 near Bassetts

🧍 🚲 🏊 🎣 🚤 👪

**Luxury rating:** 3                                      **Recreation rating:** 5

Staying in a cabin on the shore of Sardine Lake might seem just too good to be true. Unfortunately, it often is. Staying here is the closest thing to an *On Golden Pond* ambience in California. It is one of the prettiest mountain cabin settings anywhere. The lake is small but gorgeous, blue-green and sheltered, with the spiked rim of the Sierra Buttes providing a dramatic backdrop. The cabins are cute and cozy, set near the lake and sheltered in a pine forest. Some have decks with lake views. A small marina is within short walking distance and a first-class restaurant is along the shore.

How could this be too good to be true? Because it is just about impossible to get a reservation and actually spend a week at a cabin here. These cabins are always reserved far in advance. The only way to arrange a stay is to sign up on a waiting list, then hope for a cancellation. Some people who have fallen in love with the place admit to a wait of up to 10 years before getting a chance to relive *On Golden Pond*. The owners requested I leave the place out of the book because they didn't want to continue disappointing people who have to be turned away. Sorry. This place is just too good to not at least get on the waiting list.

The scenic beauty of the area is stunning. Though the lake is small, it is pristine—almost divine—set at 6,000 feet. The contrast between the calm blue-green waters and the towering granite mountain backdrop, with an army of conifers at its base, can inspire a feeling of greatness in all who see it. There is no substitute for natural beauty and there is no substitute for Sardine Lake.

On the lake, a five-mph speed limit is in effect, perfect for little boats, especially canoes. Rentals are available at the marina. The lake provides good catch rates for rainbow trout, especially trolling near the inlet along the back wall. The hiking is exceptional, with a great jaunt up to Upper Sardine Lake, where a small waterfall awaits discovery on the stream that connects Upper Sardine Lake to Lower Sardine Lake. The hiking trail to the top of the Sierra Buttes cannot be accessed directly from Sardine Lake. The trailhead is at an access point near Packer Lake.

If you take one look at this place—the mountain beauty, the little cabins, the fishing, boating, and hiking—you will want to stay here, too. Good luck in your quest.

## Facilities

Sardine Lake Resort has a series of small lakeside cabins with kitchenettes and bathrooms. A marina with boat rentals and a restaurant (reservations required) are available. A primitive, narrow dirt boat ramp is accessible only to small boats on trailers. Pets are permitted by prior arrangement. Smoking is allowed in some areas. Linens are provided.

## Reservations and Rates

Reservations are required. All cabins are always reserved in advance. You instead sign up on a waiting list and hope for a cancellation. The fees are $755–1,165 per week. The resort is open when snow clears, usually mid-May to mid-October. Contact Sardine Lake Resort, P.O. Box 216, Sierra City, CA 96125, 530/862-1196 (summer) or 530/862-1363; winter address is 3251 Virginiatown Road, Lincoln, CA 95648.

## Directions

From Truckee, drive north on Highway 89 for 20 miles to Sierraville and the Y. Turn left on Highway 49 and drive 12 miles to Bassetts Store and just beyond to Gold Lake Road. Turn right on Gold Lake Road and drive 1 mile to Sardine Lake Road. Turn left and drive a short distance, then bear left at the fork (signed Sardine Lake) and drive 1 mile to the lake.

## 9 YUBA RIVER INN

Yuba River, off Highway 49 near Sierra City

**Luxury rating:** 2                                   **Recreation rating:** 4

A mixture of the old and the new is what you'll get here. The cabins range from 1930s-era to newly built, some with kitchens, some with wood-burning stoves, some with hot tubs, and some allowing smoking. Take your pick, but you'd better choose quickly if you want a cabin with a kitchen, because those go fast. Could the fact that there's no restaurant within walking distance have anything to do with this?

Each cabin accommodates up to six, depending on the unit. The cabins without kitchens have a small refrigerator, and the fully equipped kitchens include a microwave. The Wild Plum Cabin is the most deluxe lodging, with two bedrooms, a woodburning stove, and a whirlpool tub. The cabins are surrounded by pines, cedars, and firs at an elevation of 4,100 feet.

The inn is on 20 acres with one-third mile of North Fork Yuba River frontage; you can fish for rainbow, brown, and brook trout. The Pacific Crest Trail is one-half mile east of the inn, with easy access. Well-known and popular mountain biking trails along the Yuba River are a few miles downstream, as are white-water rafting and kayaking.

This is a beautiful and relatively quiet area of California, and there's no quick and easy way to get here. Once you reach the foothills, the scenery is often outstanding and you might want to poke around some of the gold rush–era towns as you work your way to the Yuba River Inn.

## Facilities

Yuba River Inn has 10 log cabins with bathrooms and showers. Kitchen facilities are provided in some of the cabins. One cabin has a woodburning stove and whirlpool tub.

A pool is available in July and August. The cabins are suitable for children. Leashed pets are allowed, with a two-pet limit per cabin. Smoking is permitted in some of the cabins. Linens and towels are provided; there is no daily maid service.

## Reservations and Rates

Reservations are required during the summer for cabins with kitchens. The fee is $61–66 per night for up to three people for a cabin without a kitchen, and $88–165 per night for 3–6 people for a cabin with a kitchen. A pet fee of $10 per pet per night is charged. Credit cards are not accepted. The inn is open year-round. Contact Yuba River Inn, P.O. Box 236, Sierra City, CA 96125, 530/862-1122, website: www.yubariverinn.com.

## Directions

From Auburn, take Highway 49 north to Nevada City and continue (the road jogs left at Nevada City, then narrows) past Downieville to Sierra City. Continue on Highway 49 for 0.5 mile to the inn on the right.

# 10 SHORE HOUSE AT LAKE TAHOE

North shore of Lake Tahoe, off Highway 28 at Tahoe Vista

**Luxury rating:** 4          **Recreation rating:** 4

When they say they're "full service" at the Shore House at Lake Tahoe, they mean it. That's because the inn-keeper is an ordained minister and he also performs weddings at the complex. He'll make your room reservation, put on his robe, and marry you, and then he and his wife will organize your reception if you want. The rest is up to you.

But you don't have to get married to stay here. It's a quiet, romantic, lakefront hideaway for couples wanting a break from their hectic routines. Two free-standing and seven adjoining cottages have gas fireplaces, decks, feather beds, and down comforters. From your deck or balcony, you'll look out over the lawn and pier to the beautiful tourmaline waters of Lake Tahoe and the surrounding mountains.

Each cottage is unique and decorated individually; among them are Opa's Room, The Pine Room, The Moon Room, The Terrace Room, and The Studio. The Lakeview Room has floor-to-ceiling sliding glass doors with great views, and the rainbow trout and mackinaw painted on the shower walls appear to be swimming around you. The

Tree House is on the second story and situated between two large ponderosa pines; it sports a Native American decor. The Honeymoon Cottage is a separate cabin near the lakefront with a queen-size log bed, two-person whirlpool tub in the bedroom, knotty-pine walls, vaulted ceilings, and breathtaking views.

## Facilities

Shore House at Lake Tahoe has nine cottages for up to two people. There are no kitchen facilities, but a full breakfast and homemade cookies are provided. Amenities include a small refrigerator, LCD televisions, CD players, deck, and gas log fireplace. Telephones are not available in the cottages. An outdoor hot tub, pier, lawn area with chaise lounges, and wedding facilities are available. The facilities are not suitable for children. Pets are not allowed. No smoking is permitted. Linens and towels are provided.

## Reservations and Rates

Reservations are recommended. The fee is $190–290 per night per cottage. There is a two-night minimum stay most of the year. Major credit cards are accepted. Contact Shore House at Lake Tahoe, P.O. Box 499, 7170 North Lake Boulevard, Tahoe Vista, CA 96148, 530/546-7270 or 800/207-5160, website: www.tahoeinn.com.

## Directions

From Truckee, drive south on Highway 167 to Highway 28/North Lake Boulevard. Turn right (south) and drive 0.75 mile to the cottages on the left (lakeside).

# 11 THE COTTAGE INN
# AT LAKE TAHOE                         BEST 🌙

West shore of Lake Tahoe, off Highway 89 near Tahoe City

🏃 🚴 🏊 🎣 🚣 ❄️

**Luxury rating:** 3                              **Recreation rating:** 5

Lake Tahoe takes the prize as the number one romantic getaway for residents of California and Nevada. My wife and I are smitten by the place ourselves, and we even got hitched in a little chapel overlooking the lake as snowflakes fell softly from the sky. No, it wasn't near the Cottage Inn, but this facility is typical of the romantic accommodations that are so popular at Lake Tahoe.

You'll think you've stepped into a fairy tale when you arrive at The Cottage Inn at Lake Tahoe. The 15 gingerbread-type cottages were built in 1938 and are a holdover of the "old Tahoe"–style lodging, although they have been renovated with modern amenities. Each theme cottage has its own stone fireplace and knotty-pine paneling, and your fee includes a hearty breakfast, homemade cookies, and coffee.

Among the cottage offerings are Stagecoach Stop, Game Room, Rustic Retreat, Enchanted Cottage, Skier's Chalet, and Hunter's Hideout. The Old Fishin' Hole Cottage is recommended for fishermen and liars, the Tahoe Teepee Cottage has Native American decor and a lake view, and Romantic Hideaway features a natural-rock hot tub with waterfall. Whatever your mood, you should find a room to your liking.

Probably no other place in California has the variety of year-round activities that you'll find at Lake Tahoe. Within minutes, you can be boating, fishing, swimming, hiking, cycling, snowskiing, golfing, or even gambling. The summer is the busiest season at Lake Tahoe, but winter is also busy once the ski season begins. I have found June and September to be the best times for visiting; the masses of people are gone and the weather is gorgeous.

## Facilities

The Cottage Inn has 19 cabins for two people and two suites for 3–4 people. One cottage has kitchen facilities. All units have a fireplace. Breakfast, cookies, and coffee are provided. A private beach is available. The cottages are not suitable for children under age 12. Pets are not allowed. No smoking is permitted. Linens and towels are provided.

## Reservations and Rates

Reservations are recommended. The double-occupancy rate is $150–155 per night for a one-bedroom cottage, $179–210 per night for a cottage suite, and $245–255 per night for a deluxe suite. Additional people are $25 per night per person. There is a two-night minimum stay on weekends and a three-night minimum on holidays. Major credit cards are accepted. It's open year-round. Contact The Cottage Inn at Lake Tahoe, 1690 West Lake Boulevard, P.O. Box 66, Tahoe City, CA 96145, 530/581-4073 or 800/581-4073, website: www.thecottageinn.com.

## Directions

From Truckee, drive south on Highway 89 through Tahoe City. Continue south on Highway 89 for two miles to the inn on the left (lakeside).

# 12 TAHOMA MEADOWS BED AND BREAKFAST

West shore of Lake Tahoe, off Highway 89 in Tahoma

🏃 🚴 🏊 🛶 🚤 ❄️

**Luxury rating:** 3                                           **Recreation rating:** 4

The little red engine that could would fit right in among the little red cottages at Tahoma Meadows Bed and Breakfast. The cottages are all cute, quaint, and old-fashioned. Even when they compare the place to bigger, more modern resorts, some visitors prefer the comfort and feel of yesteryear that abounds here.

In addition to the bed-and-breakfast inn, there are six freestanding cottages with fully equipped kitchens. The Angler is a two-room cottage with fly-fishing decor and a claw-foot tub/shower, queen bed, and queen-size futon in the sitting room. The Boat House has a cream-colored interior, claw-foot tub/shower, queen bed, and trundle bed in the sitting room. There are two bedrooms in the Tree House, which has a fireplace, queen bed, two twin beds, and a futon in the living room; the cottage is cheerful and bright. Breakfast is not provided with a cottage rental.

The innkeeper is an avid fly fisher and is happy to give you current conditions and advice. This is a great place for cycling, since the trail from Tahoe City runs past the facilities. Rafting the Truckee River is popular in spring and summer, and many vacationers feel that their trip to the west shore isn't complete unless they've stopped to look at the giant trout at Fanny Bridge in Tahoe City.

## Facilities

Tahoma Meadows Bed and Breakfast has six cottages that can accommodate up to six people. There are also 10 duplex-style cottages. The cottages have fully equipped kitchens. Linens and towels are provided.

## Reservations and Rates

Reservations are recommended. The fee is $145–355 per night per cottage for up to four people; additional guests are $10 per night per person. The inn rooms are $95–199 per night and include breakfast. Rates for children are $10–20 per night. There is a two-night minimum stay during the summer season and a three-night minimum during the Christmas holiday. Major credit cards are accepted. It's open year-round. Contact Tahoma Meadows Bed and Breakfast, 6821 West Lake Boulevard, P.O. Box 810, Homewood, CA 96141, 530/525-1553 or 866/525-1553, website: www.tahomameadows.com.

## Directions

From Truckee, drive south on Highway 89 through Tahoe City. Continue south on Highway 89 for eight miles to the inn on the right, next to the big red-and-white barn.

# 13 TAHOMA LODGE

West shore of Lake Tahoe, off Highway 89 in Homewood

🥾 🚴 🏊 🛶 🏊 🐎 👪

**Luxury rating:** 3                              **Recreation rating:** 5

Tahoma Lodge is a good choice for a family or group vacation: you have access to a beach and pier, you have a pool, hot tub, basketball court, and play area, you have a choice of cabin sizes up to four bedrooms, and you have your pooch with you. Everybody's happy, right?

The location is a plus since it's halfway between the north and south shores, yet far enough away from Tahoe City to avoid the crowds and congestion that build up in those three areas. And in winter, you're a five-minute drive from Homewood ski and snowboard resort. When most people think of the old Tahoe, they think of the Homewood area.

And so it is with Tahoma Lodge, a not-so-fancy place with rustic cabins in a wooded setting. The accommodations are 1950s-style with a few updates; the decor is knotty pine, linoleum floors, metal roofs, and dark interiors. All of the cabins have a deck with barbecue and picnic table, television, telephone, and some have a fireplace or woodstove. For a large group, I suggest the Redwood unit, which has four bedrooms, sleeps nine, and includes a washer and dryer and a dishwasher.

The west shore is wonderful for cycling and hiking. A bike trail meanders for miles along the highway and lake from Tahoe City to Homewood. For hiking, the views along the Rubicon Trail in D.L. Bliss State Park are hard to surpass. You'll climb above Lake Tahoe for wide-open vistas of the lake and surrounding mountains and the clear, blue-green water and rocky shoreline below. Sit down on a rock for a snack or picnic lunch and you'll soon discover that this must be the chipmunk capital of California. Unbelievable how cute and quick the little ones are to steal your heart—and lunch.

## Facilities

Tahoma Lodge has 10 cabins with fully equipped kitchens. Barbecues are provided, and most units have a deck or porch and fireplace or woodstove. A heated pool (summer only) and basketball court are available. The cabins are suitable for children. Leashed pets are allowed with permission. No smoking is permitted. Linens and towels are provided.

## Reservations and Rates

Reservations are recommended. The fee is $155–355 per night per cabin; it's slightly higher for holidays, but there are discounts for the off-season. Major credit cards are accepted. It's open year-round. Contact Tahoma Lodge, 7018 West Lake Boulevard, P.O. Box 72, Tahoma, CA 96142, 530/525-7721 or 866/819-2226, website: www.tahomalodge.com.

## Directions

From Truckee, drive south on Highway 89 through Tahoe City. Continue south on Highway 89 for approximately eight miles to the lodge.

# 14 MEEKS BAY RESORT AND MARINA

West shore of Lake Tahoe, off Highway 89 near Tahoma

**Luxury rating:** 3                                     **Recreation rating:** 5

Meeks Bay Resort has developed into its own micro-universe at Lake Tahoe—it has a little bit of every-thing. At the heart of the resort are eight cabins, 12 condo-style units, a campground, and the awesome Ke-hlet Mansion. Most of the cabins have lake views, and the deck at the mansion extends over the water.

As you likely guessed, the cabins can be on the pricey side, and with a one-week minimum stay during the peak season (early July to early September), the pretty two-story jobs will set you back better than a grand. The cheapest you can get still costs $650.

But what the heck, life ain't a dress rehearsal, right? You're better off spending it on yourself and your family than at the casinos, and here you get vacation grounds set on the threshold of outstanding boating, swimming, biking, and hiking. Although the resort does not rent boats, it does have a concrete boat ramp that provides powerboats with access to nearby Emerald Bay to the south, the prettiest spot on the prettiest lake in California. A great beach and a roped-off swimming area are within a short walking distance of the cabins.

A trailhead for access to Eldorado National Forest and the Desolation Wilderness (a wilderness permit is required for overnight use) is across the highway from the re-sort. The famed West Shore Bicycle Path is nearby to the north.

## Facilities

Meeks Bay Resort and Marina has eight cabins in a variety of sizes, each with a bath and kitchen with cookware and utensils. There are also 12 condo-style units; Washoe

House, which sleeps 10; and Kehlet Mansion, which sleeps 12. Amenities include a small general store, campground, beach, roped-off swimming area, boat ramp, and marina with boat rentals. No pets are permitted. No smoking is allowed. Linens and towels are provided.

## Reservations and Rates

Reservations are recommended. Cabins rent for $120 per night for studios, $240 per night for one-bedroom and two-bedroom; rates are higher in July and August, lower in May, June, September, and October. Weekly rates range $1,350–1,825. A three-night minimum occupancy is required from the July 4 weekend through Labor Day. Contact Meeks Bay Resort and Marina, 7941 Emerald Bay Road, P.O. Box 787, Tahoma, CA 96142, 530/525-6946 or 877/326-3357, website: www.meeksbayresort.com. Bike rentals are available through West Shore Sports, 530/525-9920. Fishing charters are available in Tahoe Vista through Mac-A-Tac Charters, 530/546-2500.

## Directions

From Truckee, take the Highway 89 exit and drive to Tahoe City. Continue south on Highway 89 for 10 miles to Meeks Bay Resort at 7941 Emerald Bay Road (on the lake side of the road).

## 15 RICHARDSON'S RESORT
### Off Highway 89 near South Lake Tahoe

**Luxury rating:** 3                                    **Recreation rating:** 5

The cabins at Richardson's Resort are set amid a thin pine forest, creating an airy feel. The cabins are also within walking distance of Lake Tahoe. The camp-like setting can make it feel as if you are far away from the masses. Yet in truth you are only minutes away from many attractions. These include a great paved bicycle trail, mountain biking in a national forest, skiing at Heavenly in the winter, and gambling at the casinos year-round.

On the southwest shore of Lake Tahoe, Richardson's Resort is a perfect location for all kinds of outdoor recreation. Add 40 cabins, many with great lake views, and you have a recipe for one fantastic vacation. The cabins are rustic, complete with knotty-pine ceilings, and most have woodstoves. The resort is completely self-contained, so you don't have to drive anywhere once you get here.

A great three-mile bike route runs right through the resort, then loops around the lake for another three miles, almost all of it perfectly flat for easy biking. Depending on your level of fitness and ambition, you can extend mountain bike trips for miles and miles into the adjoining Eldorado National Forest.

In the winter, the same routes make for some of the best cross-country skiing available anywhere, crowned by awesome lake views. The experience is absolutely wondrous at night under a full moon.

Top it off with a dinner at the south shore's only lakeside restaurant, Beacon Bar & Grill (530/541-0630), and a night in your cabin, and you've got the entire package. No extra pushing needed.

## Facilities
Richardson's Resort has 40 cabins (19 are open year-round), each with a bathroom, kitchen, and woodstove with gas heater. A boat ramp, boat rentals, and marina are within walking distance. Bike rentals are also available. A grocery store is on the property, and a lakefront restaurant offers lunch and dinner. In the winter, sleigh rides and cross-country skiing take place at the resort. No pets are allowed. Linens and towels are provided, with maid service available for an extra charge.

## Reservations and Rates
Reservations are required. In the summer, cabin fees range $635–1,935 per week. Discount rates are offered in the winter, along with a reduced two-night minimum stay on weekends. A special ski package is offered in the winter and includes lift tickets, lodging, light breakfast, skier gift package, and discount coupons for dinner. Contact Richardson's Resort, P.O. Box 9028, South Lake Tahoe, CA 96158, 530/541-1801 or 800/544-1801, website: www.camprichardson.com.

## Directions
From Sacramento, take U.S. 50 to South Lake Tahoe. At the junction of U.S. 50 and Highway 89, turn north on Highway 89 and drive 2.5 miles to the resort on the right side of the road.

# 16 ZEPHYR COVE RESORT                    BEST (
South Tahoe, Nevada, off U.S. 50 near Stateline

**Luxury rating:** 3                                    **Recreation rating:** 5

A heavenly force casts a spell over many visitors at Lake Tahoe. Your heart opens to Lake Tahoe because of its immense scope and cobalt-blue waters set in high mountains. Add cabins with views of the lake, a mile of sandy beach, a one-minute walk to a marina with boat rentals, paddleboats, and headquarters for the Tahoe cruise ship MS *Dixie II,* and you can figure out why Zephyr Cove Resort has become one of the most popular spots in South Tahoe.

If you rent a cabin at Zephyr Cove, you can park your car and hide the key for as long as you stay. Zephyr Cove Resort is on the Nevada side of the south shore, just over four miles from Stateline. It offers 28 cabins of different sizes, most with a bath and kitchenette, but all are within a minute's stroll of the lakeshore and beach. Some of the cabins have lake frontage, and, of course, some are closer to the water than others.

The resort has a mile of beach frontage. Got that? A mile of beach frontage! At Tahoe? At Tahoe! This is where sand is about as valuable as gold. Like I said, it takes only about a minute to walk from the cabins to the beach. Now remember: What did I tell you to do with your car keys?

The adjacent marina provides a huge variety of water sports activities, including the lake's famous tour on the giant paddleboat MS *Dixie II*. At the marina, also within a very short walking distance, you can rent paddleboats or boats with motors, or arrange a fishing trip.

One of the best fishing spots for big mackinaw trout is at the southern end of the lake, just offshore of the casinos at a place called "the Nub." Even though the lake bottom is about 750 feet deep in this area, the Nub rises up like a giant dome to 160 feet deep, with its 50-yard crown covered with weeds and grass. This is where the big mackinaw hide out, and right at dawn, if you troll a minnow or J-Plug over the top of the grass, you have the chance of catching some huge trout.

## Facilities

Zephyr Cove Resort has 28 cabins of different sizes, each with a bath and most with a kitchenette. Five lodge rooms are also available. A small general store, restaurant, bar, and a marina with boat rentals, paddleboats, and Lake Tahoe tours on the MS *Dixie II* are available. There's a campground with both RV and tent sites. Pets are permitted, $15 per night. Linens and towels are provided.

## Reservations and Rates

Reservations are often required. Fees range $119–469 per night for cabins, depending on the number of people and size of the cabin. Rooms at the lodge range $69–139 per night, with discounts available in the off-season. Contact Zephyr Cove Resort, P.O. Box 830, Zephyr Cove, NV 89448, 775/589-4906 or 800/238-2463, website: www.tahoedixie2.com.

## Directions

From Sacramento, take U.S. 50 east and continue for 100 miles to Stateline. Continue on U.S. 50 past Stateline for 4 miles and look for the sign for Zephyr Cove Lodge on the left side of the street. Turn left (before the traffic signal) and park at an area just off the highway. Walk a short distance on a sidewalk to the resort office for check-in.

# **17** LAZY S LODGE
South shore of Lake Tahoe, off Highway 89

**Luxury rating:** 2                                              **Recreation rating:** 4

You could stay here for weeks and not run out of different activities for each day—and each night. Most of them require a short drive, walk, or bike ride. But isn't that lucky for you when you're in such a beautiful mountain setting next to one of the world's most beautiful lakes?

The accommodations are plain and simple: 1950s-era with some updating in the 1960s and 1970s. The two-room cottages have fully equipped kitchens, and some have fireplaces. The studio rooms have a wet bar, microwave, and refrigerator. The rectangular pool is big enough for lap swimming, and there's also a hot tub and large lawn area with tables and barbecue. Tall trees surround the lodge.

You're five miles from Heavenly Valley ski resort, and at least four other major ski resorts are within an hour's drive—perfect for a winter vacation. And in the summer, boy oh boy, do you have choices. You're just down the road from the south shore of Lake Tahoe, which has plenty of fine beaches, miles and miles of biking and walking paths, fishing and boat cruises, golfing, horseback riding, and some excellent hiking trails. Did I forget anything? Oh, yes, if you're so inclined and feel lucky, there are gambling casinos and plenty of nightlife in town.

You could do all of this, or then again, you could be lazy and do nothing but sit in a chaise lounge next to the pool at the Lazy S Lodge.

## Facilities
Lazy S Lodge has 20 cottages and studio rooms. The cottages have fully equipped kitchens, and the studios have kitchenettes with microwave, refrigerator, and wet bar. A heated pool, hot tub, picnic tables, and barbecues are available. The lodge is suitable for children. Pets are not allowed. Smoking is not permitted. Linens and towels are provided.

## Reservations and Rates
Reservations are recommended. The fee is $109–149 per night per cottage and $69–99 per night per inn room. Rates are higher during holidays. Rollaway cribs are $10 per

night. Ski packages are available. Major credit cards are accepted. The lodge is open year-round. Contact Lazy S Lodge, 609 Emerald Bay Road, South Lake Tahoe, CA 96150, 530/541-0230 or 800/862-8881, website: www.lazyslodge.com.

## Directions
In South Lake Tahoe at the junction of Highway 89 and U.S. 50, turn north on Highway 89 and drive one mile to the resort on the right.

# 18 ANGORA LAKES RESORT
Upper Angora Lake, South Tahoe, off Highway 89 near Fallen Leaf Lake

**Luxury rating:** 2                                                    **Recreation rating:** 5

For many people, a vacation at Angora Lakes is perfection. Unfortunately, perfection has its price. About the only way to reserve a spot here is to call in January for the coming summer and get on the cancellation waiting list.

It can take a long time on the waiting list to finally get a chance to stay at a cabin here. There are just eight of them, relatively primitive at that, but they are remote and situated on a pristine lake surrounded by Eldorado National Forest, so remote that a shuttle ride is provided for cabin guests.

The resort is absolutely beautiful. The water often seems to be almost as blue as Lake Tahoe, circled by both beach and boulders, and backed by forest. The boulders are perfect for making flying leaps into the lake for swimming if you can stand the cold water. Little rowboats are available for cruising around, the trout fishing is decent, although the fish are often small, and the hiking in the area is excellent.

But trying to get a reservation will turn even the most die-hard Tahoe lover into a prisoner of hope. First off, there is a carryover list of guests who stay here for a week each year; that locks up most of the cabins for the summer. Those left are snatched up by people on a waiting list compiled over the winter, or when there is a rare cancellation. Your best bet is to make contact with the staff at Angora Lakes Resort in January, ask for a waiting list form, fill it out, send it in, and start hoping.

Rarely do you come across a place so worth the wait. Angora Lakes is one of those places.

## Facilities
Angora Lakes Resort has eight cabins of varying design and size. Each has a kitchen, electricity, hot shower, and chemical toilet. No pets are permitted. No smoking is allowed. Rowboats are available for rent. No linens, towels, or laundry facilities are provided.

## Reservations and Rates
Reservations are required, and signing up on a cancellation list is an option. Cabin rates range $900–1,000 per week, depending on the size of the cabin. Contact Angora

Lakes Resort, P.O. Box 8897, South Lake Tahoe, CA 96158, 530/541-2092 (summer) or 805/545-9332 (winter).

## Directions
From Sacramento, take U.S. 50 east to the Highway 50/89 split in South Lake Tahoe. Turn north on Highway 89 to Fallen Leaf Lake Road. Turn left on Fallen Leaf Lake Road and drive up the hill for 2 miles. When the road forks, bear left for 0.25 mile to Forest Service Road 12N14. Bear right and drive 2.3 miles (past the Angora Fire Lookout) to the end of the road and a parking lot. A 0.5-mile shuttle ride to the cabins is available for guests and their gear; otherwise you must make the short hike uphill.

## 19 ECHO LAKE CHALET
Echo Lake, South Tahoe, off U.S. 50 near Echo Summit

**Luxury rating:** 3                                          **Recreation rating:** 5

Echo Lakes is an exquisite place—a high, blue, beautiful alpine lake set in granite and surrounded by forest. Here you will find 10 old cabins in only fair shape but with decks, great views, and such a beautiful setting that you may feel as if you have been deposited in heaven.

At an elevation of 7,500 feet in a canyon near Desolation Wilderness, it's not far from Echo Summit off U.S. 50. The lake is shaped like an hourglass, with the lower portion best for waterskiing. Boats are run in a clockwise direction around the lake. The upper portion is quiet, sprinkled with a few little islands, and is the choice for fishing and low-speed boating, like paddling in a canoe during an awesome evening sunset. The one problem at the lake is the wind in the early summer; it can absolutely howl out of the west in the afternoon.

A great adventure is to take the hiker's shuttle boat to the head of Upper Echo Lake. From there it is a fantastic hike on the Pacific Crest Trail into Desolation Wilderness, with rock-sprinkled Aloha Lake the primary destination. This is a relatively easy day hike, seven miles round-trip. There are several other lakes along the way, as well as long-distance views to the east of Echo Lakes and, once over the pass, heading north, to the east of the back side of Mount Tallac and to the west of Desolation's bare granite slopes.

For a short walk with a great view from the chalet, walk across the dam; from there, a short hike climbs up to the right. It ends with a great view of South Lake Tahoe, from the valley on out to the lake.

Fishing is good at Echo Lakes, with most anglers trolling to catch rainbow trout. The best bite is at dawn, when the lake is glassed out, and when the pools from rising trout can look like raindrops. It is one of the most beautiful places on earth.

## Facilities
Echo Lake Chalet has nine cabins with bathrooms. All but one have kitchenettes,

cookware, and utensils. A boat ramp, dock, and rental boats are nearby, as well as a small store. Small, quiet, clean pets are permitted with prior approval and $200 deposit, and must be attended at all times. Linens and towels are provided.

## Reservations and Rates

Reservations are required. Cabin rates range from $90 per night for two to $139 per night for four, and from $474 per week to $834 per week; chalet 11 for two plus a futon is $195 per night or $1,170 per week. It's open Memorial Day weekend to mid-September depending on snow conditions. Contact Echo Lake Chalet, 9900 Echo Lakes Road, Echo Lakes, CA 95721, 530/659-7207, website: www.echochalet.com.

## Directions

From South Lake Tahoe, drive south on Highway 89 for five miles to U.S. 50. Drive west on U.S. 50 for 5.5 miles to the signed turnoff for Echo Lakes on the right (one mile west of Echo Summit). Turn right and drive 0.5 mile on Johnson Pass Road to Echo Lakes Road. Turn left and drive 1 mile to a series of parking lots. Continue 0.25 mile down the hill to the Echo Lake Chalet and marina.

# 20 SORENSEN'S RESORT

Toiyabe National Forest, off Highway 88 in Hope Valley

**Luxury rating:** 4                                                          **Recreation rating:** 4

It might seem like a pipe dream to imagine a place in the high Sierra where log cabins are set amid pines and firs, with a pretty stream within walking distance and several lakes nearby for first-rate fishing.

In Hope Valley, this pipe dream is a reality at a place called Sorensen's Resort—although it is really more of a cabin village than a resort. Here you can make your base camp, using one of the cabins as your retreat, then spend as much time as you wish exploring the area by hiking or fishing at great recreation destinations such as the West Fork Carson River, Caples Lake, or the Pacific Crest Trail, among many.

Hope Valley is along Highway 88, the winding two-laner that rises out of the Central Valley at Stockton. This is the little highway that passes Lower Bear River Reservoir, Silver Lake, and Caples Lake before finally rising over Carson Pass and being routed down into Hope Valley. Here at 7,000 feet is Sorensen's, and once you set up shop in one of its cabins, you probably won't feel like going home for a long time.

There are 33 cabins, including 10 gorgeous log cabins. All but 3 have kitchens, but none have telephones or televisions to disrupt your stay. The walls are thick, and it is usually quiet, so you don't lose the sense of mountain solitude. A small but outstanding restaurant is at lodge headquarters, and in the summer an outside deck is available for dining.

Because of the high elevation, there is often snow here from late November or early December through May. This appeals to skiers in the winter, and Kirkwood Ski Area is about 15 miles west off Highway 88.

You don't have to go far for a pretty walk or fishing. Just across the road from Sorensen's is a meadow and the West Fork Carson River, which provides an easy hike and also fair fishing for rainbow trout. Several quality lakes dot the area. The best for fishing are Caples Lake, 12 miles west, and Blue Lakes, off Blue Lakes Road 12 miles east. Other nearby lakes include Woods Lake, Red Lake, Kirkwood Lake, Burnside Lake, and Tamarack Lake.

My favorite hike starts at Carson Pass, elevation 8,540 feet, at the trailhead for the Pacific Crest Trail. Heading north, the trail is routed up over a mountain rim for about two miles, with a great view below of Caples Lake. After you top the rim, the Upper Truckee River Canyon comes into view to the north along with the headwaters for the Truckee River, and if you look to the far north, you can make out giant Lake Tahoe, an unforgettable scene.

## Facilities

Sorensen's Resort has 33 cabins of various sizes, including 10 log cabins; 30 have kitchens. All provide electricity; cabins do not have telephones or televisions. Pets are permitted in selected units. No smoking is permitted, and there is a $500 fine for violations. Linens and towels are provided.

## Reservations and Rates

Reservations are recommended. Cabin fees range $115–175 for two-person cabins, $135–225 for four-person cabins, and $155–210 for six-person cabins. Log cabin fees range $175–275 per night. Discounts are available for off-season and midweek stays. A two-night minimum stay is required on weekends. Contact Sorensen's Resort, 14255 Highway 88, Hope Valley, CA 96120, 530/694-2203 or 800/423-9949, website: www.sorensensresort.com.

## Directions

From Sacramento, drive east on U.S. 50 for about 90 miles to the U.S. 50 junction with Highway 89. Turn right (south) on Highway 89 and drive over Luther Pass to Highway 88. Turn left (east) on Highway 88 and drive 1 mile to Sorensen's Resort on the right side of the road.

From Stockton, drive east on Highway 88 for about 110 miles, passing through Jackson and Kirkwood and over Carson Pass. When you reach the Highway 88 and Highway 89 junction, continue straight on Highway 88 for 1 mile to Sorensen's Resort.

# 21 CAPLES LAKE RESORT

Eldorado National Forest, off Highway 88 near Kirkwood

🚶 🚴 🛶 ⛴ ❄ 👥

**Luxury rating: 3**                                      **Recreation rating: 5**

Some people complain that they have "No place to go, nothing to do." Then I ask them, "Have you been to Caples Lake?" They usually respond with a look that resembles a deer staring into headlights. With its blue-green waters surrounded by forest at 7,800 feet with a backdrop of high wilderness peaks, Caples Lake is not only pretty, but the cabin rentals and huge array of outdoor recreation possibilities can make any vacation seem far too short. The cabins are open year-round, offering boat and bike rentals and horseback riding in the summer and snowshoes in the winter. Kirkwood Ski Area is only a few miles away.

Caples Lake Resort overlooks pretty Caples Lake, set in the high alpine country near Carson Pass. There is a beautiful view of the lake and mountains from the second floor of the lodge. The cabins have furnished kitchens, modern bathrooms, wall heaters, and bedding, and in winter, the fireplaces add a great touch. Note that Cabins 2, 3, and 5 are closest to the lake. Lodge rooms are also available and have been remodeled with private bathrooms across the hall. Two bonuses here are a dry sauna heated by a woodstove (a real plus in cold weather) and an on-site restaurant. A small marina provides boat rentals: 12- and 14-foot aluminum motorboats for fishing, as well as canoes and paddleboats.

Of the half dozen lakes in the immediate area, Caples provides not only the most consistent trout fishing, but typically the biggest fish as well. Several trails from the resort are great for biking or horseback riding. Several wilderness trails (no bikes allowed) begin nearby. The best two short hikes are from Woods Lake to Round Top Lake and from Carson Pass to Winnemucca Lake, both about four miles round-trip.

## Facilities

Caples Lake Resort has eight cabins that vary in size. Each has been remodeled to provide a private bathroom. Full kitchens with cookware, utensils, and gas stoves are provided, and a boat dock, ramp, small marina, and small store are available nearby. The lodge holds six guest rooms. You can rent boats, bikes, horses, and, in the winter, snowshoes. No pets are allowed. No smoking is allowed. Linens and towels are provided.

## Reservations and Rates

Reservations are recommended. Cottage rates are $90–360 per night, depending on the size of the cabin, number of people, day of the week, and season. Contact Caples Lake Resort, P.O. Box 88, Kirkwood, CA 95646, 209/258-8888, website: www.capleslakeresort.com.

## Directions

From Jackson, drive east on Highway 88 for 63 miles to Caples Lake, about 1.5 miles past the turnoff for Kirkwood. Turn right at the sign for Caples Lake Lodge.

# 22 KIT CARSON LODGE
### Eldorado National Forest, off Highway 88 near Silver Lake

🏃 🚴 🏊 🚣 👫

**Luxury rating:** 3                                         **Recreation rating:** 5

© NAOMI BRAZIER GILGERT

The cabins at Silver Lake look so perfect that upon first sight, you might think they are private retreats for a few lucky rich folks. Guess again. They are private retreats all right, but for anybody who wants to rent them.

There are a lot of Silver Lakes in California and all of them are beautiful, but this one might just be the most special. This Silver Lake is at 7,200 feet on the western slopes of the Sierra Nevada along Highway 88; it's pretty and blue, surrounded by granite and national forest, and well-stocked with trout. It is one of several lakes in the immediate region, along with Caples Lake, Woods Lake, Red Lake, and Kirkwood Lake, all within a few miles. With relatively short drives, you can also reach Frog Lake, Blue Lakes, Burnside Lake, and Lost Lakes to the east.

And like I said, the cabins look perfect, sprinkled about the forest along the lake's northern shore. Although they are well-equipped, it is critical that you remember to bring your own towels and dish soap because they are not provided. Several cabins have lake frontage, including Beaver, Eastern Brook, Black Bear, and Wolf, and most of the others have lake views. The view from Eastern Brook cabin, for instance, is very beautiful, with little islands in the foreground and a sky painted that magic deep blue you see only in the high country. Silver Lake laps at the shore a short distance from your front porch.

Since this is the high country, expect extraordinary amounts of snow and ice in rough winters. In typical years, Silver and the nearby lakes start melting off their ice between May and early June, with enough snowmelt in the adjacent forest for the lakes to become accessible by Memorial Day weekend.

Kit Carson Lodge provides boat rentals, but this country is suited for visitors to bring their own car-top boat, such as a canoe. With a canoe you can lake-hop for days, hitting them all—fishing, paddling, and playing.

This is also an excellent area for hiking, with several great trails available, including the short wilderness hike to Winnemucca Lake.

## Facilities

Kit Carson Lodge has 19 cabins in a variety of sizes and accommodations. Bathroom, full kitchen with utensils, fireplace, gas stove, and deck are included in each cabin.

Amenities include boat rentals, a boat dock, a small beach, and a swimming area. A store, a post office, and a coin laundry are nearby. No pets are permitted. No smoking is allowed. Linens are provided but towels, dish soap, and toiletries are not.

## Reservations and Rates

Reservations are recommended and required for discounted rates. Rates range $795–1,590 per week during summer. Prior to June 10 and after September 4, nightly rentals are available and rates range $85–240 per night, with discounts for midweek stays. Contact Kit Carson Lodge, Kit Carson, CA 95644, 209/258-8500 (summer), 530/676-1370 (winter—November–May), or at 4521 Holiday Hill Court, Shingle Springs, CA 95682, website: www.kitcarson lodge.com.

## Directions

From Jackson, drive east on Highway 88 for 50 miles to Silver Lake. Turn at the signed entrance road for Kit Carson Lodge.

## 23 KAY'S SILVER LAKE RESORT

Eldorado National Forest, off Highway 88 near Kirkwood

**Luxury rating:** 3 **Recreation rating:** 4

You want a pretty Sierra mountain lake offering fishing, hiking, and boating, and a rustic mountain cabin to go along with it? Then stop here. You'll find a traditional mountain getaway next to Silver Lake, a classic granite cirque just below the Sierra ridge at 7,200 feet.

© PENNY HUTCHINSON

The cabins come in three sizes: studio, one-bedroom, and two-bedroom. All have fully equipped kitchens, private bathrooms, and decks. The studio cabins also have a living room with double bed. With a one-bedroom cabin, add a bedroom and daybed. The two-bedroom cabins include a dining area, large living area with two daybeds, and another bedroom. A big plus is the gas heating in these cabins, since the temperatures can fluctuate greatly at this elevation.

Winter weather sometimes requires guests to walk in up to 200 yards uphill to the cabins; a trail is not maintained. If you have to hunker down during a storm, you'll be relieved to know that the resort has a store with basic supplies. Kirkwood Ski Area is a 10-minute drive east on Highway 88; downhill and cross-country skiing are available, as is snowmobiling.

During warmer weather at Silver Lake, you can rent 13-foot aluminum boats with 7.5 horsepower motors; a boat launch is available. The fishing is good. A great hike starts at the trailhead on the east side of the lake; it's a two-mile tromp to little Hidden Lake, one of several nice hikes in the area.

## Facilities

Kay's Silver Lake Resort has nine cabins with fully equipped kitchens and private bathrooms. Fire pits, gas heating, and decks are provided. A small store, bait and tackle, boat rentals, and boat launch are available. The resort is suitable for children. Pets are not allowed. Smoking is permitted. One set of linens and towels is provided; there is a $1.50 fee for each extra set. There is no daily maid service.

## Reservations and Rates

Reservations are recommended. The fee is $75–185 per night per cabin and $435–960 per week. There is a two-night minimum stay most of the year and a three-night minimum on holidays. No credit cards are accepted. Kay's is open year-round. Contact Kay's Silver Lake Resort, 48400 Kay's Road, Pioneer, CA 95666, 209/258-8598, website: www.kaysresort.com.

## Directions

From Jackson, drive east on Highway 88 for 52 miles to the resort on both sides of the road.

## 24 BEAR RIVER LAKE RESORT                    BEST (
Bear River Reservoir, off Highway 88 in Eldorado National Forest

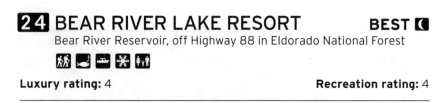

**Luxury rating:** 4                                      **Recreation rating:** 4

As you venture into the mountains on Highway 88, heading east "up the hill," Bear River Reservoir is the first of three quality mountain lakes you come to (Silver Lake and Caples Lake are the other two). For many, there is no need to drive further. This place has most everything you could want.

With a lower elevation—5,900 feet—Bear River Reservoir has an advantage over Silver and Caples Lakes. The ice here melts off sooner, and correspondingly, the spring trout stocks and fishing get going earlier, too. Yet the lake is high enough on the Sierra slopes to often get a ton of snow, creating outstanding winter recreation, including 75 miles of snowmobile trails and many snow-play areas.

Bear River Lake Resort is a complete vacation service lodge that makes a superb headquarters for a vacation getaway. The cabins are not true luxury, but they provide everything: a kitchen with all the goodies, private bedroom with fresh linens, and full bathroom. The cabins are above the west shore of the lake.

The reservoir covers 725 acres and is in a canyon on the edge of the national forest. It was put on the map because of its fishing, often excellent for rainbow, brown, and brook trout. The cobalt-blue lake gets a double-barreled dose of trout, receiving plants from both the Department of Fish and Game and the private resort here, which adds bonus trophy fish. You get the picture: lots of fish. Almost every week, someone catches a trout in the 5- to 10-pound class.

## Facilities

Bear River Lake Resort has nine deluxe cabins that sleep four. Each includes a bedroom, additional fold-out bed in the living room, full bathroom, full kitchen, and cooking utensils. A playground, volleyball, beach area, and a game room are available for children. A boat ramp, a grocery store, boat rentals, a restaurant, and a cocktail lounge are nearby. In winter, snowmobile service is available. No smoking is permitted. Pets are allowed with prior approval. Linens and towels are provided.

## Reservations and Rates

Reservations are recommended. Double-occupancy rates range from $94 per single night to $498 per week. There is a $5 charge per night for additional guests and a $100 damage deposit. Major credit cards are accepted. The resort is open year-round (call for access conditions in winter). Contact Bear River Lake Resort, 40800 Highway 88, Pioneer, CA 95666, 209/295-4868, fax 209/295-4585, website: www.bear-riverlake.com.

## Directions

From Stockton, drive east on Highway 88 for about 80 miles to the lake entrance on the right side of the road. Turn right and drive 2.5 miles to a junction (if you pass the dam, you have gone 0.25 mile too far). Turn left and drive 0.5 mile to the entrance on the right side of the road.

# 25 LAKE ALPINE LODGE AND CABINS

Stanislaus National Forest, off Highway 4 near Bear Valley

**Luxury rating: 3**                                        **Recreation rating: 5**

One of the Sierra Nevada's great summer jewels is Lake Alpine and its cabins, campsites, and lodge, as well as the hiking, fishing, and many other nearby adventures. Though hardly a secret, it still gets missed by many simply because it is on Highway 4, near Bear Valley/Mount Reba, rather than on either the I-80 or U.S. 50 corridor to Reno and Tahoe.

The lake is at 7,320 feet and covers 180 surface acres, high enough in the mountains to capture the best of the Sierra, small enough to keep the setting quiet and intimate, and big enough for low-speed boating and for the trout to grow.

All the cabins at Lake Alpine Lodge and Cabins have lake views and are within walking distance of the lake. It's not quite like finding your own Golden Pond, because the cabins are on a sloping hillside on the opposite side of the highway from the lake, but that is actually a bonus, since the distance provides privacy and quiet from the activity at the lake.

Hiking in the area is outstanding. Most visitors take two hours and hike completely around the lake, a flat four-mile trip, which was recently widened, ending conflicts among low-speed hikers, shoreline anglers, and high-speed cyclists. But better trails are available. One is the 1.3-mile climb to Osborne Ridge (the trailhead is just east of Silver Tip Campground), where you get a gorgeous view of the lake and into the Carson-Iceberg Wilderness. If you like views, this one is a must. Another must is the 1.5-mile tromp to Duck Luck (trailhead at Silver Valley Campground), a tiny, picturesque setting with some old pioneer cabins along the route. The ambitious can extend the hike into the adjacent Carson-Iceberg Wilderness to Rock Lake, a pristine lake with clear, blue water set in granite; it's an eight-mile round-trip hike.

Alpine Lake is an ideal lake for a small boat; there's a good boat ramp, and a 10-mph speed limit keeps the lake quiet. In other words, there are no Jet Skis or similar personal watercraft, no water-skiers, and no big, fast boats. Just folks putting around, trolling, and sometimes paddling canoes or oaring small inflatable rafts.

## Facilities

Lake Alpine Lodge and Cabins has six bedroom cabins and three studio cabins. All cabins have at least two beds. Most include a bathroom with shower, a refrigerator, cookware, barbecue, and decks. Tent cabins with fewer amenities are also available. A nearby lodge provides a small store, bar, and restaurant. Pets are permitted only in tent cabins and must be on a leash or in a kennel. Linens are provided.

## Reservations and Rates

Reservations are recommended. Cabin rentals are priced $110–215 per night for two people, $10 for each additional person. Contact Lake Alpine Lodge and Cabins, P.O. Box 5300, Bear Valley, CA 95223, 209/753-6358, website: www.lakealpinelodge.com.

## Directions

From Stockton, turn east on Highway 4 and drive into the Sierra Nevada. Continue east past Arnold about 25 miles to Lake Alpine (on the right) and Lake Alpine Lodge (on the left).

# Other Cabins & Cottages in the Region

**Loon Lake Chalet and Robbs Hut,** Eldorado National Forest, Information Center, 3070 Camino Heights Drive, Camino, CA 95709, 530/644-6048; Eldorado National Forest, Pacific Ranger District, 530/644-2349.

**Shinneyboo Creek Cabins,** 11820 Eagle Lakes Road, Soda Springs, CA, 530/587-5160, website: www.shineyboocreek.com.

# SAN FRANCISCO BAY AREA

COURTESY OF DILLON BEACH RESORT

## BEST CABINS & COTTAGES

◖ **Best for Beach Access**
Dillon Beach Resort, **page 222**

◖ **Most Romantic**
Dancing Coyote Beach, **page 223**

◖ **Most Luxurious**
Manka's Inverness Lodge, **page 224**

◖ **Best for Water Sports**
Snug Harbor Resort, **page 235**

◖ **Best for Families**
Costanoa, **page 236**

**It's ironic that many people who have chosen to live** in the Bay Area are often the ones who complain the most about it. I've even heard some say, "Some day I'm going to get out of here and start having a good time."

I wish I could take anyone who has ever had these thoughts on a little trip in my airplane and circle the Bay Area at 3,000 feet. What you see is that despite strips of roadways and pockets of cities where people are jammed together, most of the region is wild, unsettled, and beautiful. There is no metropolitan area in the world that offers better and more diverse recreation and open space so close to so many.

The Bay Area has 150 significant parks (including 12 with redwoods), 7,500 miles of hiking and biking trails, 45 lakes, 25 waterfalls, 100 miles of coast, mountains with incredible lookouts, bays with islands, and in all, 1.2 million acres of greenbelt with hundreds of acres being added each year with land bought by money earmarked from property taxes. The land has no limit. Enjoy it.

Along with the unique recreation possibilities here comes unique lodging. I discovered rustic cabins at Mount Tamalpais and others nearby on an ocean bluff . . . the opportunity to stay overnight on a yacht in San Francisco's Fisherman's Wharf and Oakland's Jack London Square . . . romantic cabins in the North Bay foothills and Point Reyes National Seashore . . . tent cabins at Big Basin Redwoods, the region's number-one hiking park . . . and park-model cabins in the San Joaquin Delta within walking distance of private docks and boating.

Note that proximity to a metropolitan area means two things: the demand is higher and the price is higher. So plan ahead and don't expect the midweek or off-season deals that are common in more rural areas.

The Bay Area encompasses many world-class landmarks. San Francisco alone holds the Golden Gate Bridge, Fisherman's Wharf, Alcatraz, Ghirardelli Square, Chinatown, Pacific Bell ballpark, the Crissy Field waterfront, cable cars, South Beach, Fort Point, the Cliff House and Ocean Beach, and Fort Funston.

In fact, instead of going far away for a vacation, residents of the Bay Area might consider what so many do from all over the world: stay and discover the treasures in your own backyard.

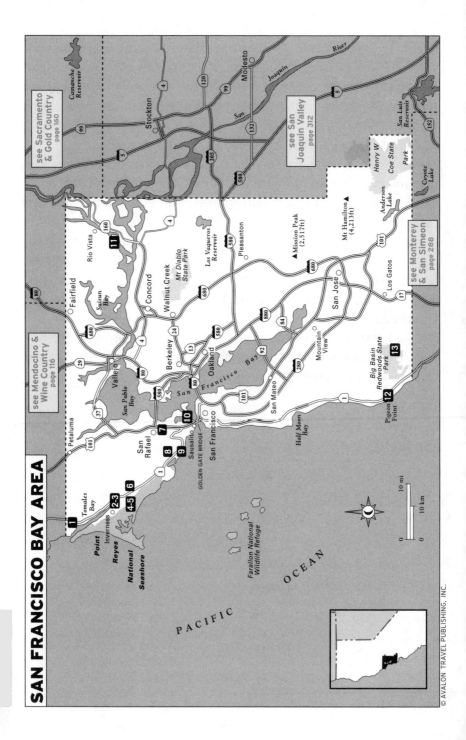

SAN FRANCISCO BAY AREA

see Sacramento & Gold Country page 160

see Mendocino & Wine Country page 116

see San Joaquin Valley page 312

see Monterey & San Simeon page 288

Camanche Reservoir

Modesto

San Joaquin River

Stockton

San Joaquin

San Luis Reservoir

Coyote Lake

Henry W Coe State Park

Anderson Lake

Mt Hamilton (4,213ft) ▲

Mission Peak (2,517ft) ▲

Rio Vista

Fairfield

Suisun Bay

Concord

Walnut Creek

Mt Diablo State Park

Los Vaqueros Reservoir

Pleasanton

Los Gatos

Big Basin Redwoods State Park

Berkeley

Oakland

San Francisco Bay

San Jose

Mountain View

Vallejo

San Pablo Bay

San Francisco

San Mateo

Half Moon Bay

Pigeon Point

Petaluma

San Rafael

Sausalito

GOLDEN GATE BRIDGE

Tomales Bay

Point Reyes National Seashore

Inverness

Farallon National Wildlife Refuge

PACIFIC OCEAN

10 mi

10 km

© AVALON TRAVEL PUBLISHING, INC.

# San Francisco Bay Area Cabins & Cottages

# 1 DILLON BEACH RESORT

BEST ☾

Dillon Beach, off Highway 1 near Tomales

**Luxury rating: 3**                          **Recreation rating: 4**

It doesn't take long to become enchanted with Dillon Beach, the oceanside community at the mouth of Tomales Bay. The cottages here provide sweeping ocean views, access to excellent beach walks, clamming (in season), beachcombing, and boat rentals just a mile away. If you can arrange to stay at Dillon Beach Resort during the week, do so; although this area is a popular Bay Area spot for weekend getaways, during the week the place attracts relatively few people. The cottages are furnished with everything but food and drink. That means you can relax in comfort; that is, unless you're out adventuring.

Weather is always a wild card, with fog common in the summer. But no matter how rough the ocean is, Tomales is often surprisingly calm, sheltered from west winds by Inverness Ridge at Point Reyes National Seashore. That makes Tomales Bay great for sea kayaks and small boats.

Other great features include some of the best clamming beds on the Bay Area coast. It requires a short boat ride to reach the best areas. Boat rentals and detailed where-to-go information are available nearby at Lawsons' Landing (707/878-2443). The best times are always during the minus low tides that arrive about every two weeks from late fall through winter to early spring.

## Facilities

Dillon Beach Resort has three cottages. Dillon Beach Property Management has 25 vacation homes. All are completely furnished, including kitchens with cookware and utensils. A grocery and tackle store is available. Pets are permitted by prior approval. Linens and towels are provided.

## Reservations and Rates

Reservations are recommended. The rate is $250–330 per night for up to six people. A two-night minimum stay is required on weekends. Off-season discounts are available. Contact Dillon Beach Resort, P.O. Box 97, Dillon Beach, CA 94929, 707/878-2094, website: www.dillonbeachresort.com. For vacation home rentals, contact Dillon Beach Property Management, P.O. Box 151, Dillon Beach, CA 94929, 707/878-2204 or 800/447-3767, website: www.DillonBeach.com.

## Directions

In Petaluma on U.S. 101, take the East Washington Boulevard exit and drive west (it turns into Bodega Avenue) for 10 miles to Tomales Road (there is a turn lane). Turn left at Tomales Road (if you reach the town of Two Rock, you've gone a mile too far) and drive 6 miles to the town of Tomales at Highway 1. At the stop sign, turn right on Highway 1 and drive 0.25 mile to Dillon Beach Road. Turn left on Dillon Beach Road and drive 4 miles to Dillon Beach Resort.

# 2 DANCING COYOTE BEACH                                    BEST ☾
Point Reyes, off Highway 1 in Inverness

🏃 🚲 🛶 🐕

**Luxury rating:** 3                                        **Recreation rating:** 3

A romantic getaway about an hour from San Francisco? Private deck and beach access? Fireplace? And it costs as little as $125 per night? No way!

Yes, you better believe it. It's Dancing Coyote Beach in Inverness, close to Point Reyes, where four adjoining cottages are about 50 feet from the beach with bay views. These are older units that have been renovated with a modern, open look on the inside.

Three of the two-story cottages are identical and have cathedral ceilings, private deck, bedroom, living area, kitchen, fireplace, and skylights. The Sky Cottage has the same amenities, plus a sleeping loft with fireplace and picture window the width of the loft, with a view of the bay. There's also an enclosed, private shower on the deck that is popular with guests. You'll find your refrigerator stocked with food items to cook yourself a full breakfast each day, and several restaurants are nearby.

Guests have access to a private, sandy beach. Inverness is a sleepy little village with an ideal location for exploring Tomales Bay and Point Reyes National Seashore. This area is good for hiking, biking, bird-watching, whale-watching, beachcombing, or reading and relaxing.

## Facilities

Dancing Coyote Beach has three adjoining cottages with fully equipped kitchens and private bathrooms, and the additional deluxe "Owners Cottage" which is occassionally available. Decks, fireplaces, and food items to prepare a full breakfast are provided. Barbecues are available near the beach; they are not allowed on the decks. Pets are allowed in one cottage with prior permission. No smoking is permitted. Linens and towels are provided.

## Reservations and Rates

Reservations are recommended. The fee is $100–250 per night per cottage for two people, plus $25 per person per night each additional person. There is a two-night minimum stay on weekends. Weekly rates are available. Credit cards are not accepted. Contact Dancing Coyote Beach, P.O. Box 98, Inverness, CA 94937, 415/669-7200.

## Directions

From U.S. 101 in Marin, take the San Anselmo/Sir Francis Drake Boulevard exit and drive west for about 20 miles to Highway 1 at Olema. Turn right (north) on Highway 1 and drive 2.3 miles to Sir Francis Drake Boulevard. Turn left and drive 3.5 miles to Inverness. Continue driving for about 100 yards to the cottages on the right at 12794 Sir Francis Drake Boulevard.

## 3 MANKA'S INVERNESS LODGE                    BEST (

Point Reyes, off Highway 1 in Inverness

**Luxury rating:** 4                              **Recreation rating:** 4

Call it rustic and elegant. Call it quirky and cozy. Call it upscale and inviting. Most people just call it Manka's Inverness Lodge.

The former hunting and fishing lodge has been transformed into one of the most romantic lodging facilities in the Bay Area. The owners say they have a simple formula: great beds, blazing fires in the lobby and in the cabins, deep reading chairs, a long wine list and a short menu, indulgent baths, quiet nights, and windows with a view of either the water or the woods. And guess what? It works.

Manka's offers two cabins, eight lodge rooms, and a suite on-site, as well as three cabins off-site. These are not ordinary cabins and rooms, though. Depending on your rental, your furnishings could include a buffalo or bear rug, antiques, unpeeled cypress or four-poster log bed, white linen curtains, plaid bedding, or stuffed animals.

The Boathouse is a restored boathouse that was built in 1911. It stands over Tomales Bay, with large decks, two bathrooms, a living room, and a two-room den. Perched over the Boathouse is the Boatman's Quarters, with fantastic views, a fireplace, and a deck with outdoor shower. Both are two blocks from the lodge.

There's also the Chicken Ranch, a renovated rose- and vine-trellised cottage from the mid-1800s, officially recognized as the oldest home in western Marin County. Originally, this building was a hunting cabin; it became part of a chicken ranch in the late 1800s. You'll feel like you've entered a time machine when you stay here. This cottage is one mile from the lodge.

The most popular cabin, by far, is the Fishing Cabin; it can take months to garner a reservation for this one. When I shot an episode of my TV show, *The Great Outdoors with Tom Stienstra,* on Point Reyes, I was lucky enough to snag it. The owners refer to this cabin as "rustic luxury," and I agree. You'll sleep in a king-size bed with a bear rug at your feet, sit in an overstuffed down and feather couch or hickory chairs in front of the ocean-rock fireplace, shower or take a hot tub on your private deck, and admire the old fishing memorabilia.

One last bit: Manka's has a superb restaurant (open for dinner Thursday–Monday only and open daily for breakfast for lodge guests only), with an assortment of unusual game entrées and an extensive wine list.

## Facilities

Manka's Inverness Lodge has two cabins, eight lodge rooms, and a suite on-site, and three cabins off-site. Full bathrooms and fully equipped kitchens are provided in two of the cabins but not in the lodge rooms. A fireplace, oversized tub or claw-foot tub, deck, and hot tub are provided in some of the rentals. There are no telephones or televisions in the rooms, but stereo/CD systems are provided. A restaurant is available. The lodge is not suitable for children. Leashed pets are allowed. No smoking is permitted. Linens and towels are provided.

## Reservations and Rates

Reservations are required. The fee is $365–565 per night per cabin, $215–385 per night for lodge rooms, and $315 per night for the suite. The pet fee is $50 per night per pet. There is a two-night minimum stay on weekends. Major credit cards are accepted. Contact Manka's Inverness Lodge, P.O. Box 1110, Inverness, CA 94937, 415/669-1034 or 800/58-LODGE (800/585-6343), website: www.mankas.com.

## Directions

From U.S. 101 in Marin, take the San Anselmo/Sir Francis Drake Boulevard exit and drive west for about 20 miles to Highway 1 at Olema. Turn right (north) on Highway 1 and drive 2 miles to Sir Francis Drake Boulevard. Turn left and drive 4 miles to Inverness. Continue one block to Argyle Way. Turn left and drive 150 feet up the curving hill road to the lodge on your right.

# 4 HOLLY TREE INN
### Point Reyes, off Highway 1 in Inverness

**Luxury rating:** 4                           **Recreation rating:** 4

So you want to be close to Point Reyes National Seashore, but you don't want to camp and you don't want a motel room? At the Holly Tree Inn, you can have your own cottage with kitchen and hot tub, and you're only one mile from the Bear Valley Visitors Center at Point Reyes.

This is a bed-and-breakfast inn with four rooms in the main house, a charming cottage on-site, and two additional cottages nearby. The private and cheerful Cottage in the Woods is on the grounds; it's a two-room retreat featuring a king-size bed, vaulted ceiling, pine floors, woodburning stove, hot tub, and an old-fashioned bathtub. A complimentary breakfast is included.

Sea Star Cottage is a few miles down Sir Francis Drake Boulevard at the end of a—er, dock. Yup, the cottage is at the end of a 75-foot dock, resting on stilts over the edge of Tomales Bay, complete with water and mountain views, including of Mount Tamalpais to the south. The little house contains a living room, kitchen, solarium with hot tub, queen-size four-poster bed draped in white linen, fresh flower arrangements, and complimentary breakfast.

A 20-minute drive from the inn is Vision Cottage, a two-bedroom cabin good for families and groups. Set beneath an old growth forest of Bishop pines, the cottage features two decks and floor-to-ceiling windows in the living room that provide a forest view. Other amenities include a fully equipped kitchen and a refrigerator stocked nightly with a fully prepared breakfast for you to heat up in the morning. You'll also have use of a gas log fireplace, hot tub, queen-size beds, down comforters, and handmade quilts. From the front door, you can walk down the path straight to Shell Beach at Tomales Bay, 1.3 miles downhill.

## Facilities

Holly Tree Inn has one on-site cottage, two off-site cottages, and four inn rooms. Fully equipped kitchens are provided in the off-site cottages, and a complimentary full breakfast is prepared and placed in the cottage refrigerators the night before. The on-site cottage does not have a full kitchen, but breakfast is brought to the front door. A private bathroom with shower is included in all units. Fireplace, hot tub, and patio are available in some of the rentals. Although the inn can accommodate children, the facilities are more suitable for adults. Pets are not allowed. No smoking is permitted. Linens and towels are provided.

## Reservations and Rates

Reservations are recommended. The fee is $190–265 per night per cottage, $130–180 for inn rooms. For more than two in a cottage, it's $30 per person per night for ages 12 and over and $15 per person per night for children under age 12. There is a two-night minimum stay on weekends. Major credit cards are accepted. Contact Holly Tree Inn, P.O. Box 642, Point Reyes Station, CA 94956, 415/663-1554 or 800/286-4655, website: www.hollytreeinn.com.

## Directions

From U.S. 101 in Marin, take the San Anselmo/Sir Francis Drake Boulevard exit and drive west for about 20 miles to Highway 1 at Olema. Turn right (north) on Highway 1 and drive 0.2 mile to Bear Valley Road. Turn left on Bear Valley Road and drive approximately 2 miles to Silverhills Road. Turn left and drive a short distance to the inn at 3 Silverhills Road.

# 5 GRAY'S RETREAT AND JASMINE COTTAGE

Point Reyes, off Highway 1 in Inverness

**Luxury rating:** 3          **Recreation rating:** 3

This place has such a secret location that the innkeeper refuses to give detailed directions until you've made reservations. Karen Gray says that privacy is the key element at the three lodging options here—Gray's Retreat, Jasmine Cottage, and a barn loft—situated on five acres and two miles from the entrance station to Point Reyes National Seashore.

Gray's Retreat is a country home with a fully equipped kitchen that sleeps up to six comfortably but can also accommodate larger groups. The home is ideal for a family, and pets are allowed. Nine-foot-high French doors and windows frame the view of Point Reyes to the west and Elephant Mountain to the east. A fireplace, barbecue, two patios, small library of Point Reyes writings, telephone, and television with VCR are provided. A high chair, jogger stroller, and children's books and games are available.

Jasmine Cottage has a romantic, intimate feel and can house up to four. You'll be surrounded by bouquets of flowers, candles on the table, a library, and a double hammock outside. Although there is a fully equipped kitchen, complimentary continental breakfast is delivered to the cottage. A fireplace, shared garden hot tub, laundry room, porch, and outdoor furniture are provided, but there are no telephones or televisions.

The barn loft has the best views on the compound, and guests enjoy the spectacular sunsets from this vantage point. Amenities include a sleeping loft with skylight, a tiny kitchen, complimentary continental breakfast, tea, and coffee, and a shared garden patio with hot tub. Wander around outside and you'll probably be greeted by the neighboring donkeys. The loft can sleep four people when the sofa bed is used.

For details about Point Reyes National Seashore, refer to the description for Point Reyes Seashore Lodge (see next listing).

## Facilities

Options at Gray's Retreat and Jasmine Cottage include a house, a cottage, and a barn loft; each comes with a fully equipped kitchen and private bathroom. The facilities are suitable for children. Well-behaved pets are allowed. No smoking is permitted. Linens and towels are provided.

## Reservations and Rates

Reservations are required. The double-occupancy rate is $145 per night for the barn loft, $220 per night for Jasmine Cottage, and $245 per night for Gray's Retreat. The seventh night is free, and additional guests are $15 per night per person. PortaCribs are provided for infants. The pet fee is $50 per stay for perfectly behaved dogs by prior approval. There is a two-night minimum stay on weekends and a three-night minimum on holidays. Major credit cards are accepted. Contact Gray's Retreat and Jasmine Cottage, P.O. Box 56, Point Reyes Station, CA 94956, 415/663-1166, website: www.jasminecottage.com.

## Directions

Directions are provided after reservations are confirmed; the innkeeper insists on privacy for guests.

# 6 POINT REYES SEASHORE LODGE
### Point Reyes, off Highway 1 in Olema

**Luxury rating:** 4          **Recreation rating:** 4

This lodge is well known to Point Reyes National Seashore visitors because they travel right past the inn on their way to the park entrance. But what is somewhat secret is that there are two cottages available. These private hideaways can sleep 4–6 people and have kitchens and spas. The two-acre property is filled with gardens, a lawn, curving pathways, and serene sitting areas. No, you won't be roughing it here.

Creekside Cottage is on Olema Creek and has a garden patio, bedroom, sofa sleeper, and television with VCR. Casa Olema is a historic building with living room, dining area, loft bedroom, television with VCR, large spa, and sleeping room for six. The decor is traditional and upscale. A restaurant is available if you don't feel like cooking.

Point Reyes Seashore Lodge is only 35 miles north of San Francisco, but it seems like you're a thousand miles from the hubbub of a city. You're midway between Tomales Bay and Stinson Beach, and the Bear Valley Visitor Center at Point Reyes is only a few miles away. Some activities at the park you shouldn't miss are viewing the tule elk at Pierce Point, visiting the old lighthouse, and hiking or biking, on the lookout all the while for the unusual white deer. For swimming or beachcombing, check out Heart's Desire Beach.

## Facilities

Point Reyes Seashore Lodge has two cottages and 21 inn rooms. Fully equipped kitchens and private bathrooms are provided in the cottages. Amenities include a restaurant, recreation room with pool table, and reception and conference facilities. The inn is suitable for children. Pets are not allowed. No smoking is permitted. One lodge room is wheelchair accessible. Linens and towels are provided.

## Reservations and Rates

Reservations are recommended. The fee is $295 per night per cottage, $135–230 per night for inn rooms, plus $25 for each additional person per night, $5 per night for children under age 12. Major credit cards are accepted. Contact Point Reyes Seashore Lodge, 10021 Coastal Highway 1, P.O. Box 39, Olema, CA 94950, 415/663-9000 or 800/404-5634 (California only), fax 415/663-9030, website: www.pointreyesseashore.com.

## Directions

From U.S. 101 in Marin, take the San Anselmo/Sir Francis Drake Boulevard exit and drive west for about 20 miles to Highway 1 at Olema. Turn right (north) on Highway 1 and drive approximately 150 feet to the lodge on the left side of the road.

# 7 GERSTLE PARK INN

San Francisco Bay, off U.S. 101 in San Rafael

**Luxury rating:** 4                                    **Recreation rating:** 3

Tucked into a hill in the heart of San Rafael is an inn with cottages that will take you back in time to the 1880s, then return you to the present. Gerstle Park Inn is a two-acre estate with a Craftsman-style home and former carriage house, barn, and cottage that have all been renovated with modern amenities, yet still retain the charm of yesteryear. The property contains a fruit orchard, and large trees are dotted around the buildings. The inn caters to vacationers as well as business travelers.

The former carriage house contains two suites, Sunrise and Sunset, about 50 yards from the inn. Both suites have a fully equipped kitchen, a living room, and a bedroom. The units share a garden patio with chaise lounges. Sunrise is decorated in shades of soft green, black, and white and features a pair of French doors that open from the living room. Sunset's decor is in earthtones and blue, with French doors that lead to a deck overlooking the garden.

Garden Cottage is a former barn, but you'd never guess that now. It houses a living room, bedroom, and galley kitchen with old-style marble countertop. The color scheme features dark and medium blues, and Adirondack chairs outside the cottage face the garden.

By far the most popular cottage is two-story Orchard, which is the most secluded lodging on the property. Downstairs, you'll find a living room with queen sofa bed, a galley kitchen, and a breakfast nook. Upstairs is a bedroom with queen-size bed, vaulted ceiling and deck, and a bathroom with tub/shower and skylight. The decor is country French with a color scheme of cream, rose, and light blue.

Eight suites are inside the inn, where a full complimentary breakfast is served each morning and wine is provided later in the day. The innkeeper has managed to combine old-fashioned comfort with modern sophistication, using a combination of antiques and upscale, traditional decorating. Gerstle Park is in the same neighborhood as the inn and offers trails, redwood trees, and a tennis court. You're only a short walk to downtown San Rafael, although once inside the grounds, you'll feel like you're miles away.

## Facilities

Gerstle Park Inn has two cottages, two suites in a carriage house, and eight inn rooms. The cottages and carriage house suites have fully equipped kitchens and private bathrooms. Telephones, televisions with VCR, and modem hookups are provided. Complimentary full breakfast and beverages are provided. A video library is available. Although the inn can accommodate children, it is more suitable for adults. Pets are not allowed. No smoking is permitted. Linens and towels are provided.

## Reservations and Rates

Reservations are recommended. The double-occupancy rates are $189–275 per night for the cottages and $179–245 per night for the inn rooms. Additional guests are $25 per night per person. A two-night minimum stay is required, and a three-night minimum stay is required on holidays. Major credit cards are accepted. Contact Gerstle Park Inn, 34 Grove Street, San Rafael, CA 94901, 415/721-7611 or 800/726-7611, website: www.gerstleparkinn.com.

## Directions

From U.S. 101 in Marin, drive north to the Central San Rafael exit. Turn left on 4th Street and drive 0.5 mile to D Street. Turn left and drive 0.2 mile to San Rafael Avenue. Turn right and drive a short distance to Grove Street. Turn left and drive approximately 300 feet to the inn on the right.

# 8 WEST POINT INN

Mount Tamalpais, off Highway 1 near Mill Valley

🚶 🚴 ❄️

**Luxury rating:** 1                                                   **Recreation rating:** 5

---

The primitive wood cabins at West Point Inn provide one of the Bay Area's lesser-known and yet most spectacular hideaways. The lodge is high on the south face of Mount Tamalpais (a.k.a. Mount Tam) in Marin. Hikers and bikers who frequent the trails know West Point Inn as the place to get lemonade on Sunday. But the refreshing drink isn't the best thing going for the inn—it is the series of woodsy, rustic cabins and inn rooms (all without electricity) that are available for lodging. The experience is a lot like camping—just throw out your sleeping bag.

The inn's location near the 2,571-foot summit of Mount Tam makes for breathtaking views and sunsets, and the nearby trail system is among the best in the Bay Area for hiking and biking. The inn is on the dirt railroad grade running up Mount Tam. In fact, most find it for the first time as a rest stop while exploring the nearby trails and fire roads on foot or bicycle. West Point Inn is a historic structure, constructed in 1904 to serve customers of the Mount Tamalpais and Muir Woods Railroad. Except for occasional repairs and paint, the inn has not changed much in the past century; it's still without electricity, though a commercial gas-powered kitchen is provided for groups who rent the entire inn.

If you want to check the place out before deciding to book a trip, drive up to the Pantoll parking area and trailhead at Mount Tamalpais State Park. From here, it's a two-mile hike to the inn. Note that it is also accessible out of Rock Springs trailhead and that mountain bikers must take fire roads to reach the inn. If there's a trick, it's to get your reservation in early. Reservations are accepted 90 days in advance, and the openings go fast.

Although temperatures are not usually cold, I have heard complaints that it can feel cold. That's because a marine layer off the ocean can pour moist, dense air across the lower slopes of the mountain. So bring a few warm layers and a good sleeping bag, of course.

That same weather phenomenon creates some of the most magical views in the Bay Area. When a layer of fog encroaches on the coast, the summit of Mount Tam often pokes through the top of the fog layer like an island. From the summit, looking out to the west, the fog appears as a pearlescent sea that extends forever. Yet at the same time, looking east, the bay can look something like the Mediterranean Sea, cobalt blue, sprinkled with islands. Every sunset from this vantage point is memorable.

The hiking and biking are outstanding, with many great trailheads. East Peak is a 330-foot climb to the Mount Tam summit. From Pantoll parking lot, a four-mile round-trip leads into Steep Ravine (stream canyon), and an eight-mile round-trip goes out Matt Davis/Coastal Trail (coastal views).

Rock Springs offers a two-mile round-trip trek to O'Rourke's Bench and Barth's

Retreat (coastal views). For a series of cascades in a wooded canyon, take Laura Dell Trail, a 2.5-mile round-trip to Cataract Falls.

Finally, a three-mile round-trip on Main Trail and Hillside through Muir Woods encompasses giant redwoods, a creek, and the forest slope.

## Facilities

West Point Inn has five cabins and seven inn rooms. Beds, a large full kitchen, and outside chemical toilets are available. No electricity is provided and smoking and candles are prohibited. Bring a sleeping bag, flashlight, and food. No pets are permitted. No linens are provided.

## Reservations and Rates

Reservations are required for weekends, available up to 90 days in advance. The fee is $35 per night, $17.50 for those under 18, and $700 for groups reserving the entire inn (for private parties of up to 20 people; no weddings, receptions, bachelor parties, or beer kegs). Payment is required in advance. No refunds or changes are allowed. West Point Inn is open for lodging Tuesday–Saturday nights. A parking permit is required at Pantoll or Rock Springs at Mount Tamalpais State Park. Contact West Point Inn, 1000 Panoramic Highway, Mill Valley, CA 94941, 415/646-0702 (24-hour recorded reservation line) or 415/388-9955; Mount Tamalpais State Park, 801 Panoramic Highway, Mill Valley, CA 94941, 415/388-2070; or California State Parks, Marin District, 415/893-1580.

## Directions

From U.S. 101 in Marin, take the Stinson Beach/Highway 1 exit. Drive west for 1 mile to the stoplight at the T intersection with Highway 1/Shoreline Highway. Turn left and drive 2.5 miles uphill to Panoramic Highway. Bear right and continue up the hill for 5.5 miles to Pantoll. Turn left at the Pantoll parking area and ranger station. Hike about 2 miles to West Point Inn (cyclists must take the old Railroad Grade).

# 9 STEEP RAVINE CABINS

Mount Tamalpais State Park, off Highway 1 near Stinson Beach

**Luxury rating:** 1          **Recreation rating:** 4

This is one of the best cabin deals in California—$75 a night for a rustic cabin on an ocean bluff overlooking the Pacific Ocean.

First, you must schedule your stay as far ahead as possible—reservations are available seven months in advance. For a weekend in August, for instance, you can book your trip in January. Do that and you get a cabin. Do anything else and you stand a chance of missing out.

The cabins are at Rocky Point on the Marin Coast, close enough to hear the waves. These are primitive cabins, but at least firewood for the stove is available. You must bring everything else: sleeping bag, pillow, lantern, flashlight, food, and anything else to keep you satisfied. Officially, they are called environmental campsites. A gate on the access road, on the ocean side of Highway 1, keeps the camp secluded and relatively hidden from many people.

There are passing ships, fishing boats, and lots of marine birds, especially in the summer when pelicans and murres are abundant. On clear days, the sunsets can be breathtaking. In the winter, you might even spot passing whales, noticeable by their spouts, which look like little puffs of smoke.

There are two beach walks from the cabins. The closest is down to the cove just north of Rocky Point and to Redrock Beach. The walk is short, with the trail routed right out of the camp. The other trail is on the south side of Rocky Point and reaches a tiny but secluded beach. To get there, you walk back up the access road, turn right, then look for the trail on the right down to the cove.

The trailhead for the gorgeous Steep Ravine Trail is across the highway from the gated access road, with a small jog to the right.

## Facilities

Steep Ravine has 10 cabins, each with a woodstove, picnic table, and flat wood surface for sleeping. There are also six walk-in campsites. Piped water and firewood are available. No pets are allowed. Linens and towels are not provided. Bring your own sleeping bag and pillow.

## Reservations and Rates

Reservations are required (call 800/444-7275 or visit website www.ReserveAmerica.com); when you call for reservations, ask for Mount Tamalpais State Park Environmental Campsites at Steep Ravine. The cabin fee is $75 per night; walk-in campsites are $15 per night. Contact Mount Tamalpais State Park, 801 Panoramic Highway, Mill Valley, CA 94941, 415/388-2070; or Marin District Headquarters, 415/893-1580. A map/brochure of Mount Tamalpais State Park is available at the Pantoll Ranger Station or by mail from the address above. A more detailed hiking map of the area is available for a fee from Olmsted Brothers Map Company, P.O. Box 5351, Berkeley, CA 94705.

## Directions

From U.S. 101 in Marin, take the Stinson Beach/Highway 1 exit and continue to the coast at Muir Beach overlook. Turn north on Highway 1 and drive about four miles to the Rocky Point access road (gated) on the left side of the highway. Directions on how to get through the gated access road are included in the reservation confirmation.

# 10 CASA MADRONA

San Francisco Bay, off U.S. 101 in Sausalito

**Luxury rating:** 4                                               **Recreation rating:** 3

Not sure what type of lodging you want? At Casa Madrona in downtown Sausalito you have a choice: cottage, casita, or hotel room. You also get to choose from a wide selection of theme decorations, amenities, and prices—all with San Francisco Bay views. And there's even a full-service European day spa on the premises.

Imagine a beautiful hillside retreat with fireplace and kitchen, watching the yachts sail by from your deck—a peaceful, terraced setting just steps away from a 100-year-old Victorian mansion housing all the hotel services you might want. At Casa Madrona, this dream can come true.

The Painter's Cottage, which sleeps four, has a Norman Rockwell theme and includes an easel, paints, and brushes. The Calico Cabin has yellow gingham bedding, pine furniture, a porch, a window seat, and a woodburning stove. In La Tonnelle Cottage, you'll find a tiled tub for two, a wood-burning stove, rattan furniture, and a garden patio.

The hotel's philosophy is to give guests a "small oasis of tranquility" next to a hectic urban setting.

## Facilities

Casa Madrona has a mix of 63 cottages, casitas, and hotel rooms. All include private bathrooms. A deck or porch is provided, and some rentals have a fireplace or wood-stove. Some of the cottages have fully equipped kitchens. Complimentary breakfast and an evening wine and cheese social hour are provided. A restaurant, hot tub, full-service European day spa, catamaran cruises, and conference and reception facilities are available. The cottages are suitable for children; the hotel is not. Pets are not allowed. No smoking is permitted. Some facilities are wheelchair accessible. Linens and towels are provided, and there is maid service twice a day.

## Reservations and Rates

Reservations are recommended. The double-occupancy rate is $255–440 per night, plus $25 per night per additional person. Children under age 12 stay free. A two-night, midweek romantic getaway package is available. Major credit cards are accepted. Contact Casa Madrona, 801 Bridgeway, Sausalito, CA 94965, 415/332-0502 or 800/567-9524, website: www.casamadrona.com.

## Directions

From San Francisco, drive north on U.S. 101 across the Golden Gate Bridge. After crossing the bridge, exit on Alexander Avenue (first exit after the bridge crossing). Bear right on Alexander Avenue (it becomes Bridgeway Road) and drive two miles to Sausalito. Continue a short distance to the hotel on the left.

## **11** SNUG HARBOR RESORT                    BEST **◖**
Ryer Island, the Delta, off Highway 12 near Rio Vista

**Luxury rating:** 4                                        **Recreation rating:** 5

If you want a romantic vacation getaway, go for the one-bedroom Snuggle Inn. If you've got a big family or group, or just need some space, go for Snuggle Inn Number 1. But do plan ahead—these units book quickly for the summer.

© STEPHANI STIENSTRA

Now, you ask, what the heck is a Snuggle Inn?

A Snuggle Inn is a park-model cabin set on prime waterfront land. Park-model cabins have been built off-site and then transported to the resort; they are small, cozy, clean, and comfortable. Snug Harbor also offers a large four-bedroom, two-bath modular home on a peninsula. The units are designed for those who want to have the feel of camping with the comforts of home. The place has a diverse clientele because it is so well suited for a family outing, a romantic getaway, or a boating or fishing adventure.

Snug Harbor is unique in many ways, and it starts with the trip here. Most visitors will need to take one of the cabled ferry rides to reach Ryer Island. So from the start, you are off the beaten path. Yet it's a nice place, with clean cabins, full-service marina, and an excellent location to explore the boating paradise of the Delta. The waterfront sites with docks give Snug Harbor the feel of a Louisiana bayou. Snug Harbor is an excellent location for fishing and water sports, especially waterskiing. Anglers will find good prospects for striped bass, largemouth bass, and catfish.

## Facilities

Snug Harbor has 18 cabins in varying sizes and a four-bedroom modular home with decks. All have furnished kitchens and bathrooms. Restrooms, hot showers, an RV dump station, a convenience store, a swimming beach, a children's play area, a boat launch, paddleboats, propane gas, and a full-service marina are available. Some facilities are wheelchair accessible. There are also waterfront sites for RVs or tents. Pets are allowed in select units only for $2 per day, plus a $50 deposit. No smoking is allowed in the Snuggle Inns. Towels and sheet sets are not included.

## Reservations and Rates

Reservations are recommended and a deposit is required. Rates range from $100 per night for a cabin for 2 to $380 per night for a cabin for 14. Extra charges apply if a cleanup is required. Other fees include $10 for boat launch and $10 for day-use visitors. Major credit cards are accepted. It's open year-round. Contact Snug Harbor Resort, 356 Snug Harbor Drive (Ryer Island), Walnut Grove, CA 95690, 916/775-1455, website: www.snugharbor.net.

## Directions

From San Francisco, take I-80 to Fairfield and Highway 12. Turn east on Highway 12 and drive to Rio Vista and Front Street. Turn left on Front Street and drive under the bridge to River Road. Turn right on River Road and drive two miles to the Real McCoy Ferry (signed Ryer Island). Take the ferry across the Sacramento River to Ryer Island and Levee Road. Turn right and drive 3.5 miles on Levee Road to Snug Harbor on the right.

## 12 COSTANOA                                           BEST ⊆

On Highway 1 near Año Nuevo

**Luxury rating:** 3                                **Recreation rating:** 5

Costanoa sits on hillside bluffs overlooking the ocean, just east of Highway 1 near Año Nuevo State Reserve and the San Mateo and Santa Cruz county line. Costanoa works as a vacation getaway because of the overnight accommodations. They feature 89 canvas bungalows with ocean views, deluxe-style lodge rooms and suites, and campsites for tents and RVs with hookups. Everything is deluxe, including an on-site store and restaurant.

When you arrive, you first notice the wood-tailored lodges and outbuildings, and that everything looks clean and new. That's because it is. The place opened in 1999, so it's one of the state's newest resort operations. Next you notice that the hillsides are peppered with little white canvas bungalows—which means you share no walls with other visitors—with ocean views from nearly everywhere on the property. A camp loop accommodates RVs and tents.

Several excellent mountain-bike rides, hikes, and wildlife-viewing spots are within short range. From the resort itself, the Whitehouse Creek/Ohlone Ridge Trail provides an easy loop hike, about 1.5 miles, for ocean views from a sub-ridge. On the west side of the highway, Atkinson Bluff Trail extends on the cliff-edge overlooking the beach and is routed in a loop out to Franklin Point and past a secluded beach and tidepools. Hikes lead through redwoods and to a ridge with long-distance views at Butano Redwoods State Park to the north.

A great mountain-bike ride can be accessed from nearby Gazos Creek Road to the north. This dirt road extends nine miles into a redwood-filled canyon, climbing much of the way, before hitting a gate that blocks vehicles. But the road then rises up and meets the China Grade, the fire road that extends to a fork to the Butano Rim to the north and all the way to Highway 9 to the southeast. This is one of the most challenging mountain-bike networks in the Bay Area, and yet with access to some of the region's wildest and prettiest lands.

The famous elephant seal tours are also available from mid-December through March, though hundreds of resident elephant seals remain year-round at Año Nuevo State Reserve to the south. Horseback riding, sea kayaking, and sailboarding are also options.

## Facilities
Costanoa has 89 canvas bungalows, cabins, deluxe lodge rooms, campsites for tents and RVs. There's a central restroom and shower area for each group of bungalows. Lodge rooms are five-star accommodations. Linens and towels are provided in lodge rooms and available for a fee for others. Amenities include a restaurant, café, small store, picnic area, spa with massage service, Wi-Fi, comfort stations with fireplaces, a sauna, hot tubs, private indoor and outdoor showers, bathrooms with showers, and heated floors. Pets and smoking are prohibited.

## Reservations and Rates
Canvas bungalows range $115–145 per night, cabins are $170–185 per night, lodge rooms cost $195–255, and a lodge suite goes for $300–350. For example, the Cypress bungalows provide a queen bed with heated mattress pad, electricity, a bathroom, towels, access to an outdoor hot tub, a breakfast buffet, and maid service; the rate is $115 per night on weekdays, $130 for weekends. Mountain bikes can be rented for $15 per hour, $45 per day; horseback riding costs $75 per 90-minute guided ride; and sea kayaks and sailboards can be rented by appointment off-site. Contact Costanoa, 2001 Rossi Road, Pescadero, CA 94060, 650/879-1100 or 877/262-7848, website: www.costanoa.com.

## Directions
From Half Moon Bay, take Highway 1 south and drive 26 miles (9 miles past the turnoff for Pescadero Road) to Rossi Road. Turn left and go 0.5 mile to parking.

# 13 BIG BASIN REDWOODS STATE PARK
Big Basin, off Highway 9 near Boulder Creek

**Luxury rating:** 1      **Recreation rating:** 5

This beautiful state park in the Santa Cruz Mountains has tent cabins available for rent, which means that you can just pick up and go without elaborate planning. The cabins are on a loop road near Huckleberry Camp, well spaced in a towering redwood forest.

Made out of wood and canvas, the tent cabins measure 12 by 14 feet and feature two full-size beds, a table, and a woodstove. If you visit during cold weather, bring a stack of firewood with you to keep warm. Duraflames, Presto Logs, and other artificial logs are not permitted; bundles of firewood (five or six small logs) are sold at $7.75 a whack at the park's General Store, but they provide warmth for only a few hours. Most visitors bring a sleeping bag, lantern, cooking gear, cooler, and firewood.

Big Basin, of course, is best known for its giant redwoods, Berry Creek Falls (a 70-foot waterfall), and excellent hiking trails. The 90 miles of hiking routes cross a largely untouched landscape; the highlight is the 4.7-mile trip (one-way) to Berry Creek Falls, a beautiful silver cascade falling under a redwood canopy. This rivals Point Reyes National Seashore as the Bay Area's best hiking parkland.

The forest is very quiet out here and sound really carries, so a quiet time at the campground is enforced 10 P.M.–8 A.M.

## Facilities

Big Basin Redwoods State Park has 35 tent cabins, each with two full-size beds with mattress pads, a table, bench, and woodstove. A picnic table, food locker, and fire pit with grill are outside each cabin. There are two restrooms nearby, one with a coin-operated shower and another with a coin-operated washer and dryer. A stocked camper store is at park headquarters. Lanterns can be rented for $6 per night and small bundles of firewood are available for $7.75 each at the Big Basin Store. Restaurants are available in Boulder Creek. Linens are not provided. Bring your sleeping bag or rent bedding for $10 per stay.

## Reservations and Rates

Reservations for cabins are required (call the tent cabin host at 800/874-8368). The fee is $50 per night per cabin. Additional vehicles are $6. Contact Urban Parks, 21600 Big Basin Way, no. 4, Boulder Creek, CA 95006, website: www.bigbasintentcabins.com. To contact Big Basin Redwoods State Park, phone 831/338-8860.

## Directions

From Santa Cruz, turn north on Highway 9 and drive approximately 12 miles to Boulder Creek. At Boulder Creek, turn left on Highway 236 and drive about 10 miles to the entrance sign for Big Basin Redwoods State Park. Continue for 1.5 miles, turn right at the sign for Huckleberry Campground, drive 0.25 mile, and then turn right again at the access road for campsites 6–41. The camp host is at site 7 in a small trailer.

# Other Cabins & Cottages in the Region

**Lundborg Landing,** P.O. Box 220, Bethel Island, CA 94511, 925/684-9351, website: www.lundborglanding.com.

**San Francisco North/Petaluma KOA,** 20 Rainsville Road, Petaluma, CA 94952, 707/763-1492, website: www.koa.com.

# YOSEMITE AND MAMMOTH

COURTESY OF TUOLUMNE MEADOWS LODGE

## BEST CABINS & COTTAGES

# Some of nature's most perfect artwork has been

created in Yosemite and the adjoining eastern Sierra near Mammoth Lakes, as well as some of the most profound natural phenomena imaginable.

Yosemite Valley is the world's greatest showpiece. It is also among the most highly visited and well-known destinations on earth. Many of the cabins and cottages listed in this section are set within close driving proximity of Yosemite National Park. In fact, it may surprise many to learn that several rental cabins are available inside the park. When it comes to cabin rentals in this region, the variety is extraordinary. At Yosemite, the zenith is Ahwahnee Cabins, where upscale lodging is coupled with the perfect location – the center of the most beautiful place on earth.

Many family recreation opportunities exist at lake-based settings, including at Lake Alpine, Pinecrest Lake on the western slopes of the Sierra, and at June Lake, Silver Lake, Lake Mary, Twin Lakes, Convict Lake, and Rock Creek Lake on the eastern Sierra.

A highlight of the Mammoth and June Lake areas is the historic setting for lodging. The high-end toppers are Double Eagle Resort at June Lake and Tamarack Lodge Resort, which is old-style but luxurious, complete with a gourmet restaurant.

The entire region is sprinkled north to south with ski resorts and snow-play areas, and that makes most of the cabin and cottage rentals a year-round opportunity. In fact, demand can be higher in winter. One of the most unusual winter offerings is at Rock Creek Lodge, where to reach your cabin, you are transported two miles by snowmobile. Another anomaly is at Tioga Lodge, where incredible demand to stay at the Soiled Dove cottage may be due to its bordello theme.

Of course, every visit to this area must start with a tour of Yosemite Valley. It is framed by El Capitan, the Goliath of Yosemite, on one side and the three-spired Cathedral Rocks on the other. As you enter the valley, Bridalveil Fall comes to view, a perfect free fall over the south canyon rim, then across a meadow. To your left you'll see the two-tiered Yosemite Falls, and finally, Half Dome, the single most awesome piece of rock in the world.

The irony is that this is all most people ever see of the region, even though it represents but a fraction of the fantastic land of wonder, adventure, and unparalleled natural beauty. Though 24,000 people jam into five square miles of Yosemite Valley each summer day, the park is actually 90 percent wilderness. Other landmark areas you can reach by car include the Wawona Grove of Giant Sequoias, Tenaya Lake, Tuolumne Meadows, and Hetch Hetchy.

But that's still only scratching the surface. For those who hike, another world will open up: Yosemite has 318 lakes, dozens of pristine streams, the Grand Canyon of the Tuolumne River, Matterhorn Peak, Benson Lake (with the largest white sand beach in the Sierra), and dozens of spectacular waterfalls.

If you explore beyond the park boundaries, the adventures just keep getting better. Over Tioga Pass, outside the park and just off Highway 120, are Tioga Lake, Ellery Lake, and Saddlebag Lake (10,087 feet), the latter of which is the highest lake in California accessible by car. To the east is Mono Lake and its weird tufa spires, which create a stark moonscape.

The nearby June Lake Loop and Mammoth Lakes area is a launch point to another orbit. Both have small lakes with on-site cabin rentals, excellent fishing, and great hiking for all levels. In addition, just east of Mammoth Lakes airport is a series of hot springs, including a famous spot on Hot Creek, something of a legend in these parts. A bonus in this region is Hunewill Guest Ranch, a 140-year-old cattle ranch – not just a dude ranch, but a working operation with everything kept historically accurate.

More hiking (and fishing) opportunities abound at Devils Postpile National Monument, where you can hike to Rainbow Falls. At nearby Agnew Meadows, you'll find a trail that hugs the pristine San Joaquin River up to Thousand Island Lake and leads to the beautiful view from Banner and Ritter Peaks in the Ansel Adams Wilderness. Many of California's best lakes for trout fishing are also in the Yosemite and Mammoth area, such as June Lake and Convict Lake.

This region has it all: beauty, variety, and a chance at the hike or fish of a lifetime. There is nothing else like it on earth.

# YOSEMITE & MAMMOTH

© AVALON TRAVEL PUBLISHING, INC.

# Yosemite and Mammoth Cabins & Cottages

# 1 THE RIVERS RESORT
Dodge Ridge, off Highway 108 east of Sonora

**Luxury rating:** 3                                          **Recreation rating:** 4

The Rivers Resort gets a thumbs up, and this is why: prime location near the Dodge Ridge Ski Area, proximity to local lakes and rivers, nearby hiking and horseback riding, and a setting right on the South Fork of the Stanislaus River at approximately 5,400 feet in elevation.

The 1960s-style cottages have full kitchens, walls and ceilings of knotty pine, rock-and-brick fireplaces, and redwood decks. The furniture is modest and simple with wagon-wheel designs popular in the decor. The cabins receive some level of upgrade virtually every year, so some cabins may be slightly more updated than others.

All of the cabins have river views, except Cabin 1, which overlooks the pool. Cabin 2 has a river view from the deck only. By far, the most popular rental is Cabin 3 because it's closest to the river, commanding a great view, but it books up quickly in the summer.

One- to four-bedroom cottages are available, and all are two stories and freestanding, which means you don't share a common wall. They are referred to as condominiums because they are privately owned and rented to the public by the resort's manager. A big plus is the large, heated swimming pool with sundeck and changing rooms that is available in the summer. Another plus is access to the Stanislaus River from the property; within a few steps of your cottage, you can go trout fishing.

Five miles from your cottage is the Dodge Ridge Ski Area, which recently underwent a $3.5 million expansion that included opening new runs. Downhill and cross-country skiing and snowboarding are available. Snowmobiling is another option. Plenty of hiking is accessible in Stanislaus National Forest and Emigrant Wilderness. Swimming and boating are popular at Pinecrest Lake (one mile from the resort) and Beardsley Reservoir; waterskiing and personal-watercraft riding are permitted at Beardsley Lake. You can also ride horses at nearby Kennedy Meadows or Aspen Meadows, or tour the state fish hatchery at Moccasin.

## Facilities
The Rivers Resort has 10 condominium cottages with fully equipped kitchens and private bathrooms. Fireplace, deck or porch, television, and barbecue are provided.

There are no telephones. Facilities include a heated swimming pool, sundeck, and changing area. The resort is suitable for children. Leashed pets are permitted in some of the cottages. Smoking is permitted in some units. One cottage is wheelchair accessible. One set of linens and towels is provided, but there is no daily maid service.

## Reservations and Rates

Reservations are recommended. The fee is $95–195 per night per cottage or $700–1,500 per week. Discounts are offered in the off-season. Additional guests are $5 per night per person, with a maximum of two extra. Major credit cards are accepted. The resort is open year-round. Contact The Rivers Resort, P.O. Box 81, Strawberry, CA 95375, 209/965-3278 or 800/514-6777, website: www.gorrr.com.

## Directions

From Sonora, drive east on Highway 108 for approximately 31 miles (near Dodge Ridge turnoff) to the resort on the right.

# 2 PINECREST LAKE RESORT

Stanislaus National Forest, off Highway 108 east of Sonora

🚶 🚴 ⛰️ 🛶 🏊 ➡️ ❄️

**Luxury rating:** 3                              **Recreation rating:** 4

No secrets here. The word is out about Pinecrest Lake as a first-class family destination for easy camping, light boating, fishing, swimming, hiking, biking, and watching outdoor movies under the stars during the summer. Pinecrest Lake is set at 5,621 feet, covers 300 acres, and is the centerpiece of a fully developed family vacation resort.

The surrounding area is beautiful, best known for its big sugar pines and cedars, with exceptional hiking and biking trails. The water is clear and cold, but by mid-summer it is good for swimming on a hot summer day. A small but excellent marina rents all types of boats. Some families rent a pontoon boat so they can enjoy a picnic or barbecue on the water, then use the boat as a swimming or fishing platform. Small sailboats, paddleboats, and rowboats (outboard motors extra, of course) are also available for rent. The lake gets regular stocks of rainbow trout, which join a small resident population of brown trout.

At the center of all the activity is Pinecrest Lake Resort. One of its main attractions is its relative proximity to the Bay Area, far closer than most mountain destinations in Northern California. The resort provides a variety of cabins, townhouses with fireplaces, and deluxe hotel rooms. This is a year-round resort, an ideal location for skiers, with Dodge Ridge Ski Area nearby and special midweek ski packages available at a discount.

The number-one adventure for families is to hike at least a portion of the Pinecrest National Recreation Trail, usually parlaying it with a picnic. It's an easy, pleasant hike around the scenic shore of Pinecrest Lake that is suitable for the entire family. Pack along your binoculars and bird book because the bird-watching is quite good. Picnic spots abound, especially near the inlet at the east end of the lake.

Bicycles are allowed along the paved bike path that goes through the Pinecrest Picnic Area along the shoreline. The same path is also wheelchair accessible. Where the pavement ends and the trail begins, bicycles are not allowed. Add two miles to the journey with an easy and peaceful hike to Catfish Lake, actually a set of shallow ponds surrounded by old-growth forest.

## Facilities

Pinecrest Lake Resort offers two-bedroom and three-bedroom cabins, accommodating four, six, or eight people. All come with wall-to-wall carpet, television, and fully equipped kitchen. Townhouse-style cabins also include a fireplace and shower-tub combination. No pets are allowed, and no smoking is permitted at any indoor resort facility. Linens, blankets, pillows, and towels are provided.

## Reservations and Rates

Reservations are recommended. Cabin rentals are priced according to season and size, as low as $120 per night Sunday–Thursday in spring and fall for a two-bedroom cabin that sleeps four, and as high as $1,645 per week in summer for a three-bedroom townhouse that sleeps eight. A one-week minimum stay is required in July and August. Motel rooms are also available. Contact Pinecrest Lake Resort, 421 Pinecrest Lake, P.O. Box 1216, Pinecrest, CA 95364, 209/965-3411, website: www.pinecrestlakeresort.com.

## Directions

From Manteca at Highway 99, drive east on Highway 120 to Oakdale and Highway 108/120. Turn east on Highway 108/120 and drive to Sonora. Continue northeast on Highway 108 for 30 miles toward Sonora Pass to the Pinecrest turnoff. Turn right onto Pinecrest Lake Road.

# ❸ PINECREST CHALET
Dodge Ridge, off Highway 108 east of Sonora

🏃 🚲 🏊 ⛵ 🚤 ❄️ 👫 ♿

**Luxury rating: 3**                                  **Recreation rating: 5**

You want to get up close and personal with Dodge Ridge Ski Area? Well, this is the closest lodging you'll find, only 3.5 miles from the ski resort. Pinecrest Chalet is only 0.5 mile from Pinecrest Lake. Summer or winter, you have plenty of recreational choices.

You'll also have plenty of choices for lodging, because Pinecrest Chalet has various cabins, townhouses, and an RV park situated on seven acres with the North Fork Tuolumne River running through the property. These may look like rustic cabins on the outside, but on the inside they are modern, with plaster board walls and contemporary decor.

The popular mini-chalets are one-room cabins with fully equipped kitchens, fireplaces, and cathedral-style, knotty pine ceilings; some chalets have hot tubs. The larger townhouses and deluxe cabins have 2–4 bedrooms, fully equipped kitchen, and living room with woodburning fireplace. For budget lodging, try a one-room economy cabin—these sleep 2–4 people and have a bathroom and limited kitchen facilities.

Pinecrest Chalet is in Stanislaus National Forest among large sugar pines, the conifers with the gigantic pine cones. Guests have use of a large pool, basketball court, play area, and volleyball court. The setting is ideal for families and groups. Fishing, boating, horseback riding, and hiking are close by. A few people have caught brown trout in the Tuolumne River, which runs by the resort, but the fishing is marginal. Winter recreation includes downhill and cross-country skiing, snowboarding, ice-skating, snowmobiling, snowshoeing, and sledding. For details about the area, see the listings for Pinecrest Lake Resort and The Rivers Resort earlier in this chapter.

## Facilities

Pinecrest Chalet has 16 cabins and seven townhouses. An RV park is on the premises. Some rentals have full kitchens, and all units have a small refrigerator, coffeemaker, and microwave. Barbecues and television are provided, but there are no telephones. A pool, laundry facilities, a basketball court, volleyball, horseshoes, and a children's play area round out the amenities. The facilities are suitable for children. Pets are not allowed. Smoking is not permitted. Some facilities are wheelchair accessible. Linens and towels are provided.

## Reservations and Rates

Reservations are recommended. The fee is $90–315 per night or $975–2,045 per week with full kitchens; $60–120 per night and $550–780 per week for studios without full kitchens. It's $5 per night per each additional person. A rollaway bed may be rented for $10 per night. There is a two-night minimum stay on weekends and a three-night minimum on holidays. Major credit cards are accepted. It's open year-round. Contact Pinecrest Chalet, 500 Dodge Ridge, P.O. Box 1279, Pinecrest, CA 95364, 209/965-3276, fax 209/965-3849, website: www.pinecrestchalet.com.

## Directions

From Manteca at Highway 99, drive east on Highway 120 to Oakdale and Highway 108/120. Turn east on Highway 108/120 and drive to Sonora. Continue east on Highway 108 to the Pinecrest exit and Pinecrest Lake Road. Bear right and drive 0.2 mile to Dodge Ridge Road. Turn right and drive 0.8 mile to the chalets on the right.

## 4 HUNEWILL GUEST RANCH BEST ◖

Off U.S. 395 near Bridgeport

🚶 🏊 🎣 👫 ♿

**Luxury rating:** 3                                              **Recreation rating:** 4

---

It's not the Ponderosa, but it sure feels like it.

That sensation will surface for anybody who remembers the old *Bonanza* show once you set your boots on Hunewill Guest Ranch, a 4,500-acre cattle ranch that was established 140 years ago. This is the real thing, a genuine cattle ranch, where life is simple and informal, and guests usually help out with cattle chores. That means you'll be horseback riding—a lot. Is your butt ready for this?

The ranch caters to families, groups, and anglers. Most vacationers stay for a week. Visitors have the option of trail rides six days a week; riders are split into groups of beginning, intermediate, and advanced, and families often divide into different groups for the day. Since riders must be at least six years of age, child care is available for the younger members of a family.

If you are concerned about oversleeping your scheduled morning wake-up, don't worry. Your cabin is next to the horse pasture, and the thundering noise of the horses galloping in each morning will awaken you. But you'll want to watch this spectacular event, because it gets your juices racing and reminds you of why you came here in the first place.

You're surrounded by about 1,200 cows, 120 horses, sheep, llamas, pigs, and authentic cowboys and cowgirls, as six generations of the Hunewill family have been raised on and worked on the ranch; they know every facet of ranch life and cattle work. On a typical day, you'll be riding through open meadows and across streams at 6,500 feet in elevation, surrounded by snowy peaks and mountains, including Yosemite National Park to the west. You may even stop at one of the ol' swimming holes for a quick dip. More advanced riders have the option of working alongside one of the Hunewills, learning the ropes of doctoring cattle, tracking a cow and not getting lost, roping, and understanding "cow logic."

Hiking and catch-and-release fishing are available for those who don't want to go riding; a four-acre, spring-fed fly-fishing pond stocked with two- to five-pound rainbow trout was established several years ago, and float tubes and rafts are allowed. An extra fee is charged for pond fishing. Excellent fishing is also available in the nearby East Walker River and in streams and lakes in Toiyabe National Forest.

The dinner bell calls you to dinner at the original 1860s-era Victorian ranch house, where you'll eat home-style meals in a large dining room. There are also creekside cookouts, campfire sing-alongs, square dancing, a talent night, roping practice, and an occasional hayride.

Cabins are simple duplex-style units with two rooms, two bathrooms, a porch, and a connecting door between rooms in case you want to join two units. Aspen, Bristlecone, Cedar, and Juniper are the newer cabins and are a little more expensive than the older cabins.

In addition to the general activities at the ranch, if you have intermediate to advanced riding skills you can sign on for special trail rides and the annual fall cattle drive. These trips are for more adventurous riders and sometimes involve camping out and riding up to 60 miles from the ranch to the herd's wintering grounds in Nevada. Check with the ranch for details.

## Facilities

Hunewill Guest Ranch has 25 cabins with no kitchen facilities, but all meals are provided. Each cabin has a private bathroom. A fly-fishing pond, coin-operated laundry, horseshoes, table tennis, volleyball, organized activities, child care, private riding lessons, aerobics, personal training, and massage are available. One room is wheelchair accessible. Pets are not allowed. No smoking is permitted. Linens and towels are provided.

## Reservations and Rates

Reservations are recommended. The fee is $1,277–1,373 per week, double occupancy. There are discounts for children. Daily rates are available on a space-available basis. Reduced rates are possible for non-riding guests and visitors bringing their own horses; special trail ride packages are available. The ranch is open May–October. Contact Hunewill Guest Ranch, P.O. Box 368, Bridgeport, CA 93517, 760/932-7710 (summer); 200 Hunewill Lane, Wellington, NV 89444, 775/465-2201 (winter), fax 775/465-2056, website: www.hunewillranch.com.

## Directions

From Bridgeport on U.S. 395, turn southwest on Twin Lakes Road and drive five miles to the signed turnoff for Hunewill Ranch on the left. Turn left and drive one mile to the ranch.

# 5 EVERGREEN LODGE

Hetch Hetchy, Yosemite National Park, off Highway 120 near Mather

**Luxury rating:** 3                                          **Recreation rating:** 5

Hetch Hetchy is the Yosemite you hear little about, and that is why the cabins at Evergreen Lodge remain a relatively well-kept secret. Hetch Hetchy is a giant lake in the dammed Tuolumne River canyon in the remote northwest sector of Yosemite National Park. Evergreen Lodge is just a mile outside the park entrance and eight miles from the lake and the site of an excellent trailhead for hiking and horseback riding. The cabins are quite old but comfortable and come complete with porches.

Evergreen Lodge is at 4,600 feet and is surrounded by Stanislaus National Forest. What makes Evergreen special is the short hop to Hetch Hetchy and the great hikes to Wapama Falls and Tueala Falls. A bonus is that lodge guests are provided free access to Camp Mather and its swimming pool; horse rentals are available there.

Every year thousands of people at overloaded Yosemite end up stuck without a spot, spending the night in their cars. Many would pay a million dollars for one of these cabins, but they just don't know they exist.

## Facilities

Evergreen Lodge has 67 lodging units, including 19 one- and two-room cabins with bathrooms, heat, and private decks. There are no kitchens or televisions in the cabins, but a lodge restaurant is nearby. A swimming pool and horseback riding outfitter are one mile away at Camp Mather, with free access provided to lodge guests. No pets are permitted. No smoking is allowed. Bed linens are provided with daily maid service.

## Reservations and Rates

Reservations are recommended. Cabin rates on weekends range from $79 for two to $229 for six, with a two-night minimum stay during peak season. Weekly and seasonal discounts are available. The season runs late April–October. Contact Evergreen Lodge, 33160 Evergreen Road, Groveland, CA 95321, 209/379-2606 or 800/935-6343, website: www.evergreenlodge.com.

## Directions

From Manteca at Highway 99, drive east on Highway 120 to Oakdale and Highway 108/120. Turn east on Highway 108/120 and drive 25 miles to the turnoff for Highway 49/120 and Chinese Camp. Turn right on Highway 49/120 and drive 12 miles to Moccasin and Highway 120. Turn left on Highway 120 and drive about 5 miles to Groveland and continue for 28 miles (6 miles past Harden Flat) to Evergreen Road. Turn left and drive 7 miles and look for Evergreen Lodge on the left side of the road.

# 6 TUOLUMNE MEADOWS LODGE
Tioga Pass, off Highway 120 in Yosemite

**Luxury rating:** 1                                    **Recreation rating:** 5

Tuolumne Meadows, at 8,600 feet on the brink of the Yosemite wilderness, is one of the best jumping-off points for an adventure of any place in North America, especially for hikes that are easy and extraordinarily beautiful.

Your base for this adventure is Tuolumne Meadows Lodge, where there are 69 canvas tent cabins that sleep up to four. This is a vast improvement compared to the

Curry Village combat camping scenario in Yosemite Valley (see Yosemite Valley Tent Cabins in this chapter). This is the high country, and
everything is different compared to
the valley scene. The air is thin and
light, the smell of pine duff is in the
air, and the magic of the next day's
adventures looms when you put your
head down on your pillow to sleep
for the night.

   Well, that is, if you have a pillow.
Many folks just bring their sleeping bags, though bedding is available for a few bucks.
This is a fairly primitive setting, with all facilities available nearby in a campground
setting. But a great bonus here is that the lodge provides a central dining tent with
extremely sumptuous breakfasts and dinners that can satiate even the most prodi-
gious appetites.

   With your body well-fueled and acclimated to the altitude, you will be ready for
some of the greatest day hikes in America. Starting from Tuolumne Meadows, an
excellent option for your first trip is to take the Pacific Crest Trail out to the north.
The trail begins with gentle walking as it follows the Tuolumne River toward the
Grand Canyon of the Tuolumne River. It stays easy to Glen Aulin, where you get a
great view of several small waterfalls and 100-foot Tuolumne Falls, pouring through
a granite slot then cascading into a foaming crater full of blue-white bubbles.

   The ambitious can continue down into the Grand Canyon of the Tuolumne, drop-
ping more than 1,000 feet in the process to see Waterwheel Falls and several other
beautiful waterfalls. This trip is eight miles one-way from Tuolumne Meadows, and
the climb out of the canyon late in the day can make it a genuine butt-kicker.

   Another option from Tuolumne Meadows is to hike south on the John Muir Trail,
up Lyell Fork toward Donohue Pass. For the first four miles, you walk along the John
Muir Trail, where it seems nearly flat, with the pretzel-like Lyell Fork running nearby.
The fishing for small brook trout is often excellent at Lyell Fork, but often best after
hiking in at least three miles.

   A sensational hike is the climb up Lembert Dome (9,450 feet) for spectacular views.
The trailhead is up the road toward Tioga Pass, on the left. It is a steady climb of about
1.5 miles, with the views of wilderness peaks and Tuolumne Meadows just incredible.
It's Rambob's favorite spot. You know ol' Rambob, right? (Okay, he's my brother.)

   Of course, you could choose instead to be waiting in the long pizza line, crowded
with all the other flatlanders, down there in the valley.

## Facilities

Tuolumne Meadows Lodge has 69 canvas tent cabins that sleep up to four. A woodstove for heat and candles for lighting are provided; there is no electricity. Restroom
facilities and showers are nearby. Breakfast and dinner are served in a central dining

tent. Smoking is permitted. No pets are allowed. Linens are provided, but there's no daily maid service.

## Reservations and Rates

Reservations are required. The rate is $75 per night for one person with an additional charge of $9 per adult and $4 per child. Major credit cards are accepted. There is a $20 park entrance fee, which is good for a week. The lodge is open June–September. Contact Yosemite Reservations, 6771 North Palm Avenue, Fresno, CA 93704, 559/252-4848 (often busy) or 559/253-5635, www.YosemitePark.com. For information about Yosemite, call 209/372-0200. For an excellent hiking map of the area, contact Tom Harrison Cartography at 415/456-7940.

## Directions

From Mariposa in the Central Valley, drive east on Highway 140 to the El Portal entrance station for Yosemite National Park. Continue east on Highway 140 to the Highway 120/140 junction. Turn left on Highway 120 and drive 8 miles to a fork and bear right on Highway 120 east. Continue east on Highway 120 for 54 miles to Tuolumne Meadows Lodge on the right. Note: An alternative route is available from Highway 120 out of Manteca/Chinese Camp.

From the eastern Sierra, take U.S. 395 to the junction with Highway 120 (just south of Lee Vining). Turn west on Highway 120 and drive to the Tioga Pass entrance station. Continue about 10 miles to Tuolumne Meadows Lodge on the left.

# **7** TIOGA PASS RESORT
Tioga Pass, off Highway 120 near Yosemite

**Luxury rating:** 4    **Recreation rating:** 5

How would you like to enjoy all the elements of Yosemite's high-country wilderness, avoid the hassles of an overcrowded park, *and* have a cozy cabin each night? That combination is exactly what makes Tioga Pass Resort a winner.

This is the high country—elevation 9,600 feet. It's a land of wilderness, granite peaks, mountain slopes sprinkled with lodgepole pine, and pristine lakes. Tioga Pass Resort is just two miles from the eastern entrance station of Yosemite National Park and within close range of Tioga and Ellery Lakes. The surrounding landscape has all the recreational qualities of Yosemite, yet is actually part of Inyo National Forest, with several nearby lakes for car-top boating, much better fishing than in the park, and excellent hiking. And if you want to make the quick getaway into Yosemite, a 5-minute drive puts you inside park borders, and another 15 minutes gets you to Tuolumne Meadows.

When you first arrive, you will discover the cabins set on a hillside behind the general store, in a variety of sizes to accommodate couples, families, or small groups. A creek runs nearby. Because this entire area is set high near the Sierra crest, it is subject to cold nights and afternoon winds. No problem, though. After all, you have a cabin to stay in, right? Right.

Within a mile or two are Ellery Lake to the east and Tioga Lake to the west, both beautiful alpine lakes that run pure, cold, and pristine; they are stocked with trout. Just four miles away, via a bumpy Forest Service road, is Saddlebag Lake. At 10,087 feet, it is the highest lake in California accessible by car, providing more alpine beauty, an excellent trailhead, and good boating and fishing. And then there is Yosemite, with outstanding hiking out of Tuolumne Meadows either up Lyell Fork, to Cathedral Lake, down to Glen Aulin along the Tuolumne River, or up Lembert Dome.

Note: In the winter, the roads to the resort are not plowed. Access is still available from Yosemite's eastern entrance, but you'll have to ski in.

## Facilities
Tioga Pass Resort provides 10 cabins in one- and two-bedroom configurations, plus four motel units. Each cabin includes a kitchen with utensils, cookware, a stove, and a refrigerator. An electric heater is included. Central kitchen and bath facilities are provided in the winter. A small store and restaurant are on-site. Pets are not allowed. Linens are provided in the summer.

## Reservations and Rates
Reservations are required. Cabin rates are graduated based on number of nights, starting at $140–210 per night. Motel-style units start at $120 per night. Contact Tioga Pass Resort, 85 Highway 120 West, P.O. Box 7, Lee Vining, CA, 93541 in summer, or P.O. Box 307 in winter, 209/372-4471, website: www.tiogapassresort.com. For an excellent hiking map of the area, contact Tom Harrison Cartography at 415/456-7940.

## Directions
From Mariposa in the Central Valley, drive east on Highway 140 to the El Portal entrance station for Yosemite National Park. Continue east on Highway 140 to the Highway 120/140 junction. Turn left on Highway 120 and drive 8 miles to a fork and bear right on Highway 120 east. Continue east on Highway 120 and drive 65 miles to the Tioga Pass entrance station. Continue 2 miles and turn left at Tioga Pass Resort. Note: An alternate route is available from Highway 120 out of Manteca/Chinese Camp.

From the eastern Sierra, take U.S. 395 to the junction with Highway 120 (just south of Lee Vining). Turn west on Highway 120 and drive 12 miles up the grade toward Yosemite National Park. After passing the Saddlebag Lake turnoff, drive about 0.25 mile and turn right at Tioga Pass Resort.

# 8 TIOGA LODGE
Mono Lake, off U.S. 395 near Lee Vining

**Luxury rating:** 2                                  **Recreation rating:** 4

Near the shores of Mono Lake sits a historic resort that was nearly comatose before it was given new life a few years ago. It would have been easy for the owners to raze the structures at Tioga Lodge and start fresh, what with the boarded up, decaying buildings that had become an eyesore. But the owners had a vision to restore the place to its former glory days—a time when Mark Twain and Ansel Adams visited and President Theodore Roosevelt's wife planted a pine tree there. Today, the restoration is well underway and some new buildings have been added, blending the old west look with the new.

Located in Mono Basin National Scenic Area, the lodge consists of 13 cottages, a restaurant, a saloon, a gift shop, and a gazebo. The 23-acre property overlooks Mono Lake and the little islands of Negit and Paoha, and includes a half mile of Mono Lake frontage. The lodge is on one side of U.S. 395, and the remainder of the property is across the road, toward the lake. Since the property is on this major highway, expect some traffic sights and sounds. Still, the grounds are lovely, with walkways, a white bridge, outdoor swing, and a creek meandering through the property. The restaurant and gift shop were transported to the Tioga Lodge site in the 19th century from the town of Bodie, now a historical ghost town.

The 14 cottages consist of two freestanding cottages, a duplex unit, an A-frame building housing five lodge rooms, and another building with four rooms. The cottages are more like inn rooms than cottages, with no kitchen facilities. The rooms are decorated in themes that reflect the history of the lodge and the area. The Mountain Man Room is designed in honor of the explorer Joseph Walker and sports a handmade aspen log bed and an elk head and long rifle mounted on the wall. The Poet's Room is where Mark Twain and Ansel Adams supposedly stayed when they visited, and it is carpeted and contains a dark metal bed and a writing credenza with chair.

Other rooms include Old California, Paiute, Mono Lake, Wilderness, Bodie, Soiled Dove, Nelly Bly, and Log Cabin Mine. The favorite? It's the wildly popular and ultra-feminine Soiled Dove, a tribute to the lodge's one-time bordello heritage. And guess what? It's women, not men, who request this room by a wide margin.

The restaurant features an outdoor rock patio overlooking Mono Lake. When the restaurant originally opened in 1918, the attire was formal—the waiters dressed in tuxedos, and the tables were decorated with silver candelabras and lace linens. Well, you can leave your tuxedo and formal clothes at home because the attire is casual now. The restaurant is open only for dinner, but breakfast is served on weekends. The saloon serves wine and beer and has the ambience of a cellar, with old stone walls, sand floor, old western movie posters, and a rustic wood ceiling.

The Mono Lake Tufa State Reserve is the highlight of this area, where you can visit Mono Lake and its strange and remarkable Tufa Towers. Resembling a moonscape, this is truly one of the most extraordinary landscapes in California. It is best seen on a one-mile loop trail or by canoe. Mono Lake is vast, covering 60 square miles, and is estimated to be more than 700,000 years old, making it one of the oldest lakes in North America. About 80 percent of California's gull population nests here.

For hikers, the fall color in Lundy Canyon is spectacular.

## Facilities

Tioga Lodge has cottages in several configurations, including two freestanding cabins, a duplex, an A-frame with five lodge rooms, and a lodge with four rooms. The cottages have private bathrooms but no kitchens. Most of the cottages and rooms have a deck or porch, and some cottages have inside sitting rooms, but there are no telephones, televisions, or radios. The lodge is suitable for children. Pets are not allowed. No smoking is permitted. Linens and towels are provided.

## Reservations and Rates

Reservations are recommended. The fee is $55–107 per night. Rollaway beds are $10 per night. Major credit cards are accepted. The lodge is open year-round. Contact Tioga Lodge, P.O. Box 580, Lee Vining, CA 93541, 760/647-6423 or 888/647-6423, fax 760/647-6074, website: www.tiogalodge.com.

## Directions

From Lee Vining, drive north on U.S. 395 for 2.5 miles to the lodge on the left.

## 9 AHWAHNEE CABINS                                BEST (

Yosemite Valley, off Highway 120 in Yosemite

**Luxury rating:** 5                                **Recreation rating:** 5

This is the kind of place where you can fall in love for keeps. Hey, it happened to us.

Yosemite Valley is the spectacle of all spectacles. Few places in this country provide more breathtaking scenery than Yosemite, with its dramatic canyon walls, rimmed by El Capitan, Cathedral Rocks, and many other glacial-carved monuments—anchored by Half Dome. This 360-degree panorama sparkles with the most spectacular waterfalls in the world.

It doesn't get any better than this. And your stay doesn't get any better than at the Ahwahnee. This is Yosemite-style luxury, with gorgeous lodging rooms and cottages within walking distance of the base of Yosemite Falls. Everything is drop-dead beautiful, from the Native American–style blankets and surrounding interior decor to the most inviting hiking trails in the world just past your front door.

In addition, the restaurant at the Ahwahnee is also world-class, the kind of place where you just have to sit there for a while to take it all in—the scenery *and* the food. The Sunday buffet, for instance, is something of a gorge; when you get done, you often feel like somebody could drill three holes in you and use you for a bowling ball.

I suggest you get up at dawn, while everybody else is in dreamland, and walk around Yosemite Valley when there is scarcely another human out and about. Across a pristine meadow is Yosemite Falls, charged full with foaming, spraying water, silver-tasseled in reflected light. At 2,425 feet long, it is the tallest waterfall in the world. Across the valley is Bridalveil Falls, 620 feet high and perhaps just as beautiful.

You might take the shuttle to Happy Isles and the trailhead for the Mist Trail. Up you go, first to Vernal Falls, a wide, free-flowing cascade of silver, 317 feet high, then with a steep, stair-step tromp upstream, you reach Nevada Falls, tumbling 594 feet at the foot of Liberty Dome.

For an easy bonus, the Mirror Lake Trail skirts the base of Half Dome and extends out to the entrance of Tenaya Canyon. In the afternoon, this trail gets inundated with people. At dawn, when all is quiet—and not a single soul is out but you—it's like walking in the beginning of time.

## Facilities

Ahwahnee Cabins has 24 cottages, four luxurious parlor rooms, and 99 luxury hotel rooms. Bathroom, small refrigerator, television, and telephone are provided. A small patio is outside. Some units have a fireplace or woodstove. The restaurant has a dress code: no jeans, shorts, or tennis shoes; men must wear coats; T-shirts are permitted for men and women. No smoking is allowed. Pets are not permitted. Linens and towels are provided.

## Reservations and Rates

Reservations are required. The rate is $379 per night (single or double occupancy) for cottages and rooms to $936 for suites with a parlor, plus $21 for each additional person. Rollaways are $11 per night. Children under 12 are free if they stay in the same room. Discounted rates are available in the off-season. Major credit cards are accepted. Ahwahnee is open year-round. There is a $20 park entrance fee, which is good for a week. Contact Yosemite Reservations, 6771 North Palm Avenue, Fresno, CA 93704, 559/252-4848 (often busy) or 559/253-5635, www.YosemitePark.com. For information about Yosemite, call 209/372-0200. For an excellent hiking map of the area, contact Tom Harrison Cartography at 415/456-7940.

## Directions
From Mariposa, drive east on Highway 140 to the El Portal entrance station for Yosemite National Park. Continue east on Highway 140 to the Highway 120/140 junction. Continue east and drive seven miles into Yosemite Valley (the Little Chapel is on the right and Yosemite Falls is on the left) to a stop sign. Turn left on Sentinel at the Stone Bridge (crossing the Merced River) and continue a short distance to another stop sign. Turn right and drive a short distance to Village Drive. Turn left and continue to Ahwahnee Road. Turn right and drive to Ahwahnee Hotel. The route is well-signed.

# 10 YOSEMITE VALLEY TENT CABINS
Curry Village, off Highway 120 in Yosemite

🥾 🚴 🏊 🛶 ❄️ 👫

**Luxury rating:** 1                                        **Recreation rating:** 5

The Yosemite Valley Tent Cabins at Curry Village embody the definition of combat camping. It's as if you hide out in your army bunker (tent cabin) all night, trying to fortify yourself as best you can; come morning, you get your courage up and head out amid the crowds—typically 24,000 people in five square miles every summer day.

© JEFFREY/SCOTT ADVERTISING

It's astounding that the park service concessionaire put 427 tent cabins in here by design. The walls are thin and you can hear other people nearby—not just in your own tent, of course, but in other tents. There are stories of one guy snoring so badly, with so many people kept awake by it, that a battalion of combat campers invaded his tent cabin, ready to kick him out to his own personal bivouac.

The irony is that for many, the tent cabins somehow do the job. They provide a place to bed down for the night in the most magical place in the world, Yosemite Valley. In turn, when you wake up in the morning, you have no need to drive anywhere. You are already there. You just hike out (the Mist Falls Trailhead at Happy Isles is nearby), rent a bike, or ride the shuttle bus to your choice of a dozen world-class destinations. The shuttle to Glacier Point, for instance, provides eye-popping views, crowned by the chance to hike the Pohono Trail on the southern rim of Yosemite Valley.

### Facilities

Curry Village has 427 tent cabins, 100 cabins with private baths, 80 cabins with a central bath, 3 specialty cabins, and 18 lodge rooms. Cabins are furnished with two beds. Some have electricity, televisions, and fireplaces. Tent cabins sleep 1–5 people. Drinking water, restrooms, and coin showers are nearby. Tent cabins have no electricity, kitchens, televisions, or phones. A few heated tent cabins are available in fall and winter. A coin laundry and a restaurant are in the area. In summer, ranger programs occur each night in a nearby amphitheater, and Curry Village Pavilion serves buffet-style breakfasts and dinners. Amenities include a gift shop, ice-skating in winter, bicycle rentals, and guided rafting trips. The smoking policy varies according to lodging and season. No pets are allowed. Linens and towels are provided.

### Reservations and Rates

Reservations are required; call 559/242-4848 (often busy). Cabin rates vary according to season and accommodations. In summer, tent cabins are $69 per night, cabins without bathrooms are $85 per night, cabins with bathrooms are $108 per night, and lodge rooms are $113 per night. Some units are available year-round. Fees range $9–11 for each additional person, with discounts available. Major credit cards are accepted. There is a $20 park entrance fee, which is good for a week. Contact Yosemite Reservations, 6771 North Palm Avenue, Fresno, CA 93704, 559/252-4848 (often busy) or 559/253-5635; www.YosemitePark.com. For information about Yosemite, call 209/372-0200. For an excellent hiking map of the area, contact Tom Harrison Cartography at 415/456-7940.

### Directions

From Mariposa, drive east on Highway 140 to the El Portal entrance station for Yosemite National Park. Continue east on Highway 140 to the Highway 120/140 junction. Continue east and drive seven miles into Yosemite Valley (the Little Chapel is on the right, Yosemite Falls on the left) to a stop sign. Continue straight to a stop signed for Curry Village. Turn right and drive a short distance to the Curry Village parking lot.

## 11 YOSEMITE HIGH SIERRA CAMPS
Yosemite National Park, off Highway 120 near Tuolumne Meadows

**Luxury rating:** 1        **Recreation rating:** 5

Here you get all the qualities of a prime wilderness experience: the dramatic beauty, the quiet, the views, and the pristine lakes, streams, and meadows of Yosemite. Yet, you get it all without the pounding physical punishment of backpacking, meal prep, or cleanup.

Five hike-to (or horseback ride–to) camps sit in the wilderness, providing meals, a bed in a tent cabin, and hot showers. These trips are so popular that a lottery is held every winter for the daily quota of positions available at each of the five camps. Yet there is often considerable availability for the tent cabins into summer because of cancellations.

The five High Sierra camps are spaced roughly 6–10 miles apart, so you can create a weeklong loop trip in the wilderness. Many also simply hike in to one of the camps, then stay there for a few days, using the location as a launch point for stellar wilderness day trips without having to carry any gear, just a canteen and trail snacks.

Here are the camp profiles at a glance:

**Glen Aulin,** at 7,800 feet, is at the head of the Grand Canyon of the Tuolumne River, an easy, near-level 5.7-mile hike on the Pacific Crest Trail heading north out of Tuolumne Meadows. Featured side trips include nearby Tuolumne Falls, Waterwheel Falls, and remote Cold Creek Canyon.

**May Lake,** at 9,700 feet, is a very pretty alpine lake at the foot of spectacular Mount Hoffman (10,850 feet), with forest and meadow backing the southern end of the lake. Reaching it requires only a 1.2-mile hike, crossing up and down a short rise. A highlight is climbing around the slopes of Hoffman for great views.

**Sunrise,** at 9,400 feet, is reached by an easy 5.3-mile hike from Tioga Road or a 7.8-mile hike from Tuolumne Meadows. The camp is adjacent to the John Muir Trail and a pristine alpine meadow that absolutely glows at sunrise, hence the name. A side trip to Cathedral Lake is a must.

**Merced Lake,** at 7,150 feet, is a shocker for newcomers. It is pristine, gorgeous, and big (for the alpine zone), situated in remote wilderness midway between Vogelsang Pass and the cutoff trail to Half Dome. A great side trip is hiking up the hill for beautiful views of the back side of Half Dome, along with visiting Emeric Lake (and other lakes).

**Vogelsang,** at 10,300 feet, is reached by a seven-mile tromp from Tuolumne Meadows, including a 1,700-foot climb (with switchbacks) out of Lyell Fork over Vogelsang Pass. The setting is somewhat stark, made up of granite, meadows, ice, and a few pines. Several nearby pristine lakes make this a fantastic base camp for day tripping.

## Facilities

Yosemite National Park has five High Sierra camps with canvas tent cabins, steel frame beds with mattresses, and restroom facilities with hot showers (subject to water availability). Exception: There are no showers at Vogelsang or Glen Aulin. Pets are not permitted. Smoking is not allowed. Pillows, woolen blankets, and comforters are provided; guests provide their own sheets, sleeping bags, and towels (also available for purchase).

## Reservations and Rates

Reservations are required. The fee is $138 per day per adult, $94 per day per child, and includes breakfast and dinner served in the main dining tent. Box lunches are available for an additional $8.50 per day. Contact High Sierra Desk, 559/253-5674. At the end of the message, leave your name, phone number, and preference for camp location and date; applications for each winter's lottery for the following summer are available October 15 to November 30. For information on saddle trips to camps, contact Yosemite Stables, 209/372-8348. To learn more about the camps via the Internet, visit www.YosemitePark.com.

## Directions

From Mariposa, drive east on Highway 140 to the El Portal entrance station for Yosemite National Park. Continue east on Highway 140 to the Highway 120/140 junction. Turn left on Highway 120 and drive eight miles to a fork and bear right on Highway 120 east. Continue east on Highway 120 and drive to the appointed trailhead for the selected High Sierra camp. Note: An alternate route is available from Highway 120 out of Manteca/Chinese Camp.

# 12 SILVER LAKE RESORT CABINS
### Silver Lake, off U.S. 395 on the June Lake Loop

🚶 🛶 🚐 ❄️ 👫

**Luxury rating:** 3                                    **Recreation rating:** 5

No television. No telephone. Cozy cabin. Pretty high-mountain lake. Little general store. Boats. Trout. Hiking trails. Stream nearby. Skiing in the winter. This is the recipe for a vacation at Silver Lake.

For most visitors, it is everything they've ever wanted. Silver Lake is less developed than June Lake—the principal lake in the June Lake Loop—but it is just as pretty, set at 7,600 feet with 10,909-foot Carson Peak looming in the background. It is one of four drive-to lakes on the loop, just west of U.S. 395 in the eastern Sierra.

A large but exposed campground and RV park is directly north of Silver Lake, but nearby, off the northwest shore, is Silver Lake Resort and its 16 cabins, each different from the next. The cabins come in all sizes and prices. You can get fresh bed linens when needed, and fresh towels are provided daily. Each cabin also has a propane wall heater. The operation is not so much a resort as it is a camp.

Silver Lake gets its name from the way the sun and afternoon winds send reflected silver flashes off its surface—a pretty scene, especially when the lake's deep blue-green colors are contrasted with the stark, ashen granite of the high mountain walls backing the Sierra Nevada.

Most people come here for the trout, and there are usually plenty, particularly near the dam, boat ramp, and in Reverse Creek near the campground. Boat and motor rentals are available through the resort. If you decide to boat here, the best advice is to set your alarm and be on the lake early. The trout not only bite best here after first light (a high sun and clear water can make them spooky at midday), but the lake is at its calmest between dawn and 9 A.M.

A great wilderness trailhead (Rush Creek Trailhead) is behind the adjacent RV park, with a trail routed 2.1 miles to Agnew Lake with a steady climb of about 1,200 feet on the way. The trail is literally cut into the granite slope, and with nothing blocking your view to the east, you get great vistas of Silver Lake. After topping the rim, you're treated to a divine look at Agnew Lake, set in granite. The trail skirts the north shore of the lake and in another mile rises to the shore of Gem Lake, which can be astonishing in its natural beauty.

## Facilities
Silver Lake Resort has 16 cabins, each furnished with a stove and refrigerator and all kitchen utensils. The cabins have propane heat but no telephones or televisions. No pets are permitted. Smoking is prohibited. Towels are provided every other day, and fresh linens are provided when needed, depending on the length of your stay.

## Reservations and Rates
Reservations are required, with a deposit of 50 percent of the total fee. Prices are $95 per night for a small cabin for two people, $105–185 per night for a cabin for 4–8 people. The Creek House costs $215 per night and the Road House $235; both of these can handle up to eight people. Contact Silver Lake Resort, Route 3, Box 116, June Lake, CA 93529, 760/648-7525, website: www.silverlakeresort.net.

## Directions
From Lee Vining, drive south on U.S. 395 and turn right at the first Highway 158/ June Lake Loop turnoff. Drive west on Highway 158 past Grant Lake at Silver Lake. Just as you arrive at Silver Lake, turn right at the small store adjacent to the RV campground and park.

## 13 LAKE FRONT CABINS                    BEST (
June Lake, off U.S. 395 on the June Lake Loop

**Luxury rating: 2**                              **Recreation rating: 4**

At Lake Front Cabins, you may be near the lake's edge, but don't expect a lake view; a row of trees on Forest Service land blocks the view. But it doesn't really matter—the accommodations are comfortable, the new owners are friendly and helpful, upgrades are ongoing, and the price is right.

Since the eight cabins surround a yard, the setup is ideal for groups who wish to rent the whole place. The cabins were originally built in the 1950s as a fishing getaway, appealing primarily to men on fishing vacations. Since the cabins have been remodeled and nicely redecorated, they now appeal to couples and families as well. The cabins feature forest green carpet and maroon-and-green bedspreads, along with the original knotty pine interior and eight-foot ceilings. The decor gives the cabins a homey, country look.  Televisions, thermostat heat, and electric blankets are provided.

The cabins are situated 400 feet from June Lake and 500 feet from the marina, an easy walk. There are studios and one- and two-bedroom cabins with full kitchens and bathrooms. These can accommodate up to six. Some of the cabins have adjoining walls. The fire pit and patio area next to the lawn make a good setup for reunions and families with small children.

You're two blocks from the village of June Lake and its restaurants, stores, and shops. And if you rent a boat for a day while you're staying at one of the cabins, you'll get a discount. For more information about June Lake, refer to description for The Four Seasons (see listing in this chapter).

## Facilities

The nine cabins come with fully equipped kitchens and bathrooms, barbecues, patios, and televisions. A fish-cleaning station is available. The cabins are suitable for children. Pets are not allowed. Smoking is not permitted. Linens, towels, and electric blankets are provided.

## Reservations and Rates

Reservations are recommended. The fee is $100 per night per studio, $115 per night per one-bedroom, and $130 per night per two-bedroom, based on occupancies of two, two, and four, respectively. Rates are slightly higher during holidays. There is at least a two-night minimum stay during the summer and on holidays. Major credit cards are accepted. Lake Front is open year-round. Contact Lake Front Cabins, P.O. Box 696, June Lake, CA 93529-0696, 760/648-7527 or 877/648-7527, fax 760/648-7810, website: www.lakefrontcabins.net/pages/1/index.htm.

## Directions

From Lee Vining, drive south on U.S. 395 (passing Highway 158 North) for 20 miles (6 miles past Highway 158 North) to June Lake Junction (a sign is posted for June Lake Village) and Highway 158 South. Turn right (west) on Highway 158 South and drive 2.5 miles to June Lake Village and Knoll Road. Turn right and drive two blocks to Brenner Street. Turn right and drive 100 feet to the cabins on the right at 32 Brenner Street.

# 14 THE HAVEN

June Lake, off U.S. 395 on the June Lake Loop

**Luxury rating:** 2                                       **Recreation rating:** 4

If you want to spend time in the gorgeous June Lake area but you're on a tight budget, The Haven should meet your needs. Here you're treated to lodging with a full kitchen, a private bathroom, and maybe a fireplace, and you're only one-half block from the marina and one block from the village. The cottages have adjoining walls and are surprisingly updated. All this is yours for as little as 65 bucks a night.

The Haven offers cottages from studios to two-bedrooms with a living room that can sleep up to four. The cottages have light-colored walls, a few antiques, and cheerful, country decor. Some of the rentals are two-story and have fireplaces or woodstoves, but you must bring your own firewood. The cottages are set around a patio and indoor spa, and you'll get a lake view from the deck.

For details about the June Lake area, refer to the description for The Four Seasons (see listing in this chapter).

## Facilities

The Haven has eight cottages with fully equipped kitchens, decks or patios, gas barbecues, and cable television. Some cottages have fireplaces or woodstoves; bring your own firewood. An enclosed spa is available for guests. The cottages are suitable for children. Pets are not allowed. Smoking is permitted. Linens and towels are provided.

## Reservations and Rates

Reservations are recommended. The fee is $65–115 per night per cottage, double occupancy. Additional guests are $10 per night per person. There is a three-night minimum stay on holidays. Major credit cards are accepted. It's open year-round. Contact The Haven, P.O. Box 157, June Lake, CA 93529, 760/648-7524 or 800/648-7524, fax 760/648-1081, website: www.mammothlakes.com.

## Directions

From Lee Vining, drive south on U.S. 395 (passing Highway 158 North) for 20 miles (6 miles past Highway 158 North) to June Lake Junction (a sign is posted for June Lake Village) and Highway 158 South. Turn right (west) on Highway 158 North and drive 2.5 miles to June Lake Village and Knoll Road. Turn right and drive one-half block to the cottages on the right.

# 15 JUNE LAKE PINES COTTAGES
## June Lake, off U.S. 395 on the June Lake Loop

**Luxury rating:** 2                                           **Recreation rating:** 5

In the old days, nobody spent the winter at June Lake. That was back in the 1920s, before the town of June Lake was established as a summer fishing village and great winter ski area. Eighty years later, it's still known for its outstanding fishing in summer, but also for its winter sports, hiking, cycling, and horseback riding. The old, white-and-royal-blue-trimmed cottages at June Lake Pines Cottages are a reminder of June Lake's beginnings and its transformation into a thriving resort town.

The one- to three-bedroom cottages are in the heart of June Lake, across from the general store, and they can accommodate up to six people. They're old, they're cute, they're wedged in between commercial businesses, and they are close to just about everything in June Lake. All of the cottages have a full kitchen, a private bathroom, and a television; some even have a fireplace. Inside, the decor is 1950s style with knotty pine walls and a few updates. The cottages are clean and functional, and the owners, Harley and Betty Wilmot, are knowledgeable and helpful.

For information about the June Lake area, refer to the description for The Four Seasons (see next listing).

## Facilities
June Lake Pines Cottages has 12 cottages with fully equipped kitchens and bathrooms. Barbecues and televisions are provided, and some units have a fireplace. Laundry facilities and ski packages are available. The facilities are suitable for children. Leashed pets are allowed during the summer only. Smoking is permitted in some of the cottages. Linens and towels are provided, and there is limited daily maid service.

## Reservations and Rates
Reservations are recommended. For two people, the rate is $75–140 per night during the summer, $55–85 per night during the winter. Holiday rates are slightly higher. Discounts are offered for stays of five nights or more. An additional fee of $10 per

night per person is charged. Pets are $10 for the first night, then $5 per night. Ski packages are available. Major credit cards are accepted. It's open year-round. Contact June Lake Pines Cottages, P.O. Box 97, June Lake, CA 93529, 800/481-3637, website: www.junelakepines.com.

## Directions

From Lee Vining, drive south on U.S. 395 (passing Highway 158 North) for 20 miles (6 miles past Highway 158 North) to June Lake Junction (a sign is posted for June Lake Village) and Highway 158 South. Turn right (west) on Highway 158 South and drive 2.5 miles to June Lake Village and the cottages on the left, across the street from the general store.

# 16 THE FOUR SEASONS

Off Highway 158 in June Lake Village

**Luxury rating:** 3                                              **Recreation rating:** 5

When a lot of people envision a cabin in the mountains, they see an A-frame, one of those high-peaked, steeply sloped cabins with a large downstairs and a loft for sleeping.

That is exactly what makes The Four Seasons so appealing to vacationers, along with a location near June Lake that's ideal for fishing, boating, hiking, and, in the winter, skiing. You get a chance to stay in an A-frame mountain chalet, complete with a woodstove and a view of the nearby high Sierra, and the opportunity to take part in your favorite outdoor sports.

Where? These cabins are less than a mile from the June Lake Ski Area, less than a mile from Reverse Creek, and only a few miles from Silver Lake to the west, and Gull and June Lakes to the east. In other words, it is in the middle of some of the best year-round recreational opportunities in the June Lake Loop.

The cabins are all electric, which means you get complete kitchen facilities, television (hey, you can always unplug the thing), and electric blankets. They are designed to sleep up to seven people, with rates adjusted according to group size and season, of course. Prime time in this area is mid-December through early March for skiing; July and August for fishing, boating, and hiking; and mid-September to mid-October for viewing the fall colors.

With the ski area less than a mile away, winter is when the cabins are most heavily booked and when reservations are most likely to be required. June Mountain is a small hill compared to nearby Mammoth to the south, but it is plenty big enough for most beginner and intermediate skiers, with six lifts, one tram, and 2,500 vertical feet of skiing.

Of the lakes, June Lake is the prettiest, but it has the most commercial development; Gull Lake is the smallest but often has the best fishing; and Silver Lake is pretty and has good fishing but is susceptible to west winds, common in the early summer.

## Facilities

The Four Seasons has all-electric A-frame chalets with full kitchens, living rooms with woodstove and television, beds with electric blankets, and bathrooms with tub/shower combinations. The cabins are designed to handle up to seven people. No pets are permitted.

## Reservations and Rates

Reservations are recommended in summer and often required in winter. Rates range from $98 per day for two people up to $195 per day for seven people. Christmas and New Year's rates range $195–255 per night, with a seven-night minimum stay. A minimum stay of two nights is required some months. The resort is open from the last Saturday in April through October, then it closes until mid-December, when it reopens for the Christmas holidays, closing again after the New Year. Contact The Four Seasons, Star Route 3, Box 8-B, June Lake, CA 93529, 760/648-7476, website: www.junelakecalifornia.com/fourseasons/foursns.htm/.

## Directions

From Lee Vining, drive south on U.S. 395 (passing Highway 158 North) for 20 miles (6 miles past Highway 158 North) to June Lake Junction (a sign is posted for June Lake Village) and Highway 158 South. Turn right (west) on Highway 158 South and drive 2 miles to June Lake. Continue for 2 miles past June Lake Village (1 mile past the ski park), and turn left at the signed driveway for The Four Seasons.

# 17 DOUBLE EAGLE RESORT AND SPA

June Lake, off U.S. 395 on the June Lake Loop

**Luxury rating:** 4                                                    **Recreation rating:** 5

You want it all? You get it all at Double Eagle Resort and Spa, but you'd better have a credit card with a high limit ready to hand over.

It's difficult to decide the best features of the place: the superb recreational opportunities nearby or the luxurious amenities at the resort. In any case, you won't be hearing complaints from your partner or your family that they're bored.

First, let's talk about the resort.

There are 13 upscale two-bedroom cabins with all the bells and whistles, including a living room with fireplace or woodstove, an outside patio with barbecue, a full kitchen with microwave, a ski locker, a telephone, and a television with VCR. Walk outside your cabin and you'll find a pool; a hot tub; a full-service spa; a state-of-the-art fitness center with yoga, meditation, and tai chi classes; catch-and-release fishing ponds, fishing guides, and a fly-fishing school for women; organized activities and day trips, including ski and snowboard trips; and a restaurant. Take your pick.

The spa features 10 different types of massage, aromatherapy, hydrotherapy, body therapies, facials and skin care, manicures, pedicures, waxing, hair stylists, and make-up lessons. And get this: Some of the private treatment rooms have fireplaces. What happened to a good, old-fashioned, sweaty hike in the mountains, followed by an invigorating hot shower?

For winter sports, the ski lodge at June Mountain is only two miles from the resort. The much larger Mammoth Mountain complex, where you can downhill or cross-country ski, is a 20-minute drive south. Ice-skating is available, and there are hundreds of miles of groomed trails for snowmobiling.

In the summer, four lakes with excellent fishing are within eight miles. Other nearby recreation opportunities include superb hiking, horseback riding, and cycling.

## Facilities

Double Eagle Resort and Spa has 13 two-bedroom cabins with fully equipped kitchens and bathrooms and 16 luxury suites. Barbecue, deck, fireplace or woodstove, ski locker, television with VCR, and telephone are provided. A pool, a hot tub, a full-service spa, fishing ponds, fly-fishing guides, a fly-fishing school for women, ski and snowboard packages, a restaurant, a fitness center, and organized activities are available. The resort is suitable for children. Leashed pets are allowed in some of the cabins. Smoking is permitted on outside decks but not in the cabins. Linens and towels are provided, and there is daily maid service.

## Reservations and Rates

Reservations are recommended. The fee is $315–349 per night per cabin during the summer, $228–271 per night during the winter. Suites run $229–249 per night. Family discount packages are available. There is a three-night minimum stay on holidays. Major credit cards are accepted. Contact Double Eagle Resort and Spa, 5587 Boulder Road/Highway 158, P.O. Box 736, June Lake, CA 93529, 760/648-7004, fax 760/648-7017, website: www.double-eagle-resort.com.

## Directions

From Lee Vining, drive south on U.S. 395 (passing Highway 158 North) for 20 miles (6 miles past Highway 158 North) to June Lake Junction (a sign is posted for June Lake Village) and Highway 158 South. Turn right (west) on Highway 158 South and drive 2 miles to June Lake. Continue for 5 miles to the resort on the right.

# 18 BIG ROCK RESORT

June Lake, off U.S. 395 on the June Lake Loop

🚶 🏊 🛶 🚐 ❄ 🐕 👪

**Luxury rating:** 3                                   **Recreation rating:** 5

If you must have June Lake water frontage and a lake view to go along with it, then Big Rock Resort is your ticket. Situated about five miles from the town of June Lake and right next to the actual lake are eight cabins with kitchens and decks. A marina with boat rentals and paddleboats is available, and guests receive complimentary launching and docking.

I think this is one heck of a deal for the price: you get a nice, comfy cabin, great location, and direct access to beautiful June Lake. And Fido can go on vacation with you, since dogs are allowed. Since new owners took over in 2002, I have felt welcome here.

The cabins range from one to three bedrooms; the two-bedroom cabins are duplexes. The one-bedroom cabin is about 20 feet from the lake, and the three-bedroom cabin is a runner-up for closest distance to the water. The duplexes are spaced farther back, about 150 feet from the lake.

In the winter, you're 1.5 miles from June Mountain Ski Area, with 2,500 vertical feet of skiing. Cross-country skiing is possible from your doorstep, and snowmobiling is offered in the June Lake Loop. You're in close proximity to Mono Lake, the ghost town of Bodie, Yosemite National Park, Devils Postpile National Monument, and Rainbow Falls.

## Facilities

Big Rock Resort has eight cabins; all have a fully equipped kitchen, barbecue, deck, and television. Some units have a fireplace. A boat slip is provided and complimentary. A full-service marina, bait and tackle shop, and boat rentals are available. The resort is suitable for children. Some pets are allowed by prior agreement only and must be leashed. No smoking is permitted. Linens and towels are provided.

## Reservations and Rates

Reservations are recommended. Rates start at $130 for one-bedroom cabin, $160 for two-bedroom cabin, and $235 for 3-bedroom cabin. Pets are $15 per night with preauthorization only. Major credit cards are accepted. It's open year-round. Contact Big Rock Resort, P.O. Box 126, June Lake, CA 93529, 760/648-7717 or 800/769-9831, fax 760/648-1067, website: www.bigrockresort.net.

## Directions

From Lee Vining, drive south on U.S. 395 (passing Highway 158 North) for 20 miles (6 miles past Highway 158 North) to June Lake Junction (a sign is posted for June Lake Village) and Highway 158 South. Turn right (west) on Highway 158 South and drive approximately 2.5 miles to the resort on the right at the west end of the lake, next to the fire station.

# 19 EDELWEISS LODGE
Mammoth Lakes, off U.S. 395

🏇 🛶 ❄️ 🐕 🎿

**Luxury rating:** 3                                                    **Recreation rating:** 4

Many people love the natural beauty and recreational activities of the Mammoth Lakes area, but they hate the crowds, the high prices, and the motel/hotel complexes. Here's my solution to enjoying the area in a reasonably priced cabin close to town, but out of the main traffic flow: Edelweiss Lodge.

Located on a wooded acre a couple of miles from town are eight cabins within walking distance of Mammoth Creek. Most of these cabins have been here for decades, and they're in much the same condition as they were years ago. You'll find knotty pine interiors, fireplaces, and high ceilings with carved beams. They all have fully equipped kitchens, televisions, and telephones, and barbecues are available in the summer.

Most of the clientele are repeat customers who've been staying here for years because of the clean, comfortable accommodations in an ideal location surrounded by towering Jeffrey pines. The cabins are popular with families and couples who like to hike and fish in the summer and ski during the winter. You can even bring your dogs, with advance permission. July and August are by far the busiest months at the lodge; make reservations months in advance if you want to stay here during peak period. The lodge is low-key, and the owners do very little advertising; they don't need to.

For details about the area, refer to the description for Crystal Crag Lodge (see listing in this chapter). The ski lifts are a five-minute drive from the lodge, and the ski shuttle is close by.

## Facilities
Edelweiss Lodge has four cabins and four suites; all feature a fully equipped kitchen, bathroom, fireplace, telephone, and television. Barbecues are available during the summer. A hot tub is available. The cabins are suitable for children. Leashed dogs at least two years of age are allowed in some of the cabins with prior permission; cats are not allowed. No smoking is permitted. Linens and towels are provided (every other day), and daily maid service is available for an additional fee with prior notice.

## Reservations and Rates
Reservations are recommended. The double occupancy rate is $70–200 per night per cabin during the summer and $150–300 per night during the winter. Pets are $15 per night. Ski packages are available. There is a two-night minimum stay, or a three- to five-day minimum stay on selected holidays. Major credit cards are accepted. The lodge is open year-round. Contact Edelweiss Lodge, P.O. Box 658, Mammoth Lakes, CA 93546, 877/233-3593, website: www.edelweiss-lodge.com.

## Directions
From Lee Vining on U.S. 395, drive south for 25 miles to Mammoth Junction and Highway 203. Turn west and drive approximately 2 miles to Old Mammoth Road. Turn left and drive 2 miles to the lodge on the right at 1872 Old Mammoth Road.

# 20 WILDYRIE RESORT
Lake Mamie, off U.S. 395 at Mammoth Lakes

🏃 🚴 🏊 🎣 🚤 👫

**Luxury rating: 2**                                          **Recreation rating: 4**

Your own spot on one of the many beautiful lakes in the Mammoth Lakes area is the highlight here, with 11 cabins next to Lake Mamie, one of the quieter lakes. The cabins are old—so old they may as well be called historic—but they're clean and comfortable.

What I like best about these cabins are the spacious front decks, with some commanding a lake view. The cabins are set on a hillside, spaced 2–3 deep. Cabins 3, 5, 6, and 7 are closest to the water, and Cabin 9 is farther away from the others. The cabins range in size from one bedroom to four bedrooms. If you have a large family or group, Cabin 1—four bedrooms and three bathrooms—can sleep 10 people. The cabins represent different time periods from old with antique furnishings to new with more modern decor. All have fully equipped kitchens and private bathrooms. There are no televisions or radios, and no daily maid service.

Lake Mamie is small and narrow with clear water, and is easily fished by boat or bank. The Department of Fish and Game stocks it with rainbow trout throughout the summer. Rowboat rentals, bait and tackle, and a launch ramp are available at the resort; no motors are allowed on the lake. For details about activities in the area, refer to the description for Crystal Crag Lodge (see listing in this chapter).

## Facilities
Wildyrie Resort has 11 cabins; each has a fully equipped kitchen and private bathroom. Lodge rooms are also available. Continental breakfast is provided. A boat dock, boat rentals, bait and tackle, and guest lounge are available. The resort is suitable for children. Pets are not allowed. No smoking is permitted. Linens and towels are provided, but there is no daily maid service.

## Reservations and Rates
Reservations are required for a minimum visit of one week. The fee is $784–1,694 per week per cabin; it's $8 per night for each extra person. Credit cards are not accepted. It's open early June through early October. Contact Wildyrie Lodge, P.O. Box 109, Mammoth Lakes, CA 93546, 760/934-2444, website: www.mammothweb.com/lodging/wildyrieresort/.

## Directions
Follow U.S. 395 to Mammoth Junction and Highway 203/Minaret Summit Road. Turn west on Highway 203 and drive four miles to Lake Mary Road. Continue straight through the intersection to Lake Mary Road and drive 2.3 miles to Twin Lakes Loop Road. Turn right and drive past Twin Lakes and Lake Mary to Lake Mamie and the resort on the left.

## 21 TAMARACK LODGE RESORT        BEST (
Twin Lakes, off U.S. 395 at Mammoth Lakes

**Luxury rating:** 3                    **Recreation rating:** 5

Every so often, you find a gem like Tamarack Lodge Resort: a historic mountain operation in a gorgeous setting that has been lovingly cared for to retain the old-style charm, yet providing upscale, modern amenities. Many of these lodges began as ski resorts, and so it is with Tamarack.

Situated in tree cover along the shoreline of Twin Lakes are 29 cabins and 11 lodge rooms. Ranging in size from studio to three bedrooms, the cabins have a kitchen, private bathroom, and gas wall heater. The amenities vary greatly from cabin to cabin; some have a fireplace. Although not all cabins have lake views, they are no more than 100–300 feet from the lake, depending on the cabin.

The deluxe cabins were constructed from 2001 to 2005. The exterior looks like your basic modern cabin with dark brown paint, large deck with Adirondack chairs, and a lake view. The inside of the two-bedroom, two-bath rental is more rustic and customized, in keeping with the traditional design of the early days of the lodge. You'll find white pine floors; wood walls; vaulted, beamed ceilings; large stone fireplaces; and Native American and western decor with area rugs and period furniture and decorations.

Tamarack is a well-known cross-country ski area offering 28 miles of groomed trails, ski skating lanes, snowshoeing, and rentals and instruction. You can ski or snowshoe from your cabin door in winter. The shuttle for Mammoth Mountain is close by, and at Mammoth, three miles away, you'll find plenty of downhill skiing terrain.

In summer, you're steps away from Twin Lakes, a pair of small lakes on little Mammoth Creek at an elevation of 8,700 feet, where you can boat, swim, and fish; they're stocked with rainbow trout. The lakes and waterfall are absolutely beautiful, set amid Sierra granite and ringed by stands of old pines. Your hiking options are almost limitless. For dining, the lodge's lakeside restaurant is known for its excellent gourmet, California-French cuisine and extensive wine list.

## Facilities

Tamarack Lodge Resort has 29 cabins with fully equipped kitchens and bathrooms, and 11 lodge rooms. Some cabins have a porch and a fireplace or woodstove. A restaurant is available. The resort is suitable for children. Pets are not allowed. No smoking is permitted. Linens, towels, and a light daily housekeeping service are provided. Daily maid service is provided in lodge rooms.

## Reservations and Rates

Reservations are recommended. The fee is $125–360 per night per cabin, or $84–230 per night for lodge rooms. Rates are higher during the Christmas holiday. Packages including breakfast and skiing are available. Multiday minimum stays are occasionally required. Contact Tamarack Lodge Resort, P.O. Box 69, Mammoth Lakes, CA 93546, 760/934-2442 or 800/626-6684, fax 760/934-2281, website: www.tamaracklodge.com.

## Directions

From Lee Vining on U.S. 395, drive south for 25 miles to Mammoth Junction and Highway 203/Minaret Summit Road. Turn west on Highway 203 and drive 4 miles to Lake Mary Road. Continue straight through the intersection and drive 2.3 miles to Twin Lakes Loop Road. Turn right and drive 0.4 mile to the resort on the left.

# 22 WOODS LODGE
### Lake George, off Highway 203 at Mammoth Lakes

🏔 🏊 🚣 🛶 🐴 🚻

**Luxury rating:** 3                                    **Recreation rating:** 5

It's picture-perfect here—the kind of place you've seen in a movie and wish you knew the location. Well, this is one of those spots, but unfortunately, it's not a secret. In summer, it can seem like you and a thousand other people are competing elbow-to-elbow for your share of paradise in this area of Mammoth Lakes.

But take heart: The big advantage you have at Woods Lodge is your location at the end of the road. That's right—it means you can carve out your own niche next to beautiful Lake George, without the general public infringing on your turf.

From the resort, at 9,200 feet in elevation, you're overlooking unparalleled beauty found in the Sierra high country—an exquisite alpine lake surrounded by trees and rocky terrain jutting up behind the forest. The cabins are spread out over a hillside, with meandering rows spaced three deep from the lake. Cabins 15, 16, and 23 are closest to the lake—and to the road and boat launch.

The one- to three-bedroom cabins range from new to old and rustic; furnishings are traditional, with some antiques. They all have fully equipped kitchens and private bathrooms. Families love it here because it's so easy to make yourself at home and wander down to the lake each day for boating, fishing, or swimming. You can bring your own boat or rent a rowboat or motorboat; lake access is simple from the boat launch at the lodge.

Lake Mary is less than a mile away, and Twin Lakes is nearby. Riding stables are close, and you're in an excellent area for hiking; you can hike a short distance from your cabin door to various trailheads.

## Facilities
Woods Lodge has 25 cabins with fully equipped kitchens and private bathrooms. A deck and a fireplace or woodstove are provided in some of the cabins. Boat launch, boat rentals, bait and tackle, and a snack shop are available. The lodge is suitable for children. Leashed pets are allowed in some cabins. No smoking is permitted. Linens and towels are provided.

## Reservations and Rates
Reservations are made for one week or longer stays only. The fee is $92–281 per night per cabin, or $595–1,792 per week. Additional guests are $8 per night per person. The pet fee is $8 per night per pet. Credit cards are not accepted. The lodge is open late May to mid-October. Contact Woods Lodge, P.O. Box 108, Mammoth Lakes, CA 93546, 760/934-2261, website: www.mammothweb.com/lodging/woodslodge.

## Directions
Drive on U.S. 395 to Mammoth Junction and Highway 203/Minaret Summit Road. Turn west on Highway 203 and drive four miles to Lake Mary Road. Continue straight through the intersection and drive four miles to Lake Mary Loop Drive. Turn left and drive one-third of a mile to Lake George Road. Turn right and drive a short distance to the lodge at the end of the road.

# 23 CRYSTAL CRAG LODGE
Lake Mary, off Highway 203 near Mammoth Lakes

**Luxury rating:** 3                                      **Recreation rating:** 5

The natural beauty of Lake Mary is astonishing. It's a deep, blue pool set in Sierra granite, with Crystal Crag, an awesome granite spire, in the background. High in the eastern Sierra at 8,900 feet, it is the largest lake in the Mammoth Lakes region. Crystal Crag Lodge makes a great vacation setting, with 21 cabins with kitchens and bathrooms set just upslope from the lake, a boat ramp and boat rentals available, decent fishing, excellent hiking trails, and many other adventures possible in the region.

And get this: This is one of the last cabin rentals in the eastern Sierra that stills accepts pets (with a fee, of course).

Newcomers to this area always want to see "Mammoth Lake." Guess what? There is no such place. The town is called Mammoth Lakes, but there is no Mammoth Lake. Instead, Lake Mary, Lake George, Lake Mamie, and Twin Lakes are all are within a 10-minute drive of each other.

Another nearby destination that makes for a great day trip is Devils Postpile National Monument and its two-hour round-trip hike to beautiful Rainbow Falls. To get there, take Minaret Summit Road over Mammoth Pass. The trailhead is at the monument, past Mammoth Mountain Ski Area. (Noncampers arriving 7:30 A.M.–5:30 P.M. are required to take a shuttle bus from Mammoth Mountain Ski Area to Devils Postpile National Monument and other nearby recreation options, including Reds Meadows, the San Joaquin River, and trailheads for the Ansel Adams Wilderness; to avoid taking the shuttle and paying the $5–9 shuttle fee, get there before 7:30 A.M. or after 5:30 P.M.)

A great short walk starts at the back of Coldwater Camp, just south of Lake Mary, and is routed up to Emerald Lake, about a mile away. A longer, more strenuous hike is accessed from the same trailhead. It runs south along Mammoth Creek up to Arrowhead Lake, and then in turn up to Skeleton Lake, Barney Lake, and finally, up to Big Duck Lake. Duck Lake is even bigger than Lake Mary, always a surprise at first sight, and is just a mile from the Pacific Crest Trail.

Fishing can also be excellent. Lake Mary receives more trout stocks than any other lake in the Mammoth region, and that includes special batches of trophy-sized fish arranged by the lodge.

Note: Because this lake is at 8,900 feet, snow can prevent the opening of Crystal Crag Lodge until late May or early June. After a heavy winter, there can be snow near the lake into July. Make sure you call ahead if you're planning a trip to Crystal Crag Lodge in late spring or early summer.

## Facilities

Crystal Crag Lodge has 21 cabins with kitchens and bathrooms. A small marina rents aluminum boats (with or without motors) by the day or week. Coin laundry is available. Leashed dogs are permitted. A small grocery store, horseback-riding facilities, and a Forest Service campground are nearby.

## Reservations and Rates

Cabin reservations are usually required, and there's a seven-night minimum stay, although some exceptions may be made. Fees range from $89 per night for one person in a studio cabin to $179 per night for up to five people in a two-bedroom cabin to $273 per night for a four-bedroom cabin that sleeps eight. Pets cost an additional $9 per night. Contact Crystal Crag Lodge, P.O. Box 88, Mammoth Lakes, CA 93546, 760/934-2436, website: www.crystalcraglodge.com.

## Directions
From Lee Vining on U.S. 395, drive south for 25 miles to Mammoth Junction and Highway 203/Minaret Summit Road. Turn west on Highway 203 and drive three miles to Lake Mary Road. Turn left on Lake Mary Road and drive three miles to Lake Mary. The road is well-signed and circles Lake Mary.

# 24 CONVICT LAKE RESORT
Inyo National Forest, off U.S. 395 near Mammoth Lakes

**Luxury rating:** 3                                   **Recreation rating:** 5

Convict Lake, in the high southeastern Sierra, is one of the most beautiful drive-to settings in North America. The lake is deep and blue-green, set below tall, sheer mountain walls and granite peaks, the kind of mountain beauty that you never forget. At the head of the lake, a small forest grows along the feeder creek, and beyond you can see a canyon that leads up to the bordering John Muir Wilderness. The air is fresh and quiet. This is the high country, 7,583 feet, and it is pristine and stunning.

Make a rustic cabin your headquarters for a mountain vacation. The cabins have names such as Loch Leven, Golden, and Steelhead, and vary in the number of people they can accommodate. Most are small, with just a kitchen, bathroom, and living space. However, giant, deluxe vacation homes can sleep up to 32. It is an ideal destination for hiking, fishing, boating, horseback riding, and exploring the nearby hot springs at Hot Creek. A small store, marina, and dinner restaurant are at Convict Lake, so you get the best of both worlds: the beauty of the high Sierra wilderness, as well as full accommodations and facilities.

The lake is small enough, about a mile long and a half-mile wide, to keep the setting intimate, yet deep enough to provide excellent fishing. Some giant brown trout are mounted in the Convict Lake store, testimonials to what is possible.

The hiking can also be spectacular. From a signed trailhead off the access road, one route follows Convict Lake's north shore, providing very pretty views. It rises in long, graded switchbacks above the lake and is routed back through the Convict Creek canyon, still climbing, but with a steady grade. Hiking up to the creek and back is a great morning trip; horseback rides are also offered.

Nearby Hot Creek has a great section where cold stream water is mixed with very hot springwater. It's about three miles off U.S. 395, east on the road just north of the airport. Floating in the hot spring is a remarkable sensation—it is possible to feel very hot water at your chest and shoulders, cold water at your thighs, and warm water at your feet; move a step in the stream and the mix changes completely. Maps of several hot springs are available at the Convict Lake Store.

## Facilities

Convict Lake Resort has 29 cabins with kitchens and bathrooms. A small marina offers 18 boats with six-horsepower motors, six pontoon boats with an eight-person capacity, and a launch ramp; other amenities include horseback riding rentals, a four-star restaurant, a general store, a fish-cleaning facility, and pay phones. Pets are permitted with an additional fee. It's open year-round. Linens, pillows, and blankets are provided.

## Reservations and Rates

Cabin reservations are strongly recommended. Fees range from $119, double occupancy, to $1,079 per night for a six-bedroom vacation house that can sleep 34. The pet fee is $10 per stay. Contact Convict Lake Resort, HCR-79, Box 204, Mammoth Lakes, CA 93546, 800/992-2260, ext. 47, website: www.convictlake.com. For reservations at The Restaurant at Convict Lake, call 760/934-3803.

## Directions

From Lee Vining, drive south on U.S. 395 (past the Mammoth Lakes turnoff) to Convict Lake Road, adjacent to the Mammoth Lakes Airport. Turn right (west) and drive two miles to the Convict Lake Store on the right.

# 25 THE REDWOODS
### Yosemite National Park, off Highway 41 in Wawona

🏃 🚲 ✳ 🐴 👫

**Luxury rating:** 3                    **Recreation rating:** 4

The biggest surprises at Yosemite National Park are not Half Dome, El Capitan, Yosemite Falls, Bridalveil Falls, or the spectacular, glaciated beauty of the valley. You already knew about them, right? Of course.

The biggest surprises at Yosemite are the 127 cabins and mountain vacation homes available for rent near Wawona at the southern border of the park. For people who have never ventured to the park's southern reaches, it can be a shock to discover there is an entire little township within park borders, complete with a grocery store.

The town is a short distance from the trailhead for the hike to Chilnualna Falls, the prettiest waterfall in Yosemite's southern region, as well as Mariposa Grove, the ancient forest of giant sequoias. Badger Pass Ski Area is 17 miles away, and it is about a 45-minute drive to either Glacier Point or Yosemite Valley. If you have never been here, you will likely be astounded to discover there is also a golf course nearby—that's right, a golf course in Yosemite National Park.

The settlement of dwellings is called The Redwoods, and it is composed of vacation cabins, cottages, and homes that vary from a one-bedroom rustic cabin to a six-bedroom mountain home. They are all privately owned but are listed with The Redwoods for vacation rentals. Since the owners occasionally use them, they are furnished with whatever they would need for their own vacations, and that includes darn near everything.

The most popular nearby hike is the traditional venture to Mariposa Grove, just east of the southern park entrance. A better romp for the ambitious is the hike out to Chilnualna Falls, with the trailhead at road's end at The Redwoods in North Wawona. It's a strenuous eight-mile round-trip, climbing 2,000 feet to the base of the falls at 6,000 feet. To reach the trailhead from Wawona, turn east on Chilnualna Falls Road and drive 1.7 miles to the road's end and park in the lot on the right side of the road; walk back to the road and look for the hiking trail at the edge of the pavement.

## Facilities

The Redwoods has 127 privately owned cabins and mountain homes for rent. Each is completely furnished, including cookware and utensils. A small grocery store is nearby. Pet policies vary by unit. Bring your own linens and towels or participate in the bed linen exchange program at the main office.

## Reservations and Rates

Reservations are required. Cabin and home rentals range $125–196 per night for a one-bedroom cabin for two to $442–662 per night for a six-bedroom mountain home for up to 18. Winter discounts are available, and different promotions are available each season. A $20 entrance fee to Yosemite National Park is charged for each vehicle; the pass is good for one week. Contact The Redwoods, P.O. Box 2085, Wawona Station, Yosemite, CA 95389, 209/375-6666, website: www.redwoodsinyosemite.com. For an excellent hiking map of the area, contact Tom Harrison Cartography at 415/456-7940. A free map/brochure of Yosemite National Park is provided at park entrance stations as part of the entrance fee.

## Directions

From Highway 99 at Merced, turn east on Highway 140 and drive to Mariposa. In Mariposa, turn south on Highway 49 and drive 30 miles to Highway 41 at Oakhurst. Turn left on Highway 41 and drive into the southern entrance station for Yosemite National Park. Continue on Highway 41 to Wawona. Turn east on Chilnualna Road and drive 1.3 miles to The Redwoods. (You will receive specific directions to your cabin at the main office when your reservation is confirmed.)

# 26 ROCK CREEK LODGE
Rock Creek, off U.S. 395 near Tom's Place

**Luxury rating:** 2                                          **Recreation rating:** 5

A winter wonderland is what you'll find most of the year at Rock Creek Lodge, one of the best lodging options in this book for accessing the outdoors experience, rustic style. Located in Inyo National Forest, the lodge was built in the 1920s as one of the first ski resorts in the country. There's still plenty of cross-country skiing and snowshoeing in winter, and you'll get a taste of the way it used to be, which is also the way it still is here.

Thirteen cabins nestle in a glacial canyon at 9,373 feet in elevation at the edge of John Muir Wilderness. All of the cabins have full kitchens, and some have private bathrooms; a central bathroom is also provided. These are rustic cabins and there's nothing fancy about them, and it's important to know what is and isn't provided because the amenities change from summer to winter. For instance, complimentary breakfast and dinner are provided in the dining room during the winter, but not in the summer. Two primitive ski-to huts are also available. In winter, snowmobiles drive you two miles from your vehicle to the lodge, since the road isn't plowed. Get the idea? You're in true backcountry.

If you like snow sports, then you'll be in winter heaven, because there are nine miles of groomed trails. The possibilities include cross-country skiing, snowshoeing, hut skiing, ski touring, and track skiing; rentals and lessons are available. For the adventurous, two ski-to huts (Mosquito Flat and Tamarack) can be accessed by skiing or snowshoeing two or three miles from the lodge. These are tent cabins with primitive cooking facilities and pit toilets, and you must haul all your own bedding, food, and equipment, much like backpacking.

But let's not forget summertime, which is equally rewarding for outdoor enthusiasts, with outstanding hiking and fishing. Hilton Lake, Tamarack Lake, Ruby Lakes, and the Little Lakes Valley are within walking distance. Ruby Lake was named for its gem-like qualities, and the Little Lakes Valley features excellent fishing for brook trout and occasional big brown trout. Many of the higher-elevation lakes nearby have golden trout.

## Facilities
Rock Creek Lodge has 14 cabins with fully equipped kitchens (summer only) and woodstoves. There are two winter ski-to huts. Breakfast and dinner, plus electric

heaters, are provided in the winter only. Eight of the cabins have private bathrooms; a central bathroom is available. A sauna, a restaurant, a general store, bait and tackle, and cross-country ski and snowshoe rentals are available. The cabins are suitable for children. Leashed pets are allowed. Linens and towels are provided during the summer only; only pillows and pillowcases are provided during the winter, so be sure to bring your own sheets and blankets.

## Reservations and Rates
Reservations are recommended. The double occupancy rate is $90–120 per night per cabin during the summer, $100–125 per night per cabin during the winter; triple occupancy is $160 per night; for more than three, it's $15 per night per person. Children ages 6–12 are half price, and children under 5 are free. The pet fee is $15 per night per pet. The Mosquito Flat ski-to hut is $35 per night per person; contact the Sierra Mountain Center, 760/873-8526, about the Tamarack ski-to hut. The winter snowmobile shuttle to and from the lodge is free. Major credit cards are accepted. It's open year-round. Contact Rock Creek Lodge, HCR 79, Box 12, Mammoth Lakes, CA 93546, 760/935-4170 or 877/935-4170, fax 760/935-4172, website: www.rockcreeklodge.com.

## Directions
From the junction of U.S. 395 and Highway 203 (the Mammoth Lakes turnoff), drive 15 miles south on U.S. 395 to Tom's Place. Turn right (south) on Rock Creek Road and drive 8 miles to the lodge on the left.

# 27 ROCK CREEK LAKES RESORT
Inyo National Forest, off U.S. 395 at Rock Creek Lake

**Luxury rating:** 2 **Recreation rating:** 5

The owners at Rock Creek Lakes Resort say that no sissies need apply. In other words, no whiners, please. This is the kind of place for down-to-earth people who can live without a telephone, television, pool, spa, and the like.

One- to three-bedroom cabins sit in a secluded lodgepole pine forest, about a quarter mile behind the resort. Two new cabins were added in 2001. Each cabin has a full kitchen, private bathroom, living room, and gas heater. In addition, the resort's café has some of the best homemade pie you'll ever taste. What Rock Creek Lakes Resort lacks in amenities, it makes up for in setting; at nearly 10,000 feet in elevation, this is one of the best locations imaginable for exploring the eastern Sierra. And it's *the* place for adventure lovers looking for a break from the urban routine.

The resort is in a dramatic canyon with towering granite peaks, just across the road from Rock Creek Lake, a natural beauty with a five-mph speed limit and great fishing. Take your pick of hiking trails that lead into the John Muir Wilderness; more than 50 lakes are within a two-hour hike of Rock Creek Canyon. If you don't want to walk, rent a horse at Rock Creek Pack Station, one-half mile from the resort. Mountain biking is also popular, and Lower Rock Creek and Sand Canyon have two of the most difficult and desirable trails around; I advise you to avoid them unless you're an experienced rider.

In addition to pies, the café serves excellent chili, burgers, and soups, but remember that it's not open for dinner; it closes at 6 P.M., but you can order a late lunch and call it dinner if you like. "Pies and skies" are what the resort is most noted for, and cyclists have been known to ride 50 miles round-trip just to get a piece of pie.

## Facilities

Rock Creek Lakes Resort has 11 cabins with fully equipped kitchens, bathrooms with showers, barbecues, decks or porches, and thermostat heating. Do not bring electrical appliances; the resort generates its own electricity. A café, a general store, and fishing supplies are available. Cabins do not have televisions or telephones. The resort is suitable for children. Pets are not allowed. Smoking is permitted in some of the cabins. One cabin is wheelchair accessible. Linens and towels are provided.

## Reservations and Rates

Reservations are recommended. The fee is $120 per night or $756 per week for a one-bedroom, $158–189 per night or $995–1,191 for a two-bedroom, and $288 per night or $1,814 per week for the two-story cabin. Additional guests are $8 per night. A four-night minimum stay is required in July and August. Major credit cards are accepted. It's open mid-May to mid-October, weather permitting. Contact Rock Creek Lakes Resort, P.O. Box 727, Bishop, CA 93515, 760/935-4311, fax 760/935-9101, website: www.rockcreeklake.com. For Rock Creek Pack Station, call 760/935-4493 (summer only).

## Directions

From the junction of U.S. 395 and Highway 203 (the Mammoth Lakes turnoff), drive 15 miles south on U.S. 395 to Tom's Place. Turn right (south) on Rock Creek Road and drive 9 miles to the resort on the right.

# Other Cabins & Cottages in the Region

**Boulder Lodge,** P.O. Box 68, 2282 Highway 158, June Lake, CA 93529, 760/648-7533 or 800/458-6355, fax 760/648-7330, website: www.boulderlodge.com.

**Fern Creek Lodge,** 4628 Highway 158, June Lake, CA 93529, 760/648-7722 or 800/621-9146, website: www.ferncreeklodge.com.

**Gull Lake Lodge,** P.O. Box 25, June Lake, CA 93529, 760/648-7516 or 800/631-9081, website: www.gulllakelodge.com.

**June Lake Motel and Cabins,** P.O. Box 98, 2716 Boulder Drive, June Lake, CA 93529, 760/648-7547 or 800/648-6835, website: www.junelakemotel.com.

**Mammoth Mountain Chalets,** P.O. Box 513, Mammoth Lakes, CA 93546, 760/934-8518 or 800/327-3681, fax 760/934-5117.

**Reverse Creek Lodge,** Route 3, Box 2, June Lake, CA 93529, 760/648-7535 or 800/762-6440, website: www.reversecreeklodge.com.

**Still Meadow Cabins,** P.O. Box 694, June Lake, CA 93529, 760/648-7794 or 800/648-2211.

**Whispering Pines,** Route 3, Box 14B, June Lake, CA 93529, 760/648-7762 or 800/648-7762, website: http://visitwhisperingpines.com.

# MONTEREY AND SAN SIMEON

COURTESY OF McALPINE LAKE AND PARK

## BEST CABINS & COTTAGES

**⟨ Best for Beach Access**
La Playa Hotel Cottages, **page 292**

**⟨ Most Luxurious**
Post Ranch Inn, **page 300**

The scenic charm seems to extend to infinity from the seaside towns of Santa Cruz, Monterey, Big Sur, and San Simeon. The primary treasure is the coast, which is rock-strewn and sprinkled with inshore kelp beds, where occasionally you can find sea otters playing Pop Goes the Weasel. The sea here is a color like no other, often more of a tourmaline than a straight green or blue.

From Carmel to Lucia alone, touring the Big Sur on Highway 1 is one of the most captivating drives anywhere. The inland strip along Highway 1 provides access to state parks, redwoods, coastal streams, Los Padres National Forest, and Ventana Wilderness. Farther south on the Pacific Coast Highway lies a largely untouched coast, encompassing San Simeon, Hearst Castle, Morro Bay, inland canyons, and three of the most fish-filled lakes anywhere: Lake San Antonio, Lake Nacimiento, and Santa Margarita Lake.

Most vacations to this region include several must-do trips, often starting in Monterey with a visit to Fisherman's Wharf and its domesticated sea lions, moving on to nearby Monterey Bay Aquarium. In addition, Carmel-by-the-Sea is well known for its shops, selling everything from small vacation mementos to high-class art worth thousands of dollars.

From there, most head south to Big Sur to take in a few brush strokes of nature's canvas, easily realizing why this area is beloved around the world. At first glance, however, it's impossible not to want the whole painting. That is where the cabin and cottage rentals come in. They provide both the ideal getaway and a launch point for adventure.

At Big Sur, the cabin accommodations are what many expect: small hideaways in the big redwoods. Some are near Big Sur River, others sit in the forest. But amid these is one like no other: Post Ranch Inn. It actually has a deluxe tree house!

Other good opportunities exist in Carmel and in the Monterey area. Most of these are midrange to high-end, and most are reserved well in advance. In the foothills, big lakes set the scene for cabin-style lodgings, which are ideal for families.

During the summer, only the fog on the coast and the intense heat just 10 miles inland keep this region from attaining perfection.

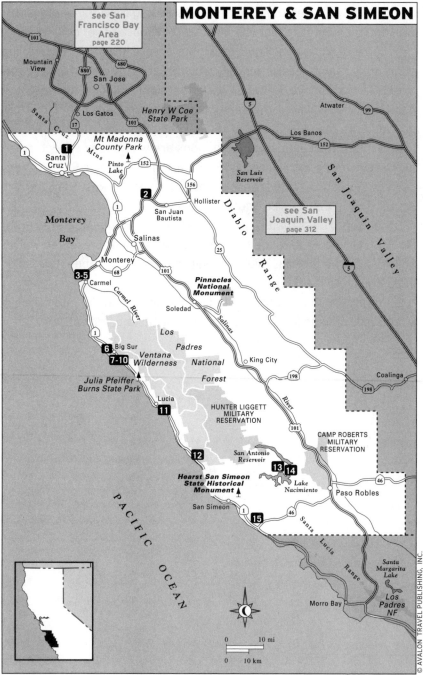

# MONTEREY & SAN SIMEON

# Monterey and San Simeon Cabins & Cottages

# 1 COTILLION GARDENS RV PARK

Santa Cruz Mountains, off Highway 9 near Felton

🏃 🐕 👪 ♿

**Luxury rating:** 2          **Recreation rating:** 4

Cotillion Gardens RV Park sits among the redwoods in the Santa Cruz Mountains, next to the San Lorenzo River. Two of the cabins are along the river—by far the best location at the park—and come with fireplaces. The others are near the forest, adjacent to an RV park with 80 sites.

The accommodations are fairly spartan; that is, you bring your own bedding or sleeping bag, along with towels, dishes, and utensils. Most cabins don't have a private bathroom, so come prepared to share one with your neighbors. One of the cabins is very primitive and we classify it as simply a sleeping unit—no, my wife and I didn't spend our wedding night here.

But a great highlight is the beauty of the redwoods, along with the many possible side trips. Since you're near the edge of the Santa Cruz Mountain redwoods, you have easy access to Henry Cowell Redwoods State Park and the San Lorenzo River. Monterey Bay is only about a 10-minute drive from the park. Other side trips include a steam train ride along the San Lorenzo River, offered by Roaring Camp Train Rides in Felton, and visiting Loch Lomond Reservoir near Ben Lomond for hiking, boat rentals, or fishing.

## Facilities

Cotillion Gardens RV Park has five camping cabins with varying accommodations. Two have fireplaces and kitchens with a microwave; all have televisions. No kitchen utensils or plates are provided. Some units have a private bathroom. Communal showers, a recreation room, a swimming pool, and a small store are on the property. Some facilities are wheelchair accessible. Leashed pets are permitted. No linens are provided.

## Reservations and Rates

Reservations are recommended. Double-occupancy cabin fees are $65, $90, and $100 per night based on size. Major credit cards are accepted. It's open year-round. Contact Cotillion Gardens RV Park, 300 Old Big Trees, Felton, CA 95018, 831/335-7669.

## Directions

From Los Gatos, drive west on Highway 17 for 20 miles toward Santa Cruz to the Mount Hermon Road exit/Scotts Valley (second exit in Scotts Valley). Take the Mount

Hermon Road exit to the stoplight. Turn right on Mount Hermon Road and drive 3.5 miles to Felton and Graham Hill Road. Turn right on Graham Hill Road and drive 50 feet to Highway 9. Turn left on Highway 9 and drive 1.5 miles to the park.

# **2** McALPINE LAKE AND PARK
McAlpine Lake, off Highway 129 near San Juan Bautista

🖼️ 🐕 👫 ♿

**Luxury rating:** 1                                      **Recreation rating:** 4

McAlpine Lake has been put on the map by its new trophy trout program, where every time you throw your line in the water, there's a chance of catching a 10-pound rainbow trout or better.

That's why the camping cabins here are designed for fishing enthusiasts. They look like miniature log cabins, cute and comfortable, and are pretty much bulletproof. You should think of your stay here as a camping trip: Bring everything you need, including sleeping bags. You share the same facilities as the campers at the park. The only difference is the privacy and security of solid walls and a roof over your head.

McAlpine Lake is no little kid's pond like you occasionally see at parks, but rather a 40-foot-deep lake. That's deep enough to provide sufficient oxygen and a food chain to support a good fishery. The highlights are trophy-size rainbow trout and catfish, and enough stocks to keep catch rates high. The success of the fishing program has rated stories in outdoor recreation newspapers. That makes this one of the best fishing opportunities in the area. The best trout fishing is in late winter and spring, with catfish taking over the top spot once the hot weather arrives for keeps.

Other highlights of the park include its proximity to Mission San Juan Bautista and the relatively short drive to the Monterey-Carmel area.

## Facilities
McAlpine Lake and Park has a campground and camping cabins with picnic tables and fire grills. Flush toilets, showers, an RV dump station, a recreation room, a swimming pool, coin laundry, propane gas, and groceries are on-site. Some facilities are wheelchair accessible. Leashed pets are permitted. Linens and towels are not provided. Bring your sleeping bag and pillow.

## Reservations and Rates
Reservations are recommended. The rate is $54 per night for cabin rentals, double

occupancy, $5 for each additional adult, $3 per child, $5 for each extra vehicle. Major credit cards are accepted. Contact McAlpine Lake and Park, 900 Anzar Road, San Juan Bautista, CA 95045, 831/623-4263, website: www.mcalpinelake.com.

## Directions
From U.S. 101, take the Highway 129 exit west and drive 100 feet. Turn left onto Searle Road (frontage road) and drive to the stop sign. Turn left again on Anzar Road and drive under the freeway to the park.

# ❸ LA PLAYA HOTEL COTTAGES          BEST (
Monterey Coast, off Highway 1 in Carmel

**Luxury rating:** 5                    **Recreation rating:** 3

You can't go wrong with these five storybook cottages, featuring either a kitchen or wet bar, right in the heart of Carmel. Not only are they centrally located, but they are tucked away about one block from the hotel, toward the ocean. It's quieter and more private at the cottages than at the hotel, but if you suddenly feel like mixing with people, you can wander over to the hotel and use its facilities, including the heated pool surrounded by gardens.

To reach the cottages, you follow a meandering path past flowers and foliage. Each cottage has 1–3 bedrooms, a television, a radio, a terrace, and a garden patio. Don't want to cook, but you don't feel like going to a restaurant? Easy. Just order the hotel's room service; your meal will soon be delivered to your quaint cottage. These upscale units have that trademark Carmel charm, from the tasteful, informally coordinated furniture, woodburning fireplace, and cheerfully painted walls to the upstairs sleeping area and deck with white Adirondack chairs.

The overall effect is inviting and serene, and it's obvious that these cottages were designed to please the most discriminating guests.

## Facilities
La Playa has five cottages with fully equipped kitchens or wet bars, televisions, and garden patios. Most of the cottages have fireplaces, and most have more than one bathroom. Up to eight people can be accommodated, depending on the cottage. Room service is available, and there is a restaurant, lounge, and heated pool at the hotel. The hotel has 75 rooms. The cottages are suitable for children, but the hotel is

more adult-oriented. Pets are not allowed. No smoking is allowed. Linens and towels are provided.

## Reservations and Rates

Reservations are recommended. The fee is $335–650 per night for cottages and $175–475 per night for hotel rooms. Additional guests are $15 per night. There is a two-night minimum stay on weekends and three-night minimum on holidays. Major credit cards are accepted. Contact La Playa Hotel Cottages, Camino Real at 8th Avenue, P.O. Box 900, Carmel-by-the-Sea, CA 93921, 831/624-6476 or 800/582-8900, fax 831/624-7966, website: www.laplayahotel.com.

## Directions

From San Jose, drive south on U.S. 101 for 40 miles to the junction with Highway 156. Turn west on Highway 156 and drive 5 miles to Highway 1. Turn south on Highway 1 and drive 15 miles to Carmel and Ocean Avenue. Turn right on Ocean Avenue and drive 0.5 mile to Camino Real. Turn left and drive two blocks to the hotel on the corner of Camino Real and 8th Avenue.

# 4 MISSION RANCH
Monterey Coast, off Highway 1 in Carmel

**Luxury rating:** 4                                        **Recreation rating:** 3

Mission Ranch is one of the few historic tracts of land in Carmel, 22 acres to be exact, that haven't been turned into shopping centers or condo complexes. Not that the developers haven't tried. Clint Eastwood bought the property in 1986, rescuing this special place from a proposed condominium development. Since then, the ranch has been painstakingly renovated, with the goal of retaining its 150-year-old history while providing modern amenities.

During the 1800s and early 1900s, the property was a 160-acre dairy ranch. Next it became an officers' club during World War II, with a well-known reputation for dance bands and a popular bar scene. Then the local school district and the state bought the property.

Nowadays, the renovated buildings reflect different architectural periods of the ranch's history, including the farmhouse built in the 1850s. The Bunkhouse is the oldest building; it sleeps up to four people. It's surrounded by large eucalyptus and cypress trees and has newly planted gardens. Other unique lodgings here include the Honeymoon Cottage and the Hay Loft.

The views from Mission Ranch are breathtaking and are sure to make your day. Looking south, you'll see undisturbed, pristine meadows, adjacent to wetlands and Carmel River Beach. Look farther and you'll spot Point Lobos across the bay. Some of the cottages have ocean views, and the restaurant and piano bar—both on-site—feature panoramic views.

It's hard to believe you're only one block from Carmel Mission, one-half mile from shopping centers, and 2.5 miles from Point Lobos State Reserve.

## Facilities

Mission Ranch has 31 varying lodging units, including a hayloft, a farmhouse, a bunkhouse, a triplex, and a cottage; all have bathrooms. Some rooms have ocean views. There are no kitchen facilities, but a complimentary continental breakfast is provided. Bed sizes vary from queen to king, and some cottages have a twin sofabed. A fireplace and hot tub are available in some rooms. A restaurant, a piano bar, six championship tennis courts, and a fitness facility are available. The ranch is not suitable for children. Pets are not allowed. Smoking is not permitted. Some facilities are wheelchair accessible. Linens and towels are provided.

## Reservations and Rates

Reservations are required. The rates range $110–290 per night per lodging unit, with a charge of $15 per each additional person per night. There is a two-night minimum stay on weekends. Major credit cards are accepted. Contact Mission Ranch, 3637B Dolores Street, Carmel, CA 93923, 831/624-6436 or 800/538-8221, fax 831/626-4163, website: www.missionranchcarmel.com.

## Directions

From San Jose, drive south on U.S. 101 for 40 miles to the junction with Highway 156. Turn west on Highway 156 and drive 5 miles to Highway 1. Turn south on Highway 1 and drive 15 miles to Carmel and Rio Road. Turn right on Rio Road and drive approximately 0.25 mile (passing Carmel Mission) to Lasuen Drive. Turn left and drive 0.5 mile to the ranch.

# 5 CARMEL RIVER INN
Carmel River, off Highway 1 in Carmel

**Luxury rating:** 3                                    **Recreation rating:** 3

This is a popular place for dogs as well as people. You see, dogs are welcome here, and their owners and families seem to like the inn, too.

You can tell you're in Carmel because of the beautifully quaint cottages, painted red with white shutters and sporting Kelly green roofs. Yes, it's bright and cheerful here at these 24 cottages set among towering cypress trees. The Carmel River Inn backs up to—what else?—the Carmel River. Although the inn is close to the highway, the trees and the river seem to buffer the traffic noise.

The cottages include lodgepole pine–crafted beds, pastel walls, and a furnished patio outside. Cottages vary in size from intimate to family size and can accommodate up to six comfortably. Bed sizes also vary, from double to king.

The grounds are landscaped and a large heated pool is big enough for lap swimming if it's not crowded. There's also plenty of decking for sunbathing.

The motto here is "great location, great rates," and I have to agree. It's definitely not a wilderness experience, but if you're looking for a cute cottage close to a popular getaway town, you've found it. You may not be able to watch deer and squirrels from your yard, but surely the neighbor's golden retriever will let you pet her.

## Facilities

Carmel River Inn has 24 cottages and 18 motel rooms varying in size and amenities. All rentals include a bathroom with shower. Some provide fully equipped kitchens, decks, and wood-burning fireplaces. A heated pool is on-site. The inn is suitable for children. Leashed pets are allowed in the cottage area only. No smoking is permitted. Some facilities are wheelchair accessible. Linens and towels are provided.

## Reservations and Rates

Reservations are recommended. The fee is $179–369 per night per cottage and $159 per night for motel rooms. The pet fee is $10 per pet per night, allowed only in cottages. There is a two-night minimum stay on weekends and a three-night minimum on holidays. Major credit cards are accepted. Contact Carmel River Inn, Highway 1 at the Bridge, P.O. Box 221609, Carmel, CA 93922, 831/624-1575 or 800/966-6490, fax 831/624-0290, website: www.carmelriverinn.com.

## Directions

From San Jose, drive south on U.S. 101 for 40 miles to the junction with Highway 156. Turn west on Highway 156 and drive 5 miles to Highway 1. Turn south on Highway 1 and drive 15 miles to Carmel and Oliver Road. Turn right on Oliver Road and drive a short distance to the inn on the right.

# 6 RIPPLEWOOD RESORT

Off Highway 1 near Big Sur

**Luxury rating:** 3                                    **Recreation rating:** 4

Everybody has a favorite chair. You know, the kind that makes you feel just right, no matter what mood you're in, what you are going through, or how long you have been away from it. Ripplewood Resort in Big Sur has entire cabins like this. In fact, they have 16 of them. Each one is different enough so that after surveying the place, you have a good chance of finding one that suits you perfectly. Just like your favorite chair.

Cabin 2 is the most secluded. Cabin 6 has a postcard view of the Big Sur River. Cabins 1, 14, and 15 have stone fireplaces. On the low end is a cabin that looks like a small motel room. On the high end is a multiple-room chalet with a redwood-beamed ceiling and stone fireplace, Cabin 15. Get the idea? Right. Take a look, survey a few, and you'll find one that's right for you.

A real bonus here is the small grocery store; most of the cabins have kitchens. That means if you don't feel like going to a restaurant or just want to spare the expense, you can make a quick shopping trip and create a meal yourself without having to drive too far. There are very few cabin settings where this is possible.

Ripplewood is along Highway 1 in the heart of Big Sur, an ideal location for a mini-vacation. The cabins are surrounded by redwoods, several of them along the Big Sur River. There is excellent hiking in the area, best of all in Andrew Molera State Beach, Point Sur State Historic Park, Julia Pfeiffer Burns State Park, Los Padres National Forest, and Ventana Wilderness.

You will remember Ripplewood's coziness and the character of the cabins.

## Facilities

Ripplewood Resort has 16 cabins of various sizes and settings that can accommodate up to five people, depending on the unit. All have bathrooms and decks, most have kitchens, and some have river views. The kitchens are not fully stocked, but kitchen kits are available for $10. A café serves breakfast and lunch, plus there's a small grocery store, a library, and a gas station. Children are suitable here, but groups are discouraged. Each person must have a bed; no sleeping bags are allowed in lieu of beds. No pets are allowed. Smoking is not permitted. Major credit cards are accepted. Linens and towels are provided.

## Reservations and Rates

Reservations are required and should be made six months in advance. The fee is $75–135 per night for two people. Children under age five are free. On weekends, there is a two-night minimum stay. Contact Ripplewood Resort, Highway 1, Big Sur, CA 93920, 831/667-2242, website: www.ripplewoodresort.com.

## Directions

From Carmel, drive 25 miles south on Highway 1. Look for Ripplewood Resort on the east side of the road. Ripplewood's small gas station and store are directional landmarks.

# 7 BIG SUR CAMPGROUND AND CABINS

Monterey Coast, off Highway 1 in Big Sur

**Luxury rating:** 3                                              **Recreation rating:** 4

This camp is like a miniature park, set in the redwoods near the Big Sur River. The cabins range from primitive tent cabins to fully furnished mini-homes—that is, two-bedroom cabins with fireplace, kitchen, and beds. You share the park with a campground and you have use of its facilities, too.

Big Sur is drop-dead gorgeous and a popular getaway, of course. These cabins provide a blessed sense of privacy. By staying in the redwoods, you have the opportunity to hike on great trails and explore nearby Pfeiffer Big Sur State Park. This is one of California's most beautiful state parks, with woods and water, forest hideaways, and coastal lookouts. It is the top adventure destination for visitors staying at this park. The must-do trip for all visitors here is the easy romp to see Pfeiffer Falls, a pretty 60-foot cascade; though a bit wispy and narrow, it still captures the attention of most. After all, it takes less than an hour to make the trip, so the payoff is definitely worth the effort.

Nearby Los Padres National Forest and Ventana Wilderness in the mountains to the east provide access to remote hiking trails with ridge-top vistas. Cruising Highway 1 south to Lucia and back offers endless views of breathtaking coastal scenery.

## Facilities

Big Sur Campground and Cabins has 19 cabins with varying levels of size and accommodation. Most have fireplaces and furnished kitchens. Four tent cabins are designed mainly as sleeping units, with few private amenities. An 80-site campground on the property has restrooms, drinking water, flush toilets, showers, an RV dump station, a playground, a small store, and a laundry room. Some facilities are wheelchair accessible. Pets are permitted in tent cabins only; no smoking or pets in the other cabins. Linens and towels are provided in some cabins; bring sleeping bags and pillows if staying in a tent cabin.

## Reservations and Rates

Reservations are recommended. Tent cabins for two people cost $59, one-bedroom cabins for two cost $105–125, two-bedroom cabins cost $210–250, a one-bedroom cabin with kitchen costs $175, and an A-frame with loft costs $190, all double occupancy rates; each additional person is $12. Major credit cards are accepted. It's open year-round. Contact Big Sur Campground and Cabins, Highway 1, Big Sur, CA 93920, 831/667-2322, website: www.campingfriend.com/bigsurcampgroundandcabins/.

## Directions

From Carmel, drive 27 miles south on Highway 1 to the campground on the right side of the road.

# 8 BIG SUR LODGE

Monterey Coast, off Highway 1 at Pfeiffer Big Sur State Park

**Luxury rating:** 3                                    **Recreation rating:** 5

You're in the heart of Big Sur here, and if you're looking for exceptional hiking among the redwoods and along the ocean, then look no further. Although these cottages aren't exceptional, Pfeiffer Big Sur State Park itself is. That doesn't mean I don't recommend the lodge; it's just that the accommodations are the predictable condo-type, and the spectacular scenery is out on the trail, not at your doorstep.

Since the park is so popular, especially during the summer months, and the lodge is inside the park, you'll probably be aware of the constant flow of people through the park. But that's easy to remedy. First, try visiting during the week and off-season—it's just as beautiful. Next, avoid the most popular trails during prime time, which is midmorning to midafternoon.

A must-see is 60-foot Pfeiffer Falls, an easy 1.5-mile round-trip hike through old redwoods and along Pfeiffer Redwood Creek. Wildlife is abundant in this park; be on the lookout for condors soaring overhead and taking rests in the redwood trees. Whale-watching is best in January and March. And for music lovers, the Big Sur Jazz Fest is held in early May.

Your room price includes admission to the park, as well as nearby Point Lobos State Reserve, Andrew Molera State Park, Julia Pfeiffer Burns State Park, and Limekiln State Park.

## Facilities

Big Sur Lodge has 61 cottages total, with 2–6 cottages per building. Each unit has a full bathroom and a deck or balcony. Fully equipped kitchens and a fireplace or woodstove are provided in some of the cottages. All beds are queen size. There are no in-room telephones, televisions, radios, or alarm clocks. A heated swimming pool, a restaurant, a grocery store, and a gift shop are on the premises. The facilities are suitable for children. Pets are not allowed. No smoking is permitted. Linens and towels are provided.

## Reservations and Rates

Reservations are recommended. The fee is $99–229 per night per cottage; add $30 for a second bedroom. A two-night minimum stay is required on weekends, and a two- to three-night minimum is required on holidays. Major credit cards are accepted. Contact Big Sur Lodge, 47225 Highway 1, Big Sur, CA 93920, 831/667-3100 or 800/424-4787, website: www.bigsurlodge.com.

## Directions

From Carmel, drive south on Highway 1 for 26 miles to the Pfeiffer Big Sur State Park entrance. Turn left and continue to the lodge.

# 9 RIVERSIDE CAMPGROUND AND CABINS

Big Sur River, off Highway 1 in Big Sur

**Luxury rating: 3**                                      **Recreation rating: 4**

When it comes to rating the quality of a cabin- or cottage-based vacation, there are really two main factors: 1) Is there a comfortable bed to sleep in? and 2) Is there a bathroom with a shower?

The answer to both is yes at Riverside Campground and Cabins. On the Big Sur Coast, there can be a fine line between nice and rustic, and rustic and camping. The privately operated Riverside Campground and Cabins is one of the nice places—one of the better opportunities designed for folks cruising Highway 1 touring the Big Sur area. This camp is amid redwoods near the Big Sur River. It's a great headquarters for hiking adventures and exploring the Big Sur Coast.

Side trips include hiking out to remote beaches at Andrew Molera State Park; rangers can often advise the best places to spot sea otters playing on the edge of kelp beds. There are also great hikes in redwood forests and to waterfalls at Julia Pfeiffer Burns State Park.

Of course, there are several fine restaurants to visit for a dining adventure. Those on a budget can try Nepenthe (831/667-2345); those who can light cigars with $100 bills can visit the Ventana Inn (831/667-4242).

## Facilities

Riverside Campground and Cabins has four stand-alone cabins, five lodge rooms. Five have bathrooms. The others share a bath house. No smoking or pets are allowed. A 44-site campground is on the property. Linens and towels are provided.

## Reservations and Rates

Reservations are recommended. The rate is $75–130 per night for two people, with $8 per additional person per night and $6 per night for each extra vehicle. Major credit cards are accepted. It's open year-round. Contact Riverside Campground and Cabins, Highway 1, P.O. Box 3, Big Sur, CA 93920, 831/667-2414, website: www.riversidecampground.com.

## Directions
From Carmel, drive 25 miles south on Highway 1 to the campground on the right.

## 🔟 POST RANCH INN                           BEST 【
Monterey Coast, off Highway 1 in Big Sur

🏃 🚲 🚹

**Luxury rating:** 5                                    **Recreation rating:** 4

© BATISTA MOON/PATRICK TREGENZA

It seems like there should be a sign when you enter Big Sur that reads, "Spectacular scenery, spectacular prices." That's certainly the case at the Post Ranch Inn, where you get an exceptional setting and accommodations with a big price tag to go along with it. Although the inn is beyond the financial realm of most of us, if you want to know how the other half lives when they go on an outdoors-oriented vacation, then read on.

What do you get on these 96 acres? Well, a lot. For starters, the cabins are spacious, contemporary, and perched about 1,200 feet above the ocean. Want an ocean view from your bed *and* bath? Then rent an Ocean House, a freestanding structure with curved roofs covered with wildflowers and grass, floor-to-ceiling windows, and a two-sided fireplace.

Feel like playing Tarzan and Jane? Try a Tree House, a triangular house on stilts, nine feet off the ground. Don't worry; a stairway leads to the door. The bed is in the center of the room, and you have tranquil views of the forest and mountain.

The circular Coast Houses and Mountain Houses are designed to replicate redwood trees. The Coast Houses have ocean views from the bed and tub and include terraces. The Mountain Houses provide views of the mountains. If you feel like soaring, try a Butterfly House, shaped like a butterfly, of course, with its wings extended.

This is a spa- and hiking-oriented resort, and the selection of services for these activities is extensive. The spa can provide everything from facials, herbal wraps, and massages to private yoga and meditation—available for an extra fee. Hiking guides can personalize private walks according to your ability and interest level. Whether it's a shorter hike to a secret spot or meadow, or a more challenging up-and-down hike to the beach for a picnic lunch, they can make it happen. Of course, you're also free to hike on your own.

When you're done with the day's activities, you can dine at the inn's gourmet restaurant, known for its four-course dinners. All the collective amenities make the Post Ranch Inn the second most expensive listing in this book.

## Facilities

Post Ranch Inn has 30 cabins; each has a private bathroom with slate spa tub, a deck, a fireplace, a king bed, a wet bar, and a small refrigerator. There are no kitchen facilities. All cabins have ocean or mountain views. A restaurant, a pool, and full spa treatments are available. There are no televisions in the cabins, but a video-viewing room is available. The facility is not suitable for children. Pets are not allowed. No smoking is permitted. Some facilities are wheelchair accessible. Linens, towels, and robes are provided.

## Reservations and Rates

Reservations are required. The fee is $525–2,000 per night per cabin, including gourmet continental buffet breakfast and a glass of wine upon arrival. For more than two people, an additional $200 per night per person is charged. A two-night minimum is required on weekends, and a three- or four-night minimum is required on holidays. Major credit cards are accepted. Contact Post Ranch Inn, P.O. Box 219, Big Sur, CA 93920, 831/667-2200 or 800/527-2200, fax 831/667-2512, website: www.postranchinn.com.

## Directions

From Carmel, drive south on Highway 1 for 30 miles to the inn on the right (west) side of the road.

# 11 LUCIA LODGE

Los Padres National Forest, off Highway 1 near Lucia

**Luxury rating:** 4                                    **Recreation rating:** 3

Lucia Lodge has been remodeled and refurbished; the direction the lodge is headed is more upscale and romantic.

Cabins 1–6 are the lowest priced; these have a queen bed. Cabins 7–9 have more amenities and ocean views. The deluxe cabin is number 10, also known as the honeymoon suite, and it has the best view. All of the cabins are only a few feet apart from each other.

The restaurant is known for its excellent food and even more excellent views and sitting decks. The setting is awesome, with the lodge on a 500-foot cliff. Don't even think about walking to the beach from here—there is no beach. There's nothing but jagged rocks and cliffs from the lodge to the rugged surf below.

Sand Dollar State Beach is about eight miles south; a day-use fee is charged per vehicle. That's where most people go if they're looking for a beach. For hiking and sightseeing, head to Limekiln State Park, 1.5 miles north of the lodge on the east side of the highway. The highlight is Limekiln Falls, a one-mile round-trip hike that starts off easy, then switches to boulder-hopping across a stream. You can also check out the limekilns, which date from the 1800s. A day-use fee is charged. A trail map is available for a fee at the entrance station.

## Facilities

Lucia Lodge has 10 cabins with full bathrooms. Two to four persons can be accommodated, depending on the cabin. There are no kitchen facilities, and some of the cabins have gas fireplaces. Complimentary continental breakfast is provided. A restaurant, communal barbecue, and horseshoe pits are on-site. The facilities are suitable for children. Pets are not allowed. No smoking is permitted. Down comforters, linens, and towels are provided.

## Reservations and Rates

Reservations are recommended. The fee is $175–250 per night per cabin during the summer season, double occupancy, plus $12.50 per additional person; discounts are available in the off-season. Major credit cards are accepted. Contact Lucia Lodge, 62400 Highway 1, Big Sur, CA 93920, 831/667-2391 or 866/424-4787, website: http://lucialodge.com.

## Directions

From Carmel, drive south on Highway 1 for 48 miles to the lodge on the right (west) side of the road.

## 12 GORDA SPRINGS RESORT

Ventana Wilderness, off Highway 1 in Gorda

🏃 ⛵ 🛶 👫 ♿

**Luxury rating: 4**                    **Recreation rating: 3**

If you're looking for a little coastal hamlet, without the congestion of Carmel or cold weather of California's north coast, try the small town of Gorda and the cottages at Gorda Springs Resort. The 10-acre resort has been around for decades, and the owners have retained the charm of the original buildings and grounds, while upgrading the accommodations with more modern decor and amenities.

The ocean-view cottages range in size from studios to two-bedrooms and can accommodate 4–6 people. The Rock House offers two bedrooms, a full kitchen, a living room, and a fireplace. The house has one queen bed, one double bed, and a sofabed in the living room. The cottages and house sit on a hill above Highway 1.

This is a beautiful area of the central coast, and the resort can accommodate weddings, receptions, and groups. Well-maintained gardens throughout the property include a garden gazebo and deck for special events.

The Whale Watcher Cafe (805/927-1590) is a treat in itself and is open for breakfast, lunch, and dinner. Located on the property, it has casual dining indoors or on the heated garden patios, where you can watch out for whales as you eat. The café is known for outstanding gourmet meals and some of the best whale-watching around. Live music events take place throughout the year.

There's no ocean access from the resort; the closest beaches are Willow Creek Beach, one mile north, and Sand Dollar State Beach, four miles north. The beach just below Gorda is a designated sanctuary for elephant seals.

## Facilities

Gorda Springs Resort has 10 ocean-view cottages with bathrooms and refrigerators, and a house with two bedrooms, living room, fireplace, and full kitchen. There are also four inn rooms. Some cottages have a spa, a private patio, and a fireplace. There are no televisions or phones in the cottages or inn rooms. A library is available. Laundry facilities, a restaurant, a gas station, a petting zoo, an antique and gift shop, and a grocery store with deli are on-site. The cottages are suitable for children. Pets are not allowed. No smoking is permitted. Some facilities are wheelchair accessible. Linens and towels are provided.

## Reservations and Rates

Reservations are recommended. The fee is $175–375 per night for a studio cottage, $225–475 per night for a two-bedroom cottage, and $250–500 per night for the house. Inn rooms are $175–350 per night. Major credit cards are accepted. Contact Gorda Springs Resort, Town of Gorda Springs, Highway 1, The South Coast, Big Sur, CA 93920, 805/927-3918 or 805/927-4600, fax 805/927-4588, website: www.bigsurgordasprings.com.

## Directions

From Carmel, drive south on Highway 1 for 65 miles to the town of Gorda. The cottages are on the left (east) side of the road. Check in at the Pacific Market, next to the cottages.

# 13 LAKE SAN ANTONIO RESORTS

Lake San Antonio, off U.S. 101 near Paso Robles

**Luxury rating:** 3 **Recreation rating:** 5

This is a fantastic year-round destination for water lovers who like good weather and lots of activities. Lake San Antonio Resorts offers mobile homes close to the water, perfect for the variety of activities that a family or group might want in the course of a day. The rentals can accommodate up to 10 people, depending on the unit, and most of the homes have lake views.

Want to fish? Good idea. This is one of the top lakes in the state for bass fishing, best in spring and early summer. It is also good for striped bass, catfish, crappie, sunfish, and bluegill.

Want to swim? Hey, it's a warm-water lake with average temperatures in the 70s during the summer. Want to boat or water-ski? The resort and the lake offer rentals, and with 60 miles of shoreline, there is plenty of room to accommodate the different water enthusiasts. In fact, Lake San Antonio is considered one of the top waterskiing lakes in California.

This lake also provides the best wintering habitat in the region for bald eagles, and eagle-watching tours are available. Closer to home (or your rental, that is), you'll find that the resort is part of a park with a playground, a volleyball court, and a grassy area right next to the mobile homes.

All in all, for a lake vacation, this setup is hard to beat.

## Facilities

Lake San Antonio Resorts has 20 mobile homes, 16 on the south shore and 4 on the north shore (units on the north shore are closed in winter). Each mobile home has a fully equipped kitchen, including dishwasher and microwave, along with a full bathroom, deck with awnings, and barbecue; one marina slip is provided. Some mobile homes have air-conditioning and daily maid service. A pool, a recreation room, a restaurant, a general store, a pay telephone, a full-service marina, and boat rentals are available. There are no telephones or televisions in the rentals. The facilities are suitable for children. Pets are not allowed. Smoking is allowed in some of the units. Linens and towels are provided.

## Reservations and Rates

Reservations are recommended. The fee is $140–160 per night or $880 per week for 4 people, $110–185 per night for 6, $150–245 per night for 8, $170–240 per night for 10, and $210–350 per night for 12; weekly rates are available. For additional people, $30 per person per night is charged. There is a two-night minimum stay on weekends. Major credit cards are accepted. Contact Lake San Antonio Resort, Star Route Box 2620, Bradley, CA 93426, 805/472-2313 or 800/310-2313, website: www.lake-sanantonioresort.com.

## Directions

To reach the north shore, on U.S. 101 (just north of King City) take the Jolon Road/G-14 exit. Turn south on Jolon Road and drive 27 miles to Pleyto Road (curvy road). Turn right and drive 3 miles to the north shore entrance of the lake. Note: When arriving from the south or east on U.S. 101 near Paso Robles, it is faster to take G-18/Jolon Road exit.

To reach the south shore from the north, on U.S. 101 (just north of King City), take the Jolon Road/G-14 exit. Turn south on Jolon Road and drive 20 miles to Lockwood and Interlake Road (G-14). Turn right and drive 13 miles to San Antonio Lake Road. Turn left and drive 3 miles to the south shore entrance of the lake.

To reach the lake from the south, on U.S. 101 at Paso Robles, take the 24th Street exit (G-14 West) and drive 14 miles to Lake Nacimiento Drive. Turn right and drive across Lake Nacimiento Dam to Interlake Road. Turn left and drive 7 miles to Lake San Antonio Road. Turn right and drive 3 miles to the south shore entrance.

# 14 LAKE NACIMIENTO RESORT
Lake Nacimiento, off U.S. 101 near Paso Robles

**Luxury rating:** 3                                   **Recreation rating:** 4

Lodging with lake views and great boating, water sports, and fishing make Lake Nacimiento Resort one of the top recreation lake destinations in California. This outstanding operation can serve as headquarters for a fun trip centered around a big lake and its 70°F summer water temperatures. The lake features 165 miles of shoreline with an incredible number of arms. Loads of high-speed boats rip around on hot summer weekends. Several five-mph zones are enforced for safety, with a boat patrol on duty. That said, some of the best waterskiing in California can be had here.

The fishing for white bass can be incredible; it's possible to catch dozens by vertical jigging a Horizon jig. Nacimiento hosts 25 fishing tournaments per year. Not only is bass fishing good, but there are also opportunities for trout (in cool months) and bluegill and catfish (in warm months).

The cabinlike lodge units are the most popular, with most designed as duplexes. Some have views of the lake. It's the kind of place where people show up with their boat, dock it for a weekend, and use the lodge units for a private retreat. Accommodations are also available for groups up to 14. The resort has a great restaurant with a lake view. Youngsters would be lucky to have their parents bring them to Lake Nacimiento.

## Facilities
Lake Nacimiento Resort has 19 lodge units, eight travel trailers, and two mobile homes. A boat ramp, boat docks, boat rentals, stables, a playground, a swimming pool, a restaurant, a recreation room, laundry facilities, a grocery store, and fishing licenses are available nearby. Swimming beaches, basketball and volleyball courts, and horseshoe pits are also on-site. Pets are not permitted, and smoking is not allowed indoors.

## Reservations and Rates
Reservations are accepted. Rates for cabinlike lodges are $135–245 for 4 people, $175–340 for 5–10 people, and $270–440 for up to 14. Travel trailers cost $70–160 per night and mobile homes cost $170–315 for 8–10 people. Discounts are available for midweek stays. Major credit cards are accepted. It's open year-round. Contact Lake Nacimiento Resort, 10625 Nacimiento Lake Drive, Bradley, CA 93426, 805/238-3256 or 800/323-3839, website: www.nacimientoresort.com.

## Directions

From U.S. 101 in Paso Robles, take the 24th Street/Lake Nacimiento exit. Turn west on 24th Street (it becomes Lake Nacimiento Road/G-14) and drive for nine miles. Bear right on Lake Nacimiento road for seven miles to the resort entrance on the left. If you cross the Lake Nacimiento dam, you've gone too far.

## 15 CAMBRIA PINES LODGE
San Simeon, off Highway 1 in Cambria

**Luxury rating:** 4  **Recreation rating:** 3

They call them one-room cabins, but I call them rooms. They range from rustic to comfy fireplace suites, with wood paneling, and you can bring your pooch. Cambria Pines Lodge has 125 lodging units on 25 acres of Monterey pine forest and gardens. Deluxe suites for two and superior rooms for four were new in 2006.

A complimentary breakfast is provided and the lodge has a restaurant. You'll share a wall with the cabin next door, but the place is quiet and comfortable. The bathrooms have showers; some cabins have tubs and showers.

The setting is ideal for weddings and special events; a garden gazebo serves this purpose. But you don't have to attend a wedding ceremony to explore and enjoy the grounds or watch the deer, squirrels, and raccoons wander.

The property overlooks the east village of Cambria, a town of about 6,000 approximately two miles from the ocean. The older section of town has a quaint village atmosphere.

For exploring, San Simeon State Beach and Hearst Castle are just five and six miles north on Highway 1. One of California's best inshore fisheries is available right here at San Simeon Bay. You'll find a wide variety of rockfish, with big bonuses of halibut in the spring and early summer and lingcod in the fall. Fishing charters are available from Virg's Landing. A rebuilt pier opened in 2001.

## Facilities

Cambria Pines Lodge has 125 lodging units ranging from duplex cabins to inn rooms and townhouse-style suites. They all have full bathrooms. A small refrigerator and microwave are provided in the suites. Fireplaces and televisions are available in some units. A complimentary buffet breakfast is included. A heated indoor pool, a spa, a sauna, an exercise room, volleyball courts, conference facilities, a restaurant, and a lounge with nightly entertainment are available. The lodge is suitable for children. Pets are allowed in some cabins by prior approval. No smoking is permitted. Some facilities are wheelchair accessible. Linens and towels are provided.

## Reservations and Rates

Reservations are recommended. The fee includes buffet breakfast and is $99–139 per night for garden cabins, $109–150 per night for fireside cabins, $119–169 per night for lodge rooms, and $199–299 per night for lodge suites. Rates are based on double occupancy; it's $10 per night for each extra person. Children under age five stay free. Pets are $25 per night per pet. There is a two-night minimum stay on weekends, and reservations should be made six months in advance for summer weekends. Major credit cards are accepted. Contact Cambria Pines Lodge, 2905 Burton Drive, Cambria, CA 93428, 805/927-4200 or 800/445-6868, fax 805/927-4016, website: www.cambria pineslodge.com. For fishing information, contact Virg's Landing, 805/772-1222.

## Directions

From Monterey, drive south on Highway 1 for about 95 miles to the town of Cambria and Burton Drive. Turn left on Burton Drive and drive 0.25 mile to the lodge on the left.

# Other Cabins & Cottages in the Region

**Centrella Inn,** 612 Central Avenue, Pacific Grove, CA 93950, 831/372-3372 or 800/233-3372, website: www.centrellainn.com.

**Deetjen's Big Sur Inn,** Highway 1, Big Sur, CA 93920, 831/667-2377.

**Paraiso Hot Springs,** Soledad, CA 93960, 831/678-2882, fax 831/678-0834.

**Santa Cruz-Monterey KOA,** 1186 San Andreas Road, Watsonville, CA 95076, 831/722-0551 or 831/722-2377, website: www.koa.com.

**Santa Margarita KOA,** 4765 Santa Margarita Lake Road, Santa Margarita, CA 93453, 805/438-5618, website: www.koa.com.

**Ventana Inn,** Highway 1, Big Sur, CA 93920, 831/667-2331 or 800/628-6500, website: www.ventanainn.com.

# SAN JOAQUIN VALLEY

COURTESY OF RANCHO BERNARDO

## BEST CABINS & COTTAGES

This section of the San Joaquin Valley is noted for its heat in summer. But that is also when the San Joaquin Delta and foothill lakes become the Garden of Eden for boating and water-sports enthusiasts. The region also offers many settings in the Sierra foothills, which can serve as launch points for short drives into the alpine beauty of Yosemite, Sequoia, and Kings Canyon National Parks.

Almost all of the cabin and cottage rentals in this region are family-oriented. The majority of them are on access roads to Yosemite. A bonus is that most have lower prices than their counterparts in the park, and like I said, are more hospitable to children. In a 10-mile radius of Groveland, I found a huge range of lodgings: cabins, cottages, historic inns, yurts, and tepees. One place that stands out, The Homestead, even provides lodging for your horse.

For those not heading to Yosemite, area lakes are the primary recreation attraction, with the refreshing, clean water revered as a tonic against the valley heat all summer long. When viewed from the air, the closeness of these lakes to the Sierra Nevada mountain range is surprising to many. Their proximity to the high country results in cool, high-quality water — the product of snowmelt sent down river canyons on the western slope. Some of these lakes are among the best around for waterskiing and powerboat recreation, including Lake Don Pedro east of Modesto, Bass Lake near Oakhurst, Lake McClure near Merced, Pine Flat Reservoir east of Fresno, and Lake Kaweah near Visalia.

In addition, Lake Don Pedro, Pine Flat Reservoir, and Lake Kaweah are among the best fishing lakes in the entire Central Valley; some anglers rate Don Pedro as the number-one all-around fishing lake in the state. The nearby Sierra rivers that feed these lakes (and others) also offer the opportunity to fly-fish for trout. In particular, the Kaweah and Kings Rivers boast many miles of ideal pocket water for fly fishers. Although only the occasional trout on these streams is large, the catch rates are often high and the rock-strewn beauty of the river canyons is exceptional.

# San Joaquin Valley Cabins & Cottages

# 1 TOWER PARK MARINA AND RESORT
San Joaquin Delta, off I-5 near Lodi

**Luxury rating:** 3  **Recreation rating:** 4

Cabins and cottages are difficult to find in the Delta, but the invention of the park-model cabin is starting a new trend here, and with it, new opportunities for vacationers. Park models are actually classified by the state of California as RVs, believe it or not, though they look nothing like RVs. The reason for this classification is that the models are built off-site, supplied with an axle and wheels, and then trailered into the park. Once in position, the wheels are removed, brick or lattice is added around the base, and decks are constructed to give them a more spacious feel.

Simply add a vacation destination nearby, and you're in business. For years, Tower Park Marina and Resort has provided exactly that as a launch point into the back San Joaquin Delta. With the addition of park models at Tower Park, this getaway can be transformed into something special. The cabins at Tower Park are the deluxe models, which means they include an operating kitchen; many of the park models at other locations offer only a barbecue outside on the deck.

The cabins are completely furnished with just about everything you need except for your food, your toothbrush, and a view of the water. The decor is comfy, and all units are heated and have air-conditioning.

The resort is on Little Potato Slough near the Mokelumne River. This huge resort is ideal for boat-in campers who desire a full-facility marina. In the summer, this is a popular waterskiing area. Some summer weekends are like a continuous party. For people who love hot weather, cool water, and water sports, this place fits the bill.

## Facilities
Tower Park Marina and Resort has four park-model cabins. Cabins are completely furnished, including kitchen and outside deck with barbecue. The resort also has a pavilion, boat rentals, overnight boat slips, a double boat launch, a playground, a restaurant, coin laundry, a gift shop, a grocery store, and propane gas. Some facilities are wheelchair accessible. Smoking is prohibited. No pets are permitted in cabins. Linens and pillows are provided.

## Reservations and Rates

Reservations are recommended. There is a $150 deposit plus a rate of $75 per night or $395 per week; it's $2 per pet per night. Major credit cards are accepted. It's open year-round. Contact Tower Park Marina and Resort, 14900 West Highway 12, Lodi, CA 95242, 209/369-1041, website: www.towerparkresort.com.

## Directions

From Stockton, head north on I-5 for 14 miles to the Lodi/Highway 12 exit. Turn west on Highway 12 and drive about 5 miles to Tower Park Way. Turn left (before the first bridge) and drive a short distance to the park.

# **2** LAKE TULLOCH RV CAMP AND MARINA
Lake Tulloch, off Highway 120 near Jamestown

**Luxury rating: 2**  **Recreation rating: 4**

Just about everybody has a yearning to find their own Golden Pond. The vision starts with a cabin on a lake, with a boat waiting just outside your private dock.

Well, there's a place where visions like this are real, and Lake Tulloch is that place. Of the 10 shoreline cabins here, 5 have their own personal docks. The other 5 have sandy beaches from which you can land a boat virtually at the foot of the cabin. Although *On Golden Pond* it's not, it still has that magic combination: cabins, docks, and boats.

The owners calls the accommodations "buck cabins," which means no showers or kitchens are provided. But they do have refrigerators and microwaves, and a full RV and tent campground is on the property; as a guest, you have use of all the facilities there. The decor is log-cabin rustic. They have two rooms and sleep up to five people.

Lake Tulloch is at an elevation of 500 feet and is adjacent to the Table Mountain range, with views and mature oaks throughout. It is a favorite destination for people who love the Central Valley's reservoir. It's a big lake, shaped like a giant X with extended lake arms adding up to 55 miles of shoreline. Unlike so many reservoirs in the foothill country, this one is nearly always full of water. In addition, it is one of the rare places where anglers and water-skiers live in harmony—well, for the most part. That is due to the many coves and one six-mile-long arm with an enforced five-mph speed limit. Because much of the lake is protected from wind, the water surface is often calm and, in turn, can offer some of the best waterskiing in California. Not only is fishing often good for bass and catfish, but a secret at Tulloch is that prospects are also good for crawdads, using bacon or chicken necks for bait.

## Facilities

Lake Tulloch RV Camp and Marina has 10 lakeside cabins that sleep up to eight, along with an adjacent RV park. A dinette, microwave, refrigerator, and electricity are provided. There is no kitchen, shower, or heater (in winter, bring your own). Just outside, a porch, picnic table, barbecue, and either a private dock or boat landing are available. The nearby resort and campground has showers, flush toilets, a laundry room, a store, RV dump station, propane gas, a restaurant (seasonal), volleyball, horseshoes, table tennis, a swimming beach, a marina, boat rentals, boat launch, and a boat ramp. Some facilities are wheelchair accessible, including three of the cabins. Pets and smoking are permitted in the cabins. Beds with mattresses are provided, but not linens or towels.

## Reservations and Rates

Reservations are recommended. Cabins rent for $100 per night or $530 per week; a $100 deposit is required. Boat trailer fee is $5 per stay. Pets are $1 per night. Credit cards are accepted. A two-night minimum stay is required on weekends. It's open year-round, with discounts October–March. Contact Lake Tulloch RV Camp and Marina, 14448 Tulloch Dam Road, Jamestown, CA 95327, 209/881-0107 or 800/894-2267 (reservations), website: www.laketullochcampground.com.

## Directions

From Manteca, drive east on Highway 120 (it becomes Highway 108) to Oakdale. Continue east for 13 miles to Tulloch Dam Road (also signed "South Shore") on the left. Turn left and drive 4.5 miles to the campground entrance and gatehouse at the end of the road at the south shore of Lake Tulloch.

# 3 THE GROVELAND MOTEL AND INDIAN VILLAGE

Groveland, off Highway 120 west of Yosemite

🏕 👪 ♿

**Luxury rating:** 2                                    **Recreation rating:** 3

---

The Groveland Motel and Indian Village's claim to fame is that it has the widest variety of accommodations along the Highway 120 route to Yosemite. You can pick from tepees, cabins, mobile homes, and campsites. Staying here is a lot like staying in a large campground or RV park, and children love it, especially if they are able to talk the adults into renting one of the tepees, which seem to have a magical effect on the little ones.

The canvas tepees sleep two and are arranged either village style around a central bonfire or set apart in a private tepee camp. Inside the tepees you'll find concrete floors, electric lights, and queen and double beds. All linens are provided and a central bathhouse with restrooms and showers is available. The facilities include a picnic table, outside light, fire ring, and water. In other words, sleeping in a tepee isn't much different from camping, except there's no tent to set up.

The cabins accommodate 2–6 people and have private bathrooms, air-conditioning, and cable television, and some have either a patio or porch. The Victorian home features three bedrooms with two queen beds and one double bed, a fully equipped kitchen, a bathroom with claw-foot tub and shower, a covered porch, and period furnishings. The mobile homes range from one to four bedrooms, and most have fully equipped kitchens. Some, but not all, mobiles have a porch, deck, and living room. The mobile homes—the largest of which is 1,600 square feet—can accommodate 6–20 people.

Within one block of The Groveland Motel and Indian Village are restaurants, a grocery store, a deli, a gas station, a community park, and a children's playground. The town of Groveland is the last full-service community before entering Yosemite National Park, so pack up on supplies if you need them. The Pine Mountain Lake airport is a 10-minute drive from the motel, and shuttle transportation is available by arrangement.

Note that this is not a hideaway with perfect quiet. Its location adjacent to Highway 120 means there is highway noise for some sites.

## Facilities

The Groveland Motel and Indian Village has 10 cabins, 14 tepees, 12 mobile homes, and campsites. A central bathhouse and restrooms are available, and small barbecues are available by request. The facilities are suitable for children. No pets are allowed. Smoking is permitted. Some of the facilities are wheelchair accessible. Linens and towels are provided.

## Reservations and Rates

Reservations are recommended. The fee is $36 per night per tepee, $80–90 per night per cabin, and $89–199 per night for a mobile home. Group rates are available. Major credit cards are accepted. It's open year-round. Contact The Groveland Motel and Indian Village, 18933 Highway 120, P.O. Box 175, Groveland, CA 95321, 209/962-7865 or 888/849-3529, fax 209/962-0664, website: www.grovelandmotel.net.

## Directions

From Manteca, drive east on Highway 120 (it becomes Highway 108) for 30 miles to the Highway 120/Yosemite exit. Bear right on Highway 120 and drive about 15 miles to Groveland. The motel is on the right, across from the Ferreti Road intersection.

# 4 YOSEMITE LAKES                                BEST ◖
Off Highway 120, near Groveland

🏃 🏊 🛶 🚤 🦌 👪 ♿

**Luxury rating: 2**                    **Recreation rating: 4**

Think big, think family-oriented, think variety of lodging options and on-site activities, and you'll be thinking of Yosemite Lakes. It's set on a 400-acre preserve at 3,400 feet in elevation, with the South Fork of the Tuolumne River running through it. Yosemite Lakes is an affiliate of Thousand Trails, a camping conglomerate with facilities around the country. At this particular location, you can choose between yurts, cabins, camping trailers, houses, a hostel, or a campground.

Although Yosemite Lakes is a membership-based facility, rentals are available to the general public for a slightly higher price than members pay. This is an unusual deal, since Thousand Trails facilities normally are completely off-limits to the general public; an exception was made in this case because the resort is so close to Yosemite National Park—five miles from the west entrance station.

All 10 cabins are small (one room) and rustic, with minimal provisions and no private bathroom or kitchen facilities. The camping trailers sleep 4–6 and come in various sizes up to 35 feet in length. This is just like RV camping, only you rent one of their RVs instead of bringing your own. Fire rings and a central bathhouse and restrooms are provided for those staying in a cabin or cottage. Linens and towels can be rented.

The cottages are a big step up from the cabins, featuring two bedrooms, fully equipped kitchens including microwave and dishwasher, private bathrooms, satellite televisions, and telephones. They sleep six. The cottages are grouped together in their own area of the preserve, so these rentals would be suitable for a large group. Some people will find this hard to believe, but some of the most deluxe accommodations here are the yurts, with floors, windows, a gas fireplace, air-conditioning, a fully equipped kitchen with microwave, a bathroom, a television, and a deck or porch with barbecue. Linens and towels are provided.

Thousand Trails is much like a resort, with a huge variety of recreational options and organized activities. It's definitely not a romantic getaway, but rather a family-oriented preserve. This is the kind of place where several generations of a family can come and spend time together, each participating in the activities that suit them, then meeting up for meals or at the end of a day. The restaurant is open for dinner on Friday and Saturday and for breakfast on Saturday and Sunday; you're on your own for meals during the rest of the week. There is 24-hour security.

The South Fork of the Tuolumne River is stocked weekly with rainbow trout. Fishing and swimming in this river are allowed. If hiking interests you, trails are available throughout the 400 acres. For details on activities in the local area, refer to the description for Yosemite Gatehouse Lodge (see next listing).

## Facilities

Yosemite Lakes has 10 bunkhouse cabins, 1 getaway cabin, 14 hillside yurts, 8 riverside yurts, 6 garden cottages, 17 trailers, a campground, and a hostel. Some lodgings have a deck or porch, fireplace, air-conditioning, and television. A convenience store, weekend restaurant, television room, recreation lodge, playground, basketball and volleyball courts, horseshoe pits, table tennis, shuffleboard, miniature golf, and laundry facilities are available. Equipment for rent includes kayaks, paddleboats, inner tubes, and bicycles. A fish-cleaning station and 24-hour security are provided. The facilities are suitable for children. Leashed pets are allowed in some facilities. Smoking is permitted in some accommodations. Some facilities are wheelchair accessible. Linens and towels are provided for the cottages, yurts, and trailers.

## Reservations and Rates

Reservations are recommended. Per night, the fee is $80 for cabins, $60 for cottages (Thousand Trails membership required), $40–50 for trailers (Thousands Trails membership required), $144 for hillside yurts, $170 for riverside yurts, and $90 for the hostel. Linens and towels can be rented for $5 per stay for two people. The pet fee is $5 per pet per stay. It's open year-round. Contact Yosemite Lakes, 31191 Hardin Flat Road, Groveland, CA 95321, 209/962-0121 or 800/533-1001, website: www.stayatyosemite.com.

## Directions

From Groveland, drive east on Highway 120 for 18 miles to the entrance road for Yosemite Lakes. Turn right and drive a short distance to the facilities.

## 5 YOSEMITE GATEHOUSE LODGE
Off Highway 120, near Groveland

**Luxury rating:** 2          **Recreation rating:** 3

Location and affordability are the buzzwords at Yosemite Gatehouse Lodge, which is just one mile from the Big Oak Flat entrance to Yosemite National Park. Four older cabins in duplex units are situated up the hill behind the lodge, nestled among ponderosa and sugar pines, cedars, redwoods, and a few oak trees. The lodge also has two motel suites and a room, one of which is a freestanding unit between the lodge and the cabins.

The dark-brown cabins here are cozy, almost 400 square feet in size. The decor is basic country. All units are heated, but there is no air conditioning. Built in the 1940s, they've been updated over the years to include everything you need to set up camp for a few days: fully equipped kitchen, private bathroom, bedroom, linens and towels, back porch—all in your own little spot in the forest. There's not much difference between the cabins, but my recommendation is Cabin 3 because it was updated most recently and has the best mattresses. A small store at the lodge supplies convenience-store fare.

Many who stay here are vacationers stopping by on their way to Yosemite National Park. Although practically everyone knows about the benefits of heading east to Yosemite, not as well-known are the attractions west on Highway 120 toward Groveland. Rainbow Pools, on the North Fork of the Tuolumne River in Stanislaus National Forest, is less than 10 miles west and is a popular swimming area, with a waterfall and series of pools created by the river. There are rock cliffs used for jumping into the water, and granite-chute slides deposit visitors into the main swimming hole. Whitewater rafting is also an option.

## Facilities

Yosemite Gatehouse Lodge has four cabins, three motel suites, and a motel room. The cabins have fully equipped kitchens, private bathrooms with showers, and porches; there is no daily maid service. The motel suites and room each have a small refrigerator and microwave. Televisions and wall heating are provided in all facilities. The facilities are suitable for children. A barbecue, campfire pit, horseshoes, and trails are available, and horseback riding is nearby. Pets are allowed, with some restrictions. Smoking is not permitted indoors. Linens and towels are provided.

## Reservations and Rates

Reservations are recommended. The fee is $106–126 per night per cabin, depending on the number of people and cabin selected, and $86–130 per night for the motel suites and room. Additional guests are $10 per night per person. Major credit cards are accepted. It is open May–November, with reduced rates starting in mid-September. Contact Yosemite Gatehouse Lodge, 34001 Highway 120, Groveland, CA 95321, 209/379-2260, website: www.yosemitecabins.com.

## Directions

From Groveland, drive east on Highway 120 for 24 miles to the lodge on the right (1 mile before the Yosemite National Park entrance station).

# 6 RANCHO BERNARDO
Off Highway 140, near Mariposa

**Luxury rating:** 3  **Recreation rating:** 3

At Rancho Bernardo, they're full of bull and proud of it. You see, this is a 40-acre cattle ranch, and the owner is a former bull rider from way back who'd be happy to tell you about the art of bull riding at the drop of a hat. In addition, the innkeepers, Barney and Kathy Lozares, are perfect hosts: friendly, helpful, and down-to-earth. And their rental facilities are stunningly beautiful, combining modern and rustic elements—you're in for a real treat when you stay here. The decor is plush and gorgeous. The bedding is high-end Ralph Lauren.

The guest house is a gorgeous, 1,000-square-foot sanctuary of towering vaulted ceilings covered in knotty pine, windows with expansive views of the rolling countryside, pine floors with area rugs, and a modern kitchenette with refrigerator, microwave, sink, and ceramic tile counters. A sitting area holds a sleeper sofa, television with VCR, woodstove on a brick hearth, a sleeping loft with plush bedding, and a full-size pool table. The cabins have heat and air-conditioning.

The barn suite has a cozy bedroom with a slightly vaulted knotty pine ceiling and pastel walls, queen-size brass bed with tastefully coordinated bedding, ceiling fan, kitchenette with microwave and refrigerator, private bathroom, television with VCR, and lots of wood accents. The retreat is inviting, bright, and cheerful. If you hear any whinnying during the night, it's not a ghost; it's probably one of the horses that reside downstairs in the barn. Both rentals have air-conditioning, which is a huge bonus, since here in foothill country—at only 1,500 feet in elevation—summers can be smoking hot. You won't be disappointed with these luxurious, spacious, down-home accommodations.

Catheys Valley is secluded, dotted with oak trees, rolling hills, ranches, and short rock walls that were constructed by Chinese laborers during the gold rush. The immigrants were promised the chance of riches in America, and instead often found themselves being used as slave labor. The little village of Hornitos is nearby, and history buffs would enjoy seeing the old pioneer church and cemetery, and ruins of the former gold-mining town where the bandit Joaquin Murietta was rumored to have hidden out in the 1800s. When I was last there, a sign at the entrance to town proclaimed, "Our town is like heaven to us, so don't drive like hell through it."

Rancho Bernardo is on the route to Yosemite National Park, about a 90-minute drive to Yosemite Valley. Closer to the ranch (a 10-minute drive) is the historic town of Mariposa, where you'll find restaurants, gold-rush-era buildings, and museums.

## Facilities

Rancho Bernardo has a guest house and a barn suite with private bathrooms. The facilities have a microwave, a refrigerator, and a sink. A complimentary breakfast is provided, as are coffee, tea, and afternoon sodas and cookies. The barn suite has a fireplace. Barbecues are available on request, and a wraparound deck and picnic area are available. The facilities are not suitable for children. Pets are not allowed. Smoking is restricted. Linens and towels are provided.

## Reservations and Rates

Reservations are recommended. For two people, the rate is $145 per night for the barn suite and $175 per night for the guesthouse. Additional guests are $35 per night per person. There is a two-night minimum stay on holidays. Major credit cards are accepted. It's open year-round. Contact Rancho Bernardo Bed and Breakfast, 2617 Old Highway South, P.O. Box 5008, Mariposa, CA 95338, 209/966-4511 or 877/930-1669, website: www.ranchobernardobnb.com.

## Directions

From Highway 99 in Merced, turn east on Highway 140 and drive to Planada. Continue on Highway 140 for approximately 13 miles to Old Highway. Turn right on Old Highway, drive exactly 4 miles to the intersection with School House Road, and enter Rancho Bernardo on the left (white rail fencing).

# **7** OWL'S NEST                              BEST **C**
Fish Camp, off Highway 41, near Yosemite

**Luxury rating:** 3                    **Recreation rating:** 4

When you pull up to Owl's Nest and see that the cabins are right along Highway 41, you might proceed with a fair amount of apprehension. After all, Owl's Nest is just a mile from the southern entrance to Yosemite National Park, and the vision of a noisy parade of vehicles might seem like a potential nightmare.

Instead, a funny thing happens at Owl's Nest: quiet, peace, and privacy.

It seems that come nightfall, the road is suddenly abandoned, with almost nobody at all going up and down that highway to Yosemite.

The A-frame cabins here at Owl's Nest are at 5,000 feet in elevation outside of Yosemite's Wawona entrance. Two of the cabins, Ponderosa and Christmas Tree, can sleep up to six and are completely furnished, with Christmas Tree providing a fireplace. The other, Tamarack, is a smaller "sleeper cabin" for two with no kitchen.

The decor is pretty and woodsy. All units are heated and have air-conditioning.

Horseback rides are available out of Fish Camp. They include scenic rides of an hour or two, along with a 5.5-hour trail ride to Mariposa Big Trees. The same destination takes about 10 minutes by car and is best visited by 8:30 A.M., before the crowds show up. Some of the best day hikes in Yosemite are along the road to Glacier Point; the drive to Glacier Point from Fish Camp is about 50 minutes. Golfing is available in Wawona and Ahwahnee.

## Facilities

Owl's Nest has three two-story cabins, two sleeper cabins, and one guest suite. All have bathrooms and a deck with a barbecue. Two have kitchens with cookware and utensils, and one has a fireplace. A small grocery store, restaurant, and other facilities are nearby. Pets are not permitted. No smoking is allowed indoors. Linens are provided.

## Reservations and Rates

Reservations are required. Cabin rates are $150 per night for two people, plus $20 for each additional person. The maximum number of people per cabin is six to eight. The sleeper cabin rents for $125 per night for two people. A three-night minimum stay is required in the summer. Major credit cards are accepted. Contact Owl's Nest, P.O. Box 33, Fish Camp, CA 93623, 559/683-3484, website: www.owlsnestlodging.com. A free map/brochure of Yosemite National Park is provided at park entrance stations as part of the $20 entrance fee. Horseback riding rentals are available at Yosemite Trails Pack Station, 559/683-7611.

## Directions

From Merced, take Highway 140 east to Mariposa and Highway 49. Turn south on Highway 49 and drive 30 miles to Highway 41 at Oakhurst. Turn left on Highway 41 and drive 13 miles to the town of Fish Camp, and look for Owl's Nest on the left side of the road.

# 8 THE HOMESTEAD                         BEST
Off Highway 49, near Oakhurst

**Luxury rating:** 4                                **Recreation rating:** 3

A unique foothill hideaway, set on 160 acres with upscale accommodations, is what you get at The Homestead. This is an adult-oriented retreat a few miles from Oakhurst in a quiet, private setting amid oaks, natural gardens, and stone walls. Nestled at

2,300 feet in elevation, the facilities consist of six adobe-and-stone cottages, a main house, and a loft room over the stable. The ranch house was made available starting in 2004, and it's usually reserved for reunions, anniversaries, and honeymoons.

The hillside cottages were built in 1992 and attest to the benefits of fine craftsmanship and attention to detail. Inside, you'll find Saltillo tile floors, hand-troweled plaster, yellow pine trim, vaulted ceilings, country kitchens, comfortable living rooms with fireplaces, ample bathrooms, and romantic bedrooms with a big log bed and an eclectic mix of antique and contemporary furnishings. Outside the 560-square-foot cottages are private patios and comfortable Adirondack chairs.

The little Star Gazing Loft is above the stable and has a picture window next to the bed. This is ideal for guests traveling with horses, since they can keep an eye on Mr. (or Mrs.) Ed from this vantage point. If you don't care for horses, or sleeping near them, one of the cottages is more suitable for you.

Even though this is a country hideaway a few miles from the nearest town, the innkeepers have ensured that their guests are not deprived of amenities usually found in a larger, more urban establishment. If you want a catered dinner, a massage, or other concierge services, it's no problem. And if you feel like going out for a special meal, the five-star Erna's Elderberry House is just a 10-minute drive down the road in Oakhurst. I was not disappointed with the gourmet food or the atmosphere, although it can get crowded.

When you decide to explore the local area, you'll discover that the southern entrance to Yosemite National Park is 21 miles away. Golfers are in luck, as two courses are nearby. The 9-hole Sierra Meadows at River Creek is less than a five-minute drive from the resort, and Sierra Meadows, an 18-hole course, is 6 miles away.

## Facilities

The Homestead has four cottages with fully equipped kitchens and private baths. Fireplace, television, air-conditioning, and picnic area with gas barbecue are included. Complimentary muffins, fruit, granola, milk, coffee, and tea are provided. Concierge services are available. There are no telephones in the cottages, but a telephone and fax machine are available in the office. The facilities are limited for children. Pets are not allowed. Horse-boarding facilities are available. No smoking is permitted. One cottage is wheelchair accessible. Linens, towels, and daily maid service are provided.

## Reservations and Rates

Reservations are recommended. The fee is $199–219 per night per cottage, $145 per night for the loft, and $349–379 for the ranch house. There is a two-night minimum stay on weekends and a three- to four-night minimum on holidays. Major credit cards are accepted. It's open year-round. Contact The Homestead, 41110 Road 600, Ahwahnee, CA 93601, 559/683-0495 or 800/483-0495, website: www.homesteadcottages.com.

## Directions

From Oakhurst, drive north on Highway 49 for 4.5 miles to Road 600. Turn left (south) and drive 2.5 miles to The Homestead on the right.

## 9 THE FORKS RESORT
### Sierra National Forest, off Highway 41 at Bass Lake

**Luxury rating:** 4                                      **Recreation rating:** 4

The Forks Resort, Miller's Landing (see next listing), and a real estate agency provide the opportunity for cabin rentals at Bass Lake. These cabins can feel like refuges of peace from the wild water sports and boating activity on Bass Lake.

Bass Lake is a long, beautiful lake in the Sierra foothills—elevation 3,400 feet—that has become a recreation center for boating and water sports. It features five campgrounds, four resorts, and two boat launches. Waterskiing, tubing, personal-watercraft riding, fishing, and swimming are all extremely popular. On a hot summer day, you can count on seeing jet boats zooming about, as the roar from their big V-8 engines echoes down the lake. The scene is wild and wet.

Sound like your kind of place? If so, book a stay at either The Forks Resort or Miller's Landing. The Forks Resort has some of the most nicely furnished cabin rentals on the lake, whereas Miller's Landing provides a range of inexpensive and rustic to well-furnished ones.

The cabins at The Forks Resort were first built in the '50s and '60s but have been recently remodeled. Most have knotty-pine interiors and are set high above the road with good views. Cabin 5 is popular because it's one of the largest cabins with more amenities, even though it has the worst view. Cabins 10, 11, 12, 14, and 15 (there's no cabin 13, heh, heh) are newest.

The decor is comfortable country-style. All are heated and the newer ones have air-conditioning.

How good are they? Good enough that reservations start being made on January 1 for the upcoming summer. Almost every day of the summer fills up. If you want to guarantee yourself a cabin, plan ahead, make your reservations early, and then get ready for the Bass Lake experience.

## Facilities
The Forks Resort has 15 one- and two-bedroom cabins, and a three-bedroom townhouse. Cabins have private bathrooms and fully equipped kitchens, most with microwaves, and a porch and televisions. One has a fireplace. They do not have telephones. Laundry facilities, a restaurant, a general store, a full-service marina, and boat rentals are available. The resort is suitable for children. Small leashed pets are allowed. No smoking is permitted. Linens and towels are provided in some cabins.

## Reservations and Rates
Reservations are recommended. The fee is $95–200 per night per cabin, or $665–1,400 per week per cabin. The pet fee is $25 per night per pet. A four-night minimum stay is required from Memorial Day weekend to Labor Day weekend. Major credit cards are accepted. It's open April–September. Contact The Forks Resort, 39150 Road 222, Bass Lake, CA 93604, 559/642-3737, website: www.theforksresort.com.

## Directions
From Fresno, drive 50 miles north on Highway 41 to Yosemite Forks. Turn right onto County Road 222 and drive 6 miles, keeping to the right at each of two Ys in the road; the resort is on the right.

## 🔟 MILLER'S LANDING
Sierra National Forest, off Highway 41 at Bass Lake

🏊 🎣 🚣 🐕 👪 ♿

**Luxury rating:** 3                                    **Recreation rating:** 4

Miller's Landing has some of the most beautiful chalets imaginable, complete with picture windows and beautiful views of Bass Lake. Or, one- and two-bedroom cabins are ideal for those who need only a cold beer to stay happy. Take your pick— for most, it'll work out just fine.

Miller's Landing has the largest marina at Bass Lake, the raucous powerboating headquarters of the Sierra foothills. This place can really rock. The high-speed boats dominate the water all summer, the sales of ice and beer are off the charts, and occasionally, folks sleep for a couple of hours each night.

That's where this place comes in. The primitive cabins are basically designed as a place to crash for the night before going back out on the water and doing it all over again. The most primitive one-bedroom cabins here have no piped water inside, just a small refrigerator and stove; a water faucet is available nearby outside the cabins. Most will just set up a camp-like existence in the cabin and use the adjacent facilities at the park's resort and camp if necessary. The most important items, beer and ice, are available nearby.

The decor is simple and rustic. The cabins are small and spaced fairly close together—about 100 feet apart. They are not winterized and are available only from May 1 to September 15.

More deluxe accommodations are available, too, for those who require them. There are several very nice units, including some with lake views and everything a visitor could ask for, like a shower, a bed with fresh sheets, and a good home-cooked meal. The six cabins with lake views are Pentwater, Cabins 1, 9A, 9B, 10A, and 10B. Because cabins 9A, 9B, 10A, and 10B are duplexes, Cabin 1 is the most popular; it's also the most spacious. These cabins have vaulted ceilings, carpeting, breakfast bars, some oak cabinetry, and knotty-pine ceilings. The good ones are drop-dead gorgeous.

The nearby marina provides boat rentals, and Miller's Landing is close to the free Wishon boat ramp.

## Facilities

Miller's Landing has 13 cabins ranging from rustic to deluxe, sized with one or two bedrooms. The 5 rustic cabins have no piped water inside, but a water faucet is outside. The rustic cabins do not have private bathrooms and linens and towels are not provided; refrigerator, stove, deck, and fire ring are provided. Other cabins have private bathrooms and fully equipped kitchens; linens and towels, a deck, a picnic table, a fire ring, and a woodstove are provided. A bathhouse, laundry facilities, a restaurant, a full-service marina, and boat rentals are available. The cabins are suitable for children. Leashed pets are allowed. Smoking is permitted. One cabin is wheelchair accessible. Linens and towels are provided in some facilities.

## Reservations and Rates

Reservations are recommended. The fee is $40–250 per night per cabin or $280–1,750 per week. For pets, a $25 cleaning fee is charged. A two-day minimum stay is required, or a one-week minimum during July and August. Major credit cards are accepted. Contact Miller's Landing, 37976 Road 222, Wishon, CA 93669, 559/642-3633, website: www.millerslanding.com.

## Directions

From Fresno, drive 50 miles north on Highway 41 to Yosemite Forks. Turn right onto County Road 222 and drive approximately 8 miles, keeping to the right at each of two Ys in the road; the resort is on the right.

# Other Cabins & Cottages in the Region

**The Pines Resort,** P.O. Box 109, Bass Lake, CA 93604, 559/642-3121 or 800/350-7463, website: www.basslake.com.

**Stockton-Lodi KOA,** 2851 East Eight Mile Road, Lodi, CA 95240, 209/941-2573 or 209/334-0309, website: www.koa.com.

**Yosemite-Mariposa KOA,** Box 545, Highway 140, Midpines, CA 95345, 209/966-2201, website: www.koa.com.

# SEQUOIA AND KINGS CANYON

COURTESY OF SILVER CITY MOUNTAIN RESORT

## BEST CABINS & COTTAGES

# The high Sierra, from Mount Whitney north through

Sequoia and Kings Canyon National Parks, is a paradise filled with deep canyons, high peaks, and fantastic natural beauty, and sprinkled with groves of the largest living things in the history of the earth – giant sequoias.

Though the area is primarily known for the national parks, the cabins available span a great variety of settings. The most popular spots, though, are in the vicinity of Sequoia and Kings Canyon National Parks, or on the parks' access roads.

Most of the cabins are historic structures, built more than 60 years ago. If you have high aspirations for luxury, you're better off taking one of the high-end inn rooms at Wuksachi Lodge in Sequoia National Park. Otherwise, get this picture of most of the cabins in focus: historic, rustic, and only modest upgrades for some. Some are even primitive. For many, that's just fine. For others, it's not. One of the most unusual experiences in the area is at Montecito-Sequoia Lodge, which has pretty basic lodging, yet where all meals are provided and where 70 employees direct full days of recreation for visitors. "Like a cruise ship in the forest," as they say.

Sooner or later, everyone will want to see the biggest tree of them all—the General Sherman Tree, estimated to be 2,300–2,700 years old with a circumference of 102.6 feet. It is in the Giant Forest at Sequoia National Park. To stand in front of it is to know true awe. That said, I found Grant Grove and Muir Grove even more enchanting.

These are among the highlights of a driving tour through both parks. A must for most is taking in the view from Moro Rock, parking and then making the 300-foot walk up a succession of stairs to reach the 6,725-foot summit. Here you can scan a series of mountain rims and granite peaks, highlighted by the Great Western Divide.

The drive out of Sequoia and into Kings Canyon features rim-of-the-world-type views as you first enter the Kings River canyon. You then descend to the bottom of the canyon, right along the Kings River, and can gaze up at the high glacial-carved canyon walls, then drive all the way out to Cedar Grove, the end of the road. The canyon rises 8,000 feet from the river to Spanish Peak, the deepest canyon in the continental United States.

Crystal Cave is another point of fascination. Among the formations are adjoined crystal columns that look like the sound pipes in the giant organ at the Mormon Tabernacle. Lights are placed strategically for perfect illumination.

This is only a start. Bears, marmots, and deer are abundant and are commonly seen in Sequoia, especially at Dorst Creek Campground. If you drive up to Mineral King and take a hike, it can seem like the marmot capital of the world.

But this region also harbors many wonderful secrets having nothing to do with the national parks. One of them, for instance, is Muir Trail Ranch near Florence Lake. The ranch in the John Muir Wilderness requires a trip by foot, boat, or horse to reach it. Other unique launch points for trips into the wilderness lie on the eastern Sierra near Bishop: Bishop Creek Lodge, Glacier Lodge, Parchers Resort, Cardinal Village Resort.

On the western slopes of the Sierra, pretty lakes with good trout fishing include Edison, Florence, and Hume Lakes. Hidden spots in Sierra National Forest provide continual fortune hunts, especially up the Dinkey Creek drainage above Courtright Reservoir. On the eastern slopes, small streams offer good vehicle access; here, too, you'll encounter beautiful Rock Creek Lake, Sabrina and South Lakes, and great wilderness trailheads at the end of almost every road.

The remote Golden Trout Wilderness on the southwest flank of Mount Whitney is one of the most pristine areas in California. Yet it is lost in the shadow of giant Whitney, elevation 14,495 feet, the highest point in the continental United States, where hiking has become so popular that reservations are required at each trailhead for overnight use, and quotas are enforced to ensure an undisturbed experience for each visitor.

In the Kernville area, cabin rentals are scattered along the Kern River. Most choose this canyon for one reason: the outstanding white-water rafting and kayaking.

# Sequoia and Kings Canyon Cabins & Cottages

# ■ VERMILION VALLEY RESORT                    BEST ◖

Sierra National Forest, off Highway 168 at Lake Edison

🕴 🏊 🎣 🚤 🐎 👫

**Luxury rating:** 1                                    **Recreation rating:** 5

This is one of the best tent-camping destinations in California. You get lakeside accommodations, boat rentals and shuttle service, horseback riding, and all the fishing and hiking you want at an elevation of 7,650 feet. The only downer is that the lake level fluctuates greatly, and you never know how full it's going to be for your trip.

The 10 tent cabins have metal frames, twin bunkbeds, wooden floors, decks, picnic tables, and fire rings—much like camping. A communal bathhouse is nearby and you can shower for $2. Cabins 1, 2, and 5 have lake views and are about 30 yards from the lake when it's full. A restaurant offers home-cooked meals and Saturday night barbecues. Motel rooms are also available, and some of them have kitchenettes.

Edison Lake is fed by Mono Creek, a cold, pure, and pristine trout stream. A 15-mph speed limit on the lake makes it ideal for those who love to fish, either by boat or from the shore. Some giant brown trout live in this lake, but they aren't easy pickings.

For hiking, explore the great trailhead at the head of the lake that travels up Mono Creek for 2.5 miles to reach the John Muir Trail. At one time, this resort provided a boat taxi to the head of the lake, an invaluable service for hikers heading to and from the John Muir Trail. That service has been discontinued.

## Facilities

Vermilion Valley Resort has 10 tent cabins and four motel rooms with kitchenettes. The tent cabins do not have electricity, kitchen facilities, or private bathrooms; a communal bathhouse is available. A small deck, picnic table, gas heater, and fire ring are provided. Amenities include a restaurant, a store, bait and tackle, a fish-cleaning station, a dock, boat rentals, and water taxi. The resort is suitable for children. Leashed pets are allowed. Smoking is permitted. Linens and towels are not provided; you must bring your own.

## Reservations and Rates

Reservations are recommended. The fee is $50 per night per tent cabin, $65–85 for trailers, and $75–85 per night for motel rooms. Shower facilities are $2 per day per person. There is no pet fee. There is a two-night minimum stay on weekends and a three-night minimum on holidays. Major credit cards are accepted. It's open mid-May through October, weather permitting. Contact Vermilion Valley Resort, P.O. Box 258, Lakeshore, CA 93634, 559/259-4000 (summer) or 559/855-6558 (winter), website: www.edisonlake.com.

## Directions

From the town of Shaver Lake, drive north on Highway 168 for 21 miles to Kaiser Pass Road/Forest Road 80. Turn right and drive 16 (narrow and twisting) miles to a fork in the road. Bear left onto Edison Lake Road and drive approximately 6 miles to the resort at the end of the road.

# 2 MONO HOT SPRINGS RESORT          BEST (
Sierra National Forest, off Highway 168 near Huntington Lake

🏞 🏊 🛶 💆 🐴 👫

**Luxury rating:** 2                                              **Recreation rating:** 4

Nobody gets here by accident. People who stay here truly want to be here—no doubt about it. It's one long drive from just about anywhere.

But the payoff for the long, winding drive is significant: a soothing mineral pool, soaking tubs, massages, and cozy cabins. Another big bonus is that you're in a magnificent area in the Ansel Adams Wilderness and Sierra National Forest.

The cabins range from studios to two-bedrooms, and the rustic cabins are primitive with absolutely no frills. The more deluxe cabins have kitchen facilities and private bathrooms, and some have siding of cobblestone instead of wood. A restaurant on the premises is open for breakfast, lunch, and dinner. The hot springs consist of a small, outside mineral pool and private, enclosed soaking tubs; water temperatures average over 100°F. The day-use fee is $4; massages are available for an extra charge. The hot springs first opened in 1934, and the same gentleman has owned and operated the facility for the past 40 years.

There is sensational hiking around here, and a must-do is the popular one-mile hike to Doris Lake for swimming; trout fishing is marginal, since the lake is no longer stocked. Tule Lake is the place to hike to for good bass fishing; plan on a fairly easy three-mile round-trip. More stream and lake fishing is available nearby. Other activities include horseback riding and day trips to Lake Edison and Florence Lake, where boat rentals are available.

## Facilities
Mono Hot Springs Resort has 15 cabins, some with fully equipped kitchens, private bathrooms, and fireplaces. There are no televisions, telephones, or microwaves. Central bathrooms are provided. Laundry facilities, a restaurant, and hot springs are on-site. The resort is suitable for children. Leashed pets are permitted. Smoking is permitted. Linens and towels are provided in some of the cabins for an extra fee.

## Reservations and Rates
Reservations are required. The fee is $55–120 per night per cabin. Additional guests are charged $8 per night. The seventh night is half price. The pet fee is $4 per night per pet. There is a $4 per day per person fee for the use of the hot springs facilities, with special packages and discounts available. There is a three-night minimum on weekends. Major credit cards are accepted. The resort is open mid-May to November. Contact Mono Hot Springs Resort, General Delivery, Mono Hot Springs, CA 93642

(summer), or P.O. Box 215, Lakeshore, CA 93634 (winter), 559/325-1710, website: www.monohotsprings.com.

## Directions
From the town of Shaver Lake, drive north on Highway 168 for 21 miles to Kaiser Pass Road/Forest Road 80. Turn right and drive 16 (narrow and twisting) miles to a fork in the road. Bear left onto Edison Lake Road and drive approximately 2.5 miles to the resort.

# ❸ LAKESHORE RESORT                    BEST ☾
Sierra National Forest, off Highway 168 at Huntington Lake

**Luxury rating:** 3                    **Recreation rating:** 4

Sailing is king here on four-mile-long Huntington Lake, even though recreational activities range from fishing, waterskiing, and swimming to downhill skiing and snowmobiling in winter. However, come June, the sailing regattas begin and continue through August. And that is why you need to reserve a cabin three months in advance for summer.

There are no cookie-cutter cabins here; each one is unique. The cabins were built between the 1920s and 1940s, but they have been updated. They're small and set on an incline, about one block from the lake and some 30 feet from each other. Situated in an old-growth forest of ponderosa and tamarack, the cabins have no lake views. The cabins are homey, with quilts on the beds, and some rentals have knotty pine interiors.

Deer Creek runs along the property, and fishing is fair for trout. Huntington Lake, at 7,000 feet in elevation, is planted with trout and kokanee salmon during spring and summer, and the fishing is good. A swimming beach is nearby. Horseback riding facilities are only about a quarter mile away at D & F Pack Station.

In winter, Sierra Summit Ski Area, 2.5 miles away, offers downhill skiing and a snowboarding hill. You also can snowmobile from your cabin, where 150 miles of trails await.

## Facilities
Lakeshore Resort has 26 cabins with private bathrooms and 20 RV sites. Some of the cabins have fully equipped kitchens. A restaurant, a saloon, a banquet room, a general store, bait and tackle, boat slips, boat rentals, and fishing licenses are available. The resort is suitable for children. Up to two leashed dogs are allowed; cats are not allowed. No smoking is permitted. Linens and towels are provided. There is no daily maid service; a linen exchange is available.

## Reservations and Rates
Reservations are recommended. The fee is $80–150 per night per cabin. A rollaway is $20, and additional people are $10 per night. The pet fee is $15 per night per dog.

There is a two-night minimum stay on weekends and a three-night minimum on holidays. Boat launching fees are $15 per day or $90 per week. Major credit cards are accepted. Contact Lakeshore Resort, P.O. Box 197, Lakeshore, CA 93634, 559/893-3193, website: www.lakeshoreresort.com.

## Directions
From the town of Shaver Lake, drive 21 miles north on Highway 168 to Huntington Lake Road. Turn left and drive approximately 1 mile to the resort on the right.

# 4 MUIR TRAIL RANCH
### Sierra National Forest, off Highway 168 near Florence Lake

**Luxury rating: 2**                                    **Recreation rating: 5**

One if by land, two if by sea, and I vote for three by land *and* sea to get to Muir Trail Ranch. Whether you take the adventurous route by trail and boat or you opt for the longer foot or horse route, you won't soon forget your ambitious trip to 200-acre Muir Trail Ranch. But before I go on, note that reservations far in advance are often required—so block out the dates, book it, and get this one locked up. This one goes fast.

Your journey begins at Florence Lake. From here, you can take a water taxi across the lake and then hike 5 miles through the John Muir Wilderness to the ranch. Or, you can pack in by horse or on foot for a total of 10 miles. Some visitors opt to have their belongings packed in, while they boat and hike their way to the ranch.

Once at the ranch, you'll be set up in a tent cabin or log cabin. The eight log cabins come with toilet and sink, whereas the four tent cabins do not. There is a communal bathroom, communal kitchen, hot springs, and a little outdoor café available to all guests.

At Muir Trail Ranch, you have the run of the place in a pristine high-mountain hideaway at over 9,000 feet in elevation. You are surrounded by the John Muir Wilderness and all it has to offer, which includes hiking and riding on your choice of quality trails, or fishing and swimming in any number of lakes and streams. You can make day trips or plan overnight excursions; guides are available.

And when you return, tuckered out, at the end of the day, you have two enclosed hot spring baths or the small outdoor hot springs pool to relax in, a café to eat at or kitchen to cook in, and your warm sleeping bag to snuggle into. As you gaze at the stars, satisfied smile on your face, you can't help wondering: is this wilderness, or is it heaven? Actually, it's both.

## Facilities
Muir Trail Ranch has eight log cabins and four tent cabins and can accommodate groups of up to 15 people; singles, couples, and small groups are welcome on a space-available basis. Kitchenette facilities are not provided in the cabins, but a communal kitchen is available. A sink with cold running water and a toilet are provided in each log cabin,

but not in the tent cabins. A communal bathroom, hot springs, an outdoor café, a small store with fishing supplies, a fire ring, and horse rentals and guide services are available. The ranch is suitable for children. Pets are not allowed. Smoking is permitted in some of the facilities. Linens and towels are not provided, so bring a sleeping bag and towels.

## Reservations and Rates

Reservations are required. For stays of one or two nights, the rate is $115–135 per night per person, including meals. For stays of a week, the rate is $595 per person, plus $150–200 per person for meals. Groups of up to 15 may reserve the entire lodge for $8,925, plus meals. Horses can be rented for $65. Credit cards are not accepted. It's open June–September. Contact Muir Trail Ranch, P.O. Box 176, Lakeshore, CA 93634-0176 (June–September), or P.O. Box 700, Ahwahnee, CA 93601 (October–May), 209/966-3195, website: www.muirtrailranch.com.

## Directions

From the town of Shaver Lake, drive north on Highway 168 for 21 miles to Kaiser Pass Road/Forest Road 80. Turn right and drive to Florence Lake Road (2 miles south of the town of Mono Hot Springs). Turn right (south) and drive 5 miles to Florence Lake. Check in at the store and park your vehicle in the trailhead parking lot.

The water taxi makes two trips a day across Florence Lake and back. The fee is $8 per person one-way and $15 round-trip; children under age 12 are $5 one-way and $10 round-trip.

# 5 BISHOP CREEK LODGE

Inyo National Forest, off U.S. 395 near Bishop

**Luxury rating:** 4                                     **Recreation rating:** 5

When spring arrives in the high Sierra, the Bishop Creek Canyon and its environs are transformed into one of the most stellar recreation lands in America. This is the high country, where visitors get a unique mix of glacial-carved granite, lakes the color of gems, great hiking, horseback riding, and good evening fishing for rainbow trout or sometimes a big brown. In the fall, the mountain slopes shimmering  golden from the turning aspens are unforgettable.

With its furnished cabins, lodge, and facilities, Bishop Creek Lodge makes an excellent headquarters for this adventure. The cabins are built to withstand tough winters, and that means they are very snug in the summer, as well as being equipped with everything you need for a comfortable stay.

For people who need a clean bed for a good night's sleep, this is the place. You will awake ready for some of the best adventures in the high country. The 13 cabins can sleep 2–8 people and include kitchens; the rental rate includes a continental breakfast at the lodge. The interiors are clean, modern, and cozy, often finished off with knotty-pine siding.

Note that Bishop Creek Lodge is down the road from Parchers Resort (see next listing) and features the same recreation options.

## Facilities
Bishop Creek Lodge has 13 cabins with fully equipped kitchens and private bathrooms. There is complimentary continental breakfast. A café, a saloon, laundry facilities, a store, bait and tackle, and boat rentals are available. The lodge is suitable for children. Leashed pets are allowed. Smoking is permitted. Linens and towels are provided.

## Reservations and Rates
Reservations are recommended. The fee is $95–265 per night per cabin or $95–250 per night for two or more nights. The seventh night is free. Additional guests are $15 per night per person. Pets are $10 per day. There is a two-night minimum stay on weekends and a three-night minimum on holidays. Major credit cards are accepted. It's open May–October. Contact Bishop Creek Lodge, 2100 South Lake Road, Bishop, CA 93514, 760/873-4484, fax 760/873-8524, website: www.bishopcreekresort.com.

## Directions
From Bishop on U.S. 395, turn west on Highway 168 and drive for approximately 13.5 miles to the South Lake turnoff. Turn left on South Lake Road and drive 1.5 miles to the lodge on the right.

# 6 PARCHERS RESORT
Inyo National Forest, off U.S. 395 near Bishop

**Luxury rating:** 3                    **Recreation rating:** 5

Since the early 1900s, Parchers Resort has been a gateway to the high Sierra wilderness, and at 9,200 feet, it offers a stellar alpine experience. It's a complete getaway for families, groups, and company retreats.

Like its friendly neighbor, Bishop Creek Lodge, this lodge features excellent cabin units that are clean, well-furnished, and comfortable. They come with all the goodies: beds, bathrooms with showers, and kitchens, all of which rate high on the comfort scale. The friendly competition between the two adjacent lodges has kept each a quality operation.

Parchers is on the same road as Bishop Creek Lodge, just a little bit higher on the mountain and, in turn, a little bit closer to nearby South Lake, the centerpiece of the area for outstanding fishing and hiking.

South Lake, at 9,755 feet, covers 166 acres. It was created by a small dam on the South Fork of Bishop Creek. A good boat ramp is available, popular among owners of trailered aluminum boats, who can launch easily and then troll adjacent to the lake's shore. A 15-mph speed limit is in effect.

In addition, more good lakes lie within a two-hour hike. A trailhead on the southeast side of the lake leads to a trail that is routed up to Bishop Pass. But the trail forks off, providing routes to three different series of lakes. If you head to the right, you will reach Treasury Lakes after about a 2.8-mile hike, a good day trip. To the left, the trail leads to Bishop Pass, in the process passing Bull Lake, Long Lake, Saddlerock Lake, and Bishop Lake. On the way up, you pass a turnoff on the left for Ruwau Lake (requiring a short but steep climb), where there are beautifully colored brook trout in the foot-long class. To catch them, cast a Met-L Fly or Panther Martin spinner, black with yellow spots, and get it deep enough so it swims just over the top of the big boulders on the bottom of the lake at the far end.

## Facilities

Parchers Resort has 13 cabins with bathrooms (most have fully equipped kitchens) and six RV sites. Complimentary continental breakfast is provided. A small store, bait and tackle, a fish cleaning station, boat rentals at South Lake, and a restaurant (breakfast and lunch only) are available. The resort is suitable for children. Leashed pets are permitted. Smoking is permitted. Two cabins are wheelchair accessible. Linens and towels are provided.

## Reservations and Rates

Reservations are recommended. The fee is $90–100 for a rustic cabin, $120–190 for a mountain cabin, with discounts available for multiple-night stays. It's $15 per night for each additional person. The pet fee is $10 per night per pet. There is a three-day minimum on holidays. Major credit cards are accepted. It's open May–October, weather permitting. Contact Parchers Resort, 2100 South Lake Road, Bishop, CA 93514, 760/873-4177, fax 760/873-8524, website: www.bishopcreekresorts.com.

## Directions

From Bishop on U.S. 395, turn west on Highway 168 and drive for approximately 13.5 miles to the South Lake turnoff. Turn left on South Lake Road and drive 5.5 miles to the resort on the left.

# 7 CARDINAL VILLAGE RESORT

Near Bishop off U.S. 395

👫 🛶 ❄️ 👪

**Luxury rating:** 3                                                   **Recreation rating:** 4

You'll take a walk through California gold-mining history when you stay at Cardinal Village Resort, site of a former mining town. The remnants of the mining village date to the late 1800s. Back then, about 100 cabins, a store, and a schoolhouse stood; today only 13 of these original buildings exist, and you can take your pick for lodging.

The cabins have been painstakingly renovated and named after local high-mountain lakes. They range from the two-person Hungry Packer to the spacious Golden Trout Cabin, which sleeps 16. Other cabins include Topsy Turvy, Loch Leven, Moonlight, and Fish Gut. These cabins have fully equipped kitchens and private bathrooms.

The mine is a short walk from the resort. Although the machinery and buildings are no longer around, you can get a look at the old foundations and the head frame of the main shaft. Guided horseback tours of the mine and beyond are available from the Fourth of July weekend into September.

The resort borders Bishop Creek, which is well-stocked with trout, including some native brown trout. The resort's pond is stocked with Alpers trout and rainbow trout. Fishing is available at nearby North Lake, well-known for its awesome aspen groves and towering granite cliffs, and at the more popular Sabrina Lake, the largest of the four lakes in the immediate vicinity of the Bishop Creek drainage. Sabrina Lake has a boat ramp and rentals, as well as some giant Alpers trout and big browns that can keep fishing enthusiasts busy.

But there's more to this area than fishing. The hiking nearby is topnotch, and there are many options. In the summer, the Saturday night barbecue at the resort is extremely popular; it costs $15 (not included in your stay) and you'll need a reservation. In winter, ice-skating is available at the resort's pond.

## Facilities

Cardinal Village Resort has 11 cabins with fully equipped kitchens and private bathrooms. A barbecue, a picnic area, a meeting room, a fishing pond, Sunday morning nondenominational church service, a restaurant, and Saturday night barbecue are available. The resort is suitable for children. Pets are not allowed. No smoking is permitted. Linens and towels are provided in some cabins; you can also bring your own or rent them for a small fee.

## Reservations and Rates

Reservations are recommended. The fee is $75–275 per night per cabin; holiday and summer rates are slightly higher. It's $15 per night per each additional person. Linens can be rented for $5 per stay per person. There is a two-night minimum stay and a three-night minimum on holidays. Major credit cards are accepted. It's open

May–October. Contact Cardinal Village Resort, Route 1, Box A3, Bishop, CA 93514, 760/873-4789, website: www.cardinalvillageresort.com.

## Directions
From Bishop on U.S. 395, turn west on Highway 168 and drive for approximately 18 miles to Aspendell and Cardinal Road. Turn right on Cardinal Road and drive 0.5 mile to the resort at the end of the road.

## 8 DINKEY CREEK INN AND CHALETS   BEST ☾
Sierra National Forest, off U.S. 168 near Shaver Lake

🏔 🛶 🚐 ❄ 🐕 ♿ &

**Luxury rating:** 3                         **Recreation rating:** 4

If you have high demands, trying to find a cabin rental in a beautiful setting can be like playing a game of mission impossible.

Say you want a pretty spot that accommodates families and pets, has a full kitchen and bathroom, won't drain your bank account, and is nice enough for Mom to feel like she's getting a special vacation—and has a variety of activities all year long to keep everyone happy. Trying to find the darned place can ruin your vacation before it's begun. Well, you can stop searching, because I found just the place, and it has every item on the checklist.

At Dinkey Creek Inn and Chalets, you get a modern A-frame chalet with fully equipped kitchen, carpeting, propane heat, and a stunning floor-to-ceiling wall of glass overlooking a large deck and a forest of pine and fir. The chalets are spaced 100 feet or more from each other. They're within 200 yards of Dinkey Creek and a historic, wood-trestle bridge built in 1938, and they're in the Sierra National Forest.

In winter, you can cross-country ski, snowshoe, or snowmobile from the inn. In the summer, you can fish along Dinkey Creek, which is stocked with trout weekly throughout the summer. Some people come here for the hiking, with most heading 12 miles northeast to the Dinkey Creek Wilderness for hikes to Mystery Lake, South Lake, Rock Lake, and others.

A big bonus here is that your pooch can go on vacation, too. And remember, the café is open for breakfast and lunch only.

## Facilities
Dinkey Creek Inn and Chalets has four chalets that can sleep up to six people, with

fully equipped kitchens and private bathrooms, and three camping cabins. A barbecue, deck, woodstove, and television are provided. A café, a grocery store, bait and tackle, and fishing licenses are available. The inn is suitable for children. Leashed pets are allowed. Smoking is permitted. One cabin is wheelchair accessible. Linens and towels are not provided, so bring your own.

## Reservations and Rates
Reservations are required. The fee is $90–110 per night per chalet during the summer, and $85 per night during the winter. The pet fee is $25 per stay for each chalet. Major credit cards are accepted. Contact Dinkey Creek Inn and Chalets, 53861 Dinkey Creek Road, Shaver Lake, CA 93664, 559/841-3435 (May–September), 559/328-8294 (October–April), website: www.dinkeycreek.com.

## Directions
From Fresno, drive north on Highway 168 for approximately 50 miles to the town of Shaver Lake and Dinkey Creek Road. Turn right (east) on Dinkey Creek Road and drive 13 miles to the inn on the right side of the road.

# 9 LAKESIDE AT THE POINT
Sierra National Forest, off Highway 168 at Shaver Lake

**Luxury rating:** 3                                    **Recreation rating:** 3

Staying here in the winter and then venturing back in the summer is like visiting with Dr. Jekyll, then Mr. Hyde. Depending on your frame of mind, in the summer you will either love it or hate it. The activity level is intense at Shaver Lake all summer, filled with fast boats, water-skiers, and personal-watercraft riders.

Since the elevation is 5,370 feet, lower than some of the neighboring lakes, the water is warmer and more appealing for water-contact sports. Spring and early summer fishing is also good because the lake is stocked with trout and kokanee salmon. The closest marina is about 1.5 miles away.

In the winter, most visitors use this place as a base for winter sports. For downhill skiers, Sierra Summit Ski Area is about 20 miles north on Highway 168, and several snow parks are even closer for cross-country skiing, snowshoeing, and snowmobiling.

Some may remember this resort as being named Shaver Lake Lodge. New owners took over in 2004 and the place has been remodeled.

The 24 1930-era rustic cabins updated with bathrooms, showers and microwaves. Three units converted to offer massage, chiropractic care, and spa with swim-resistant pool. Sizes range from studios to two-bedrooms. They are spaced close together across the road from the lake, and although every cabin has a lake view, the two cabins closest to the lake—with the best views—are Cabins 9 and 10.

The restaurant is open for lunch and dinner, and there is live music on weekends.

## Facilities

Lakeside at the Point has 24 cabins with private bathrooms. There are no kitchen facilities, but some of the rentals have refrigerators, and all have televisions. A deck or porch is provided. A restaurant, bar, and spa are available. The lodge is suitable for children. Pets are allowed. Smoking is not permitted. Linens, pillows, blankets, and towels are provided.

## Reservations and Rates

Reservations are required. The fee is $95–155 per night per cabin. Pets are charged $25 per day. Major credit cards are accepted. Contact Shaver Lakeside at the Point, 44185 Highway 168, Shaver Lake, CA 93664, 559/841-3326, website: www.shaver-lakepoint.com.

## Directions

From Fresno, drive north on Highway 168 for approximately 50 miles to Shaver Lake and the lodge on the right, past the town of Shaver Lake.

# 10 GLACIER LODGE
Inyo National Forest, off U.S. 395 near Big Pine

**Luxury rating:** 2                                           **Recreation rating:** 5

© KAREN WOLFORD

The owners of Glacier Lodge tell you straight out that if you want to be waited on and have modern conveniences, "look for the Hilton." And since there's no luxury hotel or resort anywhere near here, you'd better zip your lips and smile if you want lodging. The appeal here is the pristine beauty along with myriad recreational opportunities. If you want some phenomenal hiking, you're at the right place. You're next to trailheads that lead into the John Muir Wilderness, with scads of high-mountain lakes and incredible scenery. The Palisades Glacier, the southernmost glacier in the United States, is a few miles from the lodge. You'll see plenty of backpackers, and the lodge has an RV campground and public showers to accommodate them.

The fishing is pretty good, too. In addition to the lakes accessible by hiking, Big Pine Creek is stocked with 38,200 trout from the Sage Flat Campground to Glacier Lodge during the summer. No, that trout number is not a misprint.

The lodge and cabins are rustic and old, first built in 1917, and you're at the end of the road, surrounded by wilderness at almost 8,000 feet in elevation. Since the lodge generates its own electricity, you can't bring any appliances for safety reasons. The restaurant is closed down, but takeout meals are available at the general store on request. Private guided tours into the wilderness are available, as are pack horses and mules.

After one trip here, the only whining you'll probably do is if you can't get a reservation for your next trip.

## Facilities
Glacier Lodge has 10 cabins that can accommodate 2–9 people; note that the former lodge (with rooms) burned and a new lodge is projected for 2006 or 2007. Kitchenette facilities are provided in the cabins, but kitchen utensils are limited. The bathrooms have showers. Barbecues are provided and some cabins have decks. There are no televisions or telephones. A children's fishing pond and general store are on-site. Leashed pets are allowed. No smoking is permitted. Some facilities are wheelchair accessible. Linens and towels are supplied. There is no daily maid service in the cabins, but towels can be exchanged at the front desk.

## Reservations and Rates
Reservations are recommended. The fee is $80–95 per night per cabin, and there is a two-night minimum. For more than two people, $15 per night per person is charged. The pet fee is $15 per pet. Major credit cards are accepted, but checks are not. It's open April–November. Contact Glacier Lodge, P.O. Box 370, Big Pine, CA 93513, 760/938-2837, website: www.jewelofthesierra.com.

## Directions
From U.S. 395 in Big Pine, turn west on Crocker Street (between the Mobil and Texaco gas stations) and drive 11 miles to the lodge (check in at the general store).

# 11 GRANT GROVE VILLAGE
Sequoia National Park, off the Generals Highway east of Fresno

**Luxury rating:** 2                        **Recreation rating:** 5

Places like this were only supposed to be possible in the good old days. But when you walk amid the giant sequoias of the Grant Grove, maybe you'll soon realize these are the good ol' days—right now.

Walking around the General Grant tree has a way of making people remember this. It is 1,800 to 2,000 years old, has a circumference of 107 feet, is 267 feet tall, and is in Grant Grove, likely the world's most spectacular grove of giant trees. The ideal approach is to get up early to hike the short loop trails in the sequoia groves in the morning. At this time, light refracts through the tree limbs and makes for breathtaking scenes, with the magnitude of the girth of the giant sequoias simply breathtaking.

Many people drive long distances and camp to see this phenomenon, but it is much easier to book one of the cabins at nearby Grant Village. There are 51 cabins, but only 9 have bathrooms, heat, and electricity. That means the rest are one step up from camping. But privacy is another benefit, a rare asset in a national park that sees close to one million visitors every summer.

The Cozy Cabins (i.e., the ones with bathrooms) were originally constructed in the 1920s, but many are being renovated with modern amenities. Cabins are painted or stained dark brown with white-trimmed windows. The Rustic Cabins have carpeting, insulated walls, and battery-operated lamps (now that's progress!).

Nearby Grant Village features a small store, a gift shop, post office, and visitor center, so it is an ideal launch point for your vacation in Sequoia and Kings Canyon National Parks. The big trees in this area live 30–40 times longer than people. The big ones do not die from old age, by insects, nor by fire, but rather from falling over. They sprout not from saplings, but from tiny seeds produced from cones, often aided by fire. In addition to Grant Grove, spectacular groves of sequoias elsewhere in the park include Sherman Grove and Giant Forest (including the world's largest living thing, the Sherman Tree), Redwood Mountain Grove, Muir Grove, Lost Grove, and Converse Basin Grove.

## Facilities

Grant Grove Village has 9 Cozy Cabins, 23 Rustic Cabins, 19 tent cabins in the summer, and 30 lodge rooms. There are no kitchen facilities. A porch and picnic table are provided, and some cabins have woodstoves. A restaurant, store, and gift shop are available. The lodging is suitable for children. Pets are not allowed. No smoking is permitted. Some facilities are wheelchair accessible. Linens and towels are provided.

## Reservations and Rates

Reservations are recommended. The fees are $57.50 per night for a tent cabin, $69 for a rustic cabin, $79 per night for a deluxe rustic cabin, $115 per night for a cabin with a bathroom, and $159 per night for lodge rooms. It's $10 per night per each additional person. Children ages 12 and under are free. Major credit cards are accepted. A $10 per vehicle national park entrance fee is charged; it's good for seven days. No dogs are allowed. Contact Kings Canyon Park Service, 5755 East Kings Canyon Road, Suite 101, Fresno, CA 93727, 866/522-6966, fax 559/561-3135, website: www.sequoia-kingscanyon.com/cabins.html.

## Directions

From Fresno, drive east on Highway 180 to the Big Stump entrance station at Kings Canyon National Park. Continue 1.5 miles to the Y intersection. Bear left on Highway 180 North and drive approximately one mile to Grant Grove Village.

# **12** KINGS CANYON LODGE
Kings Canyon National Park, off Highway 180 east of Fresno

🏃 🛶 👪

**Luxury rating:** 2                                    **Recreation rating:** 4

You can search the Internet and all of the information provided by the national park, and you just plain won't find out about Kings Canyon Lodge. That's because it's not listed, it doesn't advertise, and it purposely doesn't want to be found by the collective masses. So Kings Canyon Lodge remains one of the few national park hideaways in America.

It also means that when every other place is booked in midsummer, you can often call just a week in advance and get yourself a cabin for a national park vacation. "If you're looking for a pool, HBO, and a restaurant, this isn't the place for you," might well be the mantra. Instead, it's the kind of place that caters to people who want to go hiking and have a true park experience.

About the only way you find out about Kings Canyon Lodge is to go there. It is near Yucca Point on the edge of Kings Canyon, and for those who know the area, it is roughly midway on the drive from Grant Grove in Sequoia to Cedar Grove in Kings Canyon. Upon arrival, the first thing you will notice is an antique gas pump out front. It was astonishing to me that it wasn't just for show; it actually works. Turns out it is the oldest double gravity gas pump on earth.

A lot of the place is just like this, a living time capsule. It is the oldest lodge with cabins in the area, originally built in the 1930s as a fishing and hunting lodge. It has been restored to include bathrooms with showers, paneling, and electricity (the lodge makes its own power with a generator). There is no air-conditioning, no television, and no telephone, and like they say here, "It's like stepping back in time."

Naturally, the feature adventures are heading east up the canyon on the Kings Canyon Scenic Byway. This is the deepest canyon in the continental United States, rising 8,000 feet from the Kings River to Spanish Peak. As you enter the canyon, the landscape is transformed from an oak woodland to sheer granite walls with pyramid-shaped crests that poke holes in the sky. The road edges the canyon, and once, for more than a minute while I drove at 20 mph, a golden eagle glided just above and ahead of me, riding the rising thermals out of the canyon.

The fly-fishing and hiking in the canyon are often stellar. Fly-fishing with nymphs is excellent by working pockets at the head of the canyon, though large fish are rare.

The best trail for views is up to Lookout Peak (challenging, 12 miles), and the best for waterfalls are to Roaring Falls (easy, 0.5 mile) and Mist Falls (easy, 9 miles).

## Facilities

Kings Canyon Lodge has 12 cabins of various sizes that include bathrooms with showers and electricity. Televisions, telephones, and air-conditioning are not provided. Smoking and pets are not permitted.

## Reservations and Rates

Reservations are recommended. Rates range from $69 for a cabin with double bed to $189 for a family cabin that will sleep eight. A $10 per vehicle national park entrance fee is charged and includes a brochure and map; the parking pass is good for seven days. Contact Kings Canyon Lodge, Kings Canyon National Park, P.O. Box 820, Kings Canyon National Park, CA 93633, 559/335-2405.

## Directions

From Fresno, drive east on Highway 180 for 55 miles to the Big Stump entrance station at Sequoia National Park. Continue on Highway 180 (do not turn right at Generals Highway) for 17 miles (passing both turnoffs for Hume Lake) to the lodge on the right.

## 🔢 MONTECITO-SEQUOIA LODGE           BEST 🄲
Giant Sequoia National Monument, on Generals
Highway east of Fresno

**Luxury rating:** 3                              **Recreation rating:** 5

Going to Montecito-Sequoia Lodge is like going to camp—only Mom and Dad go as well. And if Mom and Dad (or Grandma and Grandpa) like the idea of camp, then the whole family should have a great time.

This full-service vacation camp provides complimentary meals and activities for all ages from sunup to sundown, and a staff of 70 keeps it running smoothly. You can participate in as many activities as you desire. Choices include canoeing, sailing, or waterskiing in a private lake, mountain biking, swimming, horseback riding, fencing, and arts and crafts. During the winter, the emphasis is on cross-country skiing and snowshoeing. You name it, they probably have it.

"It was like being on a cruise ship, only in the forest," said one guest. There are theme nights such as Swing is King, Beach Party, Space Odyssey, Frontier Carnival, and Disco Dance. And each evening there's a campfire and sing-along.

The lodge and camps are enormously popular with families; often several generations will show up together for a family vacation or reunion. The lodge also caters to single parents. For singles and couples looking for lodging in a beautiful setting, I recommend going during the off-season when it's quieter and cheaper.

You'll have a choice between a rustic cabin with central bathhouse or a lodge room with private bathroom. You don't need kitchen facilities, since buffet meals are provided in the dining room. The cabins are dark brown, boxy structures, with a king or queen bed and bunk beds, electricity, ceiling fans, and wood-burning stoves or propane heat. Your fee includes all meals and most activities; horseback riding, mountain biking, waterskiing, and some arts and crafts cost extra. The lodge is at 7,500 feet in elevation.

## Facilities

Montecito-Sequoia Lodge has 13 cabins, 33 lodge rooms, and 3 two-room suites. Complimentary meals and activities are provided. The cabins are heated by wood-stove or propane, and do not include kitchen facilities, piped water, or bathrooms; communal bathrooms and showers are available nearby. Lodge rooms have private bathrooms. A heated pool, a spa, and tennis and volleyball courts are on-site. Water sports, winter sports, and a slew of other activities are available. A restaurant, a lounge, laundry facilities, a baby-sitting service, and a small store are available. The facilities are suitable for children. Pets are not allowed. No smoking is permitted. Some facilities are wheelchair accessible.

## Reservations and Rates

Reservations are recommended. During the summer, the cabin fee is $882 per adult for six nights, $98 for ages 2–12, and $21 for children under age 2. When there's space, daily rates are available. Winter, off-season, and midweek discounts are often available. All meals are included. Call for holiday and other rates; lodge rooms are priced higher. Reservations can be made by calling 650/967-8612 or 800/227-9900, or by writing to 2225 Grant Road, Suite 1, Los Altos, CA 94024. A $10 per vehicle national park entrance fee is charged; the pass is good for seven days. Contact Montecito-Sequoia Lodge, 8000 Generals Highway, Box 858, Kings Canyon National Park, CA 93663, 559/565-3388 or 800/227-9900, website: www.mslodge.com.

## Directions

From Fresno, drive east on Highway 180 to the Big Stump entrance station at Kings Canyon National Park. Continue 1.5 miles to the Y intersection. Turn right (south) on Generals Highway and drive eight miles to the lodge entrance road on the right. Turn right and drive 0.25 mile to the parking lot.

# 14 SEQUOIA VILLAGE INN

Sierra foothills, off Highway 198 near Sequoia National Park

🏞️ 🛶 ❄️ 🏇 👪

**Luxury rating:** 4                                      **Recreation rating:** 4

Sequoia Village Inn sits just beyond the outskirts of Sequoia National Park, literally minutes from the Ash Mountain entrance station. There are many fantastic adventures nearby—not just gazing at the giant sequoias of the famed Giant Forest, as so many newcomers might believe.

First, you need to set up Sequoia Village as your launch point. It offers five cottages and two- and three-bedroom chalets. These are fully furnished, deluxe units, and they make fine vacation accommodations for those who require facilities a clear step above rustic.

Most everyone who stays here is planning a getaway to adjacent Sequoia National Park. But on your drive into Sequoia Village, you may find yourself gawking at the Kaweah River—beautiful and trout-filled—which is ideal for fly-fishing pocket water. Highway 198 runs beside the river for miles, and the road to Mineral King provides access to the East Fork Kaweah as well.

After you enter the park, the road becomes twisty and your driving gets slower. Instead of trying to make good time, take off your watch and enjoy the drive, stopping at the lookouts to take in the spectacular Castle Rocks to the south. The drive slowly rises in the Sierra, eventually entering forest. Suddenly, a few giant trees appear, massive sequoias marked by their giant circumference; they increase in number as you enter the Giant Forest. Soon, you will turn right to witness the General Sherman Tree.

As with the giant trees in the other groves, this tree is best seen at dawn, when no one else is around, so it feels sacred. After all, the General Sherman Tree is the largest living thing on earth, estimated to be 2,300–2,700 years old. It has a circumference of 102.6 feet, is 274.9 feet tall, has a 17.5-foot diameter 60 feet above the ground, has a branch with an 8-foot diameter, and grows enough wood each year to create a 60-foot tree.

Other musts are the tour through Crystal Cave and the short and easy hike to the Moro Rock Lookout. Crystal Cave is a marbleized cave, where taking a tour is like walking back to the beginning of time. Among the formations are adjoined crystal columns resembling the sound pipes in the giant organ at the Mormon Tabernacle. Lights are strategically placed. The cave is two million years old, which is quite young in geologic time for a cave with calcium deposits.

Moro Rock provides one of the most breathtaking views in the Sierra. To get to it, you climb a succession of stairs for about 10 minutes—a 300-foot climb to reach the 6,725-foot summit. From here, the awesome Great Western Divide features prominently in the landscape, yet with a single turn, you can also take in about two-thirds of the park, the rims spiked by tower-like granite crags.

## Facilities

Sequoia Village Inn has five cottages, two chalets, and a small suite. Cabins and chalets have fully equipped kitchens, and all rentals have private bathrooms. A microwave and refrigerator are provided in the suite. Televisions, VCRs, microwaves, and telephones are provided, and barbecues are available on request. Some cottages feature a deck, patio, and fireplace. A pool, a spa, laundry facilities, and a restaurant are across the street. The inn is suitable for children. Leashed pets are allowed. Smoking is permitted outside. Linens and towels are provided.

## Reservations and Rates

Reservations are recommended. The fee is $69–259 per night per cabin, plus $8 per night per additional person. There is a three-night minimum stay on holidays. Pets are $5 per night. Major credit cards are accepted. For tours of Crystal Cave, tickets are $8 with discounts for children and seniors; tickets are sold only at the Lodgepole or Foothills visitor centers (559/565-3782 or 559/565-3135). Contact Sequoia Village Inn, 45971 Sierra Drive, P.O. Box 1014, Three Rivers, CA 93271, 559/561-3652 or 559/561-0410, website: www.sequoiavillageinn.com.

## Directions

From Visalia, drive east on Highway 198 to Three Rivers. Continue east for approximately six miles (crossing a bridge) to the inn on the left.

# 15 SILVER CITY MOUNTAIN RESORT

Sequoia National Park, off Highway 198 near Mineral King

**Luxury rating:** 3                              **Recreation rating:** 3

Just like Goldilocks, you'll find a variety of sleeping options at Silver City Mountain Resort: from small to large, from old to new, from primitive to modern. This is a long-time establishment set close to a hikers' paradise. And if you're lucky, you might even see three bears (or at least one).

The resort was built in the 1930s, and the same family has been running the place since then. How's that for tradition? The hiker's hut and the rustic cabins are original and nearly identical to when they were built. Don't expect a lot of extras in these cabins: the hut has a bed and a sink with cold water, and the rustic cabins have a stove (some even have refrigerators). A central bathroom and shower facilities are close by.

The comfy cabins are a step up from the rustic cabins and include a toilet, a refrigerator, hot and cold water, and two bedrooms that can sleep up to six. For deluxe accommodations, rent a new, modern chalet with three bedrooms, fully equipped kitchen, private bathroom, and deck.

The cabins are spaced at least 30 feet apart, set amid pine and cedar cover. Silver Creek runs alongside the resort, and some of the cabins and chalets are near the creek, including Cozy Pines, Honeymoon, Rock Cabin, and Alpine Chalet.

The restaurant is open Thursday–Monday only, so if you don't like to cook, plan your stay accordingly. The resort is known for its "Thanksgiving Dinner," held the second Saturday after Labor Day. It's a traditional, home-cooked turkey feast with all the trimmings, and you need to make reservations to be included.

Local fishing prospects include good fly-fishing for small trout on the Kaweah River, with catch-and-release fishing regulations in place.

## Facilities

Silver City Mountain Resort has 10 cabins and five chalets. Some cabins have kitchens and bathroom facilities; others do not. The chalets have fully equipped kitchens and private bathrooms. All the rentals have a deck, fire ring, and some cooking utensils and supplies. Bring paper towels and tall trash bags. A central bathroom with showers is available. The resort is suitable for children. Pets are not allowed. No smoking is permitted. Linens and towels are not provided, but blankets and pillows are, so bring your own sheets, pillowcases, and towels.

## Reservations and Rates

Reservations are recommended. The fee is $75–295 per night. Early and late season discounts are available. There is a two-night minimum stay for the chalets. Major credit cards are accepted. Open Memorial Day weekend to late October. A $10 national park entrance fee is charged for each vehicle; the pass is good for seven days. Contact Silver City Mountain Resort, P.O. Box 56, Three Rivers, CA 93271, 559/561-3223 (summer) or 805/528-2730 (winter), fax 805/528-8039 (winter), website: www.silvercityresort.com.

## Directions

From Visalia, drive east on Highway 198 to Three Rivers. Continue east for 2 miles to Mineral King Road. Turn right (east) and drive approximately 23 miles to the resort on the left. The last 23 miles of road are slow, narrow, and winding; plan on one hour of driving (note that this road is more easily driven at night when you can see the beams of headlights from oncoming cars far in advance).

# 16 WHISPERING PINES LODGE CABINS
Kern River, near Kernville

🚶 🚲 🏊 🎣 🚐 👫 ♿

**Luxury rating:** 3                              **Recreation rating:** 4

You want easy-to-reach lodging with scads of recreational opportunities available all year long? Then hustle yourself and your fanny pack to Whispering Pines Lodge Cabins, where you can choose between white-water rafting, kayaking, hiking, fishing, swimming, cycling, and—well, you get the picture.

These cabins are actually suites with common walls—more lodge room than cabin, and packed with amenities. All rentals have at least one king-size bed, and they are as close as 100 feet from the Wild and Scenic Kern River. A few of the cabins have fully equipped kitchens, and all rentals have refrigerators and coffeemakers. A complimentary full breakfast is included.

Cabins 105–108 are the most popular because they have full river views; you get a glimpse of the river from Cabins 109–114. Cabins 114 and 117 do not have fireplaces.

Several rafting companies operate out of Kernville, so it's easy to plan a rafting or kayaking trip; note that the Kern River Canyon to the north was the site of a major forest fire in 2002, and evidence of that still exists.

Take your pick of many scenic hiking and cycling trails in the area. You are near the northern shore of Lake Isabella for fishing. And in the winter, cross-country and downhill skiing and snowmobiling are less than an hour away.

Got your bags packed?

## Facilities
Whispering Pines Lodge Cabins has 17 cabins with private bathrooms with whirlpool tubs. Some of the cabins have a fully equipped kitchen, fireplace, and deck or porch. Air-conditioning, television, and telephone are provided. A pool is available. Although the lodge can accommodate children, it is more suitable for adults. Pets are not allowed. No smoking is permitted. Linens and towels are provided.

## Reservations and Rates
Reservations are recommended. The fees are $149–299 per night, and breakfast is included. For more than two people, $20 per night per person is charged. Major credit cards are accepted. Contact Whispering Pines Lodge Cabins, 13745 Sierra Way, Route 1, Box 41, Kernville, CA 93238, 760/376-3733, fax 760/376-6513, website: www.kernvalley.com/inns.

## Directions
From Kernville, drive 0.3 mile north on Sierra Way to the lodge on the left.

# Other Cabins & Cottages in the Region

**Paradise Resort,** Route 2, Bishop, CA 93514, 760/387-2370, website: www .theparadiseresort.com.

# RESOURCES

COURTESY OF DORRINGTON INN

## MAP SYMBOLS

| | | | | | |
|---|---|---|---|---|---|
| ------- | Featured Trail | 80 | Interstate Freeway | ○ | City/Town |
| — — — — | Other Trail | 101 | US Highway | ✕ ✈ | Airfield/Airport |
| ═══════ | Expressway | 29 | State Highway | ⌐ | Golf Course |
| ══════ | Primary Road | 66 | County Highway | ☟ | Waterfall |
| ────── | Secondary Road | 🄣 | Trailhead | ⊡ | Swamp |
| ········ | Unpaved Road | ★ | Point of Interest | ▲ | Mountain |
| ············ | Ferry | ℗ | Parking Area | ♠ | Park |
| —·—·—·· | National Border | ⋏ | Campground | ⑃ | Pass |
| —··—·· | State Border | ▪ | Other Location | ✚ | Unique Natural Feature |

# Resources

## ADDITIONAL CABINS AND COTTAGES

The following real estate agencies also provide rental services for privately owned cabins, homes, and chalets:

### Bass Lake Realty

P.O. Box 349
Bass Lake, CA 93604
559/642-3600
website: www.basslakerealty.com.

### Bass Lake Vacation Rentals

P.O. Box 507
Bass Lake, CA 93604
559/642-2211.

### Bodega Bay & Beyond

575 Coast Highway 1
P.O. Box 129
Bodega Bay, CA 94923-0129
707/875-3942 or 800/888-3565
website: www.sonomacoast.com.

### Clear Lake Vacation Rentals

1855 South Main Street
Lakeport, CA 95453
707/263-7188
website: www.clearlakevacations.com.

### Coastal Vistas

P.O. Box 413
Bodega Bay, CA 94923
707/875-3000 or 800/788-4782
website: www.coastalvistas.com.

### Coast Retreats of Mendocino

P.O. Box 977
Mendocino, CA 95460
707/937-1121 or 800/859-6260
website: www.coastretreats.com.

### Graeagle Vacation Rentals

P.O. Box 307
Graeagle, CA 96103
530/836-2500 or 800/836-0269
website: www.graeagleproperties.com.

### Kendall & Potter

783 Rio del Mar Boulevard, Suite 7
Aptos, CA 95003
831/688-3511 or 888/692-5331
website: www.montereycoast.com.

### Lake Tahoe Reservation Bureau

599 Tahoe Keys Boulevard
P.O. Box 16584
South Lake Tahoe, CA 96151
530/544-5397 or 800/MY-TAHOE (800/698-2463)
website: www.tahoevacationguide.com.

### Lake Valley Properties

591 Tahoe Keys Boulevard, Cedar Building, D-1
P.O. Box 7405
South Lake Tahoe, CA 96158
800/634-3397
website: www.lakevalleyproperties.com.

### McKinney & Assoc., Inc.

2196 Lake Tahoe Boulevard, Suite 1
South Lake Tahoe, CA 96150
530/542-0557 or 800/748-6857
website: www.stayintahoe.com.

### Rams Head Realty & Rentals, Inc.

1000 Annapolis Road
P.O. Box 123
The Sea Ranch, CA 95497-0123
707/785-2427 or 800/785-3455
website: www.ramshead.com.

**Russian River Vacation Homes**
14080 Mill Street
P.O. Box 418
Guerneville, CA 95446
707/869-9030 or 800/310-0804
website: www.riverhomes.com.

**Sea Ranch rentals:**
Rams Head Realty & Rentals
800/785-3455
website: www.ramshead.com

Coasting Home
800/773-8648
website: www.coastinghome.com

Ocean View Properties
707/884-3538
website: www.oceanviewprop.com

Sea Ranch Escape Vacation Home Rentals
888/732-7262
website: www.888searanch.com

Sea Ranch Vacation Rentals
800/643-8899
website: www.searanchgetaway.com

**Shoreline Properties**
18200 Old Coast Highway
Fort Bragg, CA 95437
707/964-1444 or 888/942-8284
website: www.shorelinevacations.com.

**Sierra Vacation Rentals**
7252 North Lake Boulevard, Suite 101
P.O. Box 37
Carnelian Bay, CA 96140
530/546-8222 or 800/521-6656
website: www.sierravacations.com.

**Tahoe Rental Connection**
2241 James Street, Suite 3
South Lake Tahoe, CA 96150
530/542-2777 or 800/542-2100
website: www.tahoerentalconnection.com.

**Vacation Station, Inc.**
110 Country Club Drive
P.O. Box 7180
Incline Village, NV 89452
775/831-3664 or 800/841-7443
website: www.vacationstation.com.

**West Lake Properties**
115 West Lake Boulevard
P.O. Box 1768
Tahoe City, CA 96145
530/583-0268 or 800/870-8201
website: www.westlakeproperties.com.

**Yosemite West Lodging, Inc.**
Yosemite West Reservations
P.O. Box 2325
Oakhurst, CA 93644-2325
559/642-2211
website: www.yosemitewest
reservations.com.

## INFORMATION AND SERVICES
**Amador County Chamber of Commerce and Visitors Bureau**
P.O. Box 596
Jackson, CA 95642
209/223-0350
website: www.amadorcounty
chamber.com.

**Bishop Area Chamber of Commerce and Visitors Bureau**
690 N. Main Street
Bishop, CA 93514
760/873-8405
website: www.bishopvisitor.com.

**Calaveras Visitors Bureau**
P.O. Box 637
Angels Camp, CA 95222
209/736-0049 or 800/225-3764
website: www.gocalaveras.com.

### Crescent City-Del Norte County Chamber of Commerce
1001 Front Street
Crescent City, CA 95531
707/464-3174 or 800/343-8300
website: www.northerncalifornia.net.

### El Dorado County Chamber of Commerce
542 Main Street
Placerville, CA 95667
530/621-5885 or 800/457-6279
website: www.eldoradocounty.org.

### Eureka Chamber of Commerce
2112 Broadway
Eureka, CA 95501
707/442-3738 or 800/356-6381
website: www.eurekachamber.com.

### Fort Bragg/Mendocino Coast Chamber of Commerce
P.O. Box 1141
Fort Bragg, CA 95437
707/961-6300 or 800/726-2780
website: www.mendocinocoast.com.

### Grass Valley/Nevada County Chamber of Commerce
248 Mill Street
Grass Valley, CA 95945
530/273-4667
website: www.grassvalleychamber.com.

### Lake Tahoe Basin Management Unit
870 Emerald Bay Road, Suite 1
South Lake Tahoe, CA 96150
530/573-2600
website: www.fs.fed.us/r5/ (then click on Forest Offices).

### Lee Vining Chamber of Commerce
P.O. Box 130
Lee Vining, CA 93541
760/647-6629
website: www.leevining.com.

### Mammoth Lakes Visitor Center and Ranger Station
P.O. Box 148
Mammoth Lakes, CA 93546
760/924-5500 or 888/221-1010
website: www.fs.fed.us/r5/ (then click on Forest Offices).

### Mariposa County Chamber of Commerce
P.O. Box 425
Mariposa, CA 95338
209/966-2456
website: www.mariposa.org.

### Mono Basin Scenic Area Visitor Center
P.O. Box 429, Lee Vining
CA 93541, 760/647-304
website: www.fs.fed.us/r5/ (then click on Forest Offices).

### Monterey County Convention and Visitors Bureau
P.O. Box 1770
Monterey, CA 93942-1770
831/649-1770
website: www.montereyinfo.org.

### Morro Bay Chamber of Commerce and Visitor Center
345 Embarcadero Road, Suite D
Morro Bay, CA 93442
805/772-4467 or 800/231-0592
website: www.morrobay.org.

**Mount Shasta Visitors Bureau**
300 Pine Street
Mount Shasta, CA 96067
530/926-4865 or 800/397-1519
website: www.mtshasta.com.

**Napa Chamber or Commerce**
1556 First Street
Napa, CA 94559
707/226-7455
website: www.napachamber.org.

**North Lake Tahoe**
**Chamber of Commerce**
245 North Lake Boulevard
Tahoe City, CA 96145
530/581-8795
website: www.mytahoevacation.com.

**Plumas County Visitors Bureau**
P.O. Box 4120
Quincy, CA 95971
530/283-6345 or 800/326-2247
website: www.plumascounty.org.

**Shasta Lake Visitor Center**
14250 Holiday Road
Redding, CA 96003
530/275-1589
website: www.fs.fed.us/r5/ (then click on
Forest Offices) or www.shastalake.com.

**Sonoma Valley**
**Chamber of Commerce**
651-A Broadway
Sonoma, CA 95476
707/996-1033
website: www.sonomachamber.com.

**South Lake Tahoe**
**Chamber of Commerce**
3066 Lake Tahoe Boulevard
South Lake Tahoe, CA 96150
530/541-5255
website: www.tahoeinfo.com.

**Truckee-Donner**
**Chamber of Commerce**
10065 Donner Pass Road
Truckee, CA 96161
530/587-2757
website: www.truckee.com.

**Tuolumne County Visitors Bureau**
P.O. Box 4020
Sonora, CA 95370
209/533-4420 or 800/446-1333
website: www.thegreatunfenced.com.

**West Marin**
**Chamber of Commerce**
P.O. Box 1045
Point Reyes Station, CA 94956
415/663-9232
website: www.pointreyes.org.

**Yosemite Sierra Visitors Bureau**
41969 Yosemite Highway 41
Oakhurst, CA 93644
559/683-4636
website: www.go2yosemite.net.

# Index

# Acknowledgments

Some portions of this book were written by Stephani Stienstra.
Research Editors: Lee Wilkinson, Pamela S. Padula
Assistant Research Editors: Sandy Wilkinson, Sarah Wilkinson

# MOON NORTHERN CALIFORNIA CABINS AND COTTAGES

Avalon Travel Publishing
An Imprint of
Avalon Publishing Group, Inc.

AVALON
publishing group incorporated

1400 65th Street, Suite 250
Emeryville, CA 94608, USA
www.moon.com

Editors: Ellie Behrstock, Sabrina Young,
  Cinnamon Hearst
Series Manager: Sabrina Young
Acquisitions Manager:
  Rebecca K. Browning
Copy Editor: Deana Shields
Graphics Coordinator: Stefano Boni
Production Coordinator: Darren Alessi
Cover Designer: Gerilyn Attebery
Interior Designer: Darren Alessi
Map Editor: Kevin Anglin
Cartographers: Kat Smith, Kat Bennett,
  Suzanne Service
Cartography Manager: Mike Morgenfeld
Proofreader: Cinnamon Hearst
Indexer: Greg Jewett

ISBN-10: 1-56691-587-2
ISBN-13: 978-1-56691-587-8
ISSN: 1557-2579

Printing History
1st Edition—2002
2nd Edition—April 2006
5 4 3 2 1

Text © 2006 by Tom Stienstra.
Maps © 2006 by Avalon Travel Publishing, Inc.
All rights reserved.

Some photos and illustrations are used by permission and are the property of the original copyright owners. Photographs of individual cabins and cottages are courtesy of establishment, except where otherwise credited.

Front cover photo: Double Eagle Resort and Spa
Title page photo: Gables Cedar Creek Inn
Back cover photo: © Peter Cade / Getty Images

Printed in the United States by Worzalla

Moon Outdoors and the Moon logo are the property of Avalon Travel Publishing, an imprint of Avalon Publishing Group, Inc. All other marks and logos depicted are the property of the original owners. All rights reserved. No part of this book may be translated or reproduced in any form, except brief extracts by a reviewer for the purpose of a review, without written permission of the copyright owner.

Although every effort was made to ensure that the information was correct at the time of going to press, the author and publisher do not assume and hereby disclaim any liability to any party for any loss or damage caused by errors, omissions, or any potential travel disruption due to labor or financial difficulty, whether such errors or omissions result from negligence, accident, or any other cause.

## KEEPING CURRENT

We are committed to making this book the most accurate and enjoyable cabins and cottages guide to Northern California. You can rest assured that every cabin and cottage in this book has been carefully reviewed in an effort to keep this book as up-to-date as possible. However, by the time you read this book, some of the fees listed herein may have changed and facilities may have closed unexpectedly.

If you have a favorite gem you'd like to see included in the next edition, or see anything that needs updating, clarification, or correction, please drop us a line. Send your comments via email to feedback@moon.com, or use the address above.